THE SACRED BOOKS OF THE EAST

F. MAX MULLER (ED.)

LIST OF THE 50 VOLUMES

1. Upanishads.
2. Sacred Laws of Aryas.
3. Texts of Confucianism.
4. Zend-Avesta.
5. Pahlavi Texts.
6. Qur'an.
7. Institutes of Vishnu.
8. Bhagavadgita, & c.
9. Qur'an.
10. (i) Dhammapada.
10. (ii) Sutta-Nipata.
11. Buddhist Suttas.
12. Satapatha-Brahmana.
13. Vinaya Texts.
14. Sacred Laws of Aryas.
15. Upanishads.
16. Texts of Confucianism.
17. Vinaya Texts.
18. Pahlavi Texts.
19. Fo-sho-hing-tsanking.
20. Vinaya Texts.
21. Saddharma Pundarika.
22. Gaina-Sutras.
23. Zend-Avesta.
24. Pahlavi Texts.
25. Laws of Manu.
26. Satapatha-Brahmana.
27. Texts of Confucianism (Li Ki).
28. Texts of Confucianism (Li Ki).
29. Grihya-Sutras.
30 Grihya-Sutras.
31. Zend-Avesta.
32. Vedic Hymns.
33. Minor Law-Books.
34. Vedanta-Sutras.
35. Milinda.
36. Milinda.
37. Pahlavi Texts.
38. Vedanta-Sutras.
39. Texts of Taoism
40. Texts of Taoism
41. Satapatha-Brahmana
42. Atharva-veda.
43. Satapatha-Brahmana.
44. Satapatha-Brahmana.
45. Gaina-Sutras.
46. Vedic Hymns.
47. Pahlavi Texts.
48. Vedanta-Sutras.
49. (i) Buddhakarita.
49. (ii) Mahayana Texts.
50. A General Index

The Sacred Books of the East, Vol. 49

BUDDHIST MAHAYANA TEXTS

PART–I

THE BUDDHA-KARITA

OF

ASVAGHOSHA

Translated from the Sanskrit

by

E. B. COWELL

PART–II

THE LARGER SUKHAVATI-VYUHA
THE SMALLER SUKHAVATI-VYUHA
THE VAGRAKKHEDIKA
THE LARGER
PRAGNA-PARAMITA-HRIDAYA-SUTRA
THE SMALLER
PRAGNA-PARAMITA-HRIDAYA-SUTRA

Translated by

F. MAX MULLER

THE AMITAYUR-DHYANA-SUTRA

Translated by J. TAKAKUSU

GYAN

Published by

GYAN

Gyan Publishing House
5, Ansari Road
Daryaganj, New Delhi-110002
Phone: 011-47034999, 9811692060
E-mail: books@gyanbooks.com

Distribution Network
gyanbooks.com
India, USA, Canada, UK, Australia, France

ISBN : 978-81-212-2937-1 (Set)
ISBN : 978-81-212-2754-4 (PB)
First Published, 1894

2nd Impression 2021

Printed at: Gyan Press, Delhi.

The Sacred Books of the East, Vol. 49

Buddhist Mahayana Texts, Part I
Translated by: E. B. Cowell, Translated by: F. Max Muller

THE

SACRED BOOKS OF THE EAST

TRANSLATED

BY VARIOUS ORIENTAL SCHOLARS

AND EDITED BY

F. MAX MÜLLER

VOL. XLIX

Oxford

AT THE CLARENDON PRESS

1894

CONTENTS OF THE TWO PARTS.

BUDDHIST MAHÂYÂNA TEXTS.

PART I.

PART II.

BUDDHIST MAHÂYÂNA TEXTS

PART I

THE BUDDHA-*K*ARITA

OF

A*S*VAGHOSHA

TRANSLATED FROM THE SANSKRIT

BY

E. B. COWELL

Oxford

AT THE CLARENDON PRESS

1894

INTRODUCTION.

THE Sanskrit text of the Buddha-*k*arita was published at the beginning of last year in the 'Anecdota Oxoniensia,' and the following English translation is now included in the series of 'Sacred Books of the East.' It is an early Sanskrit poem written in India on the legendary history of Buddha, and therefore contains much that is of interest for the history of Buddhism, beside its special importance as illustrating the early history of classical Sanskrit literature.

It is ascribed to A*s*vaghosha; and, although there were several writers who bore that name, it seems most probable that our author was the contemporary and spiritual adviser of Kanishka in the first century of our era. Hiouen Thsang, who left India in A.D. 645, mentions him with Deva, Nâgâr*g*una, and Kumâralabdha, 'as the four suns which illumine the world[1];' but our fullest account is given by I-tsing, who visited India in 673. He states that A*s*vaghosha was an ancient author who composed the Ala*m*kâra-*s*âstra and the Buddha-*k*arita-kâvya,—the latter work being of course the present poem. Beside these two works he also composed the hymns in honour of Buddha and the three holy beings Amitâbha, Avalokite*s*vara, and Mahâsthâma, which were chanted at the evening service of the monasteries. 'In the five countries of India and in the countries of the Southern ocean they recite these poems, because they express a store of ideas and meaning in a few words[2].' A solitary stanza (VIII, 13) is

---

[1] Julien's Translation, vol. ii, p. 214.
[2] See M. Fujishama, Journal Asiatique, 1888, p. 425.

quoted from the Buddha-*k*arita in Râyamuku*t*a's commentary on the Amarakosha I, 1. 1, 2, and also by U*gg*valadatta in his commentary on the U*n*âdi-sûtras I, 156; and five stanzas are quoted as from A*s*vaghosha in Vallabhadeva's Subhâshitâvali, which bear a great resemblance to his style, though they are not found in the extant portion of this poem [1].

The Buddha-*k*arita was translated into Chinese [2] by Dharmaraksha in the fifth century, and a translation of this was published by the Rev. S. Beal in the present series; it was also translated into Tibetan in the seventh or eighth century. The Tibetan as well as the Chinese version consists of twenty-eight chapters, and carries down the life of Buddha to his entrance into Nirvâ*n*a and the subsequent division of the sacred relics. The Tibetan version appears to be much closer to the original Sanskrit than the Chinese; in fact from its verbal accuracy we can often reproduce the exact words of the original, since certain Sanskrit words are always represented by the same Tibetan equivalents, as for instance the prepositions prefixed to verbal roots. I may here express an earnest hope that we may still ere long have an edition and translation of the Tibetan version, if some scholar can be found to complete Dr. Wenzel's unfinished labour. He had devoted much time and thought to the work; I consulted him in several of my difficulties, and it is from him that I derived all my information about the Tibetan renderings. This Tibetan version promises to be of great help in restoring the many corrupt readings which still remain in our faulty Nepalese MSS.

Only thirteen books of the Sanskrit poem claim to be A*s*vaghosha's composition; the last four books are an attempt by a modern Nepalese author to supply the loss of the original. He tells us this honestly in the colophon,

---

[1] Professor Peterson has remarked that two stanzas out of the five occur in Bhart*r*ihari's Nîti-*s*ataka.

[2] We have for the present classed the Buddha-*k*arita with the Mahâyâna Sûtras in default of more exact information.

—'having searched for them everywhere and not found them, four cantos have been made by me, Am*ri*tânanda,—the fourteenth, fifteenth, sixteenth, and seventeenth.' He adds the date 950 of the Nepalese era, corresponding to 1830 A.D.; and we have no difficulty in identifying the author. Râ*g*endralâl Mitra in his 'Nepalese Buddhist Literature' mentions Am*ri*tânanda as the author of two Sanskrit treatises and one in Newârî; he was probably the father of the old pa*nd*it of the Residency at Kâ*t*mâ*nd*u, Gu*n*ânanda, whose son Indrânanda holds the office at present. Dr. D. Wright informs me that the family seem to have been the recognised historians of the country, and keepers of the MS. treasures of sundry temples. The four books are included in this translation as an interesting literary curiosity. The first portion of the fourteenth book agrees partly with the Tibetan and Chinese, and Am*ri*tânanda may have had access to some imperfect copy of this portion of the original; but after that his account is quite independent, and has no relation to the two versions.

In my preface to the edition of the Sanskrit text I have tried to show that A*s*vaghosha's poem appears to have exercised an important influence on the succeeding poets of the classical period in India. When we compare the description in the seventh book of the Raghuva*ms*a of the ladies of the city crowding to see prince A*g*a as he passes by from the Svaya*m*vara where the princess Bho*g*yâ has chosen him as her husband, with the episode in the third book of the Buddha-*k*arita (*s*lokas 13–24); or the description of Kâma's assault on *S*iva in the Kumârasa*m*bhava with that of Mâra's temptation of Buddha in the thirteenth book, we can hardly fail to trace some connection. There is a similar resemblance between the description in the fifth book of the Râmâya*n*a, where the monkey Hanumat enters Râva*n*a's palace by night, and sees his wives asleep in the seraglio and their various unconscious attitudes, and the description in the fifth book of the present poem where Buddha on the night of his leaving his home for ever sees the same unconscious sight in his own palace. Nor may we forget that in the Râmâya*n*a the description is merely introduced as an ornamental episode; in the Buddhist poem it is an essential element in the story, as it supplies the final impulse which stirs the Bodhisattva to make his escape from the world. These different descriptions became afterwards commonplaces in Sanskrit poetry, like the catalogue of the ships in Greek or Roman epics; but they may very well have originated in connection with definite incidents in the Buddhist sacred legend.

The Sanskrit MSS. of Nepal are always negligently transcribed and abound with corrupt passages, which it is often very difficult to detect and restore. My printed text leaves many obscure lines which will have to be cleared up hereafter by more skilful emendations. I have given in the notes to the translation some further emendations of my own, and I have also added several happy conjectures which continental scholars have kindly suggested to me by letter; and I gladly take this opportunity of adding in a foot-note some which I received too late to insert in their proper places[1].

I have endeavoured to make my translation intelligible to the English reader, but many of the verses in the original are very obscure. A*s*vaghosha employs all the resources of Hindu rhetoric (as we might well expect if I-tsing is right in ascribing to him an 'ala*m*kâra-*s*âstra'), and it is often difficult to follow his subtil turns of thought and remote allusions; but many passages no doubt owe their present obscurity to undetected mistakes in the text of our MSS. In the absence of any commentary (except so far as the diffuse Chinese translation and occasional reference to the Tibetan have supplied the want) I have been necessarily left to my own resources, and I cannot fail to have sometimes missed my author's meaning,

Prâ*ms*ulabhye phale mohâd udbâhur iva vâmana*h*;

[1] Dr. von Boehtlingk suggests 'saugâ vi*k*a*k*âra' in VIII, 3, and 'vila*m*bake*s*yo' in VIII, 21,—two certain emendations. Professor Kielhorn would read 'nabhasy eva' in XIII, 47 for 'nayaty eva,' and 'tatraiva nâsînam *ri*shim' in XIII, 50. Professor Bühler would read 'priyatanayas tanayasya' in I, 87, and 'na tatyâga *k*a' in IV, 80.

but I have tried to do my best, and no one will welcome more cordially any light which others may throw on the passages which I have misunderstood.

The edition of the original text was dedicated to my old friend Professor F. Max Müller, and it is a sincere gratification to me that this translation will appear in the same volume with similar translations from his pen.

E. B. C.

CAMBRIDGE:
Feb. 1, 1894.

THE BUDDHA-*K*ARITA

OF

A*S*VAGHOSHA.

THE BUDDHA-*K*ARITA

OF

A*S*VAGHOSHA.

BOOK I.

1. That Arhat is here saluted, who has no counterpart,—who, as bestowing the supreme happiness, surpasses (Brahman) the Creator,—who, as driving away darkness, vanquishes the sun,—and, as dispelling all burning heat, surpasses the beautiful moon.

2. There was a city, the dwelling-place[1] of the great saint Kapila, having its sides surrounded by the beauty of a lofty broad table-land as by a line of clouds, and itself, with its high-soaring palaces[2], immersed in the sky.

3. By its pure and lofty system of government it, as it were, stole the splendour of the clouds of Mount Kailâsa, and while it bore the clouds which came to it through a mistake, it fulfilled the imagination which had led them thither[3].

4. In that city, shining with the splendour of gems, darkness like poverty could find no place;

---

[1] Vastu seems used here for vâstu. [2] Dhish*n*ya.
[3] They had thought that it was Kailâsa.

prosperity shone resplendently, as with a smile, from the joy of dwelling with such surpassingly excellent citizens.

5. With its festive arbours, its arched gateways and pinnacles[1], it was radiant with jewels in every dwelling; and unable to find any other rival in the world, it could only feel emulation with its own houses.

6. There the sun, even although he had retired, was unable to scorn the moon-like faces of its women which put the lotuses to shame, and as if from the access of passion, hurried towards the western ocean to enter the (cooling) water.

7. 'Yonder Indra has been utterly annihilated by the people when they saw the glories[2] acquired by the *S*âkyas,'—uttering this scoff, the city strove by its banners with gay-fluttering streamers to wipe away every mark of his existence.

8. After mocking the water-lilies even at night by the moonbeams which rest on its silver pavilions,—by day it assumed the brightness of the lotuses through the sunbeams falling on its golden palaces.

9. A king, by name *S*uddhodana, of the kindred of the sun, anointed to stand at the head of earth's monarchs,—ruling over the city, adorned it, as a bee-inmate a full-blown lotus[3].

10. The very best of kings with his train ever

---

[1] Or towers? (si*m*hakar*n*ai*h*).

[2] For the genitive ya*s*asâm, see Pâ*n*. II, 3. 52 (adhîgartha).

[3] Vâ is used for iva in *S*i*s*up. Badha, III, 63, IV, 35; Meghad. 82. (Cf. infra, IV, 44.) Purâdhirâ*g*am seems used adverbially. Cf. the line in Vikramorv. kusumâny â*s*erate sha*t*padâ*h*. Could it mean 'as a thought the lotus of the heart?'

near him [1],—intent on liberality yet devoid of pride [2]; a sovereign, yet with an ever equal eye thrown on all [3],—of gentle nature and yet with wide-reaching majesty [4].

11. Falling smitten by his arm in the arena of battle, the lordly elephants of his enemies bowed prostrate with their heads pouring forth quantities of pearls as if they were offering handfuls of flowers in homage.

12. Having dispersed his enemies by his pre-eminent majesty as the sun disperses the gloom of an eclipse, he illuminated his people on every side, showing them the paths which they were to follow.

13. Duty, wealth, and pleasure under his guidance assumed mutually each other's object, but not the outward dress; yet as if they still vied together they shone all the brighter in the glorious career of their triumphant success.

14. He, the monarch of the *S*âkyas, of native pre-eminence, but whose actual pre-eminence was brought about by his numberless councillors of exalted wisdom, shone forth all the more gloriously, like the moon amidst the stars shining with a light like its own [5].

15. To him there was a queen, named Mâyâ, as if free from all deceit (mâyâ)—an effulgence proceeding

---

[1] Also 'though the highest of mountains, yet bearing his wings (uncut).'

[2] Or if applied to an elephant, 'not in rut.'

[3] Or with a double meaning in î*s*a, 'though like *S*iva, yet with even eyes,' i. e. not three.

[4] Or 'like the moon, yet widely burning (like the sun).'

[5] Or perhaps 'shining with undiminished splendour.' If we read ak*ri*tânyathâbha*h* it would run, 'shining with its light undimmed by the stars.'

from his effulgence, like the splendour of the sun when it is free from all the influence of darkness,—a chief queen in the united assembly of all queens.

16. Like a mother to her subjects, intent on their welfare,—devoted to all worthy of reverence like devotion itself,—shining on her lord's family like the goddess of prosperity,—she was the most eminent of goddesses to the whole world.

17. Verily the life of women is always darkness, yet when it encountered her, it shone brilliantly; thus the night does not retain its gloom, when it meets with the radiant crescent of the moon.

18. 'This people, being hard to be roused to wonder in their souls, cannot be influenced by me if I come to them as beyond their senses,'—so saying, Duty abandoned her own subtile nature and made her form visible.

19. Then falling from the host of beings in the Tushita heaven[1], and illumining the three worlds, the most excellent of Bodhisattvas suddenly entered at a thought into her womb, like the Nâga-king entering the cave of Nandâ.

20. Assuming the form of a huge elephant white like Himâlaya, armed with six tusks[2], with his face perfumed with flowing ichor, he entered the womb of the queen of king *S*uddhodana, to destroy the evils of the world.

21. The guardians of the world hastened from heaven to mount watch over the world's one true ruler; thus the moonbeams, though they shine

---

[1] For tushitât kâyât, cf. tushite devanikâya upapannâ, Divyâvad. p. 83; and tushitakâyika, Lalitav. p. 142.

[2] Cf. the Pâli *kh*addanto, and the Lalitav. sha*d*danta.

everywhere, are especially bright on Mount Kailâsa.

22. Mâyâ also, holding him in her womb, like a line of clouds holding a lightning-flash, relieved the people around her from the sufferings of poverty by raining showers of gifts.

23. Then one day by the king's permission the queen, having a great longing in her mind, went with the inmates of the gynaeceum into the garden Lumbinî.

24. As the queen supported herself by a bough which hung laden with a weight of flowers, the Bodhisattva suddenly came forth, cleaving open her womb.

25. [1] At that time the constellation Pushya was auspicious, and from the side of the queen, who was purified by her vow, her son was born for the welfare of the world, without pain and without illness.

26. Like the sun bursting from a cloud in the morning,—so he too, when he was born from his mother's womb, made the world bright like gold, bursting forth with his rays which dispelled the darkness.

27. As soon as he was born the thousand-eyed (Indra) well-pleased took him gently, bright like a golden pillar; and two pure streams of water fell down from heaven upon his head with piles of Mandâra flowers.

28. Carried about by the chief suras, and delighting them with the rays that streamed from his body, he

[1] From this point the Tibetan and Chinese versions agree more or less closely with the Sanskrit text.

surpassed in beauty the new moon as it rests on a mass of evening clouds.

29. As was Aurva's birth from the thigh[1], and Prithu's from the hand[2], and Mândhâtri's, who was like Indra himself, from the forehead[3], and Kakshîvat's from the upper end of the arm[4],—thus too was his birth (miraculous).

30. Having thus in due time issued from the womb, he shone as if he had come down from heaven, he who had not been born in the natural way,—he who was born full of wisdom, not foolish,—as if his mind had been purified by countless aeons of contemplation.

31. With glory, fortitude, and beauty he shone like the young sun descended upon the earth; when he was gazed at, though of such surpassing brightness, he attracted all eyes like the moon.

32. With the radiant splendour of his limbs he extinguished like the sun the splendour of the lamps; with his beautiful hue as of precious gold he illuminated all the quarters of space.

33. Unflurried, with the lotus-sign in high relief[5], far-striding, set down with a stamp,—seven such firm footsteps did he then take,—he who was like the constellation of the seven rishis.

34. 'I am born for supreme knowledge, for the welfare of the world,—thus this is my last birth,'—

---

[1] Mahâbh. I, 2610. [2] Vishnu Pur. I, 13.

[3] According to the Mahâbh. III, l. 10450, he was born from his father's left side, but cf. Vishnu Pur. IV, 2.

[4] The MSS. vary between bhugâmsa and bhugâmsa; we might conjecture bhugâgradesât, but bhugâmsadesât is the only reading in V, 56. Beal I, 10 has 'the armpit.'

[5] Abgasamudgatâni. Cf. Beal I, 16, note.

thus did he of lion gait, gazing at the four quarters, utter a voice full of auspicious meaning.

35. Two streams of water bursting from heaven, bright as the moon's rays, having the power of heat and cold, fell down upon that peerless one's benign head to give refreshment to his body.

36. His body lay on a bed with a royal canopy and a frame shining with gold, and supported by feet of lapis lazuli, and in his honour the yaksha-lords stood round guarding him with golden lotuses in their hands.

37. The gods in homage to the son of Mâyâ, with their heads bowed at his majesty, held up a white umbrella in the sky and muttered the highest blessings on his supreme wisdom.

38. The great dragons[1] in their great thirst for the Law[2],—they who had had the privilege of waiting on the past Buddhas,—gazing with eyes of intent devotion, fanned[3] him and strewed Mandâra flowers over him.

39. Gladdened through the influence of the birth of the Tathâgata, the gods of pure natures and inhabiting pure abodes[4] were filled with joy, though all passion was extinguished, for the sake of the world[5] drowned in sorrow.

40. When he was born, the earth, though fastened down by (Himâlaya) the monarch of mountains, shook like a ship tossed by the wind; and from a cloudless sky there fell a shower full of lotuses and water-lilies, and perfumed with sandal-wood.

[1] Mahoragâ*h*.

[2] Cf. infra, *s*loka 54.

[3] Avya*g*an.

[4] *S*uddhâdhivâsâ*h*.

[5] Reading hitâya.

41. Pleasant breezes blew soft to the touch, dropping down heavenly garments; the very sun, though still the same, shone with augmented light, and fire gleamed, unstirred, with a gentle lustre.

42. In the north-eastern part of the dwelling a well of pure water appeared of its own accord, wherein the inhabitants of the gynaeceum, filled with wonder, performed their rites as in a sacred bathing-place.

43. Through the troops of heavenly visitants, who came seeking religious merit, the pool itself received strength to behold Buddha, and by means of its trees bearing flowers and perfumes it eagerly offered him worship.

44. The flowering trees at once produced their blossoms, while their fragrance was borne aloft in all directions by the wind, accompanied by the songs of bewildered female bees, while the air was inhaled and absorbed by the many snakes (gathering near)[1].

45. Sometimes there resounded[2] on both sides songs mingled with musical instruments and tabours, and lutes also, drums, tambourines, and the rest,—from women adorned with dancing bracelets.

46. '[3] That royal law which neither Bh*ri*gu nor Aṅgiras ever made, those two great seers the founders of families, their two sons *S*ukra and V*ri*haspati left revealed at the end.

---

[1] Serpents are called vâyubhaksha. See Ind. Sprüche, III, 4738, and Raghuva*ms*a XIII, 12. Cf. also infra, VII, 15.

[2] Virâ*g*itam, 'it was manifested by.' Can tat mean 'then' or 'there?'

[3] We learn from *s*loka 52 that this is a speech uttered by the Brahmans of the court.

47. 'Yea, the son of Sarasvatî[1] proclaimed that lost Veda which they had never seen in former ages,—Vyâsa rehearsed that in many forms, which Vasish*th*a helpless could not compile;

48. 'The voice of Vâlmîki uttered its poetry which the great seer *K*yavana could not compose; and that medicine which Atri never invented the wise son of Atri[2] proclaimed after him;

49. 'That Brahmanhood which Kusika never attained,—his son, O king, found out the means to gain it; (so) Sagara made a bound for the ocean, which even the Ikshvâkus had not fixed before him.

50. '*G*anaka attained a power of instructing the twice-born in the rules of Yoga which none other had ever reached[3]; and the famed feats of the grandson of *S*ûra[4] (K*ri*sh*n*a) *S*ûra and his peers were powerless to accomplish.

51. 'Therefore it is not age nor years which are the criterion; different persons win pre-eminence in the world at different places; those mighty exploits worthy of kings and sages, when left undone by the ancestors, have been done by the sons.'

52. The king, being thus consoled and congratulated by those well-trusted Brahmans, dismissed from his mind all unwelcome suspicion and rose to a still higher degree of joy;

53. And well-pleased he gave to those most excellent of the twice-born rich treasures with all

---

[1] The Vish*n*u Pur. (III, 3) says that Sârasvata arranged the Vedas in the ninth age, as Vasish*th*a in the eighth.

[2] Âtreya is the proclaimer of the *K*araka-sa*m*hitâ.

[3] Cf. *Kh*ândogya Upan. V, 3, 7.

[4] Read *S*aure*h* for *S*aurai*h*.

due honour,—'May he become the ruler of the earth according to your words, and may he retire to the woods when he attains old age.'

54. Then having learned by signs and through the power of his penances this birth of him who was to destroy all birth, the great seer Asita in his thirst for the excellent Law[1] came to the palace of the *S*âkya king.

55. Him shining with the glory of sacred knowledge and ascetic observances, the king's own priest, —himself a special student among the students of sacred knowledge,—introduced into the royal palace with all due reverence and respect.

56. He entered into the precincts of the king's gynaeceum, which was all astir with the joy arisen from the birth of the young prince,—grave from his consciousness of power, his pre-eminence in asceticism, and the weight of old age.

57. Then the king, having duly honoured the sage, who was seated in his seat, with water for the feet and an arghya offering, invited him (to speak) with all ceremonies of respect, as did Antideva[2] in olden time to Va*s*ish*th*a:

58. 'I am indeed fortunate, this my family is the object of high favour, that thou shouldst have come to visit me; be pleased to command what I should do, O benign one; I am thy disciple, be pleased to show thy confidence in me.'

59. The sage, being thus invited by the king, filled with intense feeling as was due, uttered his

[1] Cf. *s*loka 38*a*.

[2] See IX, 20, 60. C reads Atideva, i.e. Indra? [The Tibetan reads Antadeva, 'in the end dwelling god' or 'end having god.' H. W.]

deep and solemn words, having his large eyes opened wide with wonder:

60. 'This is indeed worthy of thee, great-souled as thou art, fond of guests, liberal and a lover of duty,—that thy mind should be thus kind towards me, in full accordance with thy nature, family, wisdom, and age.

61. 'This is the true way in which those seer-kings of old, rejecting through duty all trivial riches[1], have ever flung them away as was right,—being poor in outward substance but rich in ascetic endurance.

62. 'But hear now the motive for my coming and rejoice thereat; a heavenly voice has been heard by me in the heavenly path, that thy son has been born for the sake of supreme knowledge.

63. 'Having heard that voice and applied my mind thereto, and having known its truth by signs, I am now come hither, with a longing to see the banner of the *S*âkya race, as if it were Indra's banner being set up[2].'

64. Having heard this address of his, the king, with his steps bewildered with joy, took the prince, who lay on his nurse's side, and showed him to the holy ascetic.

65. Thus the great seer beheld the king's son with wonder,—his foot marked with a wheel, his fingers and toes webbed, with a circle of hair between his eyebrows, and signs of vigour like an elephant.

66. Having beheld him seated on his nurse's side,

---

[1] Or 'all riches which were trifling in comparison with duty.'

[2] In allusion to a festival in parts of India; cf. Schol. Raghuvam*s*a IV, 3. (Cf. Mrs. Guthrie's Year in an Indian Fort, vol. ii.)

like the son of Agni (Skanda) seated on Devî's side, he stood with the tears hanging on the ends of his eyelashes[1], and sighing he looked up towards heaven.

67. But seeing Asita with his eyes thus filled with tears, the king was agitated through his love for his son, and with his hands clasped and his body bowed he thus asked him in a broken voice choked with weeping,

68. 'One whose beauty has little to distinguish it from that of a divine sage[2], and whose brilliant birth has been so wonderful, and for whom thou hast prophesied a transcendent future,—wherefore, on seeing him, do tears come to thee, O reverend one?

69. 'Is the prince, O holy man, destined to a long life? Surely he cannot be born for my sorrow[3]. I have with difficulty obtained a handful of water, surely it is not death which comes to drink it.

70. 'Tell me, is the hoard of my fame free from destruction? Is this chief prize of my family secure? Shall I ever depart happily to another life,—I who keep one eye ever awake, even when my son is asleep[4]?

71. 'Surely this young shoot of my family is not born barren, destined only to wither! Speak quickly, my lord, I cannot wait; thou well knowest the love of near kindred for a son.'

72. Knowing the king to be thus agitated through his fear of some impending evil, the sage thus ad-

[1] I adopt Prof. Kielhorn's suggestion, pakshmântavilambitâsruh. (Ańkita might mean 'curved on his eyelashes.')

[2] Or, reading mune, 'one whose age is so small, O sage.'

[3] Kakkinna sokâya mama prasûtah.

[4] Obscure.

dressed him: 'Let not thy mind, O monarch, be disturbed,—all that I have said is certainly true[1].

73. 'I have no feeling of fear as to his being subject to change, but I am distressed for mine own disappointment. It is my time to depart, and this child is now born,—he who knows that mystery hard to attain, the means of destroying birth.

74. 'Having forsaken his kingdom, indifferent to all worldly objects, and having attained the highest truth by strenuous efforts, he will shine forth as a sun of knowledge to destroy the darkness of illusion in the world.

75. 'He will deliver by the boat of knowledge the distressed world, borne helplessly along, from the ocean of misery which throws up sickness as its foam, tossing with the waves of old age, and rushing with the dreadful onflow of death.

76. 'The thirsty world of living beings will drink the flowing stream of his Law, bursting forth with the water of wisdom, enclosed by the banks of strong moral rules, delightfully cool with contemplation, and filled with religious vows as with ruddy geese.

77. 'He will proclaim the way of deliverance to those afflicted with sorrow, entangled in objects of sense, and lost in the forest-paths of worldly existence, as to travellers who have lost their way.

78. 'By the rain of the Law he will give gladness to the multitude who are consumed in this world with that fire of desire whose fuel is worldly objects, as a great cloud does with its showers at the end of the hot season.

---

[1] I take **asmi** as meaning **aham** (**aham ityarthâvyayam**), or should we read **asti**?

79. 'He will break open for the escape of living beings that door whose bolt is desire and whose two leaves are ignorance and delusion,—with that excellent blow of the good Law which is so hard to find.

80. 'He, the king of the Law, when he has attained to supreme knowledge, will achieve the deliverance from its bonds of the world now overcome by misery, destitute of every refuge, and enveloped in its own chains of delusion.

81. 'Therefore make no sorrow for him,—that belongs rather, kind sire, to the pitiable world of human beings, who through illusion or the pleasures of desire or intoxication refuse to hear his perfect Law.

82. 'Therefore since I have fallen short of that excellence, though I have accomplished all the stages of contemplation, my life is only a failure; since I have not heard his Law, I count even dwelling in the highest heaven a misfortune.'

83. Having heard these words, the king with his queen and his friends abandoned sorrow and rejoiced; thinking, 'such is this son of mine,' he considered that his excellence was his own.

84. But he let his heart be influenced by the thought, 'he will travel by the noble path,'—he was not in truth averse to religion, yet still he saw alarm at the prospect of losing his child.

85. Then the sage Asita, having made known the real fate which awaited the prince to the king who was thus disturbed about his son, departed by the way of the wind as he had come, his figure watched reverentially in his flight.

86. Having taken his resolution and having seen

the son of his younger sister[1], the saint, filled with compassion, enjoined him earnestly in all kinds of ways, as if he were his son, to listen to the sage's words and ponder over them.

87. The monarch also, being well-pleased at the birth of a son, having thrown off all those bonds called worldly objects, caused his son to go through the usual birth-ceremonies in a manner worthy of the family.

88. When ten days were fulfilled after his son's birth, with his thoughts kept under restraint, and filled with excessive joy, he offered for his son most elaborate sacrifices to the gods with muttered prayers, oblations, and all kinds of auspicious ceremonies.

89. And he himself gave to the brahmans for his son's welfare cows full of milk, with no traces of infirmity, golden-horned and with strong healthy calves, to the full number of a hundred thousand.

90. Then he, with his soul under strict restraint, having performed all kinds of ceremonies which rejoiced his heart, on a fortunate day, in an auspicious moment, gladly determined to enter his city.

91. Then the queen with her babe having worshipped the gods for good fortune, occupied a costly palanquin made of elephants' tusks, filled with all kinds of white flowers, and blazing with gems.

92. Having made his wife with her child[2] enter first into the city, accompanied by the aged attendants, the king himself also advanced, saluted by the

---

[1] This was Naradatta, see Lalitavistara, ch. vii. pp. 103, 110 (Foucaux).

[2] Apatyanâthâm might also mean 'having her child as her protector.'

hosts of the citizens, as Indra entering heaven, saluted by the immortals.

93. The Sâkya king, having entered his palace, like Bhava [1] well-pleased at the birth of Kârttikeya [2], with his face full of joy, gave orders for lavish expenditure, showing all kinds of honour and liberality [3].

94. Thus at the good fortune of the birth of the king's son, that city surnamed after Kapila, with all the surrounding inhabitants, was full of gladness like the city of the lord of wealth [4], crowded with heavenly nymphs, at the birth of his son Nalakûvara.

---

[1] Sc. Siva. [2] Shanmukha.

[3] Bahuvidhapushtiyasaskaram seems used as an adverb to vyadhatta, 'he made expenditure.'

[4] Kuvera.

BOOK II.

1. From the time of the birth of that son of his, who, the true master of himself, was to end all birth and old age, the king increased day by day in wealth, elephants, horses, and friends as a river increases with its influx of waters.

2. Of different kinds of wealth and jewels, and of gold, wrought or unwrought, he found[1] treasures of manifold variety[2], surpassing even the capacity of his desires.

3. Elephants from Himavat, raging with rut, whom not even princes of elephants like Padma[3] could teach to go round in circles, came without any effort and waited on him.

4. His city was all astir with the crowds of horses, some adorned with various marks and decked with new golden trappings, others unadorned and with long flowing manes,—suitable alike in strength, gentleness, and costly ornaments[4].

5. And many fertile cows, with tall calves, gathered in his kingdom, well nourished and happy,

---

[1] I suppose avâpi to be used as a middle aorist like abodhi (cf. *S*isup. I, 3). Should we read avâpa?

[2] I take naikâtman as 'of manifold nature.'

[3] Mahâpadma is the name of the elephant which supports the world in the south.

[4] I read âptai*h*.

gentle and without fierceness, and producing excellent milk.

6. His enemies became indifferent; indifference grew into friendship; his friends became specially united; were there two sides,—one passed into oblivion.

7. Heaven rained in his kingdom in due time and place, with the sound of gentle winds and clouds, and adorned with wreaths of lightning, and without any drawback of showers of stones or thunderbolts.

8. A fruitful crop sprang up according to season, even without the labour of ploughing[1]; and the old plants grew more vigorous in juice and substance.

9. Even at that crisis which threatens danger to the body like the collision of battle, pregnant women brought forth in good health, in safety, and without sickness.

10. And whereas men do not willingly ask from others, even where a surety's property is available[2], —at that time even one possessed of slender means turned not his face away when solicited.

11. There was no ruin nor murder[3],—nay, there was not even one ungenerous to his kinsmen, no breaker of obligations, none untruthful nor injurious,—as in the days of Yayâti the son of Nahusha.

12. Those who sought religious merit performed sacred works and made gardens, temples, and

[1] Tadâ*kritenâpi krishisramena.

[2] I read pratibhvo, though it should be pratibhuvo.

[3] Could nâsaubadho (C) mean 'there was no murderer of any one?'

hermitages, wells, cisterns, lakes, and groves, having beheld heaven as it were visible before their eyes.

13. The people, delivered from famine, fear, and sickness, dwelt happily as in heaven; and in mutual contentment husband transgressed not against wife, nor wife against husband.

14. None pursued love for mere sensual pleasure; none hoarded wealth for the sake of desires; none practised religious duties for the sake of gaining wealth; none injured living beings for the sake of religious duty.

15. On every side theft and its kindred vices disappeared; his own dominion was in peace and at rest from foreign interference[1]; prosperity and plenty belonged to him, and the cities in his realm were (healthy) like the forests[2].

16. When that son was born it was in that monarch's kingdom as in the reign of Manu the son of the Sun,—gladness went everywhere and evil perished; right blazed abroad and sin was still.

17. Since at the birth of this son of the king such a universal accomplishment of all objects took place, the king in consequence caused the prince's name to be Sarvârthasiddha[3].

18. But the queen Mâyâ, having seen the great glory of her new-born son, like some *R*ishi of the

---

[1] The Tibetan seems to have read parasokamuktam for para*k*akramuktam.

[2] Cf. VIII, 13. If we read ara*n*yasya we must translate these lines, 'the cities in his kingdom seemed part of the forest champaign.' This line appears to be untranslated in the Tibetan.

[3] He by whom all objects are accomplished.

gods, could not sustain the joy which it brought; and that she might not die she went to heaven.

19. Then the queen's sister, with an influence like a mother's, undistinguished from the real mother in her affection or tenderness, brought up as her own son the young prince who was like the offspring of the gods.

20. Then like the young sun on the eastern mountain or the fire when fanned by the wind, the prince gradually grew in all due perfection, like the moon in the fortnight of brightness.

21. Then they brought him as presents from the houses of his friends costly unguents of sandalwood, and strings of gems exactly like wreaths of plants, and little golden carriages yoked with deer;

22. Ornaments also suitable to his age, and elephants, deer, and horses made of gold [1], carriages and oxen decked with rich garments, and carts [2] gay with silver and gold.

23. Thus indulged with all sorts of such objects to please the senses as were suitable to his years,—child as he was, he behaved not like a child in gravity, purity, wisdom, and dignity.

24. When he had passed the period of childhood and reached that of middle youth, the young prince learned in a few days the various sciences suitable to his race, which generally took many years to master.

25. But having heard before from the great seer Asita his destined future which was to embrace

[1] Cf. Satyavat's toy horses in Mahâbh. III, 16670.

[2] Ga*m*trî has this meaning in the Amarakosha and Hema*k*andra.

transcendental happiness, the anxious care[1] of the king of the present *S*âkya race turned the prince to sensual pleasures.

26. Then he sought for him from a family of unblemished moral excellence a bride possessed of beauty, modesty, and gentle bearing, of wide-spread glory, Ya*s*odharâ by name, having a name well worthy of her, a very goddess of good fortune.

27. Then after that the prince, beloved of the king his father, he who was like Sanatkumâra, rejoiced in the society of that *S*âkya princess as the thousand-eyed (Indra) rejoiced with his bride *S*a*k*î.

28. 'He might perchance see some inauspicious sight which could disturb his mind,'—thus reflecting the king had a dwelling prepared for him apart from the busy press in the recesses of the palace.

29. Then he spent his time in those royal apartments, furnished with the delights proper for every season, gaily decorated like heavenly chariots upon the earth, and bright like the clouds of autumn, amidst the splendid musical concerts of singing-women.

30. With the softly-sounding tambourines beaten by the tips of the women's hands, and ornamented with golden rims, and with the dances which were like the dances of the heavenly nymphs, that palace shone like Mount Kailâsa.

31. There the women delighted him with their soft voices, their beautiful pearl-garlands, their playful intoxication, their sweet laughter, and their stolen glances concealed by their brows.

---

[1] The last pâda seems spurious as it is only found in C. I have tried to make some sense by reading buddhi*h* for v*ri*ddhi*h*.

32. Borne in the arms of these women well-skilled in the ways of love, and reckless in the pursuit of pleasure, he fell from the roof of a pavilion and yet reached not the ground, like a holy sage stepping from a heavenly chariot.

33. Meanwhile the king for the sake of ensuring his son's prosperity and stirred in heart by the destiny which had been predicted for him, delighted himself in perfect calm, ceased from all evil, practised all self-restraint, and rewarded the good.

34. He turned to no sensual pleasures like one wanting in self-control; he felt no violent delight in any state of birth[1]; he subdued by firmness the restless horses of the senses; and he surpassed his kindred and citizens by his virtues.

35. He sought not learning to vex another; such knowledge as was beneficent, that only he studied; he wished well to all mankind as much as to his own subjects.

36. He worshipped also duly the brilliant (Agni) that tutelary god of the Aṅgirasas, for his son's long life; and he offered oblations in a large fire, and gave gold[2] and cows to the Brahmans.

37. He bathed to purify his body and mind with the waters of holy places and of holy feelings; and at the same time he drank the soma-juice as enjoined by the Veda, and the heartfelt self-produced happiness of perfect calm.

38. He only spoke what was pleasant and not unprofitable; he discoursed about what was true and not ill-natured; he could not speak even to himself

[1] Can *g*ananî mean mât*ri*grâma?

[2] Or pearls? (k*ris*ana.)

for very shame a false pleasant thing or a harsh truth.

39. In things which required to be done, whether they were pleasant or disagreeable, he found no reason either for desire or dislike; he pursued the advantageous which could be attained without litigation[1]; he did not so highly value sacrifice.

40. When a suppliant came to him with a petition, he at once hastened to quench his thirst with the water sprinkled on his gift[2]; and without fighting, by the battle-axe of his demeanour he smote down the arrogant armed with[3] double pride.

41. Thus he took away the one, and protected the seven; he abandoned the seven and kept the five; he obtained the set of three and learned the set of three; he understood the two and abandoned the two[4].

42. Guilty persons, even though he had sentenced them to death, he did not cause to be killed nor even looked on them with anger; he bound them with gentle words and with the reform produced in their character,—even their release was accompanied by no inflicted injury.

43. He performed great religious vows prescribed by ancient seers; he threw aside hostile feelings long cherished; he acquired glory redolent with the fragrance of virtue; he relinquished all passions involving defilement.

---

[1] Professor Max Müller would read vyavahâralabdham, 'all bliss which could be obtained in the lower or vyâvahârika sphere.'

[2] See Colebrooke's Essays, vol. ii, p. 230, note; Manu IX, 168.

[3] Cf. dvisavasam (madam), Rig-veda IX, 104, 2. Professor Kielhorn would suggest dviddarpam.

[4] The Tibetan, like the Chinese, gives no help here.

44. He desired not to take his tribute of one-sixth without acting as the guardian of his people[1]; he had no wish to covet another's property; he desired not to mention the wrong-doing of his enemies; nor did he wish to fan wrath in his heart.

45. When the monarch himself was thus employed his servants and citizens followed his example, like the senses of one absorbed in contemplation whose mind is abstracted in profound repose.

46. In course of time to the fair-bosomed Yasodharâ,—who was truly glorious in accordance with her name,—there was born from the son of Suddhodana a son named Râhula, with a face like the enemy of Râhu[2].

47. Then the king who from regard to the welfare of his race had longed for a son and been exceedingly delighted [at his coming],—as he had rejoiced at the birth of his son, so did he now rejoice at the birth of his grandson.

48. 'O how can I feel that love which my son feels for my grandson?' Thus thinking in his joy he at the due time attended to every enjoined rite like one who fondly loves his son and is about to rise to heaven.

49. Standing in the paths of the pre-eminent kings who flourished in primaeval ages, he practised austerities without laying aside his white garments, and he offered in sacrifice only those things which involved no injury to living creatures.

50. He of holy deeds shone forth gloriously, in

---

[1] Cf. Indische Sprüche, 568 (2nd ed.).

[2] I.e. the sun or the moon, as eclipsed by the demon Râhu.

the splendour of royalty and the splendour of penances, conspicuous by his family and his own conduct and wisdom, and desirous to diffuse brightness like the sun.

51. Having offered worship, he whose own glory was secure muttered repetitions of Vedic texts to Svayambhû for the safety of his son, and performed various ceremonies hard to be accomplished, like the god Ka in the first aeon wishing to create living beings.

52. He laid aside weapons and pondered the *S*âstra, he practised perfect calm and underwent various observances, like a hermit he refused all objects of sense, he viewed all his kingdoms[1] like a father.

53. He endured the kingdom for the sake of his son, his son for his family, his family for fame, fame for heaven, heaven for the soul,—he only desired the soul's continuance for the sake of duty.

54. Thus did he practise the various observances as followed by the pious and established from revelation,—ever asking himself, 'now that he has seen the face of his son, how may my son be stopped from going to the forest?'

55. The prudent[2] kings of the earth, who wish to guard their prosperity, watch over their sons in the world; but this king, though loving religion, kept his son from religion and set him free towards all objects of pleasure.

---

[1] Vishayâ*h* seems used here in two senses, 'kingdoms' and 'objects of sense.'

[2] Lit. 'self-possessed,' âtmasa*m*sthâ*h*. Or should we read âtmasa*m*sthâm, 'wishing to keep their prosperity their own?'

56. But all Bodhisattvas, those beings of pre-eminent nature, after knowing the flavour of worldly enjoyments, have departed to the forest as soon as a son is born to them; therefore he too, though he had accomplished all his previous destiny, even when the (final) motive had begun to germinate, still went on pursuing worldly pleasure up to the time of attaining the supreme wisdom.

BOOK III.

1. On a certain day he heard of the forests carpeted with tender grass, with their trees resounding with the kokilas, adorned with lotus-ponds, and which had been all bound up in the cold season.

2. Having heard of the delightful appearance of the city groves beloved by the women, he resolved to go out of doors, like an elephant long shut up in a house.

3. The king, having learned the character of the wish thus expressed by his son, ordered a pleasure-party to be prepared, worthy of his own affection and his son's beauty and youth.

4. He prohibited the encounter of any afflicted common person in the highroad; 'heaven forbid that the prince with his tender nature should even imagine himself to be distressed.'

5. Then having removed out of the way with the greatest gentleness all those who had mutilated limbs or maimed senses, the decrepit and the sick and all squalid beggars, they made the highway assume its perfect beauty.

6. Along this road thus made beautiful, the fortunate prince with his well-trained attendants came down one day at a proper time from the roof of the palace and went to visit the king by his leave.

7. Then the king, with tears rising to his eyes,

having smelt his son's head[1] and long gazed upon him, gave him his permission, saying, 'Go;' but in his heart through affection he could not let him depart.

8. He then mounted a golden chariot, adorned with reins bright like flashing lightning[2], and yoked with four gentle horses, all wearing golden trappings.

9. With a worthy retinue he entered the road which was strewn with heaps of gleaming flowers, with garlands suspended and banners waving, like the moon with its asterism entering the sky.

10. Slowly, slowly he passed along the highway, watched on every side by the citizens, and beshowered by their eyes opened wide with curiosity like blue lotuses.

11. Some praised him for his gentle disposition, others hailed him for his glorious appearance, others eulogised his beauty from his fine countenance and desired for him length of days.

12. Hump-backed men coming out from the great families, and troops of foresters and dwarfs[3], and women coming out from the meaner houses bowed down like the banners of some procession of the gods.

13. [4]Hearing the news, 'the prince is going out,' from the attendants of the female apartments, the women hastened to the roofs of the different mansions, having obtained the leave of their lords.

---

[1] Cf. Wilson, Hindu Drama, vol. ii, p. 45, note.

[2] Rasmi may mean 'rays.' For aklîva cf. Soph. Philoct. 1455, ἄρσην.

[3] These are all mentioned in the Sâhitya-darpana among the attendants in a seraglio (§ 81).

[4] With this description cf. Raghuv. VII, 5–12; Kâdambarî, p. 74.

14. Hindered by the strings of their girdles which had slipped down, with their eyes bewildered as just awakened from sleep, and with their ornaments hastily put on in the stir of the news, and filled with curiosity, they crowded round;

15. Frightening the flocks of birds which lived in the houses, with the noise of their girdles and the jingling of their anklets which resounded on the staircases and roofs of the mansions, and mutually reproaching one another for their hurry.

16. Some of these women, even in their haste as they rushed longing to see, were delayed in their going by the weight of their hips and full bosoms.

17. Another, though well able to go herself, checked her pace and forbore to run, hiding with shame her ornaments hitherto worn only in seclusion, and now too boldly displayed.

18. There they were restlessly swaying about in the windows, crowded together in the mutual press, with their earrings polished by the continual collision and their ornaments all jingling.

19. The lotus-like faces of the women gleamed while they looked out from the windows with their earrings coming into mutual proximity[1], as if they were real lotuses fastened upon the houses.

20. With the palaces all alive with crowds of damsels, every aperture thrown open in eager curiosity, the magnificent city appeared on every side like heaven with its divine chariots thronged with celestial nymphs.

21. The faces of the beautiful women shone like lotuses wreathed in garlands, while through the

[1] Parasparopâsita?

narrowness of the windows their earrings were transferred to each other's cheeks.

22. Gazing down upon the prince in the road, the women appeared as if longing to fall to the earth; gazing up to him with upturned faces, the men seemed as if longing to rise to heaven[1].

23. Beholding the king's son thus radiant in his beauty and glory, those women softly whispered, 'happy is his wife,' with pure minds and from no baser feeling.

24. 'He with the long sturdy arms, who stands in his beauty like the flower-armed god visibly present, will leave his royal pomp and devote himself to religion,' thus thinking, full of kindly feelings towards him, they all offered reverence.

25. Beholding for the first time that high-road thus crowded with respectful citizens, all dressed in white sedate garments, the prince for a while did feel a little pleasure and thought that it seemed to promise a revival of his youth.

26. But then the gods, dwelling in pure abodes[2], having beheld that city thus rejoicing like heaven itself, created an old man to walk along on purpose to stir the heart of the king's son.

27. The prince having beheld him thus overcome with decrepitude and different in form from other men, with his gaze intently fixed on him, thus addressed his driver[3] with simple confidence:

28. 'Who is this man that has come here, O charioteer, with white hair and his hand resting on a staff, his eyes hidden beneath his brows, his

---

[1] Cf. Uhland's 'Das Schloss am meere.'

[2] *S*uddhâdhivâsâ*h*.

[3] Cf. sa*m*gâhako in Pâli.

limbs bent down and hanging loose,—is this a change produced in him or his natural state or an accident?'

29. Thus addressed, the charioteer revealed to the king's son the secret that should have been kept so carefully, thinking no harm in his simplicity, for those same gods had bewildered his mind:

30. 'That is old age by which he is broken down,—the ravisher of beauty, the ruin of vigour, the cause of sorrow, the destruction of delights, the bane of memories, the enemy of the senses.

31. 'He too once drank milk in his childhood, and in course of time he learned to grope on the ground; having step by step become a vigorous youth, he has step by step in the same way reached old age.'

32. Being thus addressed, the prince, starting a little, spoke these words to the charioteer, 'What! will this evil come to me also?' and to him again spoke the charioteer:

33. 'It will come without doubt by the force of time through multitude of years even to my long-lived lord; all the world knows thus that old age will destroy their comeliness and they are content to have it so.'

34. Then he, the great-souled one, who had his mind purified by the impressions of former good actions, who possessed a store of merits accumulated through many preceding aeons, was deeply agitated when he heard of old age, like a bull who has heard the crash of a thunderbolt close by.

35. Drawing a long sigh and shaking his head, and fixing his eyes on that decrepit old man, and looking round on that exultant multitude he then uttered these distressed words:

36. 'Old age thus strikes down all alike, our memory, comeliness, and valour; and yet the world is not disturbed, even when it sees such a fate visibly impending.

37. 'Since such is our condition, O charioteer, turn back the horses,—go quickly home; how can I rejoice in the pleasure-garden, when the thoughts arising from old age overpower me?'

38. Then the charioteer at the command of the king's son turned the chariot back, and the prince lost in thought entered even that royal palace as if it were empty.

39. But when he found no happiness even there, as he continually kept reflecting, 'old age, old age,' then once more, with the permission of the king, he went out with the same arrangement as before.

40. Then the same deities created another man with his body all afflicted by disease; and on seeing him the son of *S*uddhodana addressed the charioteer, having his gaze fixed on the man:

41. 'Yonder man with a swollen belly, his whole frame shaking as he pants, his arms and shoulders hanging loose, his body all pale and thin, uttering plaintively the word "mother," when he embraces a stranger,—who, pray, is this?'

42. Then his charioteer answered, 'Gentle Sir, it is a very great affliction called sickness, that has grown up, caused by the inflammation of the (three) humours, which has made even this strong man[1] no longer master of himself.'

43. Then the prince again addressed him, looking upon the man compassionately, 'Is this evil peculiar

[1] *S*akro*s*pi.

to him or are all beings alike threatened by sickness?'

44. Then the charioteer answered, 'O prince, this evil is common to all; thus pressed round by diseases men run to pleasure, though racked with pain[1].'

45. Having heard this account, his mind deeply distressed, he trembled like the moon reflected in the waves of water; and full of sorrow he uttered these words in a low voice:

46. 'Even while they see all this calamity of diseases mankind can yet feel tranquillity; alas for the scattered intelligence of men who can smile when still not free from the terrors of disease!

47. 'Let the chariot, O charioteer, be turned back from going outside, let it return straight to the king's palace; having heard this alarm of disease, my mind shrinks into itself, repelled from pleasures.'

48. Then having turned back, with all joy departed, he entered his home, absorbed in thought; and having seen him thus return a second time, the king himself entered the city.

49. Having heard the occasion of the prince's return he felt himself as deserted by him, and, although unused to severe punishment, even when displeased, he rebuked him whose duty it was to see that the road was clear.

50. And once more he arranged for his son all kinds of worldly enjoyments to their highest point; imploring in his heart, 'Would that he might not be able to forsake us, even though rendered unable only through the restlessness of his senses[2].'

---

[1] Ru*g*âturo. [The Tibetan seems to have read ru*g*â*m*tare,—nad thar-phyin-na, 'having come to the end of illness.' H.W.]

[2] I would read api nâma sakto—.

51. But when in the women's apartments his son found no pleasure in the several objects of the senses, sweet sounds and the rest, he gave orders for another progress outside, thinking to himself[1], 'It may create a diversion of sentiment[2].'

52. And in his affection pondering on the condition of his son, never thinking of any ills that might come from his haste, he ordered the best singing-women to be in attendance, as well-skilled in all the soft arts that can please.

53. Then the royal road being specially adorned and guarded, the king once more made the prince go out, having ordered the charioteer and chariot to proceed in a contrary direction (to the previous one).

54. But as the king's son was thus going on his way, the very same deities created a dead man, and only the charioteer and the prince, and none else, beheld him as he was carried dead along the road.

55. Then spoke the prince to the charioteer, 'Who is this borne by four men, followed by mournful companions, who is bewailed, adorned but no longer breathing[3]?'

56. Then the driver,—having his mind overpowered by the gods who possess pure minds and pure dwellings,—himself knowing the truth, uttered to his lord this truth also which was not to be told:

57. 'This is some poor man who, bereft of his intellect, senses, vital airs and qualities, lying asleep

---

[1] I would read manyamâna*h*.

[2] A technical term in rhetoric. Cf. Sâhitya Darp. § 220.

[3] I would read asvâsy avarudyate.

and unconscious, like mere wood or straw, is abandoned alike by friends and enemies after they have carefully swathed and guarded him.'

58. Having heard these words of the charioteer he was somewhat startled and said to him, 'Is this an accident peculiar to him alone, or is such the end of all living creatures?'

59. Then the charioteer replied to him, 'This is the final end of all living creatures; be it a mean man, a man of middle state, or a noble, destruction is fixed to all in this world.'

60. Then the king's son, sedate though he was, as soon as he heard of death, immediately sank down overwhelmed, and pressing the end of the chariot-pole with his shoulder spoke with a loud voice,

61. 'Is this end appointed to all creatures, and yet the world throws off all fear and is infatuated! Hard indeed, I think, must the hearts of men be, who can be self-composed in such a road.

62. 'Therefore, O charioteer, turn back our chariot, this is no time or place for a pleasure-excursion; how can a rational being, who knows what destruction is, stay heedless here, in the hour of calamity[1]?'

63. Even when the prince thus spoke to him, the charioteer did not turn the chariot back; but at his peremptorily reiterated command he retired to the forest Padmakha*nd*a.

64. There he beheld that lovely forest like Nandana itself, full of young trees in flower, with intoxicated kokilas wandering joyously about, and

[1] The Tibetan has ñam thag dus-su, 'at the time of oppression (as by misfortune).' Does this imply a reading **ârtti-kâle**?

with its bright lakes gay with lotuses and well-furnished with watering-places [1].

65. The king's son was perforce carried away to that wood filled with troops of beautiful women, just as if some devotee who had newly taken his vow were carried off, feeling weak to withstand temptation, to the palace of the monarch of Alakâ [2], gay with the dancing of the loveliest heavenly nymphs.

[1] Sc. for cattle, cf. Mahâbh. XII, 9270 (in the text read -dîrghika*m*).

[2] Kuvera.

BOOK IV.

1. Then from that city-garden, with their eyes restless in excitement, the women went out to meet the prince as a newly-arrived bridegroom;

2. And when they came up to him, their eyes wide open in wonder, they performed their due homage with hands folded like a lotus-calyx.

3. Then they stood surrounding him, their minds overpowered by passion, as if they were drinking him in with their eyes motionless and blossoming wide with love.

4. Some of the women verily thought that he was Kâma incarnate,—decorated as he was with his brilliant signs as with connate ornaments.

5. Others thought from his gentleness and majesty that it was the moon with its ambrosial beams as it were visibly come down to the earth.

6. Others, smitten by his beauty, yawned[1] as if to swallow him, and fixing their eyes on each other, softly sighed.

7. Thus the women only looked upon him, simply gazing with their eyes,—they spoke not, nor did they smile, controlled by his power.

8. But having seen them thus listless, bewildered in their love, the wise son of the family priest, Udâyin, thus addressed them:

9. 'Ye are all skilled in all the graceful arts,

---

[1] Cf. Sâhitya Darp. § 155, 13.

proficients in understanding the language of amorous sentiments, possessed of beauty and gracefulness, thorough masters in your own styles.

10. 'With these graces of yours ye may embellish even the Northern Kurus, yea, even the dances [1] of Kuvera, much more this little earth.

11. 'Ye are able to move even sages who have lost all their desires, and to ensnare even the gods who are charmed by heavenly nymphs.

12. 'By your skill in expressing the heart's feelings, by your coquetry, your grace, and your perfect beauty, ye are able to enrapture even women, how much more easily men.

13. 'You thus skilled as ye are, each set [2] in her own proper sphere,—such as this is your power,—I am not satisfied with your simplicity [when you profess to find him beyond your reach].

14. 'This timid action of yours would be fit for new brides, their eyes closed through shame,—or it might be a blandishment worthy even of the wives of the cowherds [3].

15. 'What though this hero be great by his exalted glory, yet "great is the might of women," let this be your firm resolve.

16. 'In olden time a great seer, hard to be conquered even by the gods, was spurned by a harlot, the beauty of Kâsi, planting her feet upon him.

17. 'The Bhikshu Manthâlagautama was also formerly spurned by Bâlamukhyâ with her leg, and

---

[1] Professor Bühler suggests *kâkrîdam*, cf. *sloka* 28.

[2] I read niyuktânâm for viyuktânâm.

[3] Is this a reference to Krishna's story? but cf. Weber, Ind. Antiquary, vol. v, p. 254.

wishing to please her he carried out dead bodies for her sake to be buried.

18. 'And a woman low in standing and caste fascinated the great seer Gautama, though a master of long penances and old in years.

19. 'So *S*ântâ[1] by her various wiles captivated and subdued the sage's son *Ri*shyas*ri*ṅga, unskilled in women's ways.

20. 'And the great seer Vi*s*vâmitra, though plunged in a profound penance[2], was carried captive for ten years in the forests by the nymph Gh*ri*tâ*k*î[3].

21. 'Many such seers as these have women brought to shame,—how much more then a delicate prince in the first flower of his age?

22. 'This being so, boldly put forth your efforts that the prosperity of the king's family may not be turned away from him.

23. 'Ordinary women captivate similar lovers; but they are truly women who subdue the natures of high and low.'

24. Having heard these words of Udâyin these women as stung to the heart rose even above themselves for the conquest of the prince.

25. With their brows, their glances, their coquetries, their smiles, their delicate movements, they made all sorts of significant gestures like women utterly terrified.

26. But they soon regained their confidence[4] through the command of the king and the gentle temperament of the prince, and through the power of intoxication and of love.

---

[1] Râmây. I, 10 (Schleg. ed.). [2] I would read mahat tapa*h*.
[3] Râmây. IV, 35. [4] Lit. 'dispelled their want of confidence.'

27. Then surrounded by troops of women the prince wandered in the wood like an elephant in the forests of Himavat accompanied by a herd of females.

28. Attended by the women he shone in that pleasant grove, as the sun surrounded by Apsarasas in his royal garden.

29. There some of them, urged by passion, pressed him with their full firm bosoms in gentle collisions.

30. Another violently embraced him after making a pretended stumble,—leaning on him with her shoulders drooping down, and with her gentle creeper-like arms dependent.

31. Another with her mouth smelling of spirituous liquor, her lower lip red like copper, whispered in his ear, 'Let my secret be heard.'

32. Another, all wet with unguents, as if giving him her command, clasped his hand eagerly and said, 'Perform thy rites of adoration here.'

33. Another, with her blue garments continually slipping down in pretended intoxication, stood conspicuous with her tongue visible like the night with its lightning flashing.

34. Others, with their golden zones tinkling, wandered about here and there, showing to him their hips veiled with thin cloth.

35. Others leaned, holding a mango-bough in full flower, displaying their bosoms like golden jars.

36. Another, coming from a lotus-bed, carrying lotuses and with eyes like lotuses, stood like the lotus-goddess Padmâ, by the side of that lotus-faced prince.

37. Another sang a sweet song easily understood and with the proper gesticulations, rousing

him, self-subdued though he was, by her glances, as saying, 'O how thou art deluded!'

38. Another, having armed herself[1] with her bright face, with its brow-bow drawn to its full, imitated his action, as playing the hero.

39. Another, with beautiful full bosoms, and having her earrings waving in the wind[2], laughed loudly at him, as if saying, 'Catch me, sir, if you can!'

40. Some, as he was going away, bound him with strings of garlands,—others punished him with words like an elephant-driver's hook, gentle yet reproachful.

41. Another, wishing to argue with him, seizing a mango-spray, asked, all bewildered with passion, 'This flower, whose is it?'

42. Another, assuming a gait and attitude like those of a man, said to him, 'Thou who art conquered by women, go and conquer this earth!'

43. Then another with rolling eyes, smelling a blue lotus, thus addressed the prince with words slightly indistinct in her excitement,

44. 'See, my lord, this mango covered with its honey-scented flowers, where the kokila sings, as if imprisoned in a golden cage.

45. 'Come and see this a*s*oka tree, which augments lovers' sorrows,—where the bees make a noise as if they were scorched by fire.

46. 'Come and see this tilaka tree, embraced by a slender mango-branch, like a man in a white garment by a woman decked with yellow unguents.

47. 'Behold this kuruvaka in flower, bright like

---

[1] Prâv*ri*tya.

[2] I read vâtâghûr*n*ita.

fresh[1] resin-juice, which bends down as if it felt reproached by the colour of women's nails[2].

48. 'Come and see this young asoka, covered all over with new shoots, which stands as it were ashamed at the beauty of our hands.

49. 'See this lake surrounded by the sinduvâra shrubs growing on its banks[3], like a fair woman reclining, clad in fine white cloth.

50. 'See the imperial power of females,—yonder ruddy-goose in the water goes behind his mate following her like a slave.

51. 'Come and listen to the notes of this intoxicated cuckoo as he sings, while another cuckoo sings as if consenting, wholly without care.

52. 'Would that thine was the intoxication of the birds which the spring produces,—and not the thought of a thinking man, ever pondering how wise he is!'

53. Thus these young women, their souls carried away by love, assailed the prince with all kinds of stratagems.

54. But although thus attacked, he, having his senses guarded by self-control, neither rejoiced nor smiled, thinking anxiously, 'One must die.'

55. Having seen them in their real condition[4], that best of men pondered with an undisturbed[5] and stedfast mind.

---

[1] I read nirmuktam, which might mean 'just exuded,' or the whole compound may mean (cf. Kum. Sambh. V, 34) 'like a lip which has given up the use of pinguent.'

[2] Cf. Vikramorvasî, Act II, strî-nakha-pâtalam kuruvakam.

[3] I read tîragaih sinduvârakaih.

[4] For vasthânam cf. Maitri Upan. (Comm.) VI, 1.

[5] I would read asamvignena.

56. 'What is it that these women lack[1] that they perceive not that youth is fickle? for this old age will destroy whatever has beauty.

57. 'Verily they do not see any one's plunge into disease, and so dismissing fear, they are joyous in a world which is all pain.

58. 'Evidently they know nothing of death which carries all away; and so at ease and without distress they can sport and laugh.

59. 'What rational being, who knows of old age, death and sickness, could stand[2] or sit down at his ease or sleep, far less laugh?

60. 'But he verily is like one bĕreft of sense, who, beholding another aged or sick or dead, remains self-possessed and not afflicted.

61. '(So) even when a tree is deprived of its flowers and fruits, or if it is cut down and falls, no other tree sorrows.'

62. Seeing him thus absorbed in contemplation, with his desires estranged from all worldly objects, Udâyin, well skilled in the rules of policy, with kindly feelings addressed him:

63. 'Since I was appointed by the king as a fitting friend for thee, therefore I have a wish to speak to thee in this friendliness of my heart.

64. 'To hinder from what is disadvantageous,—to urge to what is advantageous,—and not to forsake in misfortune,—these are the three marks of a friend.

65. 'If I, after having promised my friendship, were not to heed when thou turnest away from the great end of man, there would be no friendship in me.

---

[1] Ki*m* vinâ. [2] I would conjecture tish*th*en.

66. 'Therefore I speak as thy friend,—such rudeness as this to women is not befitting for one young in years and graceful in person.

67. 'It is right to woo a woman even by guile,—this is useful both for getting rid of shame and for one's own enjoyment.

68. 'Reverential behaviour and compliance with her wishes are what binds a woman's heart; good qualities truly are a cause of love, and women love respect.

69. 'Wilt thou not then, O large-eyed prince, even if thy heart is unwilling, seek to please them with a courtesy worthy of this beauty of thine?

70. 'Courtesy is the balm of women, courtesy is the best ornament; beauty without courtesy is like a grove without flowers.

71. 'But of what use is courtesy by itself? let it be assisted by the heart's feelings; surely, when worldly objects so hard to attain are in thy grasp, thou wilt not despise them.

72. 'Knowing that pleasure was the best of objects, even the god Pura*m*dara (Indra) wooed in olden time Ahalyâ the wife of the saint Gautama.

73. 'So too Agastya wooed Rohi*n*î, the wife of Soma; and therefore, as *S*ruti saith, a like thing befell Lopâmudrâ[1].

74. 'The great ascetic V*ri*haspati begot Bharadvâ*g*a on Mamatâ the daughter of the Maruts, the wife of Autathya[2].

---

[1] Agastya's wife. This seems to refer to Lopâmudrâ's words to her husband in Rig-veda I, 179; cf. also Mahâbh. III, xcvii.

[2] This should be Utathya (cf. Mahâbh. I, civ). Mamatâ had Dîrghatamas by her husband and Bharadvâ*g*a by V*ri*haspati. The MSS. read Samatâ.

75. 'The Moon, the best of offerers, begat Budha of divine nature on the spouse of V*ri*haspati as she was offering a libation[1].

76. 'So too in old time Parâ*s*ara, overpowered by passion on the bank of the Yamunâ, lay with the maiden Kâlî who was the daughter of the son of the Water (Agni).

77. 'The sage Va*s*ish*th*a through lust begot a son Kapi*ñg*alâda on Akshamâlâ a despised low-caste woman[2].

78. 'And the seer-king Yayâti, even when the vigour of his prime was gone, sported in the *K*aitraratha forest with the Apsaras Vi*s*vâ*k*î.

79. 'And the Kaurava king Pâ*nd*u, though he knew that intercourse with his wife would end in death, yet overcome by the beauty and good qualities of Mâdrî yielded to the pleasures of love.

80. 'And so Karâla*g*anaka, when he carried off the Brâhman's daughter, incurred loss of caste thereby, but he would not give up his love.

81. 'Great heroes such as these pursued even contemptible desires for the sake of pleasure, how much more so when they are praiseworthy of their kind?

82. 'And yet thou, a young man, possessed of strength and beauty, despisest enjoyments which rightly belong to thee, and to which the whole world is devoted.'

83. Having heard these specious words of his, well-supported by sacred tradition, the prince made reply, in a voice like the thundering of a cloud:

---

[1] She is called Târâ, Vish*n*u Pur. IV, 6.

[2] Manu IX, 23.

84. 'This speech manifesting affection is well-befitting in thee; but I will convince thee as to where thou wrongly judgest me.

85. 'I do not despise worldly objects, I know that all mankind are bound up therein; but remembering that the world is transitory, my mind cannot find pleasure in them.

86. 'Old age, disease, and death—if these three things did not exist, I too should find my enjoyment in the objects that please the mind.

87. 'Yet even though this beauty of women were to remain perpetual, still delight in the pleasures of desire would not be worthy of the wise man.

88. 'But since their beauty will be drunk up by old age, to delight therein through infatuation cannot be a thing approved even by thyself[1].

89. 'He who himself subject to death, disease, and old age, can sport undisturbed with those whose very nature implies death, disease, and old age,—such a man is on a level with birds and beasts.

90. 'And as for what thou sayest as to even those great men having become victims to desire,—do not be bewildered by them, for destruction was also their lot.

91. 'Real greatness is not to be found there, where there is universally destruction, or where there is attachment to earthly objects, or a want of self-control.

92. 'And when thou sayest, "Let one deal with women even by guile," I know nought about guile, even if it be accompanied with courtesy.

93. 'That compliance too with a woman's wishes

[1] Or 'even by the soul.'

pleases me not, if truthfulness be not there; if there be not a union with one's whole soul and nature, then "out upon it" say I.

94. 'A soul overpowered by passion, believing in falsehood, carried away by attachment and blind to the faults of its objects,—what is there in it worth being deceived?

95. 'And if the victims of passion do deceive one another,—are not men unfit for women to look at and women for men?

96. 'Since then these things are so, thou surely wouldest not lead me astray into ignoble pleasures, —me afflicted by sorrow, and subject to old age and death?

97. 'Ah! thy mind must be very firm and strong, if thou canst find substance in the transitory pleasures of sense; even in the midst of violent alarm thou canst cling to worldly objects, when thou seest all created beings in the road of death.

98. 'But I am fearful and exceedingly bewildered, as I ponder the terrors of old age, death, and disease; I can find no peace, no self-command, much less can I find pleasure, while I see the world as it were ablaze with fire.

99. 'If desire arises in the heart of the man, who knows that death is certain,—I think that his soul must be made of iron, who restrains it in this great terror and does not weep.'

100. Then the prince uttered a discourse full of resolve and abolishing the objects of desire; and the lord of day, whose orb is the worthy centre of human eyes, departed to the Western Mountain.

101. And the women, having worn their garlands and ornaments in vain, with their graceful arts and

endearments all fruitless, concealing their love deep in their hearts[1], returned to the city with broken hopes.

102. Having thus seen the beauty[2] of the troop of women who had gone out to the city-garden, now withdrawn in the evening,—the prince, pondering the transitoriness which envelopes all things, entered his dwelling.

103. Then the king, when he heard how his mind turned away from all objects of sense, could not lie down all that night, like an elephant with an arrow in its heart; but wearied in all sorts of consultation, he and his ministers could find no other means beside these (despised) pleasures to restrain his son's purpose.

---

[1] Reading sva eva bhâve from the Tibetan.

[2] Reading sriyam for striyam.

BOOK V.

1. He, the son of the *S*âkya king, even though thus tempted by the objects of sense which infatuate others, yielded not to pleasure and felt not delight, like a lion deeply pierced in his heart by a poisoned arrow.

2. Then one day accompanied by some worthy sons of his father's ministers, friends full of varied converse,—with a desire to see the glades of the forest and longing for peace, he went out with the king's permission.

3. Having mounted his good horse Ka*m*thaka, decked with bells and bridle-bit of new gold, with beautiful golden harness and the chowrie waving[1], he went forth like the moon[2] mounted on a comet.

4. Lured by love of the wood and longing for the beauties of the ground[3], he went to a spot near at hand[4] on the forest-outskirts; and there he saw a piece of land being ploughed, with the path of the plough broken like waves on the water.

---

[1] 'The white bushy tail of the Tibet cow, fixed on a gold or ornamented shaft, rose from between the ears of the horse.' Wilson, Hindu Drama, I, p. 200.

[2] The Tibetan has tog-la ljon-dañ chu-skyes tog-can, 'like him who has the sign of a tree and water-born (lotus,) (mounted) on a comet,' but with no further explanation. Could this mean the moon as oshadhipati and as kumu e*s*a?

[3] Should we read -gu*n*e*kkh*u*h* for -gu*n*â*kkh*a*h*?

[4] Nik*ri*sh*t*atarâm; one MS. reads vik*ri*sh*t*a-, 'ploughed.'

5. Having beheld the ground in this condition, with its young grass scattered and torn by the plough, and covered with the eggs and young of little insects which were killed, he was filled with deep sorrow as for the slaughter of his own kindred.

6. And beholding the men as they were ploughing, their complexions spoiled by the dust, the sun's rays, and the wind, and their cattle bewildered with the burden of drawing, the most noble one felt extreme compassion.

7. Having alighted from the back of his horse, he went over the ground slowly, overcome with sorrow, —pondering the birth and destruction of the world, he, grieved, exclaimed, 'this is indeed pitiable.'

8. Then desiring to become perfectly lonely in his thoughts, having stopped those friends who were following him, he went to the root of a rose-apple in a solitary spot, which had its beautiful leaves all tremulous (in the wind).

9. There he sat down on the ground covered with leaves [1], and with its young grass bright like lapis lazuli; and, meditating on the origin and destruction of the world, he laid hold of the path that leads to firmness of mind.

10. Having attained to firmness of mind [2], and being forthwith set free from all sorrows such as the desire of worldly objects and the rest, he attained

---

[1] The MSS. add -khoravatyâ*m*, an obscure word, which may be connected with khura or perhaps should be altered to -koravatyâ*m*, i.e. 'covered with sharp-pointed leaves,' or 'covered with leaves and buds.' [The Tibetan has gčań-mar ldan-pai sa-gzhi der-ni de zhugs-te, 'on the pure ground here he sitting.' This might point to so*x*tra *s*au*k*avatyâ*m*. H. W.]

[2] Query, *s*amavâptamana*h*sthiti*h* for -manâ*h*sthite*h*.

the first stage of contemplation, unaffected by sin, calm, and 'argumentative[1].'

11. Having then obtained the highest happiness sprung from deliberation[2], he next pondered this meditation,—having thoroughly understood in his mind the course of the world:

12. 'It is a miserable thing that mankind, though themselves powerless[3] and subject to sickness, old age, and death, yet, blinded by passion and ignorant, look with disgust on another who is afflicted by old age or diseased or dead.

13. 'If I here, being such myself, should feel disgust for another who has such a nature, it would not be worthy or right in me who know this highest duty.'

14. As he thus considered thoroughly these faults of sickness, old age, and death which belong to all living beings, all the joy which he had felt in the activity of his vigour, his youth, and his life, vanished in a moment.

15. He did not rejoice, he did not feel remorse; he suffered no hesitation, indolence, nor sleep; he felt no drawing towards the qualities of desire; he hated not nor scorned another.

16. Thus did this pure passionless meditation grow within the great-souled one; and unobserved by the other men, there crept up a man in a beggar's dress.

17. The king's son asked him a question,—he said to him, 'Tell me, who art thou?' and the other replied, 'Oh bull of men, I, being terrified at birth

[1] *S*avitarka, cf. Yoga-sûtras I, 42. (Read anâsrava-.)

[2] Two syllables are lost in this line. [3] Arasa*h*.

and death, have become an ascetic for the sake of liberation.

18. 'Desiring liberation in a world subject to destruction, I seek that happy indestructible abode,—isolated from mankind, with my thoughts unlike those of others, and with my sinful passions turned away from all objects of sense

19. 'Dwelling anywhere, at the root of a tree, or in an uninhabited house, a mountain or a forest,—I wander without a family and without hope, a beggar ready for any fare, seeking only the highest good.'

20. When he had thus spoken, while the prince was looking on, he suddenly flew up to the sky; it was a heavenly inhabitant who, knowing that the prince's thoughts were other than what his outward form promised, had come to him for the sake of rousing his recollection.

21. When the other was gone like a bird to heaven, the foremost of men was rejoiced and astonished; and having comprehended the meaning of the term dharma[1], he set his mind on the manner of the accomplishment of deliverance.

22. Then like Indra himself, and having tamed his senses,—desiring to return home he mounted his noble steed; and having made him turn back as he looked for his friends, from that moment he sought no more the desired forest.

23. Ever seeking to make an end of old age and death, fixing his thoughts in memory on dwelling in the woods, he entered the city again but with no feelings of longing, like an elephant entering an exercise-ground[2] after roaming in a forest-land.

24. 'Happy truly and blessed is that woman whose

[1] Dharmasa*mg*ñâm?

[2] Cf. II, 3.

husband is such as thou, O long-eyed prince!' So, on seeing him, the princess exclaimed, folding her hands to welcome him, as he entered the road.

25. He whose voice was deep-sounding like a cloud heard this address and was filled with profound calm; and as he heard the word 'blessed[1]' he fixed his mind on the attainment of Nirvâ*n*a.

26. Then the prince whose form was like the peak of a golden mountain,—whose eye, voice, and arm resembled a bull, a cloud, and an elephant[2],—whose countenance and prowess were like the moon and a lion,—having a longing aroused for something imperishable,—went into his palace.

27. Then stepping like a lion he went towards the king who was attended by his numerous counsellors, like Sanatkumâra in heaven waiting on Indra resplendent in the assembly[3] of the Maruts.

28. Prostrating himself, with folded hands, he addressed him, 'Grant me graciously thy permission, O lord of men,—I wish to become a wandering mendicant for the sake of liberation, since separation is appointed for me.'

29. Having heard his words, the king shook like a tree struck by an elephant, and having seized his folded hands which were like a lotus, he thus addressed him in a voice choked with tears:

30. 'O my son, keep back this thought, it is not the time for thee to betake thyself to dharma; they say that the practice of religion is full of evils in the first period of life when the mind is still fickle.

---

[1] Sc. nirv*ri*ta.

[2] Ga*g*ameghar*sh*abhabâhunisvanâksha*h*? So Chinese translation, Beal, st. 356.

[3] I read samitau.

†

31. 'The mind of the thoughtless ignorant young man whose senses are eager for worldly objects, and who has no power of settled resolution for the hardships of vows of penance, shrinks back from the forest, for it is especially destitute of discrimination.

32. 'It is high time for me to practise religion, O my child of loved qualities[1], leaving my royal glory to thee who art well worthy to be distinguished by it; but thy religion, O firm-striding hero, is to be accomplished by heroism; it would be irreligion if thou wert to leave thine own father.

33. 'Do thou therefore abandon this thy resolution; devote thyself for the present to the duties of a householder; to a man who has enjoyed the pleasures of his prime, it is delightful to enter the penance-forest.'

34. Having heard these words of the king, he made his reply in a voice soft like a sparrow's: 'If thou wilt be my surety, O king, against four contingencies, I will not betake myself to the forest.

35. 'Let not my life be subject to death, and let not disease impair this health of mine; let not old age attack my youth, and let not misfortune destroy my weal.'

36. When his son uttered a speech so hard to be understood, the king of the *S*âkyas thus replied: 'Abandon this idea bent upon departure; extravagant desires are only ridiculous.'

37. Then he who was firm as Mount Meru addressed his father: 'If this is impossible, then this course of mine is not to be hindered; it is not right to lay hold of one who would escape[2] from a house that is on fire.

[1] Or 'lover of religion.'

[2] Read nis*k*ikramishum.

38. 'As separation is inevitable to the world, but not for Dharma[1], this separation is preferable; will not death sever me helplessly, my objects unattained and myself unsatisfied?'

39. The monarch, having heard this resolve of his son longing for liberation, and having again exclaimed, 'He shall not go,' set guards round him and the highest pleasures.

40. Then having been duly instructed[2] by the counsellors, with all respect and affection, according to the *s*âstras, and being thus forbidden with tears by his father, the prince, sorrowing, entered into his palace.

41. There he was gazed at by his wives with restless eyes, whose faces were kissed by their dangling earrings, and whose bosoms were shaken with their thick-coming sighs,—as by so many young fawns.

42. Bright like a golden mountain, and bewitching the hearts of the noble women, he enraptured their ears, limbs, eyes, and souls by his speech, touch, form, and qualities.

43. When the day was gone, then, shining with his form like the sun, he ascended the palace, as the rising sun ascends Mount Meru, desiring to dispel the darkness by his own splendour.

44. Having ascended, he repaired to a special golden seat decorated with embellishments of diamond, with tall lighted candlesticks ablaze with gold, and its interior filled with the incense of black aloe-wood.

45. Then the noblest of women waited during the

[1] This accompanies the soul at death; cf. Manu VIII, 17.

[2] Does this allude to Udâyin? or should we translate it 'being shown the way?'

night on the noblest of men who was like Indra himself, with a concert of musical instruments, as the crowds of heavenly nymphs wait on the son of the Lord of wealth [1] upon the summit of Himavat, white like the moon.

46. But even by those beautiful instruments like heavenly music he was not moved to pleasure or delight; since his desire to go forth from his home to seek the bliss of the highest end was never lulled.

47. Then by the power of the heavenly beings most excellent in self-mortification, the Akanish*th*as, who knew the purpose of his heart, deep sleep was suddenly thrown on that company of women and their limbs and gestures became distorted [2].

48. One was lying there, resting her cheek on her trembling arm; leaving as in anger her lute, though dearly loved, which lay on her side, decorated with gold-leaf.

49. Another shone with her flute clinging to her hand, lying with her white garments fallen from her bosom,—like a river whose banks are smiling with the foam of the water and whose lotuses are covered with a straight line of bees [3].

50. Another was sleeping [4], embracing her drum as a lover, with her two arms tender like the shoot of a young lotus and bearing their bracelets closely linked, blazing with gold.

51. Others, decked with new golden ornaments

---

[1] Sc. Kuvera. I follow Professor Max Müller's suggested reading himava*kk*hirasîva for the MS. himavadgirisîra.

[2] With this description of the sleeping women compare that in the Râmâya*n*a, V, 10.

[3] The bees represent the flute held in the lotus-like hand.

[4] I would read tathâparâ.

and wearing peerless yellow garments, fell down alas! helpless with sleep, like the boughs of the Kar*n*ikâra broken by an elephant.

52. Another, leaning on the side of a window, with her willow-form bent like a bow, shone as she lay with her beautiful necklace hanging down, like a statue [1] in an archway made by art.

53. The lotus-face of another, bowed down, with the pinguent-lines on her person rubbed by the jewelled earrings, appeared to be a lotus with its stalk bent into a half-circle, and shaken by a duck standing on it [2].

54. Others, lying as they sat, with their limbs oppressed by the weight of their bosoms, shone in their beauty, mutually clasping one another with their twining arms decorated with golden bracelets.

55. And another damsel lay sound asleep, embracing her big lute as if it were a female friend, and rolled it about, while its golden strings trembled, with her own face bright with her shaken earrings.

56. Another lay, with her tabour, . . .

57. Others showed no lustre with their eyes shut, although they were really full-eyed and fair-browed, —like the lotus-beds with their buds closed at the setting of the sun.

58. Another, with her hair loose and dishevelled, and her skirts and ornaments fallen from her loins, lay with her necklace in confusion, like a woman crushed by an elephant and then dropped.

59. Others, helpless and lost to shame, though

[1] *S*âlabha*mg*ikâ?

[2] This is a hard verse, but the woman's face above the bent body seems to be compared to the duck standing on the flower and bending its stalk.

naturally self-possessed and endued with all graces of person, breathed violently as they lay and yawned with their arms distorted and tossed about.

60. Others, with their ornaments and garlands thrown off,—unconscious, with their garments spread out unfastened,—their bright eyes wide open and motionless,—lay without any beauty as if they were dead.

61. Another, with fully-developed limbs, her mouth wide open, her saliva dropping, and her person exposed, lay as though sprawling in intoxication,—she spoke not, but bore every limb distorted.

62. Thus that company of women, lying in different attitudes, according to their disposition and family, bore the aspect of a lake whose lotuses were bent down and broken by the wind.

63. Then having seen these young women thus lying distorted and with uncontrolled gestures,—however excellent their forms and graceful their appearance,—the king's son felt moved with scorn.

64. 'Such is the nature of women, impure and monstrous in the world of living beings; but deceived by dress and ornaments a man becomes infatuated by a woman's attractions.

65. 'If a man would but consider the natural state of women and this change produced in them by sleep, assuredly he would not cherish his folly; but he is smitten from a right will and so succumbs to passion.'

66. Thus to him having recognised that difference there arose a desire to escape in the night; and then the gods, knowing his purpose, caused the door of the palace to fly open.

67. Then he went down from the roof of the

palace, scorning those women who lay thus distorted; and having descended, undauntedly he went out first into the courtyard[1].

68. Having awakened his horse's attendant, the swift *Kh*a*m*daka, he thus addressed him: 'Bring me quickly my horse Ka*m*thaka[2], I wish to-day to go hence to attain immortality.

69. 'Since such is the firm content which to-day is produced in my heart, and since my determination is settled in calm resolve, and since even in loneliness I seem to possess a guide,—verily the end which I desire is now before me.

70. 'Since abandoning all shame and modesty these women lay before me as they did, and the two doors opened of their own accord, verily the time is come to depart for my true health.'

71. Then, accepting his lord's command, though he knew the purport of the king's injunctions, as being urged by a higher power in his mind, he set himself to bring the horse.

72. Then he brought out for his master that noble steed, his mouth furnished with a golden bit, his back lightly touched by the bed on which he had been lying, and endued with strength, vigour, speed, and swiftness[3];

73. With a long chine, and root of the tail and heel,—gentle, with short hair, back, and ears,—with his back, belly, and sides depressed and elevated,—with broad nostrils, forehead, hips, and breast[4].

74. The broad-chested hero, having embraced him,

---

[1] Cf. Mahâbh. II, 32.
[2] Spelt in the MSS. sometimes Ka*m*t*h*aka, but not always clear.
[3] Read *g*avatvaropapannam for MS. *g*avatvalo-.
[4] Cf. the description in Shakespeare's Venus and Adonis.

and caressing him with his lotus-like hand, ordered him with a gentle-toned voice, as if he were desirous to plunge into the middle of an army:

75. 'Oftentimes have evil enemies been overthrown by the king when mounted on thee; do thou, O best of steeds, so exert thyself that I too may obtain the highest immortality[1].

76. 'Companions are easy to be found in battle or in the happiness obtained by winning worldly objects or in attaining wealth; but companions are hard for a man to find who has fallen into misfortune or when he flies for refuge to Dharma.

77. 'And yet all those who in this world are companions, whether in sinful custom or in seeking for Dharma,—as my inner soul now recognises,—they too are verily sharers in the common aim.

78. 'Since then, when I attain this righteous end, my escape from hence will be for the good of the world,—O best of steeds, by thy speed and energy, strive for thine own good and the good of the world.'

79. Thus having exhorted the best of steeds like a friend to his duty, he, the best of men, longing to go to the forest, wearing a noble form, in brightness like fire[2], mounted the white horse as the sun an autumnal cloud.

80. Then that good steed, avoiding all noises which would sound startling in the dead of night and awaken the household,—all sound of his jaws hushed and his neighing silenced,—went forth, planting his hurrying steps at full speed.

81. With their lotus-like hands, whose fore-arms

[1] Yathâvat=yathâ.

[2] Asitagati seems here used like krishnagati, 'fire.'

were adorned with golden bracelets, the Yakshas, with their bodies bent down, threw lotuses and bore up his hoofs as he rushed in startled haste.

82. The city-roads which were closed with heavy gates and bars, and which could be with difficulty opened[1] even by elephants, flew open of their own accord without noise, as the prince went through.

83. Firm in his resolve and leaving behind without hesitation his father who turned ever towards him[2], and his young son, his affectionate people and his unparalleled magnificence, he then went forth out of his father's city.

84. Then he with his eyes long and like a full-blown lotus, looking back on the city, uttered a sound like a lion, 'Till I have seen the further shore of birth and death I will never again enter the city called after Kapila.'

85. Having heard this his utterance, the troops of the court of the Lord of wealth[3] rejoiced; and the hosts of the gods, triumphing, wished him a successful accomplishment of his purpose.

86. Other heavenly beings with forms bright like fire, knowing that his purpose was hard to fulfil, produced a light on his dewy path like the rays of the moon issuing from the rift of a cloud.

87. But he with his horse like the horse of Indra, the lord of bay horses, hurrying on as if spurred in his mind, went over the leagues full of many conflicting emotions[4],—the sky all the while with its cloud-masses checkered with the light of the dawn.

---

[1] Apâdhriyante MSS., but I read apâvri-.

[2] Abhimukham.

[3] Sc. the Yakshas.

[4] Or perhaps 'six leagues.'

BOOK VI.

1. Then when the sun, the eye of the world, was just risen, he, the noblest of men, beheld the hermitage of the son of Bh*ri*gu,

2. Its deer all asleep in quiet trust, its birds tranquilly resting,—seeing it he too became restful, and he felt as if his end was attained.

3. For the sake of ending his wonder and to show reverence for the penances observed, and as expressing his own conformity therewith [1], he alighted from the back of his horse.

4. Having alighted, he stroked the horse, exclaiming, 'All is saved,' and he spoke well-pleased to *Kh*a*m*daka, bedewing him as it were with tears from his eyes:

5. 'Good friend, thy devotion to me and thy courage of soul have been proved by thy thus following this steed whose speed is like that of Târkshya [2].

6. 'Bent even though I am on other business, I am wholly won in heart by thee,—one who has such a love for his master, and at the same time is able to carry out his wish.

7. 'One can be able without affection, and affectionate though unable; but one like thee, at once affectionate and able, is hard to find in the world.

---

[1] Svâ*m* *k*ânuvartitâ*m* rakshan. [The Tibetan has the obscure raṅ·gi rjes·su bsruṅ·va la=sva+anu+rakshan? H. W.]

[2] An old mythic representation of the sun as a horse.

8. 'I am pleased with this noble action of thine; this feeling is seen towards me, even though I am regardless of conferring rewards.

9. 'Who would not be favourably disposed to one who stands to him as bringing him reward? but even one's own people commonly become mere strangers in a reverse of fortune[1].

10. 'The son is maintained for the sake of the family, the father is honoured for the sake of our own (future) support; the world shows kindness for the sake of hope; there is no such a thing as unselfishness without a motive.

11. 'Why speak many words? in short, thou hast done me a very great kindness; take now my horse and return, I have attained the desired wood.'

12. Thus having spoken, the mighty hero in his desire to show perfect gentleness[2] unloosed his ornaments and gave them to the other, who was deeply grieved.

13. Having taken a brilliant jewel whose effect illumined his diadem, he stood, uttering these words, like the mountain Mamdara with the sun resting on it:

14. 'By thee with this jewel, O *Kh*a*m*da, having offered him repeated obeisance, the king, with his loving confidence still unshaken, must be enjoined to stay his grief.

15. '"I have entered the ascetic-wood to destroy old age and death,—with no thirst for heaven, with no lack of love nor feeling of anger.

---

[1] *G*anîbhavati may be a quaint expression for para*g*ano bhavati,—this seems the meaning of the Tibetan. Or we might read *g*anyo bhavati.

[2] Ânr*i*s*am*sa (for ânr*i*s*am*sya), see Pâ*n*ini V, 1, 130 ga*n*a.

16. '"Do not think of mourning for me who am thus gone forth from my home; union, however long it may last, in time will come to an end.

17. '"Since separation is certain, therefore is my mind fixed on liberation; how shall there not be repeated severings from one's kindred?

18. '"Do not think of mourning for me who am gone forth to leave sorrow behind; it is the thralls of passion, who are attached to desires, the causes of sorrow, for whom thou shouldst mourn.

19. '"This was the firm persuasion of our predecessors,—I as one departing by a common road am not to be mourned for by my heir.

20. '"At a man's death there are doubtless heirs to his wealth; but heirs to his merit are hard to find on the earth or exist not at all.

21. '"Even though thou sayest, 'He is gone at a wrong time to the wood,'—there is no wrong time for religious duty (dharma), life being fragile as it is.

22. '"Therefore my determination is, 'I must seek my supreme good this very day;' what confidence can there be in life, when death stands as our adversary?"

23. 'Do thou address the king, O friend, with these and such-like words; and do thou use thy efforts so that he may not even remember me.

24. 'Yea, do thou repeat to the king our utter unworthiness; through unworthiness affection is lost,—and where affection is lost, there is no sorrow.'

25. Having heard these words, *Khamd*a, overwhelmed with grief, made reply with folded hands, his voice choked by tears:

26. 'At this state of mind of thine, causing afflic-

tion to thy kindred, my mind, O my lord, sinks down like an elephant in the mud of a river.

27. 'To whom would not such a determination as this of thine cause tears, even if his heart were of iron,—how much more if it were throbbing with love?

28. 'Where[1] is this delicacy of limb, fit to lie only in a palace,—and where is the ground of the ascetic-forest, covered with the shoots of rough kusa grass?

29. 'When, on hearing thy resolve, I first brought thee this horse,—it was fate only, O my lord, which made me do it, mastering my will.

30. 'But how could I, O king, by mine own will,—knowing this thy decision,—carry back the horse to the sorrow of Kapilavastu?

31. 'Surely thou wilt not abandon, O hero, that fond old king, so devoted to his son, as a heretic might the true religion?

32. 'And her, thy second mother, worn with the care of bringing thee up,—thou wilt not surely forget her, as an ingrate a benefit?

33. 'Thou wilt not surely abandon thy queen, endowed with all virtues, illustrious for her family, devoted to her husband and with a young son, as a coward the royal dignity within his reach?

34. 'Thou wilt not abandon the young son of Yasodharâ, worthy of all praise, thou the best of the cherishers of religion and fame, as a dissolute spendthrift his choicest glory?

35. 'Or even if thy mind be resolved to abandon thy kindred and thy kingdom, thou wilt not, O master, abandon me,—thy feet are my only refuge.

[1] A common expression (which occurs also in Persian poetry) to imply the incompatibility of two things.

36. 'I cannot go to the city with my soul thus burning, leaving thee behind in the forest as Sumitra[1] left the son of Raghu.

37. 'What will the king say to me, returning to the city without thee? or what shall I say to thy queens by way of telling them good news?

38. 'As for what thou saidst, "thou must repeat my unworthiness to the king"—how shall I speak what is false of thee as of a sage without a fault?

39. 'Or even if I ventured to speak it with a heart ashamed and a tongue cleaving to my mouth, who would think of believing it?

40. 'He who would tell of or believe the fierceness of the moon, might tell of or believe thy faults, O physician of faults.

41. 'Him who is always compassionate and who never fails to feel pity, it ill befits to abandon one who loves;—turn back and have mercy on me.'

42. Having heard these words of *Khamda* overcome with sorrow,—self-possessed with the utmost firmness the best of speakers answered:

43. 'Abandon this distress, *Khamda*, regarding thy separation from me,—change is inevitable in corporeal beings who are subject to different births.

44. 'Even if I through affection were not to abandon my kindred in my desire for liberation, death would still make us helplessly abandon one another.

45. 'She, my mother, by whom I was borne in the womb with great thirst and pains,—where am I now with regard to her, all her efforts fruitless, and where is she with regard to me?

46. 'As birds go to their roosting-tree and then

[1] This is the Sumantra of the Râmâya*n*a II, 57.

depart, so the meeting of beings inevitably ends in separation.

47. 'As clouds, having come together, depart asunder again, such I consider the meeting and parting of living things.

48. 'And since this world goes away, each one of us deceiving the other,—it is not right to think anything thine own in a time of union which is a dream.

49. 'Since the trees are parted from the innate colour of their leaves, why should there not still more be the parting of two things which are alien to each other?

50. 'Therefore, since it is so, grieve not, my good friend, but go; or if thy love lingers, then go and afterwards return.

51. 'Say, without reproaching us, to the people in Kapilavastu, "Let your love for him be given up, and hear his resolve.

52. '"Either he will quickly come back, having destroyed old age and death; or else he will himself perish, having failed in his purpose and lost hold of every support."'

53. Having heard his words, Ka*m*thaka, the noblest of steeds, licked his feet with his tongue and dropped hot tears.

54. With his hand whose fingers were united with a membrane and which was marked with the auspicious svastika, and with its middle part curved[1], the prince stroked him and addressed him like a friend:

55. 'Shed not tears, Ka*m*thaka, this thy perfect

[1] Professor Kielhorn suggests *k*akra-madhyena, 'with a wheel in its centre,' cf. VIII, 55.

equine nature has been proved,—bear with it, this thy labour will soon have its fruit.'

56. Then seizing the sharp jewelled sword which was in *Khamdaka*'s hand, he resolutely drew out from the sheath the blade decked with golden ornaments, like a serpent from its hole.

57. Having drawn it forth, dark blue like a blue lotus petal, he cut his decorated tiara and his hair, and he tossed it with its scattered muslin into the air as a grey goose into a lake.

58. And the heavenly beings, with a longing to worship it, seized it respectfully as it was thrown up; and the divine hosts paid it due adoration in heaven with celestial honours.

59. Having thus divorced his ornaments and banished all royal magnificence from his head, and seeing his muslin floating away like a golden goose, the stedfast prince desired a sylvan dress.

60. Then a celestial being, wearing the form of a hunter, pure in heart, knowing his thoughts, approached near him in dark-red garments; and the son of the *S*âkya king thus addressed him:

61. 'Thy red garments are auspicious, the sign of a saint; but this destructive bow is not befitting; therefore, my good friend, if there is no strong preference in the matter, do thou give me that dress and take this of mine.'

62. The hunter replied, 'It has given me my desire[1], O giver of desires, as by this I have inspired

[1] I have taken ârât as from â + râ, but Professor Kielhorn suggests that it might mean 'near.' 'Although in this dress I make the deer come confidently close to me and then kill them, yet take it if you want it.' [The Tibetan seems to have read kâmasârât,—${}_{o}$dod-pa sñin-po las, 'from essence of desire.' H.W.]

animals with confidence and then killed them; but if thou hast need of it, O thou who art like Indra, accept it at once and give me the white dress.'

63. With extreme joy he then took that sylvan dress and gave away the linen one; and the hunter, assuming his heavenly form, having taken the white garment, went to heaven.

64. Then the prince and the attendant of the horse were filled with wonder as he was thus going, and forthwith they paid great honour anew to that sylvan dress.

65. Then the great-souled one, having dismissed the weeping *Khamda*, and wearing his fame veiled by the sign of the red garment, went towards the hermitage, like the king of mountains wrapped in an evening cloud.

66. While his master, thus regardless of his kingdom, was going to the ascetic-wood in mean garments, the groom, tossing up his arms, wailed bitterly and fell on the ground.

67. Having looked again he wept aloud, and embraced the horse Ka*m*thaka with his arms; and then, hopeless and repeatedly lamenting, he went in body to the city, not in soul.

68. Sometimes he pondered, sometimes he lamented, sometimes he stumbled, and sometimes he fell; and so going along, wretched through his devoted attachment, he performed all kinds of actions in the road without conscious will.

BOOK VII.

1. Then having left the weeping tear-faced *Khamda*,—indifferent to all things in his longing for the forest, he by whom all objects are accomplished, overpowering the place by his beauty, entered that hermitage as if it were fully blessed.

2. He the prince with a gait like the lion's, having entered that arena of deer, himself like a deer,—by the beauty of his person, even though bereft of his magnificence, attracted the eyes of all the dwellers in the hermitage.

3. The drivers of wheeled carriages also, with their wives, stood still in curiosity, holding the yokes in their hands,—they gazed on him who was like Indra, and moved not, standing like their beasts of burden with their heads half bent down.

4. And the Brâhmans who had gone outside for the sake of fuel, having come with their hands full of fuel, flowers, and kusa grass,—pre-eminent as they were in penances, and proficients in wisdom, went to see him, and went not to their cells.

5. Delighted the peacocks uttered their cries, as if they had seen a dark-blue cloud rising up; and leaving the young grass and coming forward, the deer with restless eyes and the ascetics who grazed like deer [1] stood still.

---

[1] A form of ascetic observance, see Mahâbh. I, 3644; V, 4072. Cf. infra, sloka 15.

6. Beholding him, the lamp of the race of Ikshvâku, shining like the rising sun,—even though their milking was over, being filled with joy, the oblation-giving cows poured forth their milk.

7. 'It is one of the eight Vasus or one of the two Asvins, descended here,'—these words arose, uttered aloud by the sages in their astonishment at seeing him.

8. Like a second form of the lord of the gods[1], like the personified glory of the universe, he lighted up the entire wood like the sun come down of his own accord.

9. Then he, being duly honoured and invited to enter by those dwellers in the hermitage, paid his homage to the saints, with a voice like a cloud in the rainy season[2].

10. He, the wise one, longing for liberation, traversed that hermitage filled with the holy company desirous of heaven,—gazing at their strange penances.

11. He, the gentle one, having seen the different kinds of penance practised by the ascetics in that sacred grove,—desiring to know the truth, thus addressed one of the ascetics who was following him:

12. 'Since this to-day is my first sight of a hermitage I do not understand this rule of penance; therefore will your honour kindly explain to me what resolve possesses each one of you.'

13. Then the Brâhman well-versed in penance told in order to that bull of the Sâkyas, a very bull in prowess, all the various kinds of penance and the fruit thereof.

---

[1] Lekharshabha is a rare name of Indra.

[2] A conjectural reading.

14. 'Uncultivated food, growing out of the water, leaves, water, and roots and fruits,—this is the fare of the saints according to the sacred texts; but the different alternatives of penance vary.

15. 'Some live like the birds on gleaned corn, others graze on grass like the deer, others live on air with the snakes, as if turned into ant-hills[1].

16. 'Others win their nourishment with great effort from stones, others eat corn ground with their own teeth; some, having boiled for others, dress for themselves what may chance to be left.

17. 'Others, with their tufts of matted hair continually wet with water, twice offer oblations to Agni with hymns; others plunging like fishes into the water dwell there with their bodies scratched by tortoises.

18. 'By such penances endured for a time,—by the higher they attain heaven, by the lower the world of men; by the path of pain they eventually dwell in happiness,—pain, they say, is the root of merit.'

19. The king's son, having heard this speech of the ascetic, even though he saw no lofty truth in it[2], was not content, but gently uttered these thoughts to himself:

20. 'The penance is full of pain and of many kinds, and the fruit of the penance is mainly heaven at its best, and all the worlds are subject to change; verily the labour of the hermitages is spent for but little gain.

---

[1] Cf. the legend of the princess Sukanyâ, given in Wilson's note, Hindu Drama, I, p. 263.

[2] Cf. Beal, 517 (or perhaps 'though he had not himself yet attained the highest truth').

21. 'Those who abandoning wealth, kindred, and worldly objects, undertake vows for the sake of heaven,—they, when parted, only wish to go to a still greater wood of their own again[1].

22. 'He who by all these bodily toils which are called penances, seeks a sphere of action for the sake of desire,—not examining the inherent evils of mundane existence, he only seeks pain by pain.

23. 'There is ever to living creatures fear from death, and they with all their efforts seek to be born again; where there is action, there must inevitably be death,—he is always drowned therein, just because he is afraid.

24. 'Some undergo misery for the sake of this world, others meet toil for the sake of heaven; all living beings, wretched through hope and always missing their aim, fall certainly for the sake of happiness into misery.

25. 'It is not the effort itself which I blame,—which flinging aside the base pursues a high path of its own; but the wise, by all this common toil, ought to attain that state in which nothing needs ever to be done again.

26. 'If the mortification of the body here is religion, then the body's happiness is only irreligion; but by religion a man obtains happiness in the next world, therefore religion here bears irreligion as its fruit.

27. 'Since it is only by the mind's authority that the body either acts or ceases to act, therefore to control the thought is alone befitting,—without the thought the body is like a log.

---

[1] Their desired heaven will only be a fresh penance-grove.

28. 'If merit is gained by purity of food, then there is merit also in the deer; and in those men also who live as outcasts from all enjoyments, through being estranged from them by the fault of their destiny.

29. 'If the deliberate choice of pain is a cause of merit, why should not that same choice be directed to pleasure? If you say that the choice of pleasure carries no authority, is not the choice of pain equally without authority?

30. 'So too those who for the sake of purifying their actions, earnestly sprinkle water on themselves, saying, "this is a sacred spot,"—even there this satisfaction resides only in the heart,—for waters will not cleanse away sin.

31. 'The water which has been touched by the virtuous,—that is the spot, if you wish for a sacred spot on the earth; therefore I count as a place of pilgrimage only the virtues of a virtuous man[1],—water without doubt is only water.'

32. Thus he uttered his discourse full of various arguments, and the sun went down into the west; then he entered the grove where penances had now ceased and whose trees were gray with the smoke of the (evening) oblations;

33. Where the sacred fires had been duly transferred when kindled to other spots,—all crowded with the holy hermits who had performed their ablutions, and with the shrines of the gods murmuring with the muttered prayers,—it seemed all alive like the full service of religion in exercise.

34. He spent several nights there, himself like

---

[1] Gunân eva?

the moon, examining their penances; and he departed from that penance-field, feeling that he had comprehended the whole nature of penance.

35. The dwellers of the hermitage followed him with their minds fixed on the greatness of soul visible in his person, as if they were great seers beholding Religion herself, withdrawn from a land invaded by the base.

36. Then he looked on all those ascetics with their matted hair, bark garments, and rag-strips waving, and he stood considering their penances under an auspicious and noble tree by the way-side.

37. Then the hermits having approached stood surrounding the best of men; and an old man from among them thus addressed him respectfully in a gentle voice:

38. 'At thy coming the hermitage seems to have become full, it becomes as it were empty when thou art gone,—therefore, my son, thou wilt not surely desert it, as the loved life the body of one who wishes to live.

39. 'In front stands the holy mountain Himavat, inhabited by Brahmarshis, râ*g*arshis, and surarshis; by whose mere presence the merit of these penances becomes multiplied to the ascetics.

40. 'Near us also are holy spots of pilgrimage, which become ladders to heaven; loved by divine sages and saints whose souls are intent on devotion and who keep their souls in perfect control.

41. 'From hence, again, the Northern quarter is especially to be fitly followed for the sake of preeminent merit; even one who was wise starting towards the south could not advance one single step.

42. 'Hast thou seen in this sacred grove one who

neglects all ceremonies or who follows confused ceremonies or an outcast or one impure, that thou dost not desire to dwell here? Speak it out, and let the abode be welcomed.

43. 'These hermits here desire thee as their companion in penance, thee who art like a storehouse of penance,—to dwell with thee who art like Indra would bring prosperity even to V*ri*haspati.'

44. He, the chief of the wise, when thus addressed in the midst of the ascetics by their chief—having resolved in his mind to put an end to all existence—thus uttered his inward thought:

45. 'The upright-souled saints, the upholders of religion, become the very ideal of our own kindred through their delight in showing hospitality; by all these kind feelings of thine towards me affection is produced in me and the path which regards the self as supreme[1] is revealed.

46. 'I seem to be all at once bathed by these gentle heart-touching words of thine, and the joy now throbs in me once more which I felt when I first grasped the idea of dharma.

47. 'There is sorrow to me when I reflect that I shall have to depart, leaving you who are thus engaged, you who are such a refuge and who have shown such excessive kindness to me,—just as there was when I had to leave my kindred behind.

48. 'But this devotion of yours is for the sake of heaven,—while my desire is that there may be no fresh birth; therefore I wish not to dwell in this wood; the nature of cessation is different from that of activity.

49. 'It is not therefore any dislike on my part or

[1] Obscure, cf. Mahâbh. V, 1593.

the wrong conduct of another, which makes me go away from this wood; for ye are all like great sages, standing fast in the religious duties which are in accordance with former ages.'

50. Then having heard the prince's discourse, gracious and of deep meaning, gentle, strong, and full of dignity, the ascetics paid him especial honour.

51. But a certain Brâhman who was lying there in the ashes, tall and wearing his hair in a tuft, and clothed in the bark of trees, with reddish eyes and a thin long nose, and carrying a pot with water [1] in his hand, thus lifted his voice:

52. 'O sage, brave indeed is thy purpose, who, young as thou art, hast seen the evils of birth; he who, having pondered thoroughly heaven and liberation, makes up his mind for liberation,—he is indeed brave!

53. 'By all those various sacrifices, penances, and vows the slaves of passion desire to go to heaven; but the strong, having battled with passion as with an enemy, desire to obtain liberation.

54. 'If this is thy settled purpose, go quickly to Vindhyakosh*th*a; the Muni Arâ*d*a lives there who has gained an insight into absolute bliss.

55. 'From him thou wilt hear the path to truth, and if thou hast a desire for it, thou wilt embrace it; but as I foresee, this purpose of thine will go on further, after having rejected his theory.

56. 'With the nose of a well-fed horse, large long eyes, a red lower lip, white sharp teeth, and a thin red tongue,—this face of thine will drink up the entire ocean of what is to be known.

---

[1] Conjectural. Dr. von Böhtlingk suggests ku*m*d*âvahasto, 'the back of whose hand was like a ku*m*d*a.'

57. 'That unfathomed depth which characterises thee, that majesty and all those signs of thine,—they shall win a teacher's chair in the earth which was never won by sages even in a former age.'

58. The prince replied, 'Very well,' and having saluted the company of sages he departed; the hermits also having duly performed to him all the rites of courtesy entered again into the ascetic-grove.

BOOK VIII.

1. Meanwhile the attendant of the horse, in deep distress, when his unselfish master thus went into the forest, made every effort in the road to dissolve[1] his load of sorrow, and yet in spite of it all not a tear dropped from him.

2. But the road which by his lord's command he had traversed in one night with that horse,—that same road he now travelled in eight days, pondering his lord's absence.

3. And the horse Ka*m*thaka, though he still went on bravely, flagged and had lost all spirit in his heart; and decked though he was with ornaments, he had lost all his beauty when bereft of his master.

4. And turning round towards that ascetic-grove, he neighed repeatedly with a mournful sound; and though pressed with hunger, he welcomed not nor tasted any grass or water on the road, as before[2].

5. Slowly they two at last came back to the city called after Kapila, which seemed empty when deserted by that hero who was bent on the

---

[1] Vigraha seems here used in an unusual sense. Cf. Tennyson's 'Home they brought her warrior dead, &c.'

[2] I read nâbhinananda, supposing na to have been written on the margin and inserted in the wrong place, otherwise abhis must be used for abhi. [This is confirmed by the Tibetan, which translates abhinananda by mňon-par ma dga, where mňon-par is the usual translation of the preposition abhi. H.W.]

salvation of the world,—like the sky bereft of the sun.

6. Bright as it was with lotus-covered waters, adorned also with trees full of flowers, that garden of his, which was now like a forest, was no longer gay with citizens who had lost all their gladness.

7. Then those two,—who were as it were silently forbidden by the sad inhabitants who were wandering in that direction, their brightness gone and their eyes dim with tears,—slowly entered the city which seemed all bathed in gloom.

8. Having heard that they had returned with their limbs all relaxed, coming back without the pride of the *S*âkya race, the men of the city shed tears in the road, as when in old days the chariot of the son of Da*s*aratha came back.

9. Full of wrath, the people followed *Khamdaka* in the road, crying behind him with tears, 'Where is the king's son, the glory of his race and kingdom? he has been stolen away by thee.'

10. Then he said to those faithful ones, 'I have not left the king's son; but by him in the uninhabited forest I weeping and the dress of a householder were abandoned together.'

11. Having heard these words of his those crowds adopted a most difficult resolve; they did not wipe away the tears which fell from their eyes, and they blamed their own (evil) hearts on account of the consequences of their actions;

12. Then they said, 'Let us go this very day into that forest, whither he is gone, whose gait is like the king of elephants; without him we have no wish to live, like the senses when the souls depart.

13. 'This city bereft of him is a forest, and that forest which possesses him is a city; the city without him has no charms for us, like heaven without the lord of the Maruts, when V*ri*tra was slain [1].'

14. Next the women crowded to the rows of windows, crying to one another, 'The prince has returned;' but having heard that his horse had an empty back, they closed the windows again and wailed aloud.

15. But the king, having undertaken religious observances for the recovery of his son, with his mind distressed by the vow and the sorrow, was muttering prayers in the temple, and performing such rites as suited the occasion.

16. Then with his eyes filled with tears,—taking the horse, his whole soul fixed on the horse,—overcome with grief he [2] entered the palace as if his master had been killed by an enemy.

17. And entering the royal stable, looking about with his eyes full of tears, Ka*m*thaka uttered a loud sound, as if he were uttering his woe to the people.

18. Then the birds that fed in the middle of the house, and the carefully cherished horses that were tied near by, re-echoed the sound of that horse, thinking that it might be the return of the prince.

19. And the people, deceived by an excessive joy, who were in the neighbourhood of the king's inner apartments, thought in their hearts, 'Since the horse Ka*m*thaka neighs, it must be that the prince is coming.'

20. Then the women, who were fainting with

---

[1] Quoted by Uggvaladatta, on U*n*âdi-sûtras I, 156.

[2] Sc. *Kh*andaka.

sorrow, now in wild joy, with their eyes rolling to see the prince, rushed out of the palace full of hope, like flickering lightnings from an autumn cloud.

21. With their dress hanging down, and their linen garments soiled, their faces untouched by collyrium and with eyes dimmed by tears; dark and discoloured and destitute of all painting[1], like the stars in the sky, pale-red with the ending of night;

22. With their feet unstained by red, and undecked by anklets,—their faces without earrings, and their ears in their native simplicity,—their loins with only nature's fulness, and uncircled by any girdle,—and their bosoms bare of strings of pearls as if they had been robbed.

23. But when they saw *Kh*andaka standing helpless, his eyes filled with tears, and the horse, the noble women wept with pale faces, like cows abandoned by the bull in the midst of the forest.

24. Then the king's principal queen Gautamî, like a fond cow that has lost her calf, fell bursting into tears on the ground with outstretched arms, like a golden plantain-tree with trembling leaves.

25. Some of the other women, bereft of their brightness and with arms and souls lifeless, and seeming to have lost their senses in their despondency, raised no cry, shed no tear, and breathed not, standing senseless as if painted[2].

26. Others as having lost all self-control, fainting in their sorrow for their lord, their faces pouring tears from their eyes, watered their bosoms from

---

[1] Is a*ñg*anayâ used here irregularly in the fem. to distinguish it from a*ñg*ana, 'the pinguent?'

[2] Conjectural.

which all sandal-wood was banished, like a mountain the rocks with its streams.

27. Then that royal palace was illumined with their faces pelted by the tears from their eyes, as a lake in the time of the first rains with its dripping lotuses pelted by the rain from the clouds.

28. The noble women beat their breasts with their lotus-like hands, falling incessantly, whose fingers were round and plump, which had their arteries hidden and bore no ornaments,—as creepers tossed by the wind strike themselves with their shoots.

29. And again how those women shone forth, as their bosoms rose up together after the blow from the hand, and trembled with the shock,—like the streams, when their pairs of ruddy geese shake, as the lotuses on which they sit wave about with the wind from the wood[1].

30. As they pressed their breasts with their hands, so too they pressed their hands with their breasts,—dull to all feelings of pity, they made their hands and bosoms inflict mutual pains on each other.

31. Then thus spoke Yaśodharâ, shedding tears with deep[2] sorrow, her bosom heaving with her sighs, her eyes discoloured with anger, and her voice choking with emotion through the influence of despondency:

32. 'Leaving me helplessly asleep in the night, whither, O *Kh*a*m*daka, is he, the desire of my heart,

[1] This is an obscure verse,—yathâpi is not clear; I have taken yathâ as a 'how' of admiration. The latter lines seem to compare the hand swaying with the motion of the bosom to the bird seated on the tossed lotus.

[2] Is vigâdha for agâdha, or should we read vigâ*dh*a?

gone? and when thou and Kamthaka are alone come back, while three went away together, my mind trembles.

33. 'Why dost thou weep to-day, O cruel one, having done a dishonourable, pitiless, and unfriendly deed to me? Cease thy tears and be content in thy heart,—tears and that deed of thine ill agree.

34. 'Through thee, his dear obedient faithful loyal companion, always doing what was right, the son of my lord is gone never to return,—rejoice,—all hail! thy pains have gained their end.

35. 'Better for a man a wise enemy rather than a foolish friend unskilled in emergencies; by thee, the unwise self-styled friend, a great calamity has been brought upon this family.

36. 'These women are sorely to be pitied who have put away their ornaments, having their eyes red and dimmed with continuous tears, who are as it were desolate widows, though their lord still stands as unshaken as the earth or Mount Himavat.

37. 'And these lines of palaces seem to weep aloud, flinging up their dovecots for arms, with the long unbroken moan of their doves,—separated verily, with him, from all who could restrain them.

38. 'Even that horse Kamthaka without doubt desired my utter ruin; for he bore away from hence my treasure when all were sound asleep in the night,—like one who steals jewels.

39. 'When he was able to bear even the onsets of arrows, and still more the strokes of whips,—how then for fear of the fall of a whip, could he go carrying with him my prosperity and my heart together?

40. 'The base creature now neighs loudly, filling the king's palace with the sound; but when he

carried away my beloved, then this vilest of horses was dumb.

41. 'If he had neighed and so woke up the people, or had even made a noise with his hoofs on the ground, or had made the loudest sound he could with his jaws, my grief would not have been so great.'

42. Having thus heard the queen's words, their syllables choked with tears and full of lament, slowly *Khamdaka* uttered this answer, with his face bent down, his voice low with tears, and his hands clasped in supplication:

43. 'Surely, O queen, thou wilt not blame Ka*m*thaka nor wilt thou show thy anger against me,—know that we two are entirely guiltless,—that god amongst men, O queen, is gone away like a god.

44. 'I indeed, though I well knew the king's command, as though dragged by force by some divine powers, brought quickly to him this swift steed, and followed him on the road unwearied.

45. 'And this best of horses as he went along touched not the ground with the tips of his hoofs as if they were kept aloft from it; and so too, having his mouth restrained as by fate, he made no sound with his jaws and neighed not.

46. 'When the prince went out, then the gate was thrown open of its own accord; and the darkness of the night was, as it were, pierced by the sun,—we may learn from hence too that this was the ordering of fate.

47. 'When also by the king's command, in palace and city, diligent guards had been placed by thousands, and at that time they were all overcome by sleep and woke not,—we may learn from hence too that this was the ordering of fate.

48. 'When also the garment, approved for a

hermit's dwelling in the forest, was offered to him at the moment by some denizen of heaven, and the tiara which he threw into the sky was carried off, —we may learn from hence too that this was the ordering of fate.

49. 'Do not therefore assume[1] that his departure arises from the fault of either of us, O queen; neither I nor this horse acted by our own choice; he went on his way with the gods as his retinue.'

50. Having thus heard the history of the prince's departure, so marvellous in many ways, those women, as though losing their grief, were filled with wonder, but they again took up their distress at the thought of his becoming an ascetic.

51. With her eyes filled with the tears of despondency, wretched like an osprey who has lost her young,—Gautamî abandoning all self-control wailed aloud,—she fainted, and with a weeping face exclaimed:

52. 'Beautiful, soft, black, and all in great waves, growing each from its own special root,—those hairs of his are tossed on the ground, worthy to be encircled by a royal diadem.

53. 'With his long arms and lion-gait, his bull-like eye, and his beauty bright like gold, his broad chest, and his voice deep as a drum or a cloud,—should such a hero as this dwell in a hermitage?

54. 'This earth is indeed unworthy as regards that peerless doer of noble actions, for such a virtuous hero has gone away from her,—it is the merits and virtues of the subjects which produce their king.

55. 'Those two feet of his, tender, with their

[1] Should we read pratipattum for pratigantum?

beautiful web spread between the toes, with their ankles concealed, and soft like a blue lotus,—how can they, bearing a wheel marked in the middle, walk on the hard ground of the skirts of the forest?

56. 'That body, which deserves to sit or lie on the roof of a palace,—honoured with costly garments, aloes, and sandal-wood,—how will that manly body live in the woods, exposed to the attacks of the cold, the heat, and the rain?

57. 'He who was proud of his family, goodness, strength, energy, sacred learning, beauty, and youth,—who was ever ready to give, not to ask,—how will he go about begging alms from others?

58. 'He who, lying on a spotless golden bed, was awakened during the night by the concert of musical instruments,—how alas! will he, my ascetic, sleep to-day on the bare ground with only one rag of cloth interposed?'

59. Having heard this piteous lamentation, the women, embracing one another with their arms, rained the tears from their eyes, as the shaken creepers drop honey from their flowers.

60. Then Yasodharâ fell upon the ground, like the ruddy goose parted from her mate, and in utter bewilderment she slowly lamented, with her voice repeatedly stopped by sobs:

61. 'If he wishes to practise a religious life after abandoning me his lawful wife widowed,—where is his religion, who wishes to follow penance without his lawful wife to share it with him?

62. 'He surely has never heard of the monarchs of olden times, his own ancestors, Mahâsudarsa[1] and

[1] Mahâsudassana is the name of a king in Gâtaka I, 95.

the rest,—how they went with their wives into the forest,—that he thus wishes to follow a religious life without me.

63. 'He does not see that husband and wife are both consecrated in sacrifices, and both purified by the performance of the rites of the Veda, and both destined to enjoy[1] the same results afterwards,—he therefore grudges me a share in his merit.

64. 'Surely it must be that this fond lover of religion, knowing that my mind was secretly quarrelling even with my beloved, lightly and without fear has deserted me thus angry, in the hope to obtain heavenly nymphs in Indra's world!

65. 'But what kind of a thought is this of mine? those women even there have the attributes which belong to bodies,—for whose sake he thus practises austerities in the forest, deserting his royal magnificence and my fond devotion.

66. 'I have no such longing for the joy of heaven, nor is that hard for even common people to win if they are resolute[2]; but my one desire is how he my beloved may never leave me either in this world or the next.

67. 'Even if I am unworthy to look on my husband's face with its long eyes and bright smile, still is this poor Râhula never to roll about in his father's lap?

68. 'Alas! the mind of that wise hero is terribly stern,—gentle as his beauty seems, it is pitilessly cruel,—who can desert of his own accord such an infant son with his inarticulate talk, one who would charm even an enemy.

69. 'My heart too is certainly most stern, yea,

---

[1] I read bubhukshû for bubhukshu*h*.

[2] Api, I think, should properly follow *g*anasya.

made of rock or fashioned even of iron, which does not break when its lord is gone to the forest, deserted by his royal glory like an orphan,—he so well worthy of happiness.'

70. So the queen, fainting in her woe, wept and pondered and wailed aloud repeatedly,—self-possessed as she was by nature, yet in her distress she remembered not her fortitude and felt no shame.

71. Seeing Yaśodharâ thus bewildered with her wild utterances of grief and fallen on the ground, all the women cried out with their faces streaming with tears like large lotuses beaten by the rain.

72. But the king, having ended his prayers, and performed the auspicious rites of the sacrifice, now came out of the temple; and being smitten by the wailing sound of the people, he tottered like an elephant at the crash of a thunderbolt.

73. Having heard (of the arrival) of both *Kh*a*m*daka and Ka*m*thaka, and having learned the fixed resolve of his son, the lord of the earth fell struck down by sorrow like the banner of Indra when the festival is over [1].

74. Then the king, distracted by his grief for his son, being held up for a moment by his attendants all of the same race, gazed on the horse with his eyes filled with tears, and then falling on the ground wailed aloud:

75. 'After having done many dear exploits for me in battle, one great deed of cruelty, O Ka*m*thaka, hast thou done,—for by thee that dear son of mine, dear for his every virtue, has been tossed down in the wood, dear as he was, like a worthless thing.

[1] Cf. I, 63.

76. 'Therefore either lead me to-day where he is, or go quickly and bring him back again; without him there is no life left to me, as to one plunged in sickness without the true medicine.

77. 'When Suvarnanishthîvin was carried away by death, it seemed impossible that Srimgaya[1] should not die; and shall I, when my duty-loving son is gone, fear to set my soul free, like any coward?

78. 'How should not the mind of Manu himself be distracted, when parted from his dear virtuous son[2], —(Manu) the son of Vivasvat, who knew the higher and the lower, the mighty lord of creatures, the institutor of the ten chieftains[3].

79. 'I envy the monarch, that friend of Indra, the wise son of king Aga[4], who, when his son went into the forest, went himself to heaven, and dragged out no miserable life here with vain tears.

80. 'Describe to me, O beloved one, the court of that hermitage, whither thou hast carried him who is as my funeral oblation of water; these my vital airs are all ready to depart, and are eager for it, longing to drink it.'

81. Thus the king, in his grief for his separation from his son,—losing all his innate firmness which was stedfast like the earth,—loudly lamented as one distraught, like Dasaratha, a prey to his sorrow for Râma.

---

[1] See Mahâbh. XII, 31. The MSS. read Samgaya for Srimgaya.

[2] Does this refer to his losing his son Sudyumna, who was changed to a woman, Vishnu Pur. IV, 1?

[3] Dasakshatrakrit is an obscure phrase; [the Tibetan renders it by rgyal-rigs bcu byas, 'king-race ten made;' rgyal-rigs is the ordinary translation of kshatriya. H. W.]

[4] Dasaratha.

82. Then the wise counsellor, endued with religious learning, courtesy, and virtue, and the old family priest, spoke to him as was befitting in these well-weighed words, neither with their faces overwhelmed by grief nor yet wholly unmoved :

83. 'Cease, O noblest of men, thy grief, regain thy firmness,—surely thou wilt not, O firm hero, shed tears like one of no self-control; many kings on this earth have gone into the forests, throwing away their royal pomp like a crushed wreath.

84. 'Moreover, this his state of mind was all predetermined; remember those words long ago of the holy sage Asita; "He will never be made to dwell even for a moment contentedly in heaven or in an emperor's domain."

85. 'But if, O best of men, the effort must be made, quickly speak the word, we two will at once go together; let the battle be waged in every way with thy son and his fate whatever it be.'

86. Then the king commanded them both, 'Do you both go quickly hence,—my heart will not return to quiet, any more than a bird's in the woods longing for its young.'

87. With a prompt acquiescence at the king's order the counsellor and the family priest went to that forest; and then with his wives and his queen the king also, saying, 'It is done,' performed the remainder of the rites.

BOOK IX.

1. Then the two, the counsellor and the family priest, beaten by the king with his scourge of tears, went with every effort to that forest in the hurry of affection, like two noble horses goaded.

2. Having come at last full of weariness to that hermitage, accompanied by a fitting train,—they dismissed their royal pomp and with sober gestures entered the abode of Bhârgava.

3. Having saluted that Brâhman with due respect, and having been honoured by him with due reverence in return, having seated themselves, plunging at once into the subject, they addressed Bhârgava, who was likewise seated, concerning their errand.

4. 'Let your honour know us to be respectively imperfect proficients in preserving the sacred learning and in retaining the state-counsels,—in the service of the monarch of the Ikshvâku race, pure in his valour and pure and wide in his glory.

5. 'His son, who is like *G*ayanta, while he himself is like Indra, has come here, it is said, desirous to escape from the fear of old age and death,—know that we two are come here on account of him.'

6. He answered them, 'That prince of the long arms did indeed come here, but not as one unawakened; "this dharma only brings us back again," —recognising this, he went off forthwith towards Arâ*d*a, seeking liberation.'

7. Then they two, having understood the true

state of things, bade that Brâhman at once farewell, and wearied though they were, went on as if they were unwearied, thither whither the prince was gone.

8. As they were going, they saw him bereft of all ornaments[1], but still radiant with his beauty, sitting like a king in the road at the foot of a tree, like the sun under the canopy of a cloud.

9. Leaving his chariot, the family priest then went up to the prince with the counsellor, as the saint Aurva*s*eya[2] went with Vâmadeva, wishing to see Râma when he dwelt in the forest.

10. They paid him honour as was fitting, as *S*ukra and A*m*giras honoured Indra in heaven; and he in return paid due honour to them, as Indra in heaven to *S*ukra and A*m*giras.

11. Then they, having obtained his permission, sat down near him who was the banner of the *S*âkya race; and they shone in his proximity like the two stars of the asterism Punarvasû in conjunction with the moon.

12. The family priest addressed the prince who shone brightly as he sat at the foot of the tree, as V*ri*haspati addressed Indra's son *G*ayanta, seated in heaven under the heavenly tree pâri*g*âta:

13. 'O prince, consider for a moment what the king with his eyes raining tears said to thee, as he lay fainting on the ground with the arrow of thy sorrow plunged into his heart.

14. '"I know that thy resolve is fixed upon religion, and I am convinced that this purpose of thine is unchanging[3]; but I am consumed with a flame of

---

[1] Is s*rig*ayâ for sra*g*â?

[2] Agastya, the son of Urva*s*î. Vâmadeva was Da*s*aratha's counsellor.

[3] Conjectural. [The Tibetan reads the second line, khyod-kyi

anguish like fire at thy flying to the woods at an inopportune time.

15. '" Come, thou who lovest duty, for the sake of what is my heart's desire,—abandon this purpose for the sake of duty; this huge swollen stream of sorrow sweeps me away as a river's torrent its bank.

16. '" That effect [1] which is wrought in the clouds, water, the dry grass, and the mountains by the wind, the sun, the fire, and the thunderbolt,—that same effect this grief produces in us by its tearing in pieces, its drying up, its burning, and its cleaving.

17. '" Enjoy therefore for a while the sovereignty of the earth,—thou shalt go to the forest at the time provided by the *s*âstras,—do not show disregard for thy unhappy kindred,—compassion for all creatures is the true religion.

18. '" Religion is not wrought out only in the forests, the salvation of ascetics can be accomplished even in a city; thought and effort are the true means; the forest and the badge are only a coward's signs.

19. '" Liberation has been attained even by householders, Indras among men, who wore diadems, and carried strings of pearls suspended on their shoulders, whose garlands were entangled with bracelets, and who lay cradled in the lap of Fortune.

20. '" Bali and Va*g*rabâhu, the two younger brothers of Dhruva, Vaibhrâ*g*a, Âshâ*dh*a, and A*m*ti-

---

$_o$byuṅ-var $_o$gyur-var don-ni çes-pao, 'I know thy purpose which is about to arise (or which has arisen) in thy mind.' Can they have read bhâvinam or bhâvitam? H.W.]

[1] I read v*ri*tti*h*.

deva[1], and *G*anaka also, the king of the Videhas, and king Sena*g*it's son, his tree of ripe blessing[2];

21. '"Know that all these great kings who were householders were well skilled in attaining the merit which leads to final bliss,—do thou also therefore obtain both[3] simultaneously—royal magnificence and the control over the mind.

22. '"I desire,—when I have once closely embraced thee after thy kingly consecration is once performed, and while thou art still wet with the sacred water,—when I behold thee with the pomp of the royal umbrella,—in the fulness of that joy to enter the forest."

23. 'Thus did the king say to thee in a speech whose words were stopped by tears,—surely having heard it, for the sake of what is so dear to him, thou wilt with all affection follow his affection.

24. 'The king of the *S*âkyas is drowned in a deep sea of sorrow, full of waves of trouble, springing from thee; do thou therefore deliver him helpless and protectorless like an ox drowning in the sea.

25. 'Having heard that Bhîshma who sprang from Gaṅgâ's womb, Râma, and Râma the son of Bh*ri*gu,—all did what would please their fathers;—surely thou too wilt do thy father's desire.

26. 'Consider also the queen, who brought thee

---

[1] Cf. I, 57; IX, 60.

[2] My reading pâkadrumam is conjectural, Pâradrumau as two old kings would be a possible reading. Sena*g*it's son is praised for his philosophical depth in Mahâbh. XII, 6524, &c.; he is there called Medhâvin. [The Tibetan has brtan-pai (dhruva) nu vo, 'the firm one's younger brother (?);' it also has $_o$gro daṅ ljon-çin-can for pâkadruma, 'having a tree of—?' It takes sena*g*ita*sk*a râ*g*ñа*h* as acc. plural. H. W.]

[3] Ubhe*s*pi, although with prag*ri*hya e.

up, who has not yet gone to the region inhabited by Agastya[1]—wilt thou not take some heed of her, who ceaselessly grieves like a fond cow that has lost her calf?

27. 'Surely thou wilt succour thy wife by the sight of thee, who now mourns widowed yet with her lord still alive,—like a swan separated from her mate or a female elephant deserted in the forest by her companion.

28. 'Thy only son, a child little deserving such woe, distressed with sorrow, and[2] . . . . —O deliver Râhula from the grief of his kindred like the full moon from the contact of Râhu!

29. 'Burned with the fire of anguish within him, to which thy absence adds fresh fuel,—a fire whose smoke is sighs and its flame despair,—he wanders for a sight of thee through the women's apartments and the whole city.'

30. The Bodhisattva,—whose perfection was absolute,—having heard the words of the family priest, reflected for a moment, knowing all the virtues of the virtuous, and then thus uttered his gentle reply:

31. 'I well know the paternal tenderness[3] of the king, especially that which he has displayed towards me; yet knowing this as I do, still alarmed at sickness, old age, and death, I am inevitably forced to leave my kindred.

32. 'Who would not wish to see his dear kindred, if but this separation from beloved ones did not exist? but since even after it has been once, separa-

---

[1] The south,—the region of the god of death.

[2] Five syllables are here lost,—apakvasattvam?

[3] Should we read tanayaprasaktam?

tion will still come again, it is for this that I abandon my father, however loving.

33. 'I do not however approve that thou shouldst consider the king's grief as caused by me, when in the midst of his dream-like unions he is afflicted by thoughts of separations in the future.

34. 'Thus let thy thoughts settle into certainty, having seen the multiform in its various developments; neither a son nor kindred is the cause of sorrow,—this sorrow is only caused by ignorance.

35. 'Since parting is inevitably fixed in the course of time for all beings, just as for travellers who have joined company on a road,—what wise man would cherish sorrow, when he loses his kindred, even though he loves them[1]?

36. 'Leaving his kindred in another world, he departs hither; and having stolen away[2] from them here, he goes forth once more; "having gone thither, go thou elsewhere also,"—such is the lot of mankind,—what consideration can the yogin have for them[3]?

37. 'Since from the moment of leaving the womb death is a characteristic adjunct[4], why, in thy affection for thy son, hast thou called my departure to the forest ill-timed?

38. 'There may be an "ill time" in one's attaining a worldly object,—time indeed is described as

---

[1] Some letters are here lost in the original.

[2] Pralabhya, cf. Horace, 'vivens moriensque fefellit.' [The Tibetan has rab-tu bslas-nas, 'having deceived.' H.W.]

[3] The Tibetan has for the fourth line de-ltar (eva*m*) ₒdor-ldan skye-la rjes-su rten rnam ci, 'thus what kind of reliance is there on man who is of a leaving disposition?' Should we read in the original ityeva*m* *g*ane tyâgini ko*x*nurodha*h*?

[4] Can anubadhâya be wrongly used for anubandhâya?

inseparably connected with all things[1]; time drags the world into all its various times; but all time suits a bliss which is really worthy of praise[2].

39. 'That the king should wish to surrender to me his kingdom,—this is a noble thought, well worthy of a father; but it would be as improper for me to accept it, as for a sick man through greed to accept unwholesome food.

40. 'How can it be right for the wise man to enter royalty, the home of illusion, where are found anxiety, passion, and weariness, and the violation of all right through another's service?

41. 'The golden palace seems to me to be on fire; the daintiest viands seem mixed with poison; infested with crocodiles[3] [is the tranquil lotus-bed].'

. . . .

42. Having heard the king's son uttering this discourse, well suitable to his virtues and knowledge of the soul, freed from all desires, full of sound reasons, and weighty,—the counsellor thus made answer:

43. 'This resolve of thine is an excellent counsel, not unfit in itself but only unfit at the present time; it could not be thy duty, loving duty as thou dost, to leave thy father in his old age to sorrow.

44. 'Surely thy mind is not very penetrating, or it is ill-skilled in examining duty, wealth, and pleasure[4],—when for the sake of an unseen result thou departest disregarding a visible end.

[1] Cf. Pân. III, 3, 44.

[2] I.e. mukti can never be ill-timed. But this is an obscure sloka.

[3] The remainder of the prince's speech is lost. By Beal's translation from the Chinese, fifteen verses are wanting.

[4] The three well-known 'secular' ends of human action.

45. 'Again, some say that there is another birth,—others with confident assertion say that there is not; since then the matter is all in doubt, it is right to enjoy the good fortune which comes into thy hand.

46. 'If there is any activity hereafter, we will enjoy ourselves in it as may offer; or if there is no activity beyond this life, then there is an assured liberation to all the world without any effort.

47. 'Some say there is a future life, but they do not allow the possibility of liberation; as fire is hot by nature and water liquid, so they hold that there is a special nature in our power of action[1].

48. 'Some maintain that all things arise from inherent properties,—both good and evil and existence and non-existence; and since all this world thus arises spontaneously, therefore also all effort of ours is vain.

49. 'Since the action of the senses is fixed, and so too the agreeableness or the disagreeableness of outward objects,—then for that which is united to old age and pains, what effort can avail to alter it? Does it not all arise spontaneously?

50. 'The fire becomes quenched by water, and fire causes[2] water to evaporate; and different elements, united in a body, producing unity, bear up the world.

51. 'That the nature of the embryo in the womb is produced as composed of hands, feet, belly, back, and head, and that it is also united with the soul,—the wise declare that all this comes of itself spontaneously.

52. 'Who causes the sharpness of the thorn? or

[1] I.e. it cannot be abolished.

[2] I read gamayanti.

the various natures of beasts and birds? All this has arisen spontaneously; there is no acting from desire, how then can there be such a thing as will?

53. 'Others say that creation comes from Î*s*vara,—what need then is there of the effort of the conscious soul[1]? That which is the cause of the action of the world, is also determined as the cause of its ceasing to act.

54. 'Some say that the coming into being and the destruction of being are alike caused by the soul; but they say that coming into being arises without effort, while the attainment of liberation is by effort.

55. 'A man discharges his debt to his ancestors by begetting offspring, to the saints by sacred lore, to the gods by sacrifices; he is born with these three debts upon him,—whoever has liberation (from these,) he indeed has liberation.

56. 'Thus by this series of rules the wise promise liberation to him who uses effort; but however ready for effort with all their energy, those who seek liberation will find weariness.

57. 'Therefore, gentle youth, if thou hast a love for liberation, follow rightly the prescribed rule; thus wilt thou thyself attain to it, and the king's grief will come to an end.

58. 'And as for thy meditations on the evils of life ending in thy return from the forest to thy home,—let not the thought of this trouble thee, my son,—those in old time also have returned from the forests to their houses.

59. 'The king A*m*barîsha[2], though he had

[1] Purusha.

[2] Probably the son of Nâbhâga.

dwelt in the forest, went back to the city, surrounded by his children; so too Râma, seeing the earth oppressed by the base, came forth from his hermitage and ruled it again.

60. 'So too Drumâksha, the king of the *S*âlvas, came to his city from the forest with his son; and Sâ*m*k*ri*ti A*m*tideva [1], after he had become a Brahmarshi, received his royal dignity from the saint Va*s*ish*th*a.

61. 'Such men as these, illustrious in glory and virtue, left the forests and came back to their houses; therefore it is no sin to return from a hermitage to one's home, if it be only for the sake of duty.'

62. Then having heard the affectionate and loyal words of the minister, who was as the eye of the king,—firm in his resolve, the king's son made his answer, with nothing omitted or displaced [2], neither tedious [3] nor hasty:

63. 'This doubt whether anything exists or not, is not to be solved for me by another's words; having determined the truth by asceticism or quietism, I will myself grasp whatever is ascertained concerning it.

64. 'It is not for me to accept a theory which depends on the unknown and is all controverted, and which involves a hundred prepossessions; what

---

[1] This might mean A*m*tideva (cf. I, 57, IX, 20) the son of Sa*m*k*ri*ti, but in Mahâbh. XII, 1013 we have Ra*m*tideva the son of Sa*m*k*ri*ti; cf. Burnouf on Rudraka and Udraka, Introduction, p. 386. [The Tibetan takes sâ*m*k*ri*ti as sbyin·sreg·dan·bcas, 'together with burnt offering.' H. W.] Would this imply an old reading sâhuti?—For A*m*tideva's connection with Va*s*ish*th*a see Mahâbh. XII, 8591.

[2] I read avyastam.

[3] Or 'prejudiced?'

wise man would go by another's belief? Mankind are like the blind directed in the darkness by the blind.

65. 'But even though I cannot discern the truth, yet still, if good and evil are doubted, let one's mind be set on the good; even a toil[1] in vain is to be chosen by him whose soul is good, while the man of base soul has no joy even in the truth.

66. 'But having seen that this "sacred tradition" is uncertain, know that that only is right which has been uttered by the trustworthy; and know that trustworthiness means the absence of faults; he who is without faults will not utter an untruth.

67. 'And as for what thou saidst to me in regard to my returning to my home, by alleging Râma and others as examples, they are no authority,—for in determining duty, how canst thou quote as authorities those who have broken their vows?

68. 'Even the sun, therefore, may fall to the earth, even the mountain Himavat may lose its firmness; but never would I return to my home as a man of the world, with no knowledge of the truth and my senses only alert for external objects.

69. 'I would enter the blazing fire, but not my house with my purpose unfulfilled.' Thus he proudly made his resolve, and rising up in accordance with it, full of disinterestedness, went his way.

70. Then the minister and the Brâhman, both full of tears, having heard his firm determination, and having followed him awhile with despondent

---

[1] MSS. khedo.

looks, and overcome with sorrow, slowly returned of necessity to the city.

71. Through their love for the prince and their devotion to the king, they returned, and often stopped looking back[1]; they could neither behold him on the road nor yet lose the sight of him,—shining in his own splendour and beyond the reach of all others, like the sun.

72. Having placed faithful emissaries in disguise to find out the actions of him who was the supreme refuge of all, they went on with faltering steps, saying to each other, 'How shall we approach the king and see him, who is longing for his dear son?'

[1] Another reading gives 'full of reproach.'

BOOK X.

1. The prince, he of the broad and lusty chest, having thus dismissed the minister and the priest, crossed the Ganges with its speeding waves and went to Râgagriha with its beautiful palaces.

2. He reached the city distinguished by the five hills, well guarded and adorned with mountains, and supported and hallowed by auspicious sacred places[1], —like Brahman[2] in a holy calm going to the uppermost heaven.

3. Having heard of his majesty and strength, and his splendid beauty, surpassing all other men, the people of that region were all astonished as at him who has a bull for his sign and is immovable in his vow[3].

4. On seeing him, he who was going elsewhere stood still, and he who was standing there followed him in the way; he who was walking gently and gravely ran quickly, and he who was sitting at once sprang up.

5. Some people reverenced him with their hands, others in worship saluted him with their heads, some addressed him with affectionate words,—not one went on without paying him homage.

6. Those who were wearing gay-coloured dresses were ashamed when they saw him, those who were talking on random subjects fell to silence on the

---

[1] Tapoda is the name of a tîrtha in Magadha.

[2] Svayambhû.

[3] Siva.

road; no one indulged in an improper thought, as at the presence of Religion herself embodied.

7. In the men and the women on the highway, even though they were intent on other business, that conduct alone with the profoundest reverence seemed proper which is enjoined by the rules of royal homage; but his eyes never looked upon them.

8. His brows, his forehead, his mouth, or his eyes,—his body, his hands, his feet, or his gait,—whatever part of him any one beheld, that at once riveted his eyes.

9. Having beheld him with the beautiful circle of hair between his brows[1] and with long eyes, with his radiant body and his hands showing a graceful membrane between the fingers,—so worthy of ruling the earth and yet wearing a mendicant's dress,—the Goddess of Râ*g*ag*ri*ha was herself perturbed.

10. Then *S*re*n*ya[2], the lord of the court of the Magadhas, beheld from the outside of his palace the immense concourse of people, and asked the reason of it; and thus did a man recount it to him:

11. 'He who was thus foretold by the Brâhmans, "he will either attain supreme wisdom or the empire of the earth,"—it is he, the son of the king of the *S*âkyas, who is the ascetic whom the people are gazing at.'

12. The king, having heard this and perceived its meaning with his mind, thus at once spoke to that man: 'Let it be known whither he is going;' and the man, receiving the command, followed the prince.

[1] So the Tibetan. The Sanskrit text seems corrupt here. Cf. I, 65 *c*.

[2] A name of Bimbisâra, see Burnouf, Introd. p. 165.

13. With unrestless eyes, seeing only a yoke's length before him[1], with his voice hushed, and his walk slow and measured, he, the noblest of mendicants, went begging alms, keeping his limbs and his wandering thoughts under control.

14. Having received such alms as were offered, he retired to a lonely cascade of the mountain; and having eaten it there in the fitting manner, he ascended the mountain Pâ*md*ava[2].

15. In that wood, thickly filled with lodhra trees, having its thickets resonant with the notes of the peacocks, he the sun of mankind shone, wearing his red dress, like the morning sun above the eastern mountain.

16. That royal attendant, having thus watched him there, related it all to the king *S*re*n*ya; and the king, when he heard it, in his deep veneration, started himself to go thither with a modest retinue.

17. He who was like the Pâ*md*avas in heroism, and like a mountain in stature, ascended Pâ*md*ava, that noblest of mountains,—a crown-wearer, of lion-like gait, a lion among men, as a maned lion ascends a mountain.

18. There he beheld the Bodhisattva, resplendent as he sat on his hams, with subdued senses, as if the mountain were moving[3], and he himself were a peak thereof,—like the moon rising from the top of a cloud.

19. Him, distinguished by his beauty of form and perfect tranquillity as the very creation of Religion

[1] Hardy explains this 'he does not look before him further than the distance of a plough or nine spans' (Manual of Buddhism, p. 371).

[2] Cf. Lalitavistara.

[3] I.e. as if he, not the mountain, were entitled to the name a*k*ala.

herself,—filled with astonishment and affectionate regard the king of men approached, as Indra the self-existent (Brahman).

20. He, the chief of the courteous, having courteously drawn nigh to him, inquired as to the equilibrium of his bodily humours; and the other with equal gentleness assured the king of his health of mind and freedom from all ailments.

21. Then the king sat down on the clean surface of the rock, dark blue like an elephant's ear; and being seated[1], with the other's assent, he thus spoke, desiring to know his state of mind:

22. 'I have a strong friendship with thy family, come down by inheritance and well proved; since from this a desire to speak to thee, my son, has arisen in me, therefore listen to my words of affection.

23. 'When I consider thy widespread race, beginning with the sun, thy fresh youth, and thy conspicuous beauty,—whence comes this resolve of thine so out of all harmony with the rest, set wholly on a mendicant's life, not on a kingdom?

24. 'Thy limbs are worthy of red sandal-wood[2] perfumes,—they do not deserve the rough contact of red cloth; this hand is fit to protect subjects, it deserves not to hold food given by another.

25. 'If therefore, gentle youth, through thy love for thy father thou desirest not thy paternal kingdom in thy generosity,—then at any rate thy choice must not be excused,—accepting forthwith one half of my kingdom.

26. 'If thou actest thus there will be no violence

[1] N*ri*popavi*s*ya? with ârsha Sandhi.
[2] Lohita*k*andana may mean 'saffron.'

shown to thine own people, and by the mere lapse of time imperial power at last flies for refuge to the tranquil mind; therefore be pleased to do me a kindness,—the prosperity of the good becomes very powerful, when aided by the good [1].

27. 'But if from thy pride of race thou dost not now feel confidence in me, then plunge with thy arrows into countless armies, and with me as thy ally seek to conquer thy foes.

28. 'Choose thou therefore one of these ends, pursue according to rule religious merit, wealth, and pleasure; for these, love and the rest, in reverse order, are the three objects in life; when men die they pass into dissolution as far as regards this world.

29. 'That which is pleasure when it has overpowered wealth and merit, is wealth when it has conquered merit and pleasure; so too it is merit, when pleasure and wealth fall into abeyance; but all would have to be alike abandoned, if thy desired end [2] were obtained.

30. 'Do thou therefore by pursuing the three objects of life, cause this beauty of thine to bear its fruit; they say that when the attainment of religion, wealth, and pleasure is complete in all its parts, then the end of man is complete.

31. 'Do not thou let these two brawny arms lie useless which are worthy to draw the bow; they are well fitted like Mândhât*ri*'s to conquer the three worlds, much more the earth.

---

[1] [The Tibetan translates the fourth line, dam-pa-rnams dan bcas-pas dam-pai dpal ₒphel-lo, 'by being with the good the prosperity of the good increases.' H. W.]

[2] Nirvâ*n*a.

32. 'I speak this to you out of affection,—not through love of dominion or through astonishment; beholding this mendicant-dress of thine, I am filled with compassion and I shed tears.

33. 'O thou who desirest the mendicant's stage of life, enjoy pleasures now; in due time, O thou lover of religion, thou shalt practise religion;—ere old age comes on and overcomes this thy beauty, well worthy of thy illustrious race.

34. 'The old man can obtain merit by religion; old age is helpless for the enjoyment of pleasures; therefore they say that pleasures belong to the young man, wealth to the middle-aged, and religion to the old.

35. 'Youth in this present world is the enemy of religion and wealth,—since pleasures, however we guard them, are hard to hold, therefore, wherever pleasures are to be found, there they seize them.

36. 'Old age is prone to reflection[1], it is grave and intent on remaining quiet; it attains unimpassionedness with but little effort, unavoidably, and for very shame.

37. 'Therefore having passed through the deceptive period of youth, fickle, intent on external objects, heedless, impatient, not looking at the distance,—they take breath like men who have escaped safe through a forest.

38. 'Let therefore this fickle time of youth first pass by, reckless and giddy,—our early years are the mark for pleasure, they cannot be kept from the power of the senses.

39. 'Or if religion is really thy one aim, then offer

[1] Vimar*s*ayanti?

sacrifices,—this is thy family's immemorial custom, —climbing to highest heaven by sacrifices, even Indra, the lord of the winds, went thus to highest heaven.

40. 'With their arms pressed[1] by golden bracelets, and their variegated diadems resplendent with the light of gems, royal sages have reached the same goal by sacrifices which great sages reached by self-mortification.'

41. Thus spoke the monarch of the Magadhas, who spoke well and strongly like Indra[2]; but having heard it, the prince did not falter, (firm) like the mountain Kailâsa, having its many summits variegated (with lines of metals).

---

[1] Vidashta; cf. samdashta in Raghuv. XVI, 65.
[2] Valabhid, 'the smiter of the demon Vala.'

BOOK XI.

1. Being thus addressed by the monarch of the Magadhas, in a hostile speech with a friendly face,—self-possessed, unchanged, pure by family and personal purity, the son of *S*uddhodana thus made answer:

2. 'This is not to be called a strange thing for thee, born as thou art in the great family whose ensign is the lion [1]—that by thee of pure conduct, O lover of thy friends, this line of conduct should be adopted towards him who stands as one of thy friends.

3. 'Amongst the bad a friendship, worthy of their family, ceases to continue (and fades) like prosperity among the faint-hearted; it is only the good who keep increasing the old friendship of their ancestors by a new succession of friendly acts.

4. 'But those men who act unchangingly towards their friends in reverses of fortune, I esteem in my heart as true friends; who is not the friend of the prosperous man in his times of abundance?

5. 'So those who, having obtained riches in the world, employ them for the sake of their friends and religion,—their wealth has real solidity, and when it perishes it produces no pain at the end.

6. 'This thy determination concerning me, O king, is prompted by pure generosity and friendship [2];

---

[1] So the Tibetan explains haryam*k*a, señ·ges mčan·pai.

[2] The Sanskrit of this line is corrupt and does not scan. The

I will meet thee courteously with simple friendship; I would not utter aught else in my reply.

7. 'I, having experienced the fear of old age and death, fly to this path of religion in my desire for liberation; leaving behind my dear kindred with tears in their faces,—still more then those pleasures which are the causes of evil.

8. 'I am not so afraid even of serpents nor of thunderbolts falling from heaven, nor of flames blown together by the wind, as I am afraid of these worldly objects.

9. 'These transient pleasures,—the robbers of our happiness and our wealth, and which float empty and like illusions through the world,—infatuate men's minds even when they are only hoped for,—still more when they take up their abode in the soul.

10. 'The victims of pleasure attain not to happiness even in the heaven of the gods, still less in the world of mortals; he who is athirst is never satisfied with pleasures, as the fire, the friend of the wind, with fuel.

11. 'There is no calamity in the world like pleasures,—people are devoted to them through delusion; when he once knows the truth and so fears evil, what wise man would of his own choice desire evil?

12. 'When they have obtained all the earth girdled by the sea, kings wish to conquer the other side of the great ocean; mankind are never satiated

---

Tibetan renders it as follows: khyod·kyi (te) ṅes·pa (viniskayah) gaṅ·zhig bdag·la dmigs·pa ₒdi, 'whatever a determination of thine imagines of me, to this (answering I would say).' I would read vibhâvya mâm eva. The translation given above is conjectural.

with pleasures, as the ocean with the waters that fall into it.

13. 'When it had rained a golden shower from heaven, and when he had conquered the continents and the four oceans, and had even obtained the half of *S*akra's throne[1], Mândhât*ri* was still unsatisfied with worldly objects.

14. 'Though he had enjoyed the kingdom of the gods in heaven, when Indra had concealed himself through fear of V*ri*tra, and though in his pride he had made the great *Ri*shis bear his litter[2], Nahusha fell, unsatisfied with pleasures.

15. 'King (Purûravas) the son of I*d*â, having penetrated into the furthest heaven, and brought the goddess Urva*s*î into his power,—when he wished in his greed to take away gold from the *Ri*shis[3],—being unsatisfied with pleasures, fell into destruction.

16. 'Who would put his trust in these worldly objects, whether in heaven or in earth, unsettled as to lot or family,—which passed from Bali to Indra, and from Indra to Nahusha, and then again from Nahusha back to Indra?

17. 'Who would seek these enemies bearing the name of pleasures, by whom even those sages have been overcome, who were devoted to other pursuits, whose only clothes were rags, whose food was roots, fruits, and water, and who wore their twisted locks as long as snakes?

18. 'Those pleasures for whose sake even Ugrâyudha[4], armed terribly as he was with his weapon,

[1] Divyâvadâna, pp. 213–224.
[2] Mahâbh. V, 532.
[3] Mahâbh. I, 3147.
[4] See Hariva*ms*a, ch. xx. He was armed with a discus.

found death at Bhîshma's hands,—is not the mere thought of them unlucky and fatal,—still more the thought of the irreligious whose lives are spent in their service?

19. 'Who that considers the paltry flavour of worldly objects,—the very height of union being only insatiety,—the blame of the virtuous, and the certain sin,—has ever drawn near this poison which is called pleasure?

20. 'When they hear of the miseries of those who are intent on pleasure and are devoted to worldly pursuits[1], such as agriculture and the rest, and the self-content of those who are careless of pleasure,—it well befits the self-controlled to fling it away[2].

21. 'Success in pleasure is to be considered a misery in the man of pleasure, for he becomes intoxicated when his desired pleasures are attained; through intoxication he does what should not be done, not what should be done; and being wounded thereby he falls into a miserable end.

22. 'These pleasures which are gained and kept by toil,—which after deceiving leave you and return whence they came,—these pleasures which are but borrowed for a time[3], what man of self-control, if he is wise, would delight in them?

23. 'What man of self-control could find satisfaction in these pleasures which are like a torch of hay,—which excite thirst when you seek them and when you grasp them, and which they who abandon not keep only as misery[4]?

24. 'Those men of no self-control who are bitten by

---

[1] Dharmabhi*h*. (Cf. V, 5, 6.)

[2] I would read kâmâ*h*.

[3] For yâ*k*itaka cf. Pâ*n*. IV, 4, 21.

[4] I would read paripânti.

them in their hearts, fall into ruin and attain not bliss, —what man of self-control could find satisfaction in these pleasures, which are like an angry, cruel serpent?

25. 'Even if they enjoy them men are not satisfied, like dogs famishing with hunger over a bone,—what man of self-control could find satisfaction in these pleasures, which are like a skeleton composed of dry bones?

26. 'What man of self-control could find satisfaction in these pleasures which are like flesh that has been flung away, and which produce misery by their being held only in common with kings, thieves, water, and fire[1]?

27. 'What man of self-control could find satisfaction in these pleasures, which, like the senses[2], are destructive, and which bring calamity on every hand to those who abide in them, from the side of friends even more than from open enemies?

28. 'What man of self-control could find satisfaction in those pleasures, which are like the fruit that grows on the top of a tree,—which those who would leap up to reach fall down upon a mountain or into a forest, waters, or the ocean?

29. 'What man of self-control could find satisfaction in those pleasures, which are like snatching up a hot coal,—men never attain happiness, however they pursue them, increase them, or guard them?

30. 'What man of self-control could find satisfaction in those pleasures, which are like the enjoyments in a dream,—which are gained by their recipients after manifold pilgrimages and labours, and then perish in a moment?

[1] I.e. any one of these can seize them from us.

[2] Âyatana.

31. 'What man of self-control could find satisfaction in those pleasures which are like a spear[1], sword, or club,—for the sake of which the Kurus, the Vrishnis and the Amdhakas, the Maithilas and the Damdakas suffered destruction?

32. 'What man of self-control could find satisfaction in those pleasures which dissolve friendships and for the sake of which the two Asuras Sumda and Upasumda perished, victims engaged in mutual enmity?

33. 'None, however their intellect is blinded with pleasure, give themselves up, as in compassion, to ravenous beasts[2]; so what man of self-control could find satisfaction in those pleasures which are disastrous and constant enemies?

34. 'He whose intellect is blinded with pleasure does pitiable things; he incurs calamities, such as death, bonds, and the like; the wretch, who is the miserable slave of hope for the sake of pleasure, well deserves the pain of death even in the world of the living.

35. 'Deer are lured to their destruction by songs[3], insects for the sake of the brightness fly into the fire, the fish greedy for the flesh swallows the iron hook,—therefore worldly objects produce misery as their end.

36. 'As for the common opinion, "pleasures are enjoyments," none of them when examined are

[1] The Chinese translation seems to take sûla as a stake for impaling criminals in ver. 864.

[2] The text is corrupt. I would read kravyâtsu nâtmânam. The va in line 1 is for iva, a rare form, but allowed by Sanskrit lexicographers. Perhaps we should translate kâmândhasamgña, 'these men who are called "blinded with pleasure."'

[3] Cf. Kâdambarî (Calc. ed.), p. 27, l. 6 infra.

worthy of being enjoyed; fine garments and the rest are only the accessories of things,—they are to be regarded as merely the remedies for pain.

37. 'Water is desired for allaying thirst; food in the same way for removing hunger; a house for keeping off the wind, the heat of the sun, and the rain; and dress for keeping off the cold and to cover one's nakedness.

38. 'So too a bed is for removing drowsiness; a carriage for remedying the fatigue of a journey; a seat for alleviating the pain of standing; so bathing as a means for washing, health, and strength.

39. 'External objects therefore are to human beings means for remedying pain, not in themselves sources of enjoyment; what wise man would allow that he enjoys those delights which are only used as remedial?

40. 'He who, when burned with the heat of bilious fever, maintains that cold appliances are an enjoyment, when he is only engaged in alleviating pain,—he indeed might give the name of enjoyment to pleasures.

41. 'Since variableness is found in all pleasures, I cannot apply to them the name of enjoyment; the very conditions which mark pleasure, bring also in its turn pain.

42. 'Heavy garments and fragrant aloe-wood are pleasant in the cold, but an annoyance in the heat[1]; and the moonbeams and sandal-wood are pleasant in the heat, but a pain in the cold.

43. 'Since the well-known opposite pairs[2], such

[1] I have adopted Professor Kielhorn's suggested reading sukhâya sîte hy asukhâya gharme.

[2] Cf. ἡ συστοιχία of the Pythagoreans (Arist. Ethics, I, 6).

as gain and loss and the rest, are inseparably connected with everything in this world,—therefore no man is invariably happy on the earth nor invariably wretched.

44. 'When I see how the nature of pleasure and pain are mixed, I consider royalty and slavery as the same; a king does not always smile, nor is a slave always in pain.

45. 'Since to be a king involves a wider range of command, therefore the pains of a king are great; for a king is like a peg[1],—he endures trouble for the sake of the world.

46. 'A king is unfortunate, if he places his trust in his royalty which is apt to desert and loves crooked turns[2]; and on the other hand, if he does not trust in it, then what can be the happiness of a timid king?

47. 'And since after even conquering the whole earth, one city only can serve as a dwelling-place, and even there only one house can be inhabited, is not royalty mere labour for others?

48. 'And even in royal clothing one pair of garments is all he needs, and just enough food to keep off hunger; so only one bed, and only one seat; all a king's other distinctions are only for pride.

49. 'And if all these fruits are desired for the sake of satisfaction, I can be satisfied without a kingdom; and if a man is once satisfied in this world, are not all distinctions indistinguishable?

50. 'He then who has attained the auspicious road to happiness is not to be deceived in regard to pleasures; remembering thy professed friendship, tell me again and again, do they keep their promise?

---

[1] Cf. Isaiah xxii. 23, 24 (יָתֵד).

[2] Professor Kielhorn would read ra*m*kamitre.

51. 'I have not repaired to the forest through anger, nor because my diadem has been dashed down by an enemy's arrows; nor have I set my desires on loftier objects[1], that I thus refuse thy proposal.

52. 'Only he who, having once let go a malignant incensed serpent, or a blazing hay-torch all on fire, would strive again to seize it, would ever seek pleasures again after having once abandoned them.

53. 'Only he who, though seeing, would envy the blind, though free the bound, though wealthy the destitute, though sound in his reason the maniac,—only he, I say, would envy one who is devoted to worldly objects.

54. 'He who lives on alms, my good friend, is not to be pitied, having gained his end and being set on escaping the fear of old age and death; he has here the best happiness, perfect calm, and hereafter all pains are for him abolished.

55. 'But he is to be pitied who is overpowered by thirst though set in the midst of great wealth,—who attains not the happiness of calm here, while pain has to be experienced hereafter.

56. 'Thus to speak to me is well worthy of thy character, thy mode of life, and thy family; and to carry out my resolve is also befitting my character, my mode of life, and my family.

57. 'I have been wounded by the enjoyment of the world, and I have come out longing to obtain peace; I would not accept an empire free from all ill even in the third heaven, how much less amongst men?

58. 'But as for what thou saidst to me, O king, that the universal pursuit of the three objects is the

[1] Sc. as rule in heaven, &c.

supreme end of man,—and[1] thou saidst that what I regard as the desirable is misery,—thy three objects are perishable and also unsatisfying.

59. 'But that world in which there is no old age nor fear, no birth, nor death, nor anxieties[2], that alone I consider the highest end of man, where there is no ever-renewed action.

60. 'And as for what thou saidst, "wait till old age comes, for youth is ever subject to change;"—this want of decision is itself uncertain; for age too can be irresolute and youth can be firm.

61. 'But since Fate[3] is so well skilled in its art as to draw the world in all its various ages into its power,—how shall the wise man, who desires tranquillity, wait for old age, when he knows not when the time of death will be?

62. 'When death stands ready like a hunter, with old age as his weapon, and diseases scattered about as his arrows, smiting down living creatures who fly like deer to the forest of destiny, what desire can there be in any one for length of life?

63. 'It well befits the youthful son or the old man or the child so to act with all promptitude that they may choose the action of the religious man whose soul is all mercy,—nay, better still, his inactivity.

64. 'And as for what thou saidst, "be diligent in sacrifices for religion, such as are worthy of thy race and bring a glorious fruit,"—honour to such sacrifices! I desire not that fruit which is sought by causing pain to others[4]!

---

[1] I would read anartha ity âttha (for ity artha).

[2] Âdhaya*h*.

[3] Ko, 'who?' seems here used for 'fate.' Professor Kielhorn would read—Yadâ*m*tako *g*agad vaya*h*su sarveshu va*s*a*m* vikarshati.

[4] Yad ishyate is the true reading.

65. 'To kill a helpless victim through a wish for future reward,—it would be an unseemly action for a merciful-hearted good man, even if the reward of the sacrifice were eternal; but what if, after all, it is subject to decay?

66. 'And even if true religion did not consist in quite another rule of conduct, by self-restraint, moral practice and a total absence of passion,—still it would not be seemly to follow the rule of sacrifice, where the highest reward is described as attained only by slaughter.

67. 'Even that happiness which comes to a man, while he stays in this world, through the injury of another, is hateful to the wise compassionate heart; how much more if it be something beyond our sight in another life?

68. 'I am not to be lured into a course of action for future reward,—my mind does not delight, O king, in future births; these actions are uncertain and wavering in their direction, like plants beaten by the rain from a cloud.

69. 'I have come here with a wish to see next the seer Arâ*d*a who proclaims liberation; I start this very day,—happiness be to thee, O king; forgive my words which may seem harsh through their absolute freedom from passion[1].

70. '[2]Now therefore do thou guard (the world) like Indra in heaven; guard it continually like the sun by thy excellencies; guard its best happiness here;

---

[1] I read *s*amatattva.

[2] This verse is obscure,—the division of the clauses is uncertain, the Chinese translation giving only six; but ava seems to occur eight times. The Tibetan has its equivalent sruṅs nine times.

guard the earth; guard life by the noble[1]; guard the sons of the good; guard thy royal powers, O king; and guard thine own religion.

71. 'As in the midst of a sudden catastrophe arising from the flame of (fire), the enemy of cold, a bird, to deliver its body, betakes itself to the enemy of fire (water),—so do thou, when occasion calls, betake thyself, to deliver thy mind, to those who will destroy the enemies of thy home[2].'

72. The king himself, folding his hands, with a sudden longing come upon him, replied, 'Thou art obtaining thy desire without hindrance; when thou hast at last accomplished all that thou hast to do, thou shalt show hereafter thy favour towards me.'

73. Having given his firm promise to the monarch, he proceeded to the Vai*s*va*m*tara hermitage; and, after watching him with astonishment, as he wandered on in his course, the king and[3] his courtiers returned to the mountain (of Râ*g*agiri).

---

[1] So the Tibetan.

[2] This is a very hard verse, but the obscure Chinese translation helps to explain it, vv. 912–915. I read in *c*, himâri*s*atrum, i.e. water, as the enemy of the enemy of cold (fire). The bird flies to water to stop the effects of fire; as the king is to destroy his enemies by means of their enemies, cf. Manu VII, 158. Here, however, it seems to mean also that he is to destroy his passions by their opposites; the home (kshaya) is the summum bonum, nirvâ*n*a.—I read samplava for sambhava, as the two words are confused in XII, 24 and 28.

[3] *K*a seems used in a very artificial manner with the ellipsis of the substantive which should follow it; cf. Amarakosha III, 4, 1, 6 (we might also read prâpad).

BOOK XII.

1. Then the moon of the Ikshvâku race turned towards the hermitage of the sage Arâ*d*a[1] of tranquil life,—as it were, doing honour to it by his beauty.

2. He drew near, on being addressed in a loud voice 'Welcome' by the kinsman of Kâlâma, as he saw him from afar.

3. They, having mutually asked after each other's health as was fitting, sat down in a clean place on two pure wooden seats.

4. The best of sages, having seen the prince seated, and as it were drinking in the sight of him with eyes opened wide in reverence, thus addressed him:

5. 'I know, gentle youth, how thou hast come forth from thy home, having severed the bond of affection, as a wild elephant its cord.

6. 'In every way thy mind is stedfast and wise, who hast come here after abandoning royal luxury like a creeper-plant with poisonous fruit.

7. 'It is no marvel that kings have retired to the forest who have grown old in years, having given up their glory to their children, like a garland left behind after being used.

8. 'But this is to me indeed a marvel that thou art come hither in life's fresh prime, set in the open field

---

[1] Arâ*d*a holds an early form of the Sâ*m*khya doctrine.

of the world's enjoyments, ere thou hast as yet tasted of their happiness.

9. 'Verily thou art a worthy vessel to receive this highest religion; having mastered it with full knowledge, cross at once over the sea of misery.

10. 'Though the doctrine is generally efficient only after a time, when the student has been thoroughly tested, thou art easy for me to examine from thy depth of character and determination.'

11. The prince, having heard these words of Arâ*d*a, was filled with great pleasure and thus made reply:

12. 'This extreme kindliness which thou showest to me, calmly passionless as thou art, makes me, imperfect as I am, seem even already to have attained perfection.

13. 'I feel at the sight of thee like one longing to see who finds a light,—like one wishing to journey, a guide,—or like one wishing to cross, a boat.

14. 'Wilt thou therefore deign to tell me that secret, if thou thinkest it should be told, whereby thy servant may be delivered from old age, death, and disease.'

15. Arâ*d*a, thus impelled by the noble nature of the prince, declared in a concise form the tenets of his doctrine:

16. 'O best of hearers, hear this our firmly-settled theory, how our mortal existence arises and how it revolves.

17. '"The evolvent" and "the evolute," birth, old age, and death,—know that this has been called the reality by us; do thou receive our words, O thou who art stedfast in thy nature.

18. 'But know, O thou who art deep in the search

into the nature of things, that the five elements[1], egoism, intellect, and "the unmanifested" are the "evolvents;"

19. 'But know that the "evolutes" consist of intellect, external objects[2], the senses, and the hands, feet, voice, anus, and generative organ, and also the mind.

20. 'There is also a something which bears the name kshetra*gñ*a, from its knowledge of this "field" (kshetra or the body); and those who investigate the soul call the soul kshetra*gñ*a.

21. 'Kapila with his disciple became the illuminated,—such is the tradition; and he, as the illuminated, with his son is now called here Pra*g*âpati.

22. 'That which is born and grows old and is bound and dies,—is to be known as "the manifested," and "the unmanifested" is to be distinguished by its contrariety.

23. 'Ignorance, the merit or demerit of former actions, and desire are to be known as the causes of mundane existence; he who abides in the midst of this triad does not attain to the truth of things,—

24. 'From mistake[3], egoism, confusion, fluctuation, indiscrimination, false means, inordinate attachment, and gravitation.

25. 'Now "mistake" acts in a contrary manner, it does wrongly what it should do, and what it should think it thinks wrongly.

26. '"I say," "I know," "I go," "I am firmly

[1] These are the tanmâtrâ*n*i or subtile elements.

[2] Vishayân, corresponding to the gross elements. The intellect, buddhi, is both an evolver and an evolute.

[3] Should we read viparyayâd? Cf. Sâ*m*khya, aphor. III, 37.

fixed," it is thus that "egoism" shows itself here, O thou who art free from all egoism.

27. 'That state of mind is called "confusion," O thou who art all unconfused, which views under one nature, massed like a lump of clay, objects that thus become confused in their nature.

28. 'That state of mind which says that this mind, intellect, and these actions are the same as "I," and that which says that all this aggregate is the same as "I,"—is called "fluctuation."

29. 'That state of mind is called "indiscrimination," O thou who art discriminating, which thinks there is no difference between the illuminated and the unwise, and between the different evolvents.

30. 'Uttering "namas" and "vasha*t*," sprinkling water upon sacrifices, &c. with or without the recital of Vedic hymns, and such like rites,—these are declared by the wise to be "false means," O thou who art well skilled in true means.

31. 'That is called "inordinate attachment," by which the fool is entangled in external objects through his mind, speech, actions, and thoughts, O thou who hast shaken thyself free from all attachments.

32. 'The misery which a man imagines by the ideas "This is mine," "I am connected with this," is to be recognised as "gravitation,"—by this a man is borne downwards into new births.

33. 'Thus Ignorance, O ye wise, being fivefold in its character, energises towards torpor, delusion, the great delusion, and the two kinds of darkness [1].

34. 'Know, that among these indolence is "torpor," death and birth are "delusion," and be it clearly

---

[1] Cf. Sâ*m*khyakârikâ, 48.

understood, O undeluded one, that desire is the "great delusion."

35. 'Since by it even the higher beings are deluded, therefore, O hero, is this called the "great delusion."

36. 'They define anger, O thou angerless one, as "darkness;" and despondency, O undesponding, they pronounce to be the "blind darkness."

37. 'The child, entangled in this fivefold ignorance, is effused in his different births in a world abounding with misery.

38. 'He wanders about in the world of embodied existence, thinking that I am the seer, and the hearer, and the thinker,—the effect and the cause.

39. 'Through these causes[1], O wise prince, the stream of "torpor" is set in motion; be pleased to consider that in the absence of the cause there is the absence of the effect.

40. 'Let the wise man who has right views know these four things, O thou who desirest liberation,—the illuminated and the unilluminated, the manifested and the unmanifested.

41. 'The soul, having once learned to distinguish these four properly, having abandoned all (ideas of) straightness or quickness[2], attains to the immortal sphere.

42. 'For this reason the Brâhmans in the world, discoursing on the supreme Brahman, practise here a rigorous course of sacred study and let other Brâhmans live with them to follow it also.'

43. The prince, having heard this discourse from the seer, asked concerning the means and the final state.

---

[1] Cf. ver. 23.

[2] It rises above all relative ideas? The text may be corrupt.

44. 'Wilt thou please to explain to me how, how far, and where this life of sacred study is to be led, and the limit of this course of life[1]?'

45. Then Arâ*d*a, according to his doctrine, declared to him in another way that course of life clearly and succinctly.

46. 'The devotee, in the beginning, having left his house, and assumed the signs of the mendicant, goes on, following a rule of conduct which extends to the whole life.

47. 'Cultivating absolute content with any alms from any person, he carries out his lonely life, indifferent to all feelings, meditating on the holy books, and satisfied in himself.

48. 'Then having seen how fear arises from passion and the highest happiness from the absence of passion, he strives, by restraining all the senses, to attain to tranquillity of mind.

49. 'Then he reaches the first stage of contemplation, which is separated from desires, evil intentions and the like, and arises from discrimination and which involves reasoning[2].

50. 'And having obtained this ecstatic contemplation, and reasoning on various objects, the childish mind is carried away by the possession of the new unknown ecstasy.

51. 'With a tranquillity of this kind, which disdains desire or dislike, he reaches the world of Brahman, deceived by the delight.

52. 'But the wise man, knowing that these reasonings bewilder the mind, reaches a (second) stage of contemplation separate from this, which has its own pleasure and ecstasy.

[1] Dharma.

[2] Cf. Yoga-sûtras I, 42.

53. 'And he who, carried away by this pleasure, sees no further distinction, obtains a dwelling full of light, even amongst the Âbhâsura deities.

54. 'But he who separates his mind from this pleasure and ecstasy, reaches the third stage of contemplation ecstatic but without pleasure.

55. 'Upon this stage some teachers make their stand, thinking that it is indeed liberation, since pleasure and pain have been left behind and there is no exercise of the intellect.

56. 'But he who, immersed in this ecstasy, strives not for a further distinction, obtains an ecstasy in common with the *S*ubhak*ri*tsna deities.

57. 'But he who, having attained such a bliss desires it not but despises it, obtains the fourth stage of contemplation which is separate from all pleasure or pain.

58. 'The fruit of this contemplation which is on an equality with the V*ri*hatphala deities, those who investigate the great wisdom call the V*ri*hatphala[1].

59. 'But rising beyond this contemplation, having seen the imperfections of all embodied souls, the wise man climbs to a yet higher wisdom in order to abolish all body.

60. 'Then, having abandoned this contemplation, being resolved to find a further distinction, he becomes as disgusted with form itself as he who knows the real is with pleasures.

61. 'First he makes use of all the apertures of his body; and next he exerts his will to experience a feeling of void space even in the solid parts[2].

62. 'But another wise man, having contracted his soul which is by nature extended everywhere like

[1] The great fruit.

[2] An obscure verse; cf. Pâli Dict.

the ether,[1]—as he gazes ever further on, detects a yet higher distinction.

63. 'Another one of those who are profoundly versed in the supreme Self, having abolished himself by himself, sees that nothing exists and is called a Nihilist[2].

64. 'Then like the Muñga-reed's stalk[3] from its sheath or the bird from its cage, the soul, escaped from the body, is declared to be "liberated."

65. 'This is that supreme Brahman, constant, eternal, and without distinctive signs; which the wise who know reality declare to be liberation.

66. 'Thus have I shown to thee the means and liberation; if thou hast understood and approved it, then act accordingly.

67. '*G*aigîshavya[4] and *G*anaka, and the aged Parâsara, by following this path, were liberated, and so were others who sought liberation.'

68. The prince having not accepted his words but having pondered them, filled with the force of his former arguments, thus made answer:

69. 'I have heard this thy doctrine, subtil and pre-eminently auspicious, but I hold that it cannot be final, because it does not teach us how to abandon this soul itself in the various bodies.

70. 'For I consider that the embodied soul, though freed from the evolutes and the evolvents, is still subject to the condition of birth and has the condition of a seed[5].

71. 'Even though the pure soul is declared to be

---

[1] Cf. Bhâshâpari*kkh*eda, *s*loka 25.

[2] Âki*mk*anya.

[3] Cf. Ka*th*a Up. VI, 17.

[4] Mahâbh. IX, § 50; Tattvakaumudî, § 5.

[5] This is expanded in the Chinese, vv. 984, 985.

"liberated," yet as long as the soul remains there can be no absolute abandonment of it.

72. 'If we abandon successively all this triad, yet "distinction" is still perceived; as long as the soul itself continues, there this triad continues in a subtil form.

73. 'It is held (by some) that this is liberation, because the "imperfections" are so attenuated, and the thinking power is inactive, and the term of existence is so prolonged;

74. 'But as for this supposed abandonment of the principle of egoism,—as long as the soul continues, there is no real abandonment of egoism.

75. 'The soul does not become free from qualities as long as it is not released from number and the rest; therefore, as long as there is no freedom from qualities, there is no liberation declared for it.

76. 'There is no real separation of the qualities and their subject; for fire cannot be conceived, apart from its form and heat.

77. 'Before the body there will be nothing embodied, so before the qualities there will be no subject; how, if it was originally free, could the soul ever become bound[1]?

78. 'The body-knower (the soul) which is unembodied, must be either knowing or unknowing; if it is knowing, there must be some object to be known, and if there is this object, it is not liberated.

79. 'Or if the soul is declared to be unknowing, then of what use to you is this imagined soul? Even without such a soul, the existence of the absence of knowledge is notorious as, for instance, in a log of wood or a wall.

[1] I read **kasmât** for **tasmât**.

80. 'And since each successive abandonment is held to be still accompanied by qualities, I maintain that the absolute attainment of our end can only be found in the abandonment of everything.'

81. Thus did he remain unsatisfied after he had heard the doctrine of Arâda; then having decided it to be incomplete, he turned away.

82. Seeking to know the true distinction, he went to the hermitage of Udraka[1], but he gained no clear understanding from his treatment of the soul.

83. For the sage Udraka, having learned the inherent imperfections of the name and the thing named, took refuge in a theory beyond Nihilism, which maintained a name and a non-name.

84. And since even a name and a non-name were substrata, however subtil, he went even further still and found his restlessness set at rest in the idea that there is no named and no un-named;

85. And because the intellect rested there, not proceeding any further,—it became very subtil, and there was no such thing as un-named nor as named.

86. But because, even when it has reached this goal it yet returns again to the world, therefore the Bodhisattva, seeking something beyond, left Udraka.

87. Having quitted his hermitage, fully resolved in his purpose, and seeking final bliss, he next visited the hermitage, called a city, of the royal sage Gaya.

88. Then on the pure bank of the Nairañganâ the saint whose every effort was pure fixed his dwelling, bent as he was on a lonely habitation.

89. Five mendicants, desiring liberation, came

[1] Cf. Burnouf, Introd. p. 386 n. It is written Rudraka in XV, 89.

up to him when they beheld him there, just as the objects of the senses come up to a percipient who has gained wealth and health by his previous merit.

90. Being honoured by these disciples who were dwelling in that family, as they bowed reverently with their bodies bent low in humility, as the mind is honoured by the restless senses,

91. And thinking, 'this may be the means of abolishing birth and death,' he at once commenced a series of difficult austerities by fasting.

92. For six years, vainly trying to attain merit[1], he practised self-mortification, performing many rules of abstinence, hard for a man to carry out.

93. At the hours for eating, he, longing to cross the world whose farther shore is so difficult to reach, broke his vow with single jujube fruits, sesame seeds, and rice.

94. But the emaciation which was produced in his body by that asceticism, became positive fatness through the splendour which invested him.

95. Though thin, yet with his glory and his beauty unimpaired, he caused gladness to other eyes, as the autumnal moon in the beginning of her bright fortnight gladdens the lotuses.

96. Having only skin and bone remaining, with his fat, flesh and blood entirely wasted, yet, though diminished, he still shone with undiminished grandeur like the ocean.

97. Then the seer, having his body evidently emaciated to no purpose in a cruel self-mortifica-

[1] This is the Tibetan reading [las-ni thob-bzhed lo drug-tu, 'wishing to obtain (the fruits of good) works, during six years.' H.W.]

tion,—dreading continued existence, thus reflected in his longing to become a Buddha:

98. 'This is not the way to passionlessness, nor to perfect knowledge, nor to liberation; that was certainly the true way which I found at the root of the *G*ambu[1] tree.

99. 'But that cannot be attained by one who has lost his strength,'—so resuming his care for his body, he next pondered thus, how best to increase his bodily vigour:

100. 'Wearied with hunger, thirst, and fatigue, with his mind no longer self-possessed through fatigue, how should one who is not absolutely calm reach the end which is to be attained by his mind?

101. 'True calm is properly obtained by the constant satisfaction of the senses; the mind's self-possession is only obtained by the senses being perfectly satisfied.

102. 'True meditation is produced in him whose mind is self-possessed and at rest,—to him whose thoughts are engaged in meditation the exercise of perfect contemplation begins at once.

103. 'By contemplation are obtained those conditions[2] through which is eventually gained that supreme calm, undecaying, immortal state, which is so hard to be reached.'

104. Having thus resolved, 'this means is based upon eating food,' the wise seer of unbounded wisdom, having made up his mind to accept the continuance of life,

105. And having bathed, thin as he was, slowly

---

[1] The rose apple, see V, 8. [2] Dharmâ*h*.

came up the bank of the Nairañgana, supported as by a hand by the trees on the shore, which bent down the ends of their branches in adoration.

106. Now at that time Nandabalâ, the daughter of the leader of the herdsmen, impelled by the gods, with a sudden joy risen in her heart, had just come near,

107. Her arm gay with a white shell, and wearing a dark blue woollen cloth, like the river Yamunâ, with its dark blue water and its wreath of foam.

108. She, having her joy increased by her faith, with her lotus-like eyes opened wide, bowed down before him and persuaded him to take some milk.

109. By partaking that food having made her obtain the full reward of her birth, he himself became capable of gaining the highest knowledge, all his six senses being now satisfied,

110. The seer, having his body now fully robust, together with his glorious fame, one beauty and one majesty being equally spread in both, shone like the ocean and the moon [1].

111. Thinking that he had returned to the world the five mendicants left him, as the five elements leave the wise soul when it is liberated.

112. Accompanied only by his own resolve, having fixed his mind on the attainment of perfect knowledge, he went to the root of an Asvattha tree [2], where the surface of the ground was covered with young grass.

113. Then Kâla [3], the best of serpents, whose

[1] Fame is often compared for its brightness to the moon.

[2] Ficus religiosa or pipul tree.

[3] He is the Nâga king, *G*âtaka I, 72.

majesty was like the lord of elephants, having been awakened by the unparalleled sound of his feet, uttered this praise of the great sage, being sure that he was on the point of attaining perfect knowledge:

114. 'Inasmuch as the earth, pressed down by thy feet, O sage, resounds repeatedly, and inasmuch as thy splendour shines forth like the sun, thou shalt assuredly to-day enjoy the desired fruit.

115. 'Inasmuch as lines of birds fluttering in the sky offer thee reverential salutation, O lotus-eyed one, and inasmuch as gentle breezes blow in the sky, thou shalt certainly to-day become the Buddha.'

116. Being thus praised by the best of serpents, and having taken some pure grass from a grass-cutter, he, having made his resolution, sat down to obtain perfect knowledge at the foot of the great holy tree.

117. Then he sat down on his hams in a posture, immovably firm and with his limbs gathered into a mass like a sleeping serpent's hood, exclaiming, 'I will not rise from this position on the earth [1] until I have obtained my utmost aim.'

118. Then the dwellers in heaven burst into unequalled joy; the herds of beasts and the birds uttered no cry; the trees moved by the wind made no sound, when the holy one took his seat firm in his resolve.

[1] For tâvat read yâvat.

BOOK XIII.

1. When the great sage, sprung from a line of royal sages, sat down there with his soul fully resolved to obtain the highest knowledge, the whole world rejoiced; but Mâra, the enemy of the good law, was afraid.

2. He whom they call in the world Kâmadeva, the owner of the various weapons, the flower-arrowed, the lord of the course of desire,—it is he whom they also style Mâra the enemy of liberation.

3. His three sons, Confusion, Gaiety, and Pride, and his three daughters, Lust, Delight, and Thirst[1], asked of him the reason of his despondency, and he thus made answer unto them:

4. 'This sage, wearing the armour of resolution, and having drawn the arrow of wisdom with the barb of truth, sits yonder intending to conquer my realms,—hence is this despondency of my mind.

5. 'If he succeeds in overcoming me and proclaims to the world the path of final bliss, all this my realm will to-day become empty, as did that of the disembodied lord when he violated the rules of his station[2].

6. 'While, therefore, he stands within my reach

---

[1] For these cf. also ver. 14, and XV, 13.

[2] This probably refers to the legend of Nimi-videha, see Vishnu Pur. IV, 5; it might be 'the king of the Videhas.' There may be also a secondary allusion to the legend of Ananga and *S*iva.

and while his spiritual eyesight is not yet attained, I will assail him to break his vow as the swollen might of a river assails a dam.'

7. Then having seized his flower-made bow and his five infatuating arrows, he drew near to the root of the A*s*vattha tree with his children, he the great disturber of the minds of living beings.

8. Having fixed his left hand on the end of the barb and playing with the arrow, Mâra thus addressed the calm seer as he sat on his seat, preparing to cross to the further side of the ocean of existence:

9. 'Up, up, O thou Kshatriya, afraid of death! follow thine own duty and abandon this law of liberation! and having conquered the lower worlds by thy arrows, proceed to gain the higher worlds of Indra.

10. 'That is a glorious path to travel, which has been followed by former leaders of men; this mendicant life is ill-suited for one born in the noble family of a royal sage to follow.

11. 'But if thou wilt not rise, strong in thy purpose,—then be firm if thou wilt and quit not thy resolve,—this arrow is uplifted by me,—it is the very one which was shot against Sûryaka[1], the enemy of the fish.

12. 'So too, I think, when somewhat probed by this weapon, even the son of I*d*â[2], the grandson of the moon, became mad; and *S*â*m*tanu[3] also lost

---

[1] The sun, alluding to his amour with Va*d*avâ. (The lake is called vipannamînam in *Ri*tusa*m*hâra I, 20.)

[2] Purûravas. (Professor Bühler suggests sp*r*ish*t*a*h*.)

[3] Does this mean Vi*k*itravîrya the grandson of *S*a*m*tanu, see Vish*n*u Pur. IV, 20?

his self-control, — how much more then one of feebler powers now that the age has grown degenerate?

13. 'Therefore quickly rise up and come to thyself,—for this arrow is ready, darting out its tongue, which I do not launch even against the *k*akravâka birds, tenderly attached as they are and well deserving the name of lovers.'

14. But when, even though thus addressed, the *S*âkya saint unheeding did not change his posture, then Mâra discharged his arrow at him, setting in front of him his daughters and his sons[1].

15. But even when that arrow was shot he gave no heed and swerved not from his firmness; and Mâra, beholding him thus, sank down, and slowly thus spoke, full of thought:

16. 'He does not even notice that arrow by which the god *S*ambhu was pierced with love for the daughter of the mountain[2] and shaken in his vow; can he be destitute of all feeling? is not this that very arrow?

17. 'He is not worthy of my flower-shaft, nor my arrow "gladdener," nor the sending of my daughter Rati (to tempt him); he deserves the alarms and rebukes and blows from all the gathered hosts of the demons.'

18. Then Mâra called to mind his own army, wishing to work the overthrow of the *S*âkya saint; and his followers swarmed round, wearing different forms and carrying arrows, trees, darts, clubs, and swords in their hands;

19. Having the faces of boars, fishes, horses, asses,

---

[1] See ver. 3. [2] Umâ.

and camels, of tigers, bears, lions, and elephants,—one-eyed, many-faced, three-headed,—with protuberant bellies and speckled bellies;

20. Blended with goats, with knees swollen like pots, armed with tusks and with claws, carrying headless trunks in their hands, and assuming many forms, with half-mutilated faces, and with monstrous mouths;

21. Copper-red, covered with red spots, bearing clubs in their hands, with yellow or smoke-coloured hair, with wreaths dangling down, with long pendulous ears like elephants, clothed in leather or wearing no clothes at all;

22. Having half their faces white or half their bodies green,—red and smoke-coloured, yellow and black,—with arms reaching out longer than a serpent, and with girdles jingling with rattling bells.

23. Some were as tall as palm-trees, carrying spears,—others were of the size of children with projecting teeth, others birds with the faces of rams, others with men's bodies and cats' faces;

24. With dishevelled hair, or with topknots, or half-bald, with rope-garments or with head-dress all in confusion,—with triumphant faces or frowning faces,—wasting the strength or fascinating the mind.

25. Some as they went leaped about wildly, others danced upon one another, some sported about in the sky, others went along on the tops of the trees.

26. One danced, shaking a trident, another made a crash, dragging a club, another bounded for joy like a bull, another blazed out flames from every hair.

27. Such were the troops of demons who encircled the root of the Bodhi tree on every side, eager to

seize it and to destroy it, awaiting the command of their lord.

28. Beholding in the first half of the night that battle of Mâra and the bull of the *S*âkya race, the heavens did not shine and the earth shook and the (ten) regions of space flashed flames and roared.

29. A wind of intense violence blew in all directions[1], the stars did not shine, the moon gave no light, and a deeper darkness of night spread around, and all the oceans were agitated.

30. The mountain deities[2] and the Nâgas who honoured the Law, indignant at the attack on the saint, rolling their eyes in anger against Mâra, heaved deep sighs and opened their mouths wide.

31. But the god-sages, the *S*uddhâdhivâsas[3], being as it were absorbed in the perfect accomplishment of the good Law, felt only a pity for Mâra in their minds and through their absolute passionlessness were unruffled by anger.

32. When they saw the foot of the Bodhi tree crowded with that host of Mâra, intent on doing harm,—the sky was filled with the cry raised by all the virtuous beings who desired the world's liberation.

33. But the great sage[4] having beheld that army of Mâra thus engaged in an attack on the knower of the Law[5], remained untroubled and suffered no perturbation, like a lion seated in the midst of oxen.

---

[1] Vi*s*vak should be corrected vishvak.

[2] Mahîbh*ri*ta*h*. This might mean simply 'the rulers of the earth.'

[3] In Pâli Suddhâvâsâ. Cf. III, 26.

[4] Buddha himself, viewing all this ab extra.

[5] The Tibetan seems to read dharmavidhe*h* for dharmavida*h*, as it has chos-kyi cho-ga de-ni, '(injurer) of that law of dharma.'

34. Then Mâra commanded his excited army of demons to terrify him; and forthwith that host resolved to break down his determination with their various powers.

35. Some with many tongues hanging out and shaking, with sharp-pointed savage teeth and eyes like the disk of the sun, with wide-yawning mouths and upright ears like spikes,—they stood round trying to frighten him.

36. Before these monsters standing there, so dreadful in form and disposition, the great sage remained unalarmed and untroubled, sporting with them as if they had been only rude children [1].

37. Then one of them, with his eyes rolling wildly, lifted up a club against him; but his arm with the club was instantly paralysed, as was Indra's of old with its thunderbolt [2].

38. Some, having lifted up stones and trees, found themselves unable to throw them against the sage; down they fell, with their trees and their stones, like the roots of the Vindhya shattered by the thunderbolt.

39. Others, leaping up into the sky, flung rocks, trees, and axes; these remained in the sky and did not fall down, like the many-coloured rays of the evening clouds.

40. Another hurled upon him a mass of blazing straw as big as a mountain-peak, which, as soon as it was thrown, while it hung poised in the sky, was shattered into a hundred fragments by the sage's power.

41. One, rising up like the sun in full splendour, rained down from the sky a great shower of live

[1] Prof. Bühler suggests svabâlebhya*h*, 'as with his own tossed hair.'

[2] Cf. *S*atap. Br. XII, 7, 3; Vish*n*u Pur. V, 30; Kum. Sambh. II, 20.

embers, as at the end of an aeon blazing Meru showers down the pulverised scoriae of the golden valleys.

42. But that shower of embers full of sparks, when scattered at the foot of the Bodhi tree, became a shower of red lotus-petals through the operation of the great saint's boundless charity.

43. But with all these various scorching assaults on his body and his mind, and all these missiles showered down upon him, the *S*âkya saint did not in the least degree move from his posture, clasping firmly his resolution as a kinsman.

44. Then others spat out serpents from their mouths as from old decayed trunks of trees; but, as if held fast by a charm, near him they neither breathed nor discharged venom nor moved.

45. Others, having become great clouds, emitting lightning and uttering the fierce roar of thunderbolts, poured a shower of stones upon that tree,—but it turned to a pleasant shower of flowers.

46. Another set an arrow in his bow,—there it gleamed but it did not issue forth, like the anger which falls slack [1] in the soul of an ill-tempered impotent man.

47. But five arrows shot by another stood motionless and fell not, through the saint's ruling guidance, —like the five senses of him who is well experienced in the course of worldly objects and is afraid of embodied existence.

48. Another, full of anger, rushed towards the great saint, having seized a club with a desire to

[1] Dhûryamâ*n*o is a difficult word, connected with √dhv*ri* or √dhûrv.

smite him; but he fell powerless without finding an opportunity, like mankind in the presence of faults which cause failure [1].

49. But a woman named Meghakâlî, bearing a skull in her hand, in order to infatuate the mind of the sage, flitted about unsettled and stayed not in one spot, like the mind of the fickle student over the sacred texts.

50. Another, fixing a kindling eye, wished to burn him with the fire of his glance like a poisonous serpent; but he saw the sage and lo! he was not there, like the votary of pleasure when true happiness is pointed out to him [2].

51. Another, lifting up a heavy rock, wearied himself to no purpose, having his efforts baffled,—like one who wishes to obtain by bodily fatigue that condition of supreme happiness which is only to be reached by meditation and knowledge.

52. Others, wearing the forms of hyenas and lions, uttered loudly fierce howls, which caused all beings round to quail with terror, as thinking that the heavens were smitten with a thunderbolt and were bursting.

53. Deer and elephants uttering cries of pain ran about or lay down,—in that night as if it were day screaming birds flew around disturbed in all directions.

54. But amidst all these various sounds which they made, although all living creatures were shaken, the saint trembled not nor quailed, like Garu*d*a at the noise of crows.

---

[1] Cf. randhropanipâtino*narthâ*h*, *S*akunt. VI.

[2] He had not eyes to see the object which he looked for.

55. The less the saint feared the frightful hosts of that multitude, the more did Mâra, the enemy of the righteous, continue his attacks in grief and anger.

56. Then some being of invisible shape, but of preeminent glory, standing in the heavens,—beholding Mâra thus malevolent against the seer,—addressed him in a loud voice, unruffled by enmity:

57. 'Take not on thyself, O Mâra, this vain fatigue,—throw aside thy malevolence and retire to peace[1]; this sage cannot be shaken by thee any more than the mighty mountain Meru by the wind.

58. 'Even fire might lose its hot nature, water its fluidity, earth its steadiness, but never will he abandon his resolution, who has acquired his merit by a long course of actions through unnumbered aeons.

59. 'Such is that purpose of his, that heroic effort, that glorious strength, that compassion for all beings,—until he attains the highest wisdom, he will never rise from his seat, just as the sun does not rise, without dispelling the darkness.

60. 'One who rubs the two pieces of wood obtains the fire, one who digs the earth finds at last the water,—and to him in his perseverance there is nothing unattainable,—all things to him are reasonable and possible.

61. 'Pitying the world lying distressed amidst diseases and passions, he, the great physician, ought not to be hindered, who undergoes all his labours for the sake of the remedy knowledge.

62. 'He who toilsomely pursues the one good path, when all the world is carried away in devious

---

[1] Or 'go to thy home.'

tracks,—he the guide should not be disturbed, like a right informant when the caravan has lost its way.

63. 'He who is made a lamp of knowledge when all beings are lost in the great darkness,—it is not for a right-minded soul to try to quench him,—like a lamp kindled in the gloom of night.

64. 'He who, when he beholds the world drowned in the great flood of existence and unable to reach the further shore, strives to bring them safely across,—would any right-minded soul offer him wrong?

65. 'The tree of knowledge, whose roots go deep in firmness, and whose fibres are patience,—whose flowers are moral actions and whose branches are memory and thought,—and which gives out the law as its fruit,—surely when it is growing it should not be cut down.

66. 'Him whose one desire is to deliver mankind bound in soul by the fast snares of illusion,—thy wish to overthrow him is not worthy, wearied as he is for the sake of unloosing the bonds of the world.

67. 'To-day is the appointed period of all those actions which have been performed by him for the sake of knowledge,—he is now seated on this seat just as all the previous saints have sat.

68. 'This is the navel of the earth's surface, endued with all the highest glory; there is no other spot of the earth than this,—the home of contemplation, the realm of well-being.

69. 'Give not way, then, to grief but put on calm; let not thy greatness, O Mâra, be mixed with pride; it is not well to be confident,—fortune

is unstable,—why dost thou accept a position on a tottering base?'

70. Having listened to his words, and having seen the unshaken firmness of the great saint, Mâra departed dispirited and broken in purpose[1] with those very arrows by which, O world, thou art smitten in thy heart.

71. With their triumph at an end, their labour all fruitless, and all their stones, straw, and trees thrown away, that host of his fled in all directions, like some hostile army when its camp has been destroyed by the enemy.

72. When the flower-armed god[2] thus fled away vanquished with his hostile forces and the passionless sage remained victorious, having conquered all the power of darkness, the heavens shone out with the moon like a maiden with a smile, and a sweet-smelling shower of flowers fell down wet with dew.

73. [3] When the wicked one thus fled vanquished, the different regions of the sky grew clear, the moon shone forth, showers of flowers fell down from the sky upon the earth, and the night gleamed out like a spotless maiden[4].

---

[1] I read hatodyamo.

[2] Mâra as identified with Kâmadeva, cf. ver. 2.

[3] Should we read tathâ hi for tathâpi?

[4] Here the original work of Asvaghosha ends according to the gloss at the close of the Cambridge MS. C; the four remaining books were added, to supply an old lacuna, by Amritânanda, a modern Nepalese author. The Chinese and Tibetan translations seem to agree with the Sanskrit for part of the fourteenth book, but they soon diverge widely from it. The four books are included in the translation as a literary curiosity.

BOOK XIV.

1. Then, having conquered the hosts of Mâra by his firmness and calmness, he the great master of meditation set himself to meditate, longing to know the supreme end.

2. And having attained the highest mastery in all kinds of meditation, he remembered in the first watch the continuous series of all his former births.

3. 'In such a place I was so and so by name, and from thence I passed and came hither,' thus he remembered his thousands of births, experiencing each as it were over again.

4. And having remembered each birth and each death in all those various transmigrations, the compassionate one then felt compassion for all living beings.

5. Having wilfully rejected the good guides in this life and done all kinds of actions in various lives, this world of living beings rolls on helplessly, like a wheel.

6. As he thus remembered, to him in his strong self-control came the conviction, 'All existence is unsubstantial, like the fruit of a plantain.'

7. When the second watch came, he, possessed of unequalled energy, received a pre-eminent divine sight, he the highest of all sight-gifted beings.

8. Then by that divine perfectly pure sight he beheld the whole world as in a spotless mirror.

9. As he saw the various transmigrations and rebirths of the various beings with their several lower or higher merits from their actions, compassion grew up more within him.

10. 'These living beings, under the influence of evil actions, pass into wretched worlds,—these others, under the influence of good actions, go forward in heaven.

11. 'The one, being born in a dreadful hell full of terrors, are miserably tortured, alas! by many kinds of suffering;

12. 'Some are made to drink molten iron of the colour of fire, others are lifted aloft screaming on a red-hot iron pillar;

13. 'Others are baked like flour, thrown with their heads downwards into iron jars; others are miserably burned in heaps of heated charcoal;

14. 'Some are devoured by fierce dreadful dogs with iron teeth, others by gloating crows with iron beaks and all made as it were of iron;

15. 'Some, wearied of being burned, long for cold shade; these enter like bound captives into a dark blue wood with swords for leaves.

16. 'Others having many arms are split like timber with axes, but even in that agony they do not die, being supported in their vital powers by their previous actions.

17. 'Whatever deed was done only to hinder pain with the hope that it might bring pleasure, its result is now experienced by these helpless victims as simple pain.

18. 'These who did something evil for the sake

of pleasure and are now grievously pained,—does that old taste produce even an atom of pleasure to them now?

19. 'The wicked deed which was done by the wicked-hearted in glee,—its consequences are reaped by them in the fulness of time with cries.

20. 'If only evil doers could see the fruits of their actions, they would vomit hot blood as if they were smitten in a vital part.

21. 'And worse still than all these bodily tortures in hell seems to me the association of an intelligent man with the base.

22. 'Others also, through various actions arising from the spasmodic violence of their minds, are born miserable in the wombs of various beasts.

23. 'There the poor wretches are killed even in the sight of their kindred, for the sake of their flesh, their skin, their hair, or their teeth, or through hatred or for mere pleasure.

24. 'Even though powerless and helpless, oppressed by hunger, thirst, and fatigue, they are driven along as oxen and horses, their bodies wounded with goads.

25. 'They are driven along, when born as elephants, by weaker creatures than themselves for all their strength,—their heads tormented by the hook and their bodies kicked by foot and heel.

26. 'And with all these other miseries there is an especial misery arising from mutual enmity and from subjection to a master.

27. 'Air-dwellers are oppressed by air-dwellers, the denizens of water by the denizens of water, those that dwell on dry land are made to suffer by the dwellers on dry land in mutual hostility.

28. 'And others there are who, when born again, with their minds filled with envy, reap the miserable fruit of their actions in a world of the Pit*ri*s destitute of all light;

29. 'Having mouths as small as the eye of a needle and bellies as big as a mountain, these miserable wretches are tortured with the pains of hunger and thirst.

30. 'If a man only knew that such was the consequence of selfishness, he would always give to others even pieces of his own body like *S*ibi.

31. 'Rushing up filled with hope but held back by their former deeds, they try in vain to eat anything large, however impure.

32. 'Others, having found a hell in an impure lake called the womb, are born amongst men and there suffer anguish.

33. 'Others, ascetics, who have performed meritorious actions go to heaven; others, having attained widely extended empire, wander about on the earth[1];

34. 'Others as Nâgas in the subterranean regions become the guardians of treasures,—they wander in the ocean of existence, receiving the fruits of their deeds.'

35. Having pondered all this, in the last watch he thus reflected, 'Alas for this whole world of living beings doomed to misery, all alike wandering astray!

36. 'They know not that all this universe, destitute of any real refuge, is born and decays through that existence which is the site of the skandhas and pain;

---

[1] Heaven and earthly empire are alike transient.

37. 'It dies and passes into a new state and then is born anew.' Then he reflected, 'What is that which is the necessary condition for old age and death?'

38. He saw that when there is birth, there is old age and death, then he pondered, 'What is that which is the necessary condition for a new birth[1]?'

40. He perceived that where there has been the attachment to existence[2] there arises a (previous) existence; then he pondered, 'What is that which is the necessary condition for the attachment to existence?'

41. Having ascertained this to be desire, he again meditated, and he next pondered, 'What is that which is the necessary condition for desire?'

42. He saw that desire arises where there is sensation, and he next pondered, 'What is that which is the necessary condition for sensation?'

43. He saw that sensation arises where there is contact[3], and he next pondered, 'What is that which is the necessary condition for contact?'

44. He saw that contact arises through the six organs of sense; he then pondered, 'Where do the six organs of sense arise?'

45. He reflected that these arise in the organism[4], he then pondered, 'Where does the organism arise?'

---

[1] A verse (39) is omitted here containing the third step bhava (cf. Chinese translation, 1150, 1151), 'He perceived that when there has been a (previous) existence [involving previous actions] there is a new birth; then he pondered, "What is that which is the necessary condition for a previous existence arising?"' (Cf. Burnouf, Introd. pp. 485–506; Childers in Colebrooke's Essays, vol. i, 1873.)

[2] Upâdânam. [3] Sc. between the senses and their objects.

[4] Nâmarûpa, sc. 'name and form,' i.e. the individual consisting of mind and body, as the embryo in the womb.

46. He saw that the organism arises where there is incipient consciousness; he then pondered, 'Where does incipient consciousness arise?'

47. He reflected that incipient consciousness arises where there are the latent impressions left by former actions; and he next pondered, 'Where do the latent impressions arise?'

48. He reflected exhaustively that they arise in ignorance; thus did the great seer, the Bodhisattva, the lord of saints,

49. After reflecting, pondering, and meditating, finally determine, 'The latent impressions start into activity after they are once developed from ignorance.

50. 'Produced from the activity of the latent impressions incipient consciousness starts into action; (the activity) of the organism starts into action on having an experience[1] of incipient consciousness;

51. 'The six organs of sense become active when produced in the organism; sensation is produced from the contact of the six organs (with their objects);

52. 'Desire starts into activity when produced from sensation; the attachment to existence springs from desire; from this attachment arises a (continued) existence;

53. 'Birth is produced where there has been a (continued) existence; and from birth arise old age, disease, and the rest; and scorched by the flame of old age and disease the world is devoured by death;

54. 'When it is thus scorched by the fire of

---

[1] Sa*m*parîkshya is a doubtful reading; I supply *vri*tti*h* with nâmarûpasya.

death's anguish great pain arises; such verily is the origin of this great trunk of pain.'

55. Thus having ascertained it all, the great Being was perfectly illuminated; and having again meditated and pondered, he thus reflected,

56. 'When old age and disease are stopped, death also is stopped; and when birth is stopped, old age and disease are stopped;

57. 'When the action of existence is stopped, birth also is stopped; when the attachment to existence is stopped, the action of existence is stopped;

58. 'So too when desire is stopped, the attachment to existence is stopped; and with the stopping of sensation desire is no longer produced;

59. 'And when the contact of the six organs is stopped, sensation is no longer produced; and with the stopping of the six organs their contact (with their objects) is stopped;

60. 'And with the stopping of the organism the six organs are stopped; and with the stopping of incipient consciousness the organism is stopped;

61. 'And with the stopping of the latent impressions incipient consciousness is stopped; and with the stopping of ignorance the latent impressions have no longer any power.

62. 'Thus ignorance is declared to be the root of this great trunk of pain by all the wise; therefore it is to be stopped by those who seek liberation.

63. 'Therefore by the stopping of ignorance all the pains also of all existing beings are at once stopped and cease to act.'

64. The all-knowing Bodhisattva, the illuminated one, having thus determined, after again pondering and meditating thus came to his conclusion:

65. 'This is pain, this also is the origin of pain in the world of living beings; this also is the stopping of pain; this is that course which leads to its stopping.' So having determined he knew all as it really was.

66. Thus he, the holy one, sitting there on his seat of grass at the root of the tree, pondering by his own efforts attained at last perfect knowledge.

67. Then bursting the shell of ignorance, having gained all the various kinds of perfect intuition, he attained all the partial knowledge of alternatives which is included in perfect knowledge[1].

68. He became the perfectly wise, the Bhagavat, the Arhat, the king of the Law, the Tathâgata, He who has attained the knowledge of all forms, the Lord of all science.

69. Having beheld all this, the spirits standing in heaven spoke one to another, 'Strew flowers on this All-wise Monarch of Saints.'

70. While other immortals exclaimed, who knew the course of action of the greatest among the former saints, 'Do not now strew flowers—no reason for it has been shown.'

71. Then the Buddha, mounted on a throne, up in the air to the height of seven palm-trees, addressed all those Nirmitâ Bodhisattvâ*h*[2], illumining their minds,

72. 'Ho! ho! listen ye to the words of me who have now attained perfect knowledge; everything is achieved by meritorious works, therefore as long as existence lasts[3] acquire merit.

[1] Doubtful. I suppose it means that he knew all hypothetical as well as categorical propositions.

[2] These Nirmitâ Bodhisattvâ*h* seem to be the nimmâ*n*aratî devâ of the southern Buddhists with their nimmitâ kâmâ or self-created pleasures.

[3] Âbhavam.

73. 'Since I ever acted as liberal, pure-hearted, patient, skilful, devoted to meditation and wisdom,—by these meritorious works I became a Bodhisattva.

74. 'After accomplishing in due order the entire round of the preliminaries of perfect wisdom,—I have now attained that highest wisdom and I am become the All-wise Arhat and *G*ina.

75. 'My aspiration is thus fulfilled; this birth of mine has borne its fruit; the blessed and immortal knowledge which was attained by former Buddhas, is now mine.

76. 'As they through the good Law achieved the welfare of all beings, so also have I; all my sins are abolished, I am the destroyer of all pains.

77. 'Possessing a soul now of perfect purity, I urge all living beings to seek the abolition of worldly existence through the lamps of the Law.' Having worshipped him as he thus addressed them, those sons of the *G*inas disappeared.

78. The gods then with exultation paid him worship and adoration with divine flowers; and all the world, when the great saint had become all-wise, was full of brightness.

79. Then the holy one descended and stood on his throne under the tree; there he passed seven days filled with the thought, 'I have here attained perfect wisdom.'

80. When the Bodhisattva had thus attained perfect knowledge, all beings became full of great happiness; and all the different universes were illumined by a great light.

81. The happy earth shook in six different ways like an overjoyed woman, and the Bodhisattvas, each

dwelling in his own special abode, assembled and praised him.

82. 'There has arisen the greatest of all beings, the Omniscient All-wise Arhat—a lotus, unsoiled by the dust of passion, sprung up from the lake of knowledge;

83. 'A cloud bearing the water of patience, pouring forth the ambrosia of the good Law, fostering all the seeds of merit, and causing all the shoots of healing to grow;

84. 'A thunderbolt with a hundred edges, the vanquisher of Mâra, armed only with the weapon of patience; a gem fulfilling all desires, a tree of paradise, a jar of true good fortune[1], a cow that yields all that heart can wish;

85. 'A sun that destroys the darkness of delusion, a moon that takes away the scorching heat of the inherent sins of existence,—glory to thee, glory to thee, glory to thee, O Tathâgata;

86. 'Glory to thee, O Lord of the whole world, glory to thee, who hast gone through the ten (Balas[2]); glory to thee, O true hero amongst men, O Lord of righteousness, glory to thee!'

87. Thus having praised, honoured, and adored him, they each returned to their several homes, after making repeated reverential circumambulations, and recounting his eulogy.

88. Then the beings of the Kâmâva*k*ara worlds, and the brilliant inhabitants of the Pure Abodes, the

---

[1] The bhadrakumbha was the golden jar filled with consecrated water, used especially at the inauguration of a king.

[2] The ten balas are ten kinds of spiritual knowledge peculiar to a Buddha; but 'the ten' may be the ten dharmas, see Childers.

Brahmakâyika gods, and those sons of Mâra who favoured the side of truth [1],

89. The Paranirmitava*s*avarti beings, and the Nirmâ*n*aratayа*h*; the Tushita beings, the Yâmas, the Trayastri*ms*ad Devas, and the other rulers of worlds,

90. The deities who roam in the sky, those who roam on the earth or in forests, accompanying each their own king, came to the pavilion of the Bodhi tree,

91. And having worshipped the *G*ina with forms of homage suitable to their respective positions, and having praised him with hymns adapted to their respective degrees of knowledge, they returned to their own homes.

---

[1] These terms are all explained in Childers' Dict. sattaloko. For the better-inclined sons of Mâra, cf. the dialogue between those of the right side and the left side before Mâra in the Lalitav. XXI, cf. also XXIII.

BOOK XV.

1. Daily praised by all the various heavenly beings, the perfectly Wise One[1] thus passed that period of seven days which is designated 'the aliment of joy[2].'

2. He then passed the second week, while he was bathed with jars full of water by the heavenly beings, the Bodhisattvas and the rest.

3. Then having bathed in the four oceans and being seated on his throne, he passed the third week restraining his eyes from seeing.

4. In the fourth week, assuming many forms, he stood triumphant on his throne, having delivered a being who was ready to be converted.

5. A god named Sama*m*takusuma, bearing an offering of flowers, thus addressed with folded hands the great Buddha who was seated there:

6. 'What is the name, O holy one, of this meditation, engaged in which thou hast thus passed four whole weeks with joy, deeply pondering?'

7. 'This is designated, O divine being, "the array[3] of the aliment of great joy," like an inaugurated king, who has overcome his enemies and enjoys prosperity.'

8. Having said this, the saint possessing the ten

---

[1] Sa*m*buddha.

[2] Prîtyâhâra; this book corresponds closely with Lalitav. XXIV.

[3] Vyûha.

pre-eminent powers, full of joy, continued, 'The former perfect Buddhas also did not leave the Bodhi tree.

9. 'Here the Kle*s*as and the Mâras together with ignorance and the Âsravas have been conquered by me; and perfect wisdom has been attained able to deliver the world.

10. 'I too, resolved to follow the teaching of the former Buddhas, remained four whole weeks in the fulfilment of my inauguration[1].'

11. Then Mâra, utterly despondent in soul, thus addressed the Tathâgata, 'O holy one, be pleased to enter Nirvâ*n*a, thy desires are accomplished.'

12. 'I will first establish in perfect wisdom worlds as numerous as the sand, and then I will enter Nirvâ*n*a,' thus did the Buddha reply, and with a shriek Mâra went to his home.

13. Then the three daughters of Mâra, Lust, Thirst, and Delight[2], beholding their father with defeated face, approached the Tathâgata.

14. Lust, with a face like the moon and versed in all the arts of enchantment, tried to infatuate him by her descriptions of the pleasures of a householder's life.

15. 'Think, "If I abandon an emperor's happiness, with what paltry happiness shall I have to content myself? When success is lost, what shall I have to enjoy?"—and come and take refuge with us.

16. 'Else, in bitter repentance, thou wilt remember me hereafter, when thou art fallen.'—But he listened

---

[1] Query abhishekâdikâryata*h*?

[2] Cf. XIII, 3 and 14. Cf. also Lalitav. XXIV (arati?).

not to her words, closing his eyes in deep meditation like one who is sleepy.

17. Then Thirst, shameless like one distressed with thirst, thus addressed him who was free from all thirst: 'Fie, fie, thou hast abandoned thy family duties, thou hast fallen from all social obligations;

18. 'Without power no asceticism, sacrifice, or vow can be accomplished,—those great *Ri*shis Brahman and the rest, because they were endowed with power, enjoy their present triumph.

19. 'Know me to be the power called Thirst[1], and worship thirst accordingly; else I will clasp thee with all my might and fling away thy life.'

20. Motionless as one almost dead, he continued in meditation, remembering the former Buddhas; then Delight next tried to win him who was indeed hard to be won by evil deeds.

21. 'O holy one, I am Delight by name, fostering all practicable delights,—therefore making me the female mendicant's tutelary power, bring delight within thy reach.'

22. But whether flattered or threatened, whether she uttered curses or blessings, he remained absorbed in meditation, perfectly tranquil like one who has entered Nirvâ*n*a.

23. Then the three, with despondent faces, having retired together on one side, consulted with one another and came forward wearing the appearance of youthful beauty.

24. Folding their hands in reverence they thus addressed the Tathâgata, 'O holy one, receive us as religious mendicants, we are come to thy one refuge.

[1] Sc. Desire.

25. 'Having heard the fame of thy achievements, we, the daughters of Namuki, have come from the golden city, abandoning the life of a household.

26. 'We are desirous of repressing the teaching of our five hundred brothers,—we would be freed from a master, as thou thyself art freed from all passions.'

27. Having his mind continually guided by the conduct which leads to Nirvâna, and setting himself to remember the (former) Buddhas, he kept his eyes closed, absorbed in meditation.

28. Then again, having resolved on their new plan in concert, these enchantresses, assuming an older aspect, approached once more to delude him.

29. 'We have come here after wandering under the dismal avatâra of slaves[1],—thou art the avatâra of Buddha,—do thou establish us, mature, in the true Bauddha doctrine.

30. 'We are women of older age, much to be pitied, bewildered by the fear of death,—we are therefore worthy to be established in that doctrine of Nirvâna which puts an end to all future births.'

31. These words of the enchantresses were heard by him, yet he felt no anger; but they all became the victims of old age, through the manifestation of his divine power.

32. Having beheld him plunged in meditation, immovable like the mountain Meru,—they turned away their faces and they could not retain their beauty.

33. Bending their feet, with decrepit limbs, they

[1] I read dâsa- for dasa-; could there be a reference to the ten avatâras?

thus addressed their father: 'O father, do thou, the lord of the world of Desire, restore us to our own forms.'

34. His daughters were dear, but he had no power to alter the effect of the will of Buddha; then their father said to them, 'Go to the refuge which he gives.'

35. Then they in various guises, bent humbly at his feet, implored the perfect Buddha, 'Pardon our transgression, whose minds were intoxicated with youth.'

36. The teacher, that mine of Forgiveness, in silence restored them by his will; and having repeatedly worshipped and praised him they went joyfully to their home.

37. Then again Mâra, the lord of the world of Desire, lost to shame, taking the form of the head of a family, thus addressed him from the sky:

38. 'I worshipped thee long ago, foretelling that thou wouldest become a Buddha; and by my blessings thou hast to-day become Buddha Tathâgata.

39. 'As thou didst come from thine own kingdom, so now having returned as Tathâgata, with a name corresponding to the reality be a king Tathâgata.

40. 'Having gone to that royal station, do thou meditate on the three jewels, and cherish thy father and mother, and delight Yasodharâ,—

41. 'Possessed of a thousand sons, and able to deliver the world, be successively the supreme lord of every world from the Yâma heaven onwards[1].

42. 'Having become also the supreme lord of all

[1] Mâra rules the four heavens from the Yâma to the Paranirmitavasavartin, Mahâbrahman the twenty Brahmalokas above them.

Bodhisattvas, thou shalt attain Nirvâna ; O wise seer, repair to the hermitage of Kapila in order to beget those sons.

43. 'As thou art the king of the Law, so shall thy sons also be all Tathâgatas, and all the activity and cessation of existence shall depend upon thee, O Gina.'

44. To him thus speaking the All-wise replied, 'Hear, O shameless one; thou art Mâra, not the head of a clan, the upholder of the race of the Sâkyas.

45. 'A host like thee, though they came in myriads, could not harm me,—I will go to my kingdom gradually, I will bring the world to perfect happiness.

46. 'Thou art utterly vanquished, O Namuki, go back to thy own home; I will go hence to turn the wheel of the Law in Vârânasî.'

47. He, on hearing this command, saying with a deep sigh, 'Alas! I am crushed,' left him and went despondent and companionless through the sky to his home.

48. Then he, the conqueror of Mâra, rising from that throne, set forth to journey alone to the holy Vârânasî.

49. The heavens became covered with clouds when they saw the chief of saints, and the king of the Nâgas Mukilinda made a petition in reverential faith :

50. 'O holy one, thou art all-wise, there will be stormy weather for seven days,—wind, rain, and darkness,—dwell for the time in my abode.'

51. Though himself possessed of all supernatural power, the holy one thought of the world still involved in embodied existence, and sitting on that jewel-seat he remained absorbed in contemplation.

52. That king of the Nâgas there protected the Buddha, who is himself the source of all protection, from the rain, wind, and darkness, covering his body with his own hood.

53. When the seven days were past and the Nâga had paid his homage and was gone, the *G*ina proceeded to the bank of a river, near a forest of goat-herds[1].

54. As the Sugata stayed there during the night, a deity, who bore the name of the Indian fig-tree, came up to him, illumining the spot where he was, and thus addressed him with folded hands:

55. 'The fig-tree was planted by me when I was born as a man, bearing the name of Buddha; and it has been fostered like the Bodhi tree in the hope of delivering myself from evil.

56. 'By the merit of that action I myself have been born in heaven; in kindness to me, O my lord, do thou dwell seven days in triumph here.'

57. 'So be it,' said the chief of all saints, the true Kalpa tree to grant the wishes of the faithful votary, and he stayed under the fig-tree, absorbed in contemplation, spreading lustre around like a full moon.

58. There he dwelt seven days; and then in a forest of Datura trees, sitting at the foot of a palm, he remained absorbed in contemplation.

59. Spending thus in different spots his weeks of meditation, day and night, the great saint, pondering and fasting, went on in his way, longing to accomplish the world's salvation.

60. Then two wealthy merchants from the land

[1] Agapâlaka is in Pâli Costus speciosus; but it may here be a proper name.

of Uttara Utkala[1], named Trapusha and Bhallika, journeying with five hundred waggons,

61. Being freed from a sin which involved a birth as pretas[2], both joyfully worshipped Buddha with an offering of the three sweet substances[3] and milk; and they obtained thereby auspicious blessings.

62. They obtained pieces of his nails and hairs for a *K*aitya and they also received a prophecy of their future birth, and having received the additional promise, 'Ye shall also obtain a stone[4],' they then proceeded on their way elsewhere.

63. Then Buddha accepted alms in his bowl, offered by the goddess who dwelt in the Datura grove, and he blessed her with benedictions.

64. The *G*ina then blessed the four bowls as one, which were offered by the four Mahârâ*g*as[5], and ate with pleasure the offering of milk.

65. Then one day the *G*ina ate there an Harîtakî fruit[6] which was offered to him by *S*akra, and having planted the seed he caused it to grow to a tree.

66. The king of the Devas carried the news thereof joyfully to the Deva-heavens; and gods, men, and demons watered it with reverential circumambulations.

67. On hearing the news of the Harîtakî seed, and remembering the whole history from first to last, a daughter of the gods named Bhadrikâ, who had been a cow in her former birth[7], came from heaven.

---

[1] Northern Orissa.

[2] Pretadosha? or the evil inflicted by a preta?

[3] Sc. sugar, honey, and ghee.

[4] With the mark of Buddha's feet on it?

[5] The rulers of the lowest devaloka.

[6] Terminalia chebula.

[7] Cf. Mahâbh. V, 7553.

68. She, the daughter of the gods, smiling with her companions, thus addressed the *G*ina, bringing him a garment of rags, dependent from a bough:

69. 'I beg to bring to thy notice—what? O Buddha!—accept this garment of rags, by whose influence I am now a daughter of heaven named Bhadrikâ.'

70. 'By the further development of this merit thou shalt become a Bodhisattva'—uttering this blessing the Teacher accepted the rags.

71. Beholding the tattered rags, the gods, crowding in the sky, filled with wonder, and uttering cries of hî hî, flung down upon him garments of heavenly silk.

72. 'These are not fit for a religious mendicant,'—so saying, he did not accept even one of them,—only thinking in his calm apathy, 'these are fit for imperial pomp and a householder's luxury.'

73. He desired a stone slab and some water in order to wash the dirt away,—*S*akra at that moment dug out a great river full of water;

74. And four stones are brought to him by the four Mahârâ*g*as,—on one he himself sat, on another he performed the washing;

75. On another he performed the drying, and another he flung up into the sky; the stone as it flew up reached the blazing city[1] and astonished all the worlds.

76. After paying their worship in many ways, Trapusha and Bhallika duly raised an excellent *K*aitya and they called it *S*ilâgarbha.

77. The ascetics of that neighbourhood paid their

[1] The sun? or the sphere of fire?

homage to the 'Three Stones' when they were made into a *K*aitya, and the noble stream flowed widely-known as the 'Holy River.'

78. Those who bathe and offer their worship in the holy river and reverence the *K*aitya of the three stones, become great-souled Bodhisattvas and obtain Nirvâ*n*a.

79. Then seated under a palm-tree the holy one pondered: 'The profound wisdom so hard to be understood is now known by me.

80. 'These sin-defiled worlds understand not this most excellent (Law), and the unenlightened shamelessly censure both me and my wisdom.

81. 'Shall I proclaim the Law? It is only produced by knowledge; having attained it thus in my lonely pondering, do I feel strong enough to deliver the world?'

82. Having remembered all that he had heard before, he again pondered; and resolving, 'I will explain it for the sake of delivering the world,'

83. Buddha, the chief of saints, absorbed in contemplation, shone forth, arousing[1] the world, having emitted in the darkness of the night a light from the tuft of hair between his eyebrows.

84. When it became dawn, Brahman and the other gods, and the various rulers of the different worlds, besought Sugata to turn the wheel of the Law.

85. When the *G*ina by his silence uttered an assenting 'so be it,' they returned to their own abodes; and the lion of the *S*âkyas also shone there, still remaining lost in contemplation.

86. Then the four divinities (of the Bodhi tree),

---

[1] Cf. *s*loka 118.

Dharmaruki and the rest, addressed him, 'Where, O teacher of the world, will the holy one turn the wheel of the Law?'

87. 'In Vârânasî, in the Deer Park will I turn the wheel of the Law; seated in the fourth posture[1], O deities, I will deliver the world.'

88. There the holy one, the bull of the Sâkya race, pondered, 'For whom shall I first turn the wheel of the Law?'

89. The glorious one reflected that [2] Rudraka and Arâda were dead[3], and then he remembered those others, the five men united in a worthy society[4], who dwelt at Kâsî.

90. Then Buddha set out to go joyfully to Kâsî, manifesting as he went the manifold supernatural course of life of Magadha.

91. Having made a mendicant (whom he met) happy in the path of those who are illustrious through the Law, the glorious one went on, illumining the country which lies to the north of Gayâ.

92. (Having stayed) in the dwelling of the prince of the Nâgas, named Sudarsana, on the occurrence of night, he ate a morning meal consisting of the five kinds of ambrosia, and departed, gladdening him with his blessing.

93. Near Vanârâ[5] he went under the shadow

---

[1] Sc. the padmâsana (Yoga-sûtras II, 46), described as that in which the left foot is bent between the right leg and thigh, and the right foot is bent between the left foot and thigh.

[2] It is written thus here, cf. XII, 86. [3] Nirvâtau.

[4] Bhadravargîyâh, also called Pamkavargîyâh, cf. XII, 89.

[5] Query Varanâ, one of the rivers from which Benares is said to derive its name,—or is it a village near Vârânasî, the Anâla of the Lalitav. p. 528?

of a tree and there he established a poor Brâhman named Nandin in sacred knowledge.

94. In Va*n*ârâ in a householder's dwelling he was lodged for the night; in the morning he partook of some milk and departed, having given his blessing.

95. In the village called Vu*m*dadvîra he lodged in the abode of a Yaksha named Vu*m*da[1], and in the morning after taking some milk and giving his blessing he departed.

96. Next was the garden named Rohitavastuka, and there the Nâga-king Kama*nd*alu with his courtiers also worshipped him.

97. Having delivered various beings in every place, the compassionate saint journeyed on to Gandhapura and was worshipped there by the Yaksha Gandha.

98. When he arrived at the city Sârathi, the citizens volunteered to be charioteers in his service; thence he came to the Ganges, and he bade the ferryman cross.

99. 'Good man, convey me across the Ganges, may the seven blessings be thine.' 'I carry no one across unless he pays the fee.'

100. 'I have nothing, what shall I give?' So saying he went through the sky like the king of birds; and from that time Bimbisâra abolished the ferry-fee for all ascetics.

101. Then having entered Vârâ*n*asî, the *G*ina, illumining the city with his light, filled the minds of all the inhabitants of Kâ*s*î with excessive interest.

---

[1] This may be *K*u*m*da.

102. In the *S*aṅkhamedhîya garden, the king of righteousness, absorbed in meditation, passed the night, gladdening like the moon all those who were astonished at his appearance.

103. The next day at the end of the second watch[1], having gone his begging round collecting alms, he, the unequalled one, like Hari, proceeded to the Deer Park.

104. The five disciples united in a worthy society[2], when they beheld him, said to one another, 'This is Gautama who has come hither, the ascetic who has abandoned his self-control.

105. 'He wanders about now, greedy[3], of impure soul, unstable and with his senses under no firm control, devoted to inquiries regarding the frying-pan.

106. 'We will not ask after his health, nor rise to meet him, nor address him, nor offer him a welcome, nor a seat, nor bid him enter into our dwelling.'

107. Having understood their agreement, with a smiling countenance, spreading light all around, Buddha advanced gradually nearer, holding his staff and his begging-pot.

108. Forgetful of their agreement, the five friends, under his constraining majesty, rose up like birds in their cages when scorched by fire.

109. Having taken his begging-bowl and staff, they gave him an arghya, and water for washing his feet and rinsing his mouth; and bowing

---

[1] Does this yâmadvaye mean at noon, counting the ahorâtra from sunrise to sunrise?

[2] Cf. supra, 89.

[3] Or perhaps 'irregular.'

reverentially they said to him, 'Honoured Sir, health to thee.'

110. 'Health in every respect is ours,—that wisdom has been attained which is so hard to be won,'—so saying, the holy one thus spoke to the five worthy associates:

111. 'But address me not as "worthy Sir,"—know that I am a *G*ina,—I have come to give the first wheel of the Law to you. Receive initiation from me,—ye shall obtain the place of Nirvâ*n*a.'

112. Then the five, pure in heart, begged leave to undertake his vow of a religious life; and the Buddha, touching their heads, received them into the mendicant order.

113. Then at the mendicants' respectful request the chief of saints bathed in the tank, and after eating ambrosia he reflected on the field of the Law[1].

114. Remembering that the Deer Park and the field of the *G*ina were there, he went joyfully with them and pointed out the sacred seats.

115. Having worshipped three seats, he desired to visit the fourth, and when the worthy disciples asked about it, the teacher thus addressed them:

116. 'These are the four seats of the Buddhas of the (present) Bhadra Age,—three Buddhas have passed therein, and I here am the fourth possessor of the ten powers.'

117. Having thus addressed them the glorious one bowed to that throne of the Law, decked with tapestries of cloth and silk, and having its stone

[1] Does this mean the country round Benares, as the land where all Buddhas turned the wheel of the Law?

inlaid with jewels, like a golden mountain, guarded by the kings of kings,

In the former fortnight of Âshâ*dh*a, on the day consecrated to the Regent of Jupiter, on the lunar day sacred to Vish*n*u, and on an auspicious conjunction, under the asterism Anurâdhâ[1], and in the muhûrta called the Victorious, in the night,—he took his stand on the throne.

118. The five worthy disciples stood in front, with joyful minds, paying their homage, and the son of *S*uddhodana performed that act of meditation which is called the Arouser of all worlds;

Brahman and the other gods came surrounded by their attendants, summoned each from his own world; and Maitrîya[2] with the deities of the Tushita heaven came for the turning of the wheel of the Law.

119. So too when the multitude of the sons of the *G*inas and the Suras gathered together from the ten directions of space, there came also the noble chief of the sons of the *G*inas, named Dharma-*k*akra[3], carrying the wheel of the Law;

With head reverentially bowed, having placed it, a mass of gold and jewels, before the Buddha and having worshipped him, he thus besought him, 'O thou lord of saints, turn the wheel of the Law as it has been done by (former) Sugatas.'

---

[1] The seventeenth Nakshatra.

[2] Is this the same as Maitreya, who is to be the future Buddha and who now awaits his time in the Tushita heaven? The Cambridge MS. interchanges Maitreya and Maitrîya in XVI, 53.

[3] 'Ein Buddha (der das Rad des Gesetzes in Bewegung setzt), Trikâ*nd*a*s*. I, 1, 8.' St. Petersburg Dict.

BOOK XVI.

1. The omniscient lion of the *S*âkyas then caused all the assembly, headed by those who belonged to the company of Maitrîya[1], to turn the wheel of the Law.

2. 'Listen, O company belonging to Maitrîya[1], ye who form one vast congregation,—as it was proclaimed by those past arch-saints, so is it now proclaimed by Me.

3. 'These are the two extremes, O mendicants, in the self-control of the religious ascetic,—the one which is devoted to the joys of desire, vulgar and common,

4. 'And the other which is tormented by the excessive pursuit of self-inflicted pain in the mortification of the soul's corruptions,—these are the two extremes of the religious ascetic, each devoted to that which is unworthy and useless.

5. 'These have nothing to do with true asceticism, renunciation of the world, or self-control, with true indifference or suppression of pain, or with any of the means of attaining deliverance.

6. 'They do not tend to the spiritual forms of knowledge, to wisdom, nor to Nirvâ*n*a; let him who is acquainted with the uselessness of inflicting pain and weariness on the body,

---

[1] The Maitrîya-vargîyâ*h*?

7. 'Who has lost his interest[1] in any pleasure or pain of a visible nature, or in the future, and who follows this middle Path for the good of the world,—

8. 'Let him, the Tathâgata, the teacher of the world, proclaim the good Law, beginning that manifestation of the good Law which consists of the (four) noble truths,

9. 'And let the Buddha proclaim the Path with its eight divisions. I too who am now the perfectly wise, and the Tathâgata in the world,

10. 'Will proclaim the noble Law, beginning with those sublime truths and the eightfold Path which is the means to attain perfect knowledge.

11. 'Instructing all the world I will show to it Nirvâ*n*a; those four noble truths must be heard first and comprehended by the soul.

12. 'That must be understood and thoroughly realised by the true students of wisdom, which has been known here by me, through the favour of all the Buddhas.

13. 'Having known the noble eightfold Path, and embraced it as realised with joy,—thus I declare to you the first means for the attainment of liberation.

14. 'Having thus commenced the noble truths, I will describe the true self-control; this noble truth is the best of all holy laws.

15. 'Walk as long as existence lasts, holding fast the noble eightfold Path,—this noble truth is the highest law for the attainment of true liberation.

16. 'Having pondered and held fast the noble

[1] Nirata seems used here for virata.

eightfold Path, walk in self-control; others, not understanding this, idle talkers full of self-conceit,

17. 'Say according to their own will that merit is the cause of corporeal existence, others maintain that the soul must be preserved (after death) for its merit is the cause of liberation.

18. 'Some say that everything comes spontaneously; others that the consequence was produced before; others talk loudly that all also depends on a Divine Lord.

19. 'If merit and demerit are produced by the good and evil fortune of the soul, how is it that good fortune does not always come to all embodied beings (at last), even in the absence of merit?

20. 'How is the difference accounted for, which we see in form, riches, happiness, and the rest,—if there are no previous actions, how do good and evil arise here?

21. 'If karman is said to be the cause of our actions, who would imagine cogency in this assumption? If all the world is produced spontaneously, who then would talk of the ownership of actions?

22. 'If good is caused by good, then evil will be the cause of evil,—how then could liberation from existence be produced by difficult penances[1]?

23. 'Others unwisely talk of Îsvara as a cause,—how then is there not uniformity in the world if Îsvara be the uniformly acting cause?

24. 'Thus certain ignorant people, talking loudly "he is," "he is not,"—through the demerits of their false theories, are at last born wretched in the different hells.

---

[1] I. e. viewed as an evil in themselves.

25. 'Through the merits of good theories virtuous men, who understand noble knowledge, go to heavenly worlds, from their self-restraint as regards body, speech, and thought.

26. 'All those who are devoted to existence are tormented with the swarms of its evils, and being consumed by old age, diseases, and death, each one dies and is born again.

27. 'There are many wise men here who can discourse on the laws of coming into being; but there is not even one who knows how the cessation of being is produced.

28. 'This body composed of the five skandhas, and produced from the five elements, is all empty and without soul, and arises from the action of the chain of causation.

29. 'This chain of causation is the cause of coming into existence, and the cessation of the series thereof is the cause of the state of cessation.

30. 'He who knowing this desires to promote the good of the world, let him hold fast the chain of causation, with his mind fixed on wisdom;

31. 'Let him embrace the vow of self-denial for the sake of wisdom, and practise the four perfections[1], and go through existence always doing good to all beings.

32. 'Then having become an Arhat and conquered all the wicked, even the hosts of Mâra, and attained the threefold wisdom, he shall enter Nirvâ*n*a.

33. 'Whosoever therefore has his mind indifferent

[1] The four brahmavihârâ*h*, sc. charity, compassion, sympathy with others' joy, and stoicism.

and is void of all desire for any further form of existence, let him abolish one by one the several steps of the chain of causation[1].

34. 'When these effects of the chain of causation are thus one by one put an end to, he at last, being free from all stain and substratum, will pass into a blissful Nirvâ*n*a.

35. 'Listen all of you for your own happiness, with your minds free from stain,—I will declare to you step by step this chain of causation.

36. 'The idea of ignorance is what gives the root to the huge poison-tree of mundane existence with its trunk of pain.

37. 'The impressions[2] are caused by this, which produce [the acts of] the body, voice, and mind; and consciousness arises from these impressions, which produces as its development the five senses and the mind (or internal sense).

38. 'The organism[3] which is sometimes called sa*mgñ*â or sa*m*dar*s*ana[4], springs from this; and from this arises the six organs of the senses, including mind.

39. 'The association of the six organs with their objects is called "contact;" and the consciousness of these different contacts is called "sensation[5];"

40. 'By this is produced thirst, which is the desire

---

[1] Cf. Childers in Colebrooke's Essays, I, p. 453.

[2] These sa*m*skârâ*h* constitute predispositions or tendencies.

[3] Literally 'the name and the form,' the individual, consisting of mind and body.

[4] The Nâmarûpa is properly the organised body (rûpa) and the three mental skandhas, vedanâ, sa*mgñ*â, and the sa*m*skârâ*h*, which are together called nâma.

[5] Vedanâ.

of being troubled[1] by worldly objects; "attachment to continued existence," arising from this, sets itself in action towards pleasure and the rest;

41. 'From attachment springs continued existence, which is sensual, possessing form, or formless[2]; and from existence arises birth through a returning to various wombs.

42. 'On birth is dependent the series of old age, death, sorrow and the like; by putting a stop to ignorance and what follows from it, all these successively surcease.

43. 'This is the chain of causation, having many turns, and whose sphere of action is created by ignorance,—this is to be meditated upon by you who enjoy the calm of dwelling tranquilly in lonely woods[3];

'He who knows it thoroughly reaches at last to absolute tenuity; and having become thus attenuated he becomes blissfully extinct.

44. 'When you have thus learned this, in order to be freed from the bond of existence, you must cut down with all your efforts the root of pain, ignorance.

45. 'Then, being set free from the bonds of the prison-house of existence, as Arhats, possessing natures perfectly pure, you shall attain Nirvâ*n*a.'

46. Having heard this lesson preached by the chief of saints, all the mendicants comprehended the course and the cessation of embodied existence.

---

[1] Sa*m*kle*s*a,—should we read sa*ms*lesha?

[2] I.e. in the eleven kâmalokas, the sixteen rûpabrahmalokas, and the four arûpabrahmalokas.

[3] The metre shows that two short syllables are wanting in the line, vi*g*ana (vana) vi*s*râma*s*amibhi*h*.

47. As these five ascetics listened to his words, their intellectual eye was purified for the attainment of perfect wisdom:

48. The eye of dharma[1] was purified in six hundred millions of gods, and the eye of wisdom in eight hundred millions of Brahmans[2].

49. The eye of dharma was purified in eighty thousand men, and even in all beings an ardour for the Law was made visible.

50. Everywhere all kinds of evil became tranquillised, and on every side an ardour for all that helps on the good Law manifested itself.

51. In the heavens everywhere the heavenly beings with troops of Apsarases uttered forth great shouts, 'Even so, O noble being of boundless energy!'

52. Then Maitreya addressed the holy one, 'O great mendicant, in what form has the wheel been turned by thee?'

53. Having heard this question asked by the great-souled Maitreya, the holy one looked at him and thus addressed him:

54. 'The profound subtil wheel of the Law, so hard to be seen, has been turned by me, into which the disputatious Tîrthikas cannot penetrate.

55. 'The wheel of the Law has been turned, which has no extension, no origin, no birth, no home, isolated, and free from matter;

56. 'Having many divisions, and not being without divisions[3], having no cause, and susceptible of no definition,—that wheel, which is described as

[1] Dharma*k*akshu*h*, the eye to discern the Law?
[2] The divine inhabitants of the Brahmalokas.
[3] Anirvyûha*m*?

possessing perfect equilibrium, has been proclaimed by the Buddha.

57. 'Everything subject to successive causation is like a delusion, a mirage, or a dream, like the moon seen in water or an echo,—it lies stretched out on the surface, not to be extirpated, but not eternal.

58. 'The wheel of the Law has been described as that in which all false doctrines are extirpated; it is always like the pure ether, involving no doubts, ever bright.

59. 'The wheel of the Law is described as without end or middle, existing apart from "it is" or "it is not," separated from soul or soullessness.

60. 'The wheel of the Law has been here set forth, with a description according to its real nature, —as it has a limit and as it has not a limit, in its actual quantity and quality.

61. 'The wheel of the Law has been here set forth, described as possessing unique attributes, apart from the power of the eye and so too as regards the sense of hearing or smell;

62. 'Apart from the tongue, the touch, or the mind,—without soul or exertion;

'Such is this wheel of the Law which has been turned by me;

63. 'He makes wise all the ignorant,—therefore is he called the Buddha[1]; this knowledge of the laws of reality has been ascertained by me of myself,

64. 'Apart from all teaching by another, therefore is he called the self-existent,—having all laws under his control, therefore is he called the lord of Law.

65. 'He knows what is right (naya) and wrong (anaya) in laws, therefore is he called Nâyaka; he

[1] Buddha seems here to identify himself with his Law.

teaches unnumbered beings as they become fit to be taught.

66. 'He has reached the furthest limit of instruction, therefore is he called Vinâyaka, from his pointing out the best of good paths to beings who have lost their way.

67. 'He has reached the furthest limit of good teaching, he is the guide to all the Law,—attracting all beings by his knowledge of all the means of conciliation;

68. 'He has passed through the forest of mundane existence, therefore is he called the Leader of the Caravan; the absolute ruler over all law, therefore he is the *G*ina, the lord of Law.

69. 'From his turning the wheel of the Law he is the lord of all the sovereigns of Law; the master-giver of the Law, the teacher, the master of the Law, the lord of the world;

70. 'He who has offered the sacrifice, accomplished his end, fulfilled his hope, achieved his success, the consoler, the loving regarder, the hero, the champion, the victorious one in conflict;

71. 'He has come out from all conflict, released himself and the releaser of all,—he is become the light of the world, the illuminator of the knowledge of true wisdom;

72. 'The dispeller of the darkness of ignorance, the illuminer of the great torch, the great physician, the great seer, the healer of all evils,

73. 'The extractor of the barb of evil from all those who are wounded by evil,—he who is possessed of all distinctive marks and adorned with all signs,

74. 'With his body and limbs every way perfect,

of pure conduct and perfectly clear mind, possessed of the ten powers, having great fortitude, learned with all learning,

75. 'Endowed with all the independent states[1], he who has attained the great Yâna, the lord of all Dharma, the ruler, the monarch of all worlds, the sovereign,

76. 'The lord of all wisdom, the wise, the destroyer of the pride of all disputers, the omniscient, the Arhat, possessed of the perfect knowledge, the great Buddha, the lord of saints;

77. 'The victorious triumphant overthrower of the insolence and pride of the evil Mâra, the perfect Buddha, the Sugata, the wise one, he who brings the desired end to all beings,

78. 'Ever cognisant of past acts, never speaking falsely, a mine of perfect excellence and of all good qualities, the destroyer of all evil ways, the guide in all good ways[2],

79. 'The ruler of the world, the bearer of the world, the master of the world, the sovereign of the world, the teacher of the world, the preceptor of the world, he who brings to the world the Law, virtue, and its true end,

80. 'The fount of an ambrosia which quenches the scorching of the flame of all pain, and the powerful luminary which dries up the great ocean of all pain,

81. 'He who brings all virtue and all true wealth, the possessor of perfect excellence and all good qualities, the guide on the road of wisdom, he who shows the way to Nirvâ*n*a,

---

[1] Eighteen in all. See Burnouf, Lotus, pp. 648, &c.

[2] Query sadv*ri*tti for sa*m*v*ri*tti?

82. 'The Tathâgata, without stain, without attachment, without uncertainty.—This is the compendious declaration in the turning of the wheel of the Law.

83. 'A concise manifestation of a Tathâgata's qualities is now declared by me; for a Buddha's knowledge is endless, unlimited like the ether;

84. 'A narrator might spend a Kalpa, but the virtues of the Buddha would not come to an end,—thus by me has the multitude of the virtues of the Buddha been described.

85. 'Having heard this and welcomed it with joy go on ever in happiness; this, Sirs, is the Mahâyâna, the instrument of the Law of the perfect Buddha, which is the establisher of the welfare of all beings, set forth by all the Buddhas.

86. 'In order that this methodical arrangement of the Law may be always spread abroad, do you yourselves always proclaim it and hand it on.

87. 'Whosoever, Sirs, hears, sees, and welcomes with joy this methodical arrangement of the Law, which is a mine of happiness and prosperity, and honours it with folded hands,

88. 'Shall attain pre-eminent strength with a glorious form and limbs, and a retinue of the holy, and an intelligence of the highest reach,

89. 'And the happiness of perfect contemplation, with a deep calm[1] of uninterrupted bliss, with his senses in their highest perfection, and illuminated by unclouded knowledge.

90. 'He shall assuredly attain these eight pre-eminent perfections, who hears and sees this Law

[1] I read naishkarmya for naishkramya.

with a serene soul and worships it with folded hands.

91. 'Whosoever in the midst of the assembly shall gladly offer a pulpit to the high-minded teacher of the great Law,

92. 'That virtuous man shall assuredly attain the seat of the most excellent, and also the seat of a householder, and the throne of a universal monarch;

93. 'He shall also attain the throne of one of the guardian-spirits of the world, and also the firm throne of *S*akra, and also the throne of the Va*s*avartina*h* gods, aye, and the supreme throne of Brahman;

94. 'And also with the permission of the Bodhisattva who is seated on the Bodhi throne he shall obtain the throne of a teacher of the good Law who has risen to perfect knowledge.

95. 'These eight seats shall the pure-souled one attain who offers joyfully a seat to him who proclaims the Law.

96. 'Whosoever with a believing heart, after examination, shall utter applause to the pious man who proclaims this carefully arranged Law;

97. 'Shall become a truthful and pure speaker, and one whose words are to be accepted,—one whose utterances are welcome and delightful, whose voice is sweet and gentle;

98. 'Having a voice like a Kalaviṅka bird [1], with a deep and sweet tone, having also a pure voice like Brahman's [2], and a loud voice with a lion's sound.

99. 'He as an all-wise and truthful speaker shall

[1] A kind of sparrow.

[2] Or 'having a voice of pure spiritual truth?'

obtain these eight excellences of speech, who utters applause to one who proclaims the good Law.

100. 'And whosoever, after writing this method of the Law in a book, shall set it in his house and always worship it and honour it with all reverential observances,

101. 'And uttering its praises shall hand the doctrine onward on every side, he, the very pious man, shall obtain a most excellent treasure of memory,

102. 'And a treasure of insight[1], and a treasure of prudence[2], and a treasure of good spells, and a treasure full of intelligence,

103. 'And a treasure of the highest wisdom, and the most excellent treasure of the Law, and a treasure of knowledge, the means to attain the excellences of the good Law,—

104. 'These eight treasures shall that high-minded man attain who joyfully writes this down and sets it in a sure place and always worships it.

105. 'And he who, himself holding this method of the Law in his mind, sets it going around him, shall obtain a complete supply for liberality for the good of the world,

106. 'Next, a complete supply of virtuous dispositions, a most excellent supply of sacred knowledge, a supply of perfect calmness, and that which is called spiritual insight,

107. 'A supply of the merit caused by the good Law, a most excellent supply of knowledge, a supply of boundless compassion, which is the means to attain the virtues of the perfect Buddha.

---

[1] I read mahâmatinidhânam for mahâprati-.

[2] Gati? 'resources?'

108. 'He, full of joy, shall obtain these eight supplies who himself holds this method of the Law in his mind and sets it going abroad.

109. 'And he who shall declare this method of the Law to others, shall have himself purified by great merit and shall be prosperous and possessed of supernatural powers.

110. 'He shall become a universal monarch, a king of kings, and even a ruler among the guardians of the world [1], an Indra ruler of the gods [2], and even the ruler of the Yâma heaven [3],

111. 'Yea, the ruler of the Tushita heaven, and the ruler of the Sunirmitâ*h*, and the king of the Va*s*avartina*h* [4], and the lord of the Brahmaloka;

112. 'Yea, Mahâbrahman, the highest of Sages,—and in the end he shall even become a Buddha,—he, possessing a thoroughly pure intelligence, shall obtain these eight sublime rewards of merit.

113. 'And he who, thoroughly intent, with a believing heart, and filled with faith and devotion, shall hear this method of the Law as it is preached,

114. 'He shall have his intellect made perfectly pure, his mind calmed with boundless charity, and his soul happy with boundless compassion, and he shall be filled with boundless joy;

115. 'His soul constantly calm with universal indifference, rejoicing in the four contemplations, having reached the ecstatic state of absolute indifference [5], and with his senses abolished,

116. 'With the five transcendent faculties attained,

[1] Sc. the Mahârâ*g*as of the first heaven.

[2] In the second Devaloka.

[3] The third Devaloka.

[4] These are the fourth, fifth, and sixth Devalokas.

[5] Samârûpya?

and destroying the aggregate of latent impressions, he, endowed with supernatural powers, will attain the samâdhi called *S*ûra*m*gama.

117. 'He, having his soul pure, will attain these eight forms of absolute spotlessness; yea, wherever this method of the Law will prevail universally,

118. 'There will be no fear of any disturbance in the kingdom, no fear of evil-minded thieves, nor fear of evil beasts;

119. 'There will be no fear of plagues, famines, or wildernesses; and no alarm shall spread, caused by quarrel or war;

120. 'There shall be no fear from the gods nor from Nâgas, Yakshas, and the like, nor shall there be anywhere any fear of any misfortune.

121. 'These eight fears shall not be found there where this Law extends; it is all briefly explained, my friends,—all that arises from holding it stedfastly.

122. 'A yet higher and most excellent merit is declared by all the Buddhas, even although all living beings were to practise complete self-restraint.

123. 'Let a man worship the Buddhas, honouring them always with faith; from that comes this pre-eminent merit, as is declared by the *G*inas.

124. 'And whosoever joyfully worships a Pratyeka-Buddha, they shall become themselves Pratyeka-Buddhas; therefore let every one worship them.

125. 'There is pre-eminent merit from the worship of one Bodhisattva, and they shall all themselves become Bodhisattvas, let every one worship them;

126. 'Therefore there is pre-eminent merit from the worship of one Buddha,—they shall all them-

selves become *G*inas, let every one devoutly worship them; and he too shall obtain this pre-eminent merit who hears this or causes others to hear it.

127. 'And whosoever in days when the good Law is abolished abandons love for his own body and life and proclaims day and night these good words,—pre-eminent is his merit from this.

128. 'He who wishes to worship constantly the lords of saints, the Pratyeka-Buddhas and the Arhats, let him resolutely produce in his mind the idea of true wisdom and proclaim these good words and the Law.

129. 'This jewel of all good doctrines, which is uttered by the Buddhas for the good of all beings,—even one who lives in a house will be a Tathâgata for it, where this good doctrine prevails.

130. 'He obtains a glorious and endless splendour who teaches even one word thereof; he will not miss one consonant nor the meaning who gives this Sûtra to others.

131. 'He is the best of all guides of men, no other being is like unto him; he is like a jewel, of imperishable glory, who hears this Law with a pure heart.

132. 'Therefore let those who are endowed with lofty ambitions, always hear this Law which causes transcendent merit; let them hear it and gladly welcome it and lay it up in their minds and continually worship the three jewels with faith.'

BOOK XVII.

[1 [1]. When the heavenly beings with Brahman at their head and the Bodhisattvas intent on self-mortification [2] heard this glorification of the Law uttered by the lion of the *S*âkyas, they were desirous to hear again this which is so difficult to find, and they went to the city and worshipped him, propitiating his favour; in the dark fortnight of the month Âsha*dh*a on the lunar day sacred to Agni, with the moon in the constellation called Kar*n*a (?) and on an auspicious day,—he, remembering the Buddha worlds and being desirous to save all creatures, set off on his journey, longing for disciples with his father at their head.]

2. The associated Brâhmans, accompanied by the inhabitants of Kâ*s*î who had gone to the Deer Park, and the mendicants to the number of thirty, were rendered resplendent by the chief of saints; Kâ*s*ikâ the harlot of Kâ*s*î went to the heaven of the gods, after she had worshipped the *G*ina and attached her sons to the service of the glorious one; the conqueror of the world then made thirty rejoicing officiating priests of Kâ*s*î his disciples, initiating them in the course of perfect wisdom; and the son of Maitrâya*n*î [3] and Maitra, the preceptor of hosts of the twice-born, named Pûr*n*a, obtained true wisdom from the chief of saints and became a noble mendicant.

3. The priest of the lord of the city Marakata, a

---

[1] This is a doubtful verse, the metre is faulty.

[2] I read tapasyâpare.

[3] Burnouf, Lotus, p. 489.

Brâhman named A*g*aya, and his son Nâlaka, well versed in sacred learning and full of answers to questions, and an ascetic named Dh*ri*ti, dwelling in the Vindhya, and an invincible Brâhman ascetic Sa*m*gayin with his disciples,—these all, dwellers in the Vindhya,—when they came to him for refuge, the chief of saints initiated as mendicants, touching them with his hand bearing the mark of a wheel; moreover the Nâga Elapatra came to the abode of the best of saints, and stood resplendent there, perfectly calm in his demeanour and worshipping him with his rosaries.

4. There was also a female ascetic of Mathurâ named Trikavya*m*gikâ, and a Brâhman named Vidyâkara,—their son was named Sabhya, a dweller in the district called *S*vetabâlârka, a wise ascetic, proud of his wisdom,—he went into the Deer Park, wearing the aspect of one perfectly illumined, and desiring the highest wisdom from the chief of mendicants; seeking from the omniscient admission to the noble life, he became renowned as the mendicant Sabhya in all assemblies.

5. The son of Lalitâprabudhâ, born after worship paid to the best of trees on the bank of the stream Vara*n*â,—renowned in the world as Ya*s*oda,—wise from the besprinkling of the ambrosia of the words of the king of heaven,—remembering all former discourses which he had heard, came with his friends to the wood in the Deer Park, accompanied by his glory; and the holy one, touching his head with his hand, made him the guru of the chief Bhikshus.

6. The glorious one, named the great Buddha, proceeded with the mendicants in an auspicious company, and having manifested his triumphal march for the salvation of the world, entered the city of Kâ*s*î.

A poor Brâhman, named Svastika, a native of Vârâ*n*asî, obtained riches from heaven through the favour of the glorious one, and having received adoption as a slave in the *G*ina faith, became a mendicant and an Arhat at the hands of the great teacher.

7. Blessing the king of Kâ*s*î[1] Divodâsa and the citizens with gold, corn, and other riches,—taking up his abode in different places in forests, caves, mountains, he at last came in his rambles to the river *G*âhnavî. The boatman who conveyed the *G*ina across the Ganges worshipped him and offered him milk with due services of reverence, and became a mendicant through his favour and by the *G*ina's command found a dwelling in the Buddha's hermitage in the grove.

8. The glorious one, after he had crossed the Ganges, went to the hermitage of Kâ*s*yapa at Gayâ, called Uruvilva; there, having shown his supernatural power, he received as Bhikshus the Kâ*s*yapas, Uruvilva, and others, with more than a thousand of their disciples, having endued them forthwith with all kinds of spiritual knowledge and with the power to abandon all worldly action; then accompanied by three hundred disciples Upasena at the command of his maternal uncle became an ascetic.

9. The glorious one made seven hundred ascetics enter Nirvâ*n*a who dwelt in the wood Dharma; and the lord of the Law also caused the daughters of Na*m*dika, Su*g*âtâ and others, who dwelt in the village, to become the first female ascetics; and in the city of Râ*g*ageha, having enlightened in right action and in activity the king Bimbisâra,

[1] Kâ*s*ikâ.

the monarch, who is to be considered as the elder-born in perfect knowledge, he made him who was the devoted follower of the Buddha, a Bodhisattva and a Sak*ri*dâgâmin.

10. In another village named Nâradya there was a Brâhman Dharmapâlin and a Brâhman woman named *S*âlyâ; their seventh son named Upatishya[1], who had studied the entire Veda, became a Buddhist mendicant; so too there was a great pa*nd*it, a Brâhman named Dhânyâyana, who dwelt in the village Kolata, and his son;—him and the son of *S*âlî named Maudgalya the great saint received as the best of Bhikshus, pre-eminent disciples.

11. Next he ordained as a mendicant the keen-witted maternal uncle of *S*âliputra[1], Dîrghânakha by name; then travelling in the realm of Magadha, the glorious one, being honoured by the inhabitants with alms and other signs of devotion, and delivering them from evil, dwelt in the convent given by the seer *G*eta, attracting to himself many of the monks; and after ordaining as a mendicant a native of Mithilâ, named Ânanda, with his companions, he dwelt there a year.

12. The Brâhman named Kâ*s*yapa, a very Kuvera for wealth, and a master in all the sciences connected with the Veda, an inhabitant of Râ*g*ageha, being pure-minded and wearing only one garment, left all his kindred and came seeking wisdom in asceticism;—when this noble youth came to the Bodhi tree and practised for six years a penance hard to carry out, then he paid worship to the chief of saints who had attained perfect knowledge, and he became the well-

[1] Sc. *S*âriputra.

known Kâsyapa, the chief of ascetics, the foremost of the Arhats.

13. The saint Naradatta, dwelling on Mount Himavat, remembering the wholesome words of his maternal uncle, came to the Sugata with his disciples, and the holy one admitted them all into the order of the *G*ina; then a woman named *S*akti, and another named Kamalâ, pre-eminent in Brâhmanical power, came to the Sugata and fell down at his feet, and then standing before him they were received by the saint, and made happy with the staff and begging-bowl.

14. Seven hundred disciples of the ascetic Rudraka, remembering the noble words of their teacher, becoming mendicants according to the doctrine of the *G*ina, flocked round him paying him their homage and carrying their staves; next a seer, named Raivata, joyfully uttering his praises, having finished his course of discipline, became a mendicant, full of devotion to the guru, counting gold and clay as the same, well versed in sacred spells and meditation, and able to counteract the three kinds of poisons and other fatal harms.

15. Having received as followers and disciples certain householders of *S*râvastî, Pûr*n*a and others, and given them alms-vessels,—and having made many poor wretches as rich as Kuvera, and maimed persons with all their limbs perfect, and paupers and orphans affluent,—and having proclaimed the Law, and dwelt two years in the forest *G*etaka delivering the suppliants, the glorious one, having taught again the saint *G*eta, and established the Bhikshu Pûr*n*a, once more proceeded on his way.

16. Then the glorious one went on, protecting

the merchant-caravans by the stores of his own treasures from the troops of robbers, next he went into the neighbourhood of Râ*g*ageha wandering with his begging-vessel which had been given by the merchants. In the wood called Ve*n*u, filled with *S*âl trees, he ate an offering of food prepared by the enriched robbers, and he received as mendicants five hundred of them and gave them their begging-vessels and the other requisites.

17. At the invitation of Buddha's son, *S*uddhodana gave this message to his envoys *Kh*andaka and Udâyin, 'Thy father and mother, some noble ladies, headed by Ya*s*od*ri*h, and this my young son have come in the hope of seeing thee, under the idea that thou art devoted to the world's salvation; what shall I tell them?' They two went, and reverentially saluting the Buddha in the vihâra called Ve*n*u, they told him the message with their eyes filled with tears.

18. *Kh*andaka and Udâyin accepted his counsel, and, being delighted at the mighty power of Buddha, became great ascetics; and the great *G*ina took them with him and proceeded from that wood with the disciples, the mendicants, and the saints. Going on from place to place, and dwelling in each for a while and conferring deliverance and confirming the disciples, the mendicants, and the Arhats, he at last reached the wood Nigrodha, illuminating the district by his glory, shaking the earth and putting an end to misery.

19. [1] He again stirred up his followers in the doctrine of the Buddha, and then went on with the

[1] Several phrases are obscure in this verse.

crowds of inhabitants gathered round him, instructing his shaven mendicant-followers, as they begged alms, while the gods brought his precepts to their minds [1]. He forbade the mendicants to enter the city and went to Râ*g*ageha himself with his own followers; and then the king who dwells apart from all doubt [2], the *G*ina, who knows at once all the history of every Bhikshu, instructed the ascetic (Udâyin) in proclaiming wisdom to others.

20. In accordance with the *G*ina's command that prince of ascetics, Udâyin, went to the city of Kapila; there he, the lord of all possessors of supernatural powers, instructed the king as he stood in the assembly in the boon of the eight hundred powers; and coming down from heaven he uttered to the king and his court a discourse on the four sublime truths, and the king, with his mind enlightened, having worshipped him, held intercourse with him, attended by his courtiers, offering every form of homage.

21. The monarch, rejoiced at the sight of the *G*ina, praised his feet, worshipping them with eight hundred presents; and the Sugata departed, and made manifest in the sky in his one person a form comprehending the universe; first as fire, then ambrosia, then the king of beasts, an elephant, the king of horses, the king of peacocks [3], the king of birds, Maghavan, the ten rulers of the world headed by Yama, the sun, the moon, the hosts of stars, Brahman, Vish*n*u, and *S*iva.

22. The sons of Diti, the four (Mahârâ*g*as) with

---

[1] Obscure. [2] Dvâpare*stha?

[3] *S*ikhirâ*t* might mean 'the king of flames,' &c.

Dh*ri*tarâsh*t*ra at their head, the hosts of Yogins with the king Drumasiddha, the (heavenly) ascetics, the Vasus, the Manus, the sons of the forest, the creatures of the waters headed by the makara, the birds headed by Garu*d*a, and all the kings in the different worlds with the lord of the Tushita heaven at their head, and those in the world of the dead[1] the domain of Bali,—whatever is conspicuous in the universe the holy one created it all, becoming the universal one.

23. When the king had thus been instructed, the lord of saints went to the Satya heaven, and then from the sky, seated on his own throne[2], he proclaimed the twelvefold Law; then he restored Gautamî and Anugopâ and many other women to sight, and filled all the assembled people with joy; and established others in Nirvâ*n*a and in the Law. Then *S*uddhodana full of joy invited him to a feast given to the whole assembly, and he accepted it by his silence.

24. The lion of the *S*âkyas, having been thus invited, went with the congregation of his followers to the place, after having shown a mighty miracle. Then the earth shook, a shower of flowers fell, the various quarters of space became illumined and a wind blew; and the heavenly beings, Brahman, *S*iva, Vish*n*u, Indra, Yama, Varu*n*a, Kuvera, the lord of Bhûtas, the lord of the winds, Nir*ri*ti, Fire with his seven flames, and the rest, stood resting their feet on the serpent *S*esha, and followed leading the gods and gandharvas in their dance in the sky.

25. Making millions of ascetics, disciples, Arhats,

---

[1] Martya seems here to be used for m*ri*ta.

[2] Or must we take sva as put for svar, 'in heaven?'

sages, mendicants, and fasters,—and delivering from their ills the blind, the humpbacked, the lame, the insane, the maimed as well as the destitute,—and having established many persons of the fourth caste in the true activity and inaction and in the three yânas[1], with the four samgrahas[2] and the eight amgas[3],—going on from place to place, delivering, and confirming the Bhikshus, in the twelfth year he went to his own city.

26. Day by day confirming the Bhikshus, and providing food for the congregation, in an auspicious moment he made a journey to Lumbinî with the Bhikshus and the citizens, Brahman and Rudra being at their head, with great triumph and noise of musical instruments. There he saw the holy fig-tree and he stood by it remembering his birth, with a smile; and rays of light streamed from his mouth and went forth illumining the earth; and he uttered a discourse to the goddess of the wood, giving her the serenity of faith.

27. [4]Having come to the Lumbinî fig-tree he spoke to Paurvikâ the daughter of Râhula, and Gopikâ the daughter of Maitra, and his own Saudhanî Kausikâ; and he uttered an affectionate discourse honouring his mother by the tank Vasatya; then speaking with Ekasâmgî the daughter of Mahâkautuka and Sautasomî in the wood Nigrodha, he received into the community some members of his own family, headed by Sundarânanda, and one hundred and seven citizens.

---

[1] Burnouf, Lotus, p. 315.

[2] Apparently the four means of conciliating dependents.

[3] The eightfold path of Buddhist morality.

[4] Much of this stanza is obscure.

28. Having declared the glory of the Law of Buddha, he built a round Stûpa and gave a royal coronation to Saunu[1], sending him into the wood pre-eminent with the holiest saints and *K*aityas, and bidding him worship the sacred relics; and having commanded Râhula, Gautamî, and the other women led by Gopikâ, with staves in their hands, as shaven ascetics, to practise the vow of fasting called ahoratra[2], and after that the Laksha*k*aitya ceremony[3] and then the rite called *Sri*ṅgabheri[4], and that called Vasu*m*dhârikâ[5].

29. The Ash*t*asâhasrikâ of sacred authority[6],—the Geya[7] and the Gâthâ, the Nidâna and the Avadâna, and that which is called the Sûtra of the great Yâna, the Vyâkara[8] and the Ityukta, the *G*âtaka, the work called Vaipulya, the Adbhuta[9] and the Upade*s*a, and also the Udânaka[10] as the twelfth.—Teaching (these sacred texts) and making current the Yâna for common disciples, that for Pratyeka Buddhas, and the Mahâyâna, and proclaiming them all around, accompanied by thirteen and a half bodies of mendicants, the conqueror of the world went out of the city of Kapila.

30. After displaying miracles in the city of Ka-

---

[1] Or the grandson of the king?

[2] See Râ*g*endralâl Mitra, Nepalese Buddhist Literature, p. 221.

[3] Ibid. p. 275. [4] Ibid. p. 230. [5] Ibid. p. 271.

[6] Naigamâ? The Ash*t*asâhasrikâ seems not to be reckoned here among the following twelve texts of peculiar authority with the Northern Buddhists. But Burnouf's authorities include it in that called 'Sûtra.'

[7] For the following twelve names see Burnouf, Introd. pp. 51–66.

[8] More properly Vyâkara*n*a.

[9] Burnouf calls it adbhutadharma.

[10] Burnouf, Introd. p. 58.

pila, and having paid honour to his father, and having made Râhula and his companions Arhats, and also the Bhikshu*n*îs with Gautamî and Gopikâ at their head, and various women of all the four castes; and having established Saunu[1] on his imperial throne, and the people in the *G*ina doctrine, and having abolished poverty and darkness, and then remembering his mother, he set forth, after worshipping Svaya*m*bhû, towards the northern region with Brahman, Vish*n*u, and *S*iva as mendicants in his train.

31. The glory of the Avadâna of the birth of the lion of the *S*âkyas has thus been described by me at length and yet very concisely; it must be corrected by pa*nd*its wherever anything is omitted,—my childish speech is not to be laughed at, but to be listened to with pleasure.

Whatever virtue I may have acquired from describing the king of the Law, the deliverer from mundane existence, who assumes all forms,—may it become a store of merit for the production of right activity and inactivity in others, and for the diffusion of delight among the six orders of beings[2].

Thus ends the seventeenth sarga, called the Progress to Lumbinî, in the great poem made by A*s*vaghosha, the Buddha-*k*arita[3].

---

[1] Or Saunava, see *s*loka 28.

[2] Sc. the sha*d* *g*atayas, the 'six paths,' are gods, men, Asuras, &c., Pretas, brutes, and the inhabitants of the different hells.

[3] C adds here on the last page the following lines: 'The poem about Buddha, very difficult to obtain, was written by Am*ri*tânanda in the year indicated by a cipher, the arrows (of Kâma), and a nine [=Newâr Sa*m*vat 950, or A.D. 1830], in the dark fortnight of the month Mârga*s*îrsha (Nov.-Dec.) and on the day ruled by the

seventh astrological house Smara. Having searched for them everywhere and not found them, four sargas have been made by me,—the fourteenth, fifteenth, sixteenth, and seventeenth.' The beginning of another version of these lines is given in P, but D omits them. The name of Am*ri*tânanda occurs in Râ*g*endralâl Mitra's Nepalese Buddhist Literature as the author of three treatises,—two in Sanskrit, the *K*handoݥm*ri*talatâ (p. 79), the Kalyâ*n*apa*mk*avi*ms*atikâ (p. 99), translated in Wilson's Works, vol. ii, and the Vîraku*s*âvadâna (p. 274) in Newârî. Compare Cowell and Eggeling's Catalogue, pp. 18, 24; in p. 18 he is associated with the date N.S. 916 (A.D. 1796).

INDEX OF PROPER NAMES[1].

[1] This Index omits some of the obscure names in the last book.

NOTES AND CORRECTIONS.

Page 11, note 2 (I, 63). Professor Jacobi writes, 'Indra's banner is intimately connected with the *G*aina legend of king Domuha (see my Ausgew. Erzähl. in Mâhârâsh*t*rî, p. 40); the old *G*aina legends originated in the East; cf. also Râmây. II, 74, 36; IV, 16, 37; 17, 2 (Bombay ed.).'

P. 21, l. 30 (II, 31 *b*). I have read in the translation madai*h* for the printed ma*m*dai*h*.

P. 33, l. 30 (III, 50 *c*). If we read api nâma sakto, the translation should run, 'would that he might not be able to forsake us, even though he remained attached to us only through the restlessness of the senses.'

P. 49, note 2, l. 4, read kumude*s*a.

P. 60, l. 31 (V, 80 *d*). This might be rendered 'planting his footsteps without alarm,' but I have taken *k*akita as meaning 'hurrying' from the *k*akitagate*h* of the next *s*loka.

P. 83 (VIII, 31 *d*), add to note 2, 'there is a similar confusion of vigâdha and vigâ*dh*a in the MSS. in VIII, 76.'

BUDDHIST MAHÂYÂNA TEXTS

PART II

THE LARGER SUKHÂVATÎ-VYÛHA

THE SMALLER SUKHÂVATÎ-VYÛHA

THE VA*G*RA*KKH*EDIKÂ

THE LARGER
PRA*G*Ñ*Â-PÂRAMITÂ-H*R*I*DAYA-SÛTRA

THE SMALLER
PRA*G*Ñ*Â-PÂRAMITÂ-H*R*I*DAYA-SÛTRA

TRANSLATED BY F. MAX MÜLLER

THE AMITÂYUR-DHYÂNA-SÛTRA

TRANSLATED BY J. TAKAKUSU

Oxford
AT THE CLARENDON PRESS
1894

CONTENTS TO PART II.

INTRODUCTION.

THE LARGER SUKHÂVATÎ-VYÛHA.

ACCORDING to the census of 1891 Japan has about forty millions of inhabitants, of whom more than thirty millions are Buddhists. Of these Buddhists the Shin-shiu sect claims about ten millions of followers, with 19,208 temples, and 11,958 preachers, with ten chief priests, and 3,593 students. The books on which the members of this sect chiefly found their faith are the two Sukhâvatî-vyûhas, the large and the small, and the Amitâyur-dhyâna-sûtra. They are sometimes called the Large Sûtra, the Small Sûtra, and the Sûtra of Meditation[1].

According to the Buddhists of Japan, Buddha preached the Amitâyur-dhyâna-sûtra to queen Vaidehî in the city of Râ*g*ag*ri*ha. This was during the fifth period of his life; i.e. when he was between the age of seventy-one and seventy-nine.

The outline given of this Sûtra is as follows: 'Vaidehî, consort of king Bimbisâra of Magadha, seeing the wicked actions of her son A*g*âta*s*atru, began to feel weary of this world Sahâ (here as elsewhere explained as the patient, much-enduring earth). *S*âkyamuni then taught her how to be born in the Pure Land Sukhâvatî, instructing her in the method of being born in that world, enumerating three kinds of good actions. The first is worldly goodness, which includes good actions in general, such as filial piety, respect

[1] See Sukhâvatî-vyûha, in Anecdota Oxoniensia, p. ix.

for elders, loyalty, faithfulness, &c. The second is the goodness of *S*îla or morality, in which there are differences between the priesthood and the laity. In short, however, all who do not oppose the general rule of reproving wickedness and exhorting to the practice of virtue are included in this goodness. The third is the goodness of practice, which includes that of the four Satyas or truths, and the six Pâramitâs or perfections. Besides these, all other pure and good actions, such as the reading and recital of the Mahâyâna-sûtras, persuading others to hear the Law, and thirteen kinds of goodness to be practised by fixed thought, are comprised in this. Towards the end of the Sûtra, Buddha says: "Let not one's voice cease, but ten times complete the thought, and repeat the words Namo-mitâbhâya Buddhâya, or adoration to Amitâbha Buddha. This practice is the most excellent of all."

'At seventy-eight years of age Buddha is said[1] to have composed the Samanta-bhadra-bodhisattva-*k*aryâ-dharma-sûtra, in the city of Vai*s*âlî. At the age of seventy-nine he is supposed to have ascended to the Trayastri*ms*a heaven in order to preach to his mother, and after descending on earth again, he only published two more Sûtras, the Nirvâ*n*a-sûtra and the Sukhâvatî-vyûha. Very soon after he died.'

The same three books, that is, the two Sukhâvatî-vyûhas and the Amitâyur-dhyâna-sûtra, form also the chief authority of the *G*ôdoshiu sect, the sect of the Pure Land. The followers of this sect state[2] that in the year 252 A.D. Saṅghavarman, an Indian student of the Tripi*t*aka, came to China and translated the great Amitâyu*h*-sûtra, i.e. the Larger Sukhâvatî-vyûha, in two volumes. This is the first and largest of their sacred books.

In the year 400 A.D. another teacher, Kumâra*g*îva, came from India to China, and produced a translation of the

---

[1] These are the statements of the Buddhists in Japan as recorded by Bunyiu Nanjio in 'Short History of the Twelve Japanese Buddhist Sects,' Tokyo, 1886, p. xviii.

[2] Loc. cit. p. 104.

small Amitâyu*h*-sûtra, or Smaller Sukhâvatî-vyûha, in one volume. This is the smallest of the three sacred books.

In 424 A.D. Kâlayasas arrived in China from India, and translated the Amitâyur-dhyâna-sûtra in one volume.

Chinese translations of these texts were known to exist not only in China, but also in Japan, and there were in several cases more than one translation of the same text. But it was not known, nor even suspected, that the Sanskrit originals of some of them had been preserved in the temples and monasteries of that distant island.

In the year 1880 I read a paper before the Royal Asiatic Society in London, 'On Sanskrit Texts discovered in Japan' (Selected Essays, vol. ii, pp. 213–271), and in it and in the preface to my edition of the Sanskrit texts of the Sukhâvatî-vyûha in the Anecdota Oxoniensia, 1883, I explained how I discovered the existence and came into the possession of Sanskrit MSS. and copies of Sanskrit MSS. from the Buddhist monasteries in Jápan.

I had long suspected the existence of old Sanskrit MSS. in China, and had asked my friends there to search for them, and as it was well known from the works of Siebold and others that there were short invocations in Sanskrit of Buddha hung up in the Buddhist temples of Japan or written on their walls, I entertained a hope that in Japan also some real and ancient MSS. might still be discovered. The alphabet in which these short invocations are written was known by the name of Shidda, the Sanskrit Siddha[1]. It may be seen in Siebold's works and in an article published in 1880 in the Annales du Musée Guimet, vol. i, pp. 322–336, by MM. Ymaizoumi and Yamata. What was not known, however, was that there had been a period in

[1] Siddham, lit. what is successfully achieved, seems to have been used by Buddhists like siddhi*h*, success, as an auspicious invocation at the beginning of literary works. Thus we see that the alphabet on the Hôriuzhi palm-leaves begins with siddham, and this siddham may afterwards have become the name of the alphabet itself. In Siddhânta, meaning dogma, grammar, siddha conveys the sense of settled; in Siddhârtha, a name of Buddha, it means fulfilled, i.e. he whose desires have all been fulfilled, the perfect man, free from desires and passions.

the history of Japan when Sanskrit was studied systematically by native priests, nay, that some of the MSS. which had travelled from India to China, and from China to Japan were still in existence there. Of these MSS. I gave an account in 1884 in the Anecdota Oxoniensia, 'The Ancient Palm-Leaves.' Though hitherto no new discoveries of Sanskrit MSS. have been made, it is most desirable that the search for them should not be given up in China, in Japan, and in Corea also. But even thus a new and important chapter has been added to the history of Buddhism, and the fact been established once for all that Buddhist literature found a home in Japan, and was studied there for many generations not only in Chinese translations, but in the original Sanskrit also. Let us hope that through the efforts of my pupils, such as Bunyiu Nanjio, Kenjiu Kasawara (died 1883), and others, a new school of Sanskrit students has been planted in Japan which will enable the followers of Buddha there to derive their knowledge of his doctrine from the original and undefiled source of the ancient Tripi*t*aka.

I thought it best for the sake of completeness, and in compliance with the wishes of my friends in Japan, to give in this volume the translation both of the Larger and the Smaller Sukhâvatî-vyûha. They differ from each other on several smaller points. The Larger Sukhâvatî-vyûha is represented as having been preached on the G*ri*dhrakû*t*a hill near Râ*g*ag*ri*ha, the Smaller Sukhâvatî-vyûha in the *G*eta-grove near *S*râvastî. In the former the chief interlocutors are the Bhagavat, i. e. the Buddha *S*âkyamuni, Ânanda, and A*g*ita; in the latter the Bhagavat and *S*âriputra. There is one point, however, which is of great importance in the eyes of the followers of the Shin-shiu sect, on which the two treatises differ.

The Smaller Sukhâvatî-vyûha lays great stress on the fact that people can be saved or can be born in the Land of Bliss, if only they remember and repeat the name of Buddha Amitâbha two, three, four, five, six or more nights before their death, and it distinctly denies that people are born in the Paradise of Amitâbha as a reward or necessary result of good works performed in the present life. This would seem to take away one of the fundamental doctrines of Buddhism, namely the doctrine of karman, or of the continuous working of our deeds whether good or bad. Instead of the old doctrine, As a man soweth, so he shall reap, a new and easier way of salvation is here preached, viz. As a man prayeth, so he shall be saved. It is what is known to us as salvation by faith rather than by works. The Larger Sukhâvatî-vyûha lays likewise great stress on prayer and faith in Amitâbha, but it never neglects 'the stock of merit' as essential for salvation. It would almost seem as if this popular and easy doctrine had secured to itself the name of Mahâyâna, as meaning the Broad Way, in opposition to the Narrow Way, the Hînayâna.

The historical relation between the Hînayâna and the Mahâyâna schools of Buddhism is to me as great a puzzle as ever. But that the teaching of *S*âkyamuni as represented in the Hînayâna comes first in time seems to be shown by the Mahâyâna-sûtras themselves. Even in our Sukhâvatî-vyûha the teacher, the Bhagavat, is *S*âkyamuni, whom we know as the son of the Lord of Kapilavastu, the husband of Ya*s*odharâ, the father of Râhula. We begin with a dialogue between this Buddha and his famous disciple Ânanda. Ânanda observes that Buddha is in a state of spiritual exaltation and asks him what he is seeing or thinking. Thereupon Buddha relates how there was a line of eighty-one Tathâgatas or Buddhas beginning with Dîpaṅkara and ending with Loke*s*vararâ*g*a. During the period of this Tathâgata Loke*s*vararâ*g*a, a Bhikshu or Buddhist mendicant of the name of Dharmâkara formed the intention of becoming a Buddha. He therefore went to the Tathâgata Loke*s*vararâ*g*a, praised him in several verses, and then asked him to become his teacher and to describe to him what a Buddha and a Buddha country ought to be. After having received instruction, Dharmâkara comprehended all the best qualities of all the Buddha countries, and prayed that they should all be concentrated in his own country when he himself had become a Buddha. After long meditations Dharmâkara returns to Buddha Loke*s*vararâ*g*a and tells him in a long prayer what he wishes and wills his own Buddha country to be. This prayer forms really the nucleus of the Sukhâvatî-vyûha; it is in fact, under the form of a prayer, a kind of prophecy of what, according to Dharmâkara's ideas, Sukhâvatî or the Land of Bliss ought to be. Dharmâkara then became a Bodhisattva, a candidate for Buddhahood, and lastly a real Buddha (§ 9). All this is related by Buddha *S*âkyamuni to Ânanda, as a kind of vision of what happened ten kalpas ago (§ 14, s. f.). When Ânanda asks *S*âkyamuni what has become of this Bodhisattva Dharmâkara, Buddha answers that this original mendicant is now reigning in Sukhâvatî as the Buddha Amitâbha. He then proceeds to describe Sukhâvatî where Amitâbha dwells, and his description of Amitâbha's country is very much the fulfilment of all that Dharmâkara has prayed for. Once (§ 17) Ânanda is reproved by Buddha for not implicitly believing all he says about the marvels of Sukhâvatî, but afterwards the praises of Sukhâvatî and of its inhabitants are continued till nearly the end. In some verses recited by Buddha *S*âkyamuni, Amitâbha himself, when questioned by the Buddha-son Avalokite*s*vara, explains that Sukhâvatî is what it is in fulfilment of his prayers, when he was as yet living on earth (§§ 31, 13; 17). At last Ânanda expresses a wish to see Amitâbha, whereupon that Buddha sends a ray of light from the palm of his hand so that the whole world was inundated by its light, and not only Ânanda, but every living being could see Amitâbha and his retinue of Bodhisattvas in the Land of Bliss, while they in Sukhâvatî could see *S*âkyamuni and the whole world Sahâ. Then begins the conversation between *S*âkyamuni and A*g*ita (instead of Ânanda). Buddha explains to him how some of the blessed spirits in Sukhâvatî sit cross-legged in lotus-flowers, while others dwell shut up in the calyx of these flowers, the former being the firm believers in Amitâbha, the latter those who have entertained some doubt, and who have therefore to wait for five hundred years inside the calyx before they become full-blown, being debarred during all that time from seeing and hearing the Buddha.

In conclusion Buddha *S*âkyamuni exhorts A*g*ita to teach

this treatise, the Sukhâvatî-vyûha, to all beings, and promises great rewards to all who will learn it, copy it, teach and explain it.

I need not repeat here what I have said in the preface to my edition of the Sanskrit text of the Sukhâvatî-vyûha about the difficulties of translating a text which in many places is corrupt and imperfect. But I may point out another difficulty, namely how almost impossible it is to find in English a sufficient number of nouns and adjectives to render the superabundant diction of this Description of the Land of Bliss. An exact rendering of all the words of its gushing eloquence is out of the question. Often I should have liked to shorten some turgid sentence, but I was afraid of exposing myself once more to the frivolous charge of representing the Sacred Books of the East as more beautiful, as more free from blemishes, than they really are. No more unfounded charge could have been brought against these translations of the Sacred Books of the East. Whatever else they may be or not be, they are certainly faithful, as faithful as an English translation of an Oriental original can possibly be. That they are free from mistakes, I should not venture to say, and no Oriental scholar would expect it. Those who venture to translate Oriental texts that have never been translated before are few in number, and they have to do the work of pioneers. Those who follow in their track find it very easy, no doubt, to do over again what has been done before, and even to point out here and there what they consider and represent as mistakes; nay, they evidently imagine that because they can discover a mistake, they themselves could have done the pioneer's work as well or much better. If only they would try for once to find their way through the jungle and the brushwood of an unexplored forest they would become more just to their predecessors, and more humble in judging of their own performances. Nay, they might possibly find that often when they differ from the translation of others, they themselves may be wrong, and their precursors right.

This at all events I may say in my own name and in the name of my fellow-workers, that the idea of representing the Sacred Books of the East as better, purer, and more beautiful than they are, could never enter into the head of a scholar, and has never proved even a temptation to the translators of the Sacred Books of the East.

THE SMALLER SUKHÂVATÎ-VYÛHA.

The translation of the Smaller Sukhâvatî-vyûha has been published by me before in my Selected Essays, vol. ii, p. 348, where a fuller account may be found of the discovery of Sanskrit MSS. in Japan, and of the way by which they travelled from India to China, and from China to Japan. I have made a few corrections in my translation, and have added some notes and omitted others.

THE VA*G*RA*KKH*EDIKÂ.

In order to make this collection of Mahâyâna works more complete and useful to students in Japan I have added a translation of the Va*g*ra*kkh*edikâ, which is much studied in Japan, and the Sanskrit text of which was published by me in an editio princeps—in the Anecdota Oxoniensia, 1881.

The Va*g*ra*kkh*edikâ, or the Diamond-cutter, is one of the most widely read and most highly valued metaphysical treatises in Buddhist literature. In Japan the Va*g*ra*kkh*edikâ and the Pra*gñ*âpâramitâ-h*ri*daya are read chiefly by the followers of the Shin-gon sect, founded by Kô-Bô, the great disciple of the famous Hiouen-thsang, in 816 A.D. The temples of this sect in Japan amount to 12,943. Written originally in Sanskrit, it has been translated into Chinese, Tibetan, Mongol, and Mandshu. Its full title is Va*g*ra*kkh*edikâ Pra*gñ*â-pâramitâ, i.e. the Diamond-cutter, the perfection of wisdom, or, as it has sometimes been rendered, 'the

Transcendent Wisdom.' Mr. Bunyiu Nanjio in his Catalogue of the Tripi*t*aka, p. 1, has shown that it forms the ninth section of the Mahâpra*g*ñâ-pâramitâ-sûtra, and that it agrees with the Tibetan translation of the text in 300 *s*lokas.

An account of the Tibetan translation was given as far back as 1836 by Csoma Körösi in his Analysis of the Sher-chiu, the second division of the Kanjur, published in the Asiatic Researches, vol. xx, p. 393 seq. Our text is there described as the Diamond-cutter or the Sûtra of wonderful effects, in which *S*âkya in a colloquial manner instructs Subhûti, one of his principal disciples, in the true meaning of the Pra*g*ñâ-pâramitâ. The Tibetans, we are told, pay great respect to this Sûtra, and copies of it are found in consequence in great abundance [1].

The first Chinese translation [2] is ascribed to Kumâra*g*îva of the latter Tsin dynasty (A.D. 384–417). An English translation of this Chinese translation was published by the Rev. S. Beal in the Journal of the Royal Asiatic Society, 1864–5.

There are several more Chinese translations, one by Bodhiru*k*i (A. D. 509), one by Paramârtha (A. D. 562), one by Hiouen-thsang (A. D. 648), one by I-tsing (A. D. 703), one by Dharmagupta of the Sui dynasty (A. D. 589–618).

The text and German translation of the Tibetan translation were published in 1837 by M. Schmidt in the Mémoires de l'Académie de St. Pétersbourg, tom. iv, p. 186.

The Mongolian translation was presented by the Baron Schiling de Canstadt to the Library of the Institut de France.

The Mandshu translation is in the possession of M. de Harlez, who with the help of the Tibetan, Mandshu, and Chinese versions has published a valuable French translation of the Sanskrit text of the Va*g*ra*kkh*edikâ in the Journal Asiatique, 1892.

[1] See also L. Feer in Annales du Musée Guimet, vol. ii, p. 201.
[2] See preface to my edition of the Va*g*ra*kkh*edikâ, Anecd. Oxon., 1881.

At first sight it may seem as if this metaphysical treatise hardly deserved the world-wide reputation which it has attained. Translated literally into English it must often strike the Western reader as sheer nonsense, and hollow repetition. Nor can anything be said in defence of the form or style adopted in this treatise by the Buddhist philosophers who wished to convince their hearers of the truth of their philosophy. This philosophy, or, at least, its underlying doctrine, is not unknown to us in the history of Western philosophy. It is simply the denial of the reality of the phenomenal world. Considering how firmly a belief in phenomenal objects is established in the ordinary mind, it might well have seemed that such a belief could not be eradicated except by determined repetition. But that the theory had been fully reasoned out before it was stated in this practical, but by no means attractive form, may be gathered from the technical terminology which pervades our treatise. There are two words, in particular, which are of great importance for a right apprehension of its teaching, dharma and sa*mg*ñâ. Dharma, in the ordinary Buddhist phraseology, may be correctly rendered by law. Thus the whole teaching of Buddha is called the Good Law, Saddharma. But in our treatise dharma is generally used in a different sense. It means form (εἶδος), and likewise what is possessed of form, what is therefore different from other things, what is individual, in fact, what we mean by a thing or an object. This meaning has escaped most of the translators, both Eastern and Western, but if we were always to translate dharma by law, it seems to me that the whole drift of our treatise would become unintelligible. What our treatise wishes to teach is that all objects, differing one from the other by their dharmas, are illusive, or, as we should say, phenomenal and subjective, that they are in fact of our own making, the products of our own mind. When we say that something is large or small, sweet or bitter, these dharmas or qualities are subjective, and cannot be further defined. What is large to me, may be small to another. A mile may seem short or long, according to the state of our muscles, and no one can determine the point where smallness ends and length begins. This applies to all things which we are supposed to know, that is, which we are able to name. And hence the Buddhist metaphysician tells us that all things are but names, sa*m*g*ñ*âs[1], and that being names they are neither what they seem to be nor what they do not seem to be. This extreme Pyrrhonism is afterwards applied to everything. Dust is not dust, because we cannot draw a line between the smallest molecules, the smallest granules, the smallest dust, and the smallest gravel. There are no signs (no τεκμήρια or σημεῖα) by which we can know or distinguish these objects. There are in fact no objects, independent of us; hence whoever speaks of things, of beings, of living beings, of persons, &c., uses names only, and the fact that they are names implies that the normal things are not what they seem to be. This, I believe, is the meaning of the constantly recurring phrase: What is spoken of as 'beings, beings indeed' that was preached or called by Buddha as no-beings; that is, every name and every concept is only a makeshift, if it is not altogether a failure; it is certainly not true. We may speak of a dog, but there is no such thing as a dog. It is always either a greyhound or a spaniel, this or that dog, but dog is only an abstraction, a name, a concept of our mind. The same applies to quadruped, animal, living being, and being; they are all names with nothing corresponding to them. This is what is meant by the highest perfect knowledge, in which nothing, not even the smallest thing, is known, or known to be known (par. 22). In that knowledge there is no difference, it is always the same and therefore perfect (par. 23). He who has attained this knowledge believes neither in the idea, i. e. the name of a thing, nor in the idea of a no-thing, and Buddha by using the expression, the idea, or name (sa*m*g*ñ*â) of a thing, implies thereby that it is not the idea of a thing (par. 31). This metaphysical Agnosticism is represented as perfectly familiar even to children and ignorant persons (par. 30),

[1] Sa*m*g*ñ*â and dharma correspond in many respects to the Vedântic nâmarûpe.

and if it was meant to be so, the endless repetition of the same process of reasoning may find its explanation.

That this extreme scepticism or Pyrrhonism is really the popular view of the present followers of the Mahâyâna Buddhism, was clearly stated at the Congress of Religions, held in Chicago, in September, 1893. A Deputy sent by the leading sects in Japan, submitted to the Congress an outline of the doctrines of the Mahâyâna Buddhists drawn up by Mr. S. Kuroda. This outline had been carefully examined and approved by scholars belonging to six of the Buddhist sects in Japan, and was published with authority at Tokyo in 1893. This is what he writes of the Mahâyâna metaphysics:

'The distinction between pure and impure is made by the mind; so are also all the changes in all things around us. All things that are produced by causes and conditions, are inevitably destined to extinction. There is nothing that has any reality; when conditions come things begin to appear, when conditions cease these things likewise cease to exist. Like the foam of the water, like the lightning flash, and like the floating, swiftly vanishing clouds they are only of momentary duration[1]. As all things have no constant nature of their own, so there is no actuality in pure and impure, rough and fine, large and small, far and near, knowable and unknowable, &c. On this account it is sometimes said that all things are nothing. The apparent phenomena around us are, however, produced by mental operations within us, and thus distinctions are established.

'These distinctions produced by mental operations are, however, caused by fallacious reasoning nurtured by the habits of making distinctions between ego and non-ego, good and bad, and by ignorance of the fact that things have no constant nature of their own and are without distinctions (when things thought of have no corresponding reality, such thinking is called fallacious. It may be compared to the action of the ignorant monkey that tries to catch the image of the moon upon water). Owing to this fallacious reasoning, a variety of phenomena constantly

[1] Cf. Vagrakkhedikâ, par. 32.

appear and disappear, good and bad actions are done, and the wanderings through the six ways or states of life are thus caused and maintained.

'All things are included under subject and object. The subject is an entity in which mental operations are awakened whenever there are objects, while the object consists of all things, visible and invisible, knowable and unknowable, &c. The subject is not something that occupies some space in the body alone, nor does the object exist outside of the subject. The innumerable phenomena of subject and object, of ego and non-ego, are originated by the influence of fallacious thinking, and consequently various principles, sciences, and theories are produced.

'To set forth the principle of "Vidyâmâtra" (all things are nothing but phenomena in mind), phenomena of mind are divided into two kinds:—"Gosshiki" (unknowable) and "Fumbetsujishiki" (knowable). They are also divided into eight kinds:—1. *K*akshur-vig*ñ*âna (mental operations depending on the eye), 2. *S*rotra-vig*ñ*âna (those depending on the ear), 3. Ghrâ*n*a-vig*ñ*âna (those depending on the olfactory organs), 4. *G*ihvâ-vig*ñ*âna (those depending on the taste), 5. Kâya-vig*ñ*âna (those depending on the organs of touch), 6. Manovig*ñ*âna (thinking operations), 7. Klish*t*a-mano-vig*ñ*âna (subtile and ceaseless operations), 8. Âlaya-vig*ñ*âna (all things come from and are contained in this operation; hence its name, meaning receptacle).

'According to the former division, the various phenomena which appear as subjects and objects are divided into two kinds:—the perceptible and knowable, the imperceptible and unknowable. The imperceptible and unknowable phenomena are called "Gosshiki," while the perceptible and knowable phenomena are called "Fumbetsujishiki." Now what are the imperceptible and unknowable phenomena? Through the influence of habitual delusions, boundless worlds, innumerable varieties of things spring up in the mind. This boundless universe and these subtile ideas are not perceptible and knowable; only Bodhisattvas believe, understand, and become perfectly convinced of these through the contemplation of "Vidyâmâtra;" hence they are called imperceptible and unknowable. What are the knowable and perceptible phenomena? Not knowing that these imperceptible and unknowable phenomena are the productions of their own minds, men from their habitual delusions invest them with an existence outside of mind, as perceptible mental phenomena, as things visible, audible, &c. These phenomena are called perceptible and knowable. Though there are thus two kinds, perceptible and imperceptible phenomena, they occur upon the same things, and are inseparably bound together even in the smallest particle. Their difference in appearance is caused only by differences both in mental phenomena, and in the depth of conviction. Those who know only the perceptible things without knowing the imperceptible, are called the unenlightened by Buddha. Of the eight mental operations, the eighth, Âlaya-vi*gñ*âna, has reference to the imperceptible, while the first six (sic) refer to the perceptible phenomena. All these, however, are delusive mental phenomena.

'In contradistinction to the fallacious phenomena, there is the true essence of mind. Underlying the phenomena of mind, there is an unchanging principle which we call the essence of mind; the fire caused by fagots dies when the fagots are gone, but the essence of fire is never destroyed. The essence of mind is the entity without ideas and without phenomena, and is always the same. It pervades all things, and is pure and unchanging. It is not untrue or changeable, so it is also called "Bhûtatathatâ" (permanent reality).

'The essence and the phenomena of mind are inseparable; and as the former is all-pervading and ever-existing, so the phenomena occur everywhere and continually, wherever suitable conditions accompany it. Thus the perceptible and imperceptible phenomena are manifestations of the essence of mind that, according to the number and nature of conditions, develop without restraint. All things in the universe, therefore, are mind itself. By this we do not mean that all things combine into a mental unity called mind, nor that all things are emanations from it, but that without changing their places or appearance, they are mind itself everywhere. Buddha saw this truth and said that the whole universe was his own. Hence it is clear that where the essence of mind is found, and the necessary conditions accompany it, the phenomena of mind never fail to appear. So the essence of mind is compared to water, and its phenomena to waves. The water is the essence, the waves are the phenomena; for water produces waves when a wind of sufficient strength blows over its surface. The waves, then, are the phenomena, the water is the essence; but both are one and the same in reality. Though there is a distinction between the essence and the phenomena of mind, yet they are nothing but one and the same substance, that is, mind. So we say that there exists nothing but mind. Though both the world of the pure and impure, and the generation of all things, are very wide and deep, yet they owe their existence to our mind. Men, however, do not know what their own minds are; they do not clearly see the true essence, and, adhering to their prejudices, they wander about between birth and death. They are like those who, possessing invaluable jewels, are, nevertheless, suffering from poverty. Heaven and hell are but waves in the great sea of the universe; Buddhas and demons are not different in their essence. Let us, therefore, abide in the true view and reach the true comprehension of the causality of all things.'

I hope that this will justify the view I have taken of the Vagra*kkh*edikâ, and that my translation, though it differs considerably from former translations, will be found to be nearest to the intentions of the author of this famous metaphysical treatise.

THE PRAGÑÂ-PÂRAMITÂ-HRIDAYA-SÛTRA.

(THE LARGER AND THE SMALLER TEXT.)

As the short text and translation of these Sûtras were published in the Anecdota Oxoniensia, 1884, with Introduction and full notes, I did not at first intend to include them in this volume. But as I was told that this Sûtra is really the most widely read Buddhist text in Japan, to be seen everywhere on shrines, temples and monasteries, more admired, it may be, than understood by the Buddhist laity, I yielded to the wishes of my Buddhist friends, and have reprinted it so as to make this volume a really complete repository of all the important sacred texts on which Buddhism takes its stand in Japan. We have heard so much of late of a Buddhist propaganda for the conversion of the East and the West to the doctrines of Buddha, that it may be useful to see what the doctrines of the historical Buddha have become in the Mahâyâna-school, more particularly in the monasteries of Japan.

THE AMITÂYUR-DHYÂNA-SÛTRA.

As I did not succeed in getting possession of a MS. of the original Sanskrit text of this Sûtra, I had given up all hope of being able to give in this volume a translation of all the classical texts used by the two leading sects of the Buddhists in Japan. Fortunately at the last moment a young Japanese scholar who is reading Sanskrit with me at Oxford, Mr. J. Takakusu, informed me that he possessed the Chinese translation of this Sûtra, and that he felt quite competent to translate it. It so happens that the style of this Sûtra is very simple, so that there is less fear of the Chinese translator, Kâlayasas, having misunderstood the Sanskrit original. But though I feel no doubt that this translation from the Chinese gives us on the whole a true idea of the Sanskrit original, I was so much disappointed at the contents of the Sûtra, that I hesitated for some time whether I ought to publish it in this volume.

What determined me at last to do so was partly the wish of my friends in Japan who expected a complete translation of their three sacred books, partly my own wish that nothing should be suppressed that might lead us to form a favourable or unfavourable, if only a correct judgment of Buddhism in its Mahâyâna dress, as professed by millions of people in China and Japan.

What gives to these Sûtras their highest interest in the eyes of Sanskrit scholars is their date, which can be determined with considerable certainty. Those who know how few certain dates there are in the history of Sanskrit literature will welcome these Mahâyâna Sûtras as a new sheet-anchor in the chronology of Sanskrit literature. We have as yet only three, the date of *K*andragupta (Sandrokyptos) as fixed by Greek historians, and serving to determine the dates of A*s*oka and his inscriptions in the third, and indirectly of Buddha in the fifth century. The second was supplied by Hiouen-thsang's travels in India, 629–645 A. D., and the third by I-tsing's travels in India in the years 671–690 A. D.

I was able to show in my lectures on 'India, what can it teach us?' delivered at Cambridge in 1882, that Hiouen-thsang, while in India, had been the pupil of *G*ayasena and Mitrasena, which supplied scholars with a fixed date for the literary activity of Gu*n*aprabha, Vasubandhu, and their contemporaries and immediate predecessors and successors. Still more important was the date which I-tsing supplied for Bhart*ri*hari and the literary period in which he moved. Bhart*ri*hari's death, fixed by I-tsing at 650 A. D., has served as a rallying-point for a number of literary men belonging to what I called the Renaissance of Sanskrit literature.

I pointed out at the same time that the period between the end of the Vedic literature, represented in its last efforts by the numerous Sûtra-works, and the beginning of the Renaissance in the fourth century A. D., would have to be filled to a great extent by Buddhist works. I hardly thought then that Mahâyâna texts like the Sukhâvatî-vyûha, which seemed to be of so secondary a character, would claim a foremost place in that period. But there can be little doubt that the first Chinese translation of it by Lokaraksha was made between the years 147–186 A. D.; the second by *K' Kh*ien between 223–253 A. D.; and the third and best by Saṅghavarman, an Indian *S*rama*n*a of Tibetan origin, in 252 A. D., whereas the first translation of a Sanskrit text into Chinese, that of the Sûtra in forty-two sections by Kâ*s*yapa Mâtaṅga, is ascribed to the year 67 A. D. I need hardly say that there are no Sanskrit texts the date of which can be fixed with so much certainty as those of the Sanskrit originals of the Chinese translations.

The doctrine of Amitâbha and his paradise Sukhâvatî seems to have acquired great popularity in China and afterwards in Japan. We need not wonder when we see how easy salvation was made by it, particularly according to the teaching of the Smaller Sukhâvatî-vyûha and the Amitâyur-dhyâna-sûtra.

The Buddhists who, as I have pointed out on several occasions, are the debtors of the Brâhmans in almost all their philosophical speculations, seem to me to have borrowed also their half-mythological conception of Sukhâvatî or the Land of Bliss from the same source. In the Vish*n*u and other Purâ*n*as, when the cities of the Lokapâla-gods are mentioned, in the different quarters of the sky, the city of Varu*n*a is placed in the West, and it is called Mukhyâ, the chief, or Sukhâ, the happy, or Nimlo*k*anî, the city of sunset. This Sukhâ is, I think, the prototype of Sukhâvatî[1]. Though it would be rash to conclude that therefore the Purâ*n*as, as we now possess them, because they mention the Land of Bliss or Sukhâ, must be older than our text of the Sukhâvatî, say 100 A. D., we may say that Paurâ*n*ik legends must certainly have existed at that early time, and this is a matter of some importance. I have not found any Brahmanic antecedents of Avalokite*s*vara,

[1] See also Ânandagiri on *S*aṅkara's commentary on the *Kh*ândogya-upanishad, III, 10, 4, ed. Calc. p. 172.

but the occurrence of his name in the Sukhâvatî-vyûha shows that he was known much earlier than is commonly supposed, that is about 100 A.D.

In Japan, where Buddhism was introduced by way of Corea in 552 A.D., we hear of the Sukhâvatî-vyûha for the first time in 640 A.D., when the emperor Jŏmei held a religious service at his palace to hear an exposition of the Sûtra on Sukhâvatî from the lips of Ye-yin, a *S*rama*n*a invited from China. Many works were composed in Japan as well as in China on Amitâbha and his Paradise, as may be seen from the Catalogue of the Chinese Tripi*t*aka, published by my friend and former pupil Bunyiu Nanjio in 1883 (Clarendon Press).

I have to thank Dr. Winternitz and Mr. Takakusu for their kind help in preparing the indices and reading the proof-sheets of this volume.

F. MAX MÜLLER.

OXFORD:
Jan. 26, 1894.

THE FOLLOWING LIST OF BUDDHIST TEXTS, TRANSLATED IN THE SACRED BOOKS OF THE EAST, MAY BE USEFUL TO STUDENTS IN CHINA AND JAPAN:

SANSKRIT TITLE.	CHINESE TITLE.	NUMBER IN THE CATALOGUE OF THE TRIPI*T*AKA[1].
I. Buddha*k*arita (-kâvya), 'Life of Buddha,' a poem, by A*s*vaghosha, of India. See Anecdota Oxoniensia, Aryan Series, vol. i, part vii, 1893. Translated by E. B. Cowell, S. B. E., vol. xlix.	佛所行讚經 Translated into Chinese by Dharmaraksha, A. D. 420. From Chinese into English by S. Beal, Fo-sho-hing-tsan-king, S. B. E., vol. xix.	No. 1351; another of the same name No. 680. To be found in the India Office and the Bodleian Library. The Nishi-Hongwanji (大學林) Library possesses a very good separate copy.
II. Larger Sukhâvatî (-vyûha), 'The Land of Bliss.' See Anecdota Oxoniensia, Aryan Series, vol. i, part ii, 1883. Translation by F. Max Müller, S. B. E., vol. xlix.	大無量壽經 Translated into Chinese by Saṅghavarman, A. D. 252. The chief of the three Sûtras of the Pure Land sects in China and Japan.	No. 27; for comparison of the five existing texts (out of twelve) see Anecdota Oxoniensia, vol. i, part ii, Introduction, vii seq.
III. Smaller Sukhâvatî (-vyûha). See Appendix to the (Larger) Sukhâvatî, Anecdota Oxoniensia, also Max Müller's Selected Essays, pp. 348–362. Translation by F. Max Müller, S. B. E., vol. xlix.	阿彌陀經 Translated by Kumâra*g*îva, A. D. 402. Into French, by Imaizumi and Yamata, Annales M. G., vol. ii, 1881.	No. 200; another of the same name by *K'Kh*ien, i. e. No. 26.
IV. Va*g*ra*kkh*edikâ, 'The Diamond-cutter.' See Anecdota Oxoniensia, Aryan Series, vol. i, part i, 1881. Translation by F. Max Müller, S. B. E., vol. xlix.	金剛般若波羅蜜經 Translated by Kumâra*g*îva, A.D. 384–417. From Chinese into English, by S. Beal, J. R. A. S., 1864–65, Art. I. Into French, by Mons. C. de Harlez, 1892. Translation by F. Max Müller, S. B. E., vol. xlix.	No. 10; another of the same name by Bodhiru*k*i, i. e. No. 11; and many others under different names.
V. Pra*g*ñâ-pâramitâ-h*ri*daya (two texts, shorter and fuller). See Anecdota Oxoniensia, Aryan Series, vol. i, part iii. Translation by F. Max Müller, S. B. E., vol. xlix.	般若心經 1. By Kumâra*g*îva (No. 19), A.D. 400. 2. By Hiouen-thsang (No. 20), A.D. 649. 3. By Sh'-hu, A.D. 980–1000 (No. 935). 4. By Pra*g*ña, A. D. 785–810. The most popular text, but not found in the India Office collection. Translation by F. Max Müller, S. B. E., vol. xlix.	
VI. Amitâyur-dhyâna-sûtra, 'Meditation on Buddha Amitâyus.' For this, see Anecdota Oxoniensia, Aryan Series, vol. i, part ii, Introduction, ix. Translated by J. Takakusu, S. B. E., vol. xlix.	觀無量壽經 Translated by Kâlaya*s*as, A. D. 424, only translation that exists.	No. 198; another lost.

[1] Published by Bunyiu Nanjio (Clarendon Press, 1883).

OTHER BUDDHIST TEXTS TRANSLATED IN THE SACRED BOOKS OF THE EAST:

SANSKRIT TITLE.	CHINESE TITLE.
Dhammapada, by F. Max Müller, vol. x. Sutta-Nipâta, by Fausböll.	法句經 Nos. 1321, 1353, 1365, 1439. Some parts of Max Müller's translation were retranslated into Japanese by S. Katô, Nanjio's pupil.
Buddhist Suttas, by Rhys Davids, vol. xi.	
1. Mahâparinibbâna Suttanta.	1. 大般湼槃經 Nos. 113, 114, 115, 120, 123, 118, 119, 552, though they do not agree.
2. Dhamma-*k*akka-ppavattana.	2. 轉法輪經 Nos. 657, 658.
3. Tevi*gg*a Suttanta.	3. 三明經
4. Âkaṅkeya Sutta.	4. 阿康祇經
5. *K*etokhila Sutta.	5. 心愚經
6. Mahâsudassana Suttanta.	6. 大善見經
7. Sabbâsava Sutta.	7. 總煩惱經
Vinaya Texts, by Rhys Davids and Oldenberg, vol. xiii.	
1. The Pâtimokkha.	1. 解脫戒本經 See No. 1108. Cf. also 1110 and 1160.
2. The Mahâvagga.	2. 大會部
Vinaya Texts, by Rhys Davids and Oldenberg, vol. xvii.	
1. The Mahâvagga.	1. 大會部
2. The *K*ullavagga.	2. 小會部
Vinaya Texts (*K*ullavagga), by Rhys Davids and Oldenberg, vol. xx.	小會部
Fo-sho-hing-tsan-king, 'Life of Buddha,' by S. Beal, vol. xix.	佛所行讚經 No. 1351, also 680. See above.
Saddharmapu*nd*arîka, 'Lotus of the True Law,' by Kern, vol. xxi.	妙法蓮華經 Nos. 134, 136, 138, 139. It is this book which gave birth to a Japanese sect called Nichiren—the number of temples being about 5,000. It is also read by many other sects. Into French by Julien; the same from Sanskrit by Burnouf.
Milinda Prasna, 'Questions of King Milinda.' From Pâli, by Rhys Davids, vols. xxxv and xxxvi.	那先比丘經 No. 1358. Very interesting dialogue between Greek King Menander and Bhikshu Nâgasena. The Pâli text is far more interesting and fuller than the Chinese.

SACRED BOOKS OF CHINA:

Sacred Books of China, Texts of Confucianism, by James Legge, vol. iii.	書經, 詩經, 孝經
Sacred Books of China, Texts of Confucianism, by James Legge, vol. xvi.	易經
Sacred Books of China, Texts of Confucianism, by James Legge, vols. xxvii and xxviii.	禮記
Sacred Books of China, Texts of Tâoism, by James Legge, vols. xxxix and xl. The doctrine of Tâo, its history, its influence, and its relation to the other two religions of China are fully treated in these volumes.	老子道德經, 莊子書, 太上感應篇, 清淨經, 陰符經, 玉樞經, 日用經, 林西仲評論莊子數篇, 薛道衡老子廟碑, and 蘇軾莊子祠堂記. Legge's translation practically includes all the evidences of 司馬遷, 列子, 韓非子, and 班固.

THE LARGER
SUKHÂVATÎ-VYÛHA.

THE LARGER SUKHÂVATÎ-VYÛHA.

DESCRIPTION OF SUKHÂVATÎ, THE LAND OF BLISS.

OM. Adoration to the Three Treasures! Om. Adoration to all the glorious Buddhas and Bodhisattvas! Adoration to all Buddhas, Bodhisattvas, Âryas, *S*râvakas, and Pratyekabuddhas, past, present, and to come, who dwell in the unlimited and endless Lokadhâtus of the ten quarters! Adoration to Amitâbha! Adoration to him whose soul is endowed with incomprehensible virtues!

Adoration to Amitâbha, to the *G*ina, to thee, O Muni!
I go to Sukhâvatî through thy compassion also;
To Sukhâvatî, with its groves, resplendent with gold,
The delightful, adorned with the sons of Sugata,—
I go to it, which is full of many jewels and treasures;
And the refuge of thee, the famous and wise.

---

§ 1. Thus it was heard by me. At one time the Bhagavat[1] dwelt in Râ*g*ag*ri*ha, on the mountain G*ri*dhrakû*t*a, with a large assembly of Bhikshus,

[1] The Blessed, i. e. Buddha *S*âkyamuni.

with thirty-two thousands of Bhikshus, all holy (arhat), free from frailties and cares, who had performed their religious duties, whose thoughts had been thoroughly freed through perfect knowledge, with inquiring thoughts, who had broken the fetters of existence, who had obtained their desires, who had conquered, who had achieved the highest self-restraint, whose thoughts and whose knowledge were unfettered, Mahânâgas (great heroes), possessed of the six kinds of knowledge, self-controlled, meditating on the eight kinds of salvation, possessed of the powers, wise in wisdom, elders, great disciples, viz. 1. Â*gñ*âtakau*nd*inya, 2. A*s*va*g*it, 3. Vâshpa, 4. Mahânâman, 5. Bhadra*g*it, 6. Ya*s*odeva, 7. Vimala, 8. Subâhu, 9. Pûr*n*a Maitrâya*n*îputra [1], 10. Uruvilvâ-kâ*s*yapa, 11. Nadî-kâ*s*yapa, 12. Gayâ-kâ*s*yapa, 13. Kumâra-kâ*s*yapa, 14. Mahâ-kâ*s*yapa, 15. *S*âriputra [2], 16. Mahâmaudgalyâyana, 17. Mahâkaush*th*ilya, 18. Mahâkaphila, 19. Mahâ*k*unda, 20. Aniruddha [3], 21. Nandika, 22. Kampila [4], 23. Subhûti, 24. Revata, 25. Khadirava*n*ika [5], 26. Vakula, 27. Svâgata, 28. Amoghara*g*a, 29. Pârâya*n*ika, 30. Patka, 31. *K*ullapatka, 32. Nanda, 33. Râhula, and 34. the blessed Ânanda,—with these and with other elders, and great disciples, who were wise in wisdom, with the exception of one person who had still to be advanced on the path of the disciples, viz. the blessed Ânanda;—and with many noble-minded Bodhisattvas, led by Maitreya.

[1] These two names refer to one and the same person.

[2] Nos. 15 and 16 are taken as one in the MSS. A B.

[3] Frequently called Anuruddha.

[4] Kimbila is mentioned with Anuruddha and Nandiya in the Mahâvagga X, 4, 2.

[5] See Pâ*n*. VIII, 4, 5.

§ 2. Then the blessed Ânanda, having risen from his seat, having put his cloak on one shoulder, and knelt on the earth with his right knee, making obeisance with folded hands in the direction of the Bhagavat, spoke thus to the Bhagavat: 'Thy organs of sense, O Bhagavat, are serene, the colour of thy skin is clear, the colour of thy face bright and yellowish. As an autumn cloud is pale, clear, bright and yellowish, thus the organs of sense of the Bhagavat are serene, the colour of his face is clear, the colour of his skin bright and yellowish. And as, O Bhagavat, a piece of gold coming from the *G*âmbû river, having been thrown into a furnace by a clever smith or by his apprentice, and well fashioned, when thrown on a pale cloth, looks extremely clear, bright and yellowish, thus the organs of sense of the Bhagavat are serene, the colour of his face is clear, and the colour of his skin bright and yellowish. Moreover, I do not know, O Bhagavat, that I have ever seen the organs of sense of the Tathâgata so serene, the colour of his face so clear, and the colour of his skin so bright and yellowish before now. This thought occurs to me, O Bhagavat: probably, the Tathâgata[1] dwells to-day in the state of a Buddha, probably the Tathâgata dwells to-day in the state of a *G*ina, in the state of omniscience, in the state of a Mahânâga; and he contemplates the holy and fully enlightened Tathâgatas of the past, future, and present.'

After these words, the Bhagavat thus spoke to the blessed Ânanda: 'Well said! well said! Ânanda. Did the gods suggest this matter to you? or the

[1] That is, Buddha *S*âkyamuni.

blessed Buddhas? Or do you know this through the philosophical knowledge which you possess?'

After these words the blessed Ânanda spoke thus to the Bhagavat: 'The gods, O Bhagavat, do not suggest this matter to me, nor the blessed Buddhas, but this thought occurs to me by my own philosophy alone, viz. that probably the Tathâgata dwells to-day in the state of a Buddha, probably the Tathâgata dwells to-day in the state of a *G*ina, in the state of omniscience, [in the state of a Mahânâga][1]; or he contemplates [the venerable Buddhas] of the past, future, and present.'

After these words the Bhagavat spoke thus to the blessed Ânanda: 'Well said! well said! Ânanda; excellent indeed is your question[2], good your philosophy, and beautiful your understanding! You, O Ânanda, have arrived for the benefit and happiness of many people, out of compassion for the world, for the sake of the great body of men, for the benefit and happiness of gods and men, as you think it right to ask the Tathâgata this matter[3]: Thus, indeed, Ânanda might pile up[4] intellectual knowledge under immeasurable and innumerable blessed, holy, and fully enlightened Tathâgatas, and yet the knowledge of the Tathâgata would not be exceeded thereby. And why? Because, O Ânanda, one who possesses the knowledge of a Tathâgata possesses an intellectual knowledge of causes that cannot be

[1] This is left out here. Mahânâga, technical term for greatness.

[2] Unmi*ñg*a, all the Chinese translators translate as 'question.'

[3] One expects tathâgatam etam artham.

[4] I have adopted the reading of B, in order to have a subject for upasa*m*haret, but A C P read ânanda.

exceeded[1]. If[2] the Tathâgata wished, O Ânanda, he could live for a whole kalpa (age) on one alms-gift, or for a hundred kalpas, or for a thousand kalpas, or for a hundred thousand kalpas, to a hundred thousand niyutas of ko*t*îs of kalpas[3], nay, he could live beyond, and yet the organs of nature of the Tathâgata would not perish, the colour of his face would not be altered, nor would the colour of his skin be injured. And why? Because, O Ânanda, the Tathâgata has so fully obtained the Pâramitâs[4] which arise from Samâdhi[5]. The appearance of fully enlightened Buddhas is very difficult to be obtained in this world, O Ânanda. As the appearance of Audumbara-flowers is very difficult to be obtained in this world; thus, O Ânanda, the appearance of Tathâgatas who desire welfare, wish for what is beneficial, are compassionate, and have arrived at the highest compassion, is very difficult to be obtained. But, O Ânanda, it is (owing to) the grace of the Tathâgata himself that you think that the Tathâgata should be asked this question, so that there may arise in this world beings who can be teachers of all the world, for the sake of noble-minded Bodhisattvas. Therefore, O Ânanda, listen, and take it well and rightly to heart! I shall tell you.'

---

[1] I am not satisfied with this translation, but I do not think that *g*ñâna, even in Buddhist Sanskrit, could ever be used as a masculine, and I therefore take tathâgata*g*ñâna*h* as a Bahuvrîhi.

[2] Read *g*ñâna*h*. Âkâṅkshan.

[3] Large numbers, constantly recurring in the text. Niyuta is explained as a million, ko*t*î as ten millions.

[4] The highest perfection.

[5] Deep meditation.

'Yes, O Bhagavat,' so did the blessed Ânanda answer the Bhagavat.

§ 3. The Bhagavat then spoke to Ânanda: 'At the time, O Ânanda, which was long ago in the past, in an innumerable and more than innumerable, enormous, immeasurable, and incomprehensible kalpa before now,—at that time, and at that moment, there arose in the world a holy and fully enlightened Tathâgata called 1. Dîpaṅkara. Following after Dîpaṅkara, O Ânanda, there was a Tathâgata 2. Pratâpavat, and after him, 3. Prabhâkara, 4. *K*andanagandha, 5. Sumerukalpa, 6. *K*andana, 7. Vimalânana, 8. Anupalipta, 9. Vimalaprabha, 10. Nâgâbhibhû, 11. Sûryodana, 12. Girirâ*g*aghosha, 13. Merukû*t*a, 14. Suvar*n*aprabha, 15. *G*yotishprabha, 16. Vai*d*ûryanirbhâsa, 17. Brahmaghosha, 18. *K*andâbhibhû, 19. Tûryaghosha, 20. Muktakusumapratima*n*-*d*itaprabha, 21. *S*rîkû*t*a, 22. Sâgaravarabuddhivikrî*d*itâbhi*gñ*a, 23. Varaprabha, 24. Mahâgandharâ*g*anirbhâsa, 25. Vyapagatakhilamalapratighosha, 26. *S*ûrakû*t*a, 27. Ra*n*a*ñg*aha, 28. Mahâgu*n*adharabuddhiprâptâbhi*gñ*a, 29. *K*andrasûrya*g*ihmîkara*n*a, 30. Uttaptavai*d*ûryanirbhâsa, 31. *K*ittadhârâbuddhisaṅkusumitâbhyudgata, 32. Pushpâvatîvanarâ*g*asaṅkusumitâbhi*gñ*a, 33. Pushpâkara, 34. Udaka*k*andra, 35. Avidyândhakâravidhva*m*sanakara, 36. Lokendra, 37. Mukta*kkh*atrapravâtasad*ri*s*a, 38. Tishya, 39. Dharmamativinanditarâ*g*a, 40. Si*m*hasâgarakû*t*avinanditarâ*g*a, 41. Sâgarameru*k*andra, 42. Brahmasvaranâdâbhinandita, 43. Kusumasambhava, 44. Prâptasena, 45. *K*andrabhânu, 46. Merukû*t*a, 47. *K*andraprabha, 48. Vimalanetra, 49. Girirâ*g*aghoshe*s*vara, 50. Kusumaprabha, 51. Kusumav*ri*sh*t*yabhiprakîr*n*a, 52. Ratna*k*andra, 53. Padmabimbyupa*s*obhita, 54.

*K*andanagandha, 55. Ratnâbhibhâsa, 56. Nimi, 57. Mahâvyûha, 58. Vyapagatakhiladosha, 59. Brahmaghosha, 60. Saptaratnâbhivr*i*sh*t*a, 61. Mahâ*g*u*n*adhara, 62. Mahâtamâlapatra*k*andanakardama, 63. Kusumâbhi*gñ*a, 64. A*gñ*ânavidhva*m*sana, 65. Kesarin, 66. Mukta*kkh*atra, 67. Suvar*n*agarbha, 68. Vai*d*ûryagarbha, 69. Mahâketu, 70. Dharmaketu, 71. Ratnaketu, 72. Ratna*s*rî, 73. Lokendra, 74. Narendra, 75. Kâru*n*ika, 76. Lokasundara, 77. Brahmaketu, 78. Dharmamati, 79. Si*m*ha, 80. Si*m*hamati. After Si*m*hamati, a holy and fully enlightened Tathâgata arose in the world, Loke*s*vararâ*g*a by name, perfect in knowledge and conduct, a Sugata, knowing the world, without a superior, charioteer of men whose passions have to be tamed, teacher of gods and men, a Buddha, a Bhagavat. And again during the time of the preaching of this holy and fully enlightened Tathâgata Loke*s*vararâ*g*a, O Ânanda, there was a Bhikshu, Dharmâkara by name, richly endowed with memory, with understanding, prudence, and wisdom,—richly endowed with vigour, and of noble character.

§ 4. 'Then, O Ânanda, that Bhikshu Dharmâkara, having risen from his seat, having put his cloak on one shoulder, and knelt on the earth with his right knee, stretching forth his folded hands to where the Bhagavat Tathâgata Loke*s*vararâ*g*a was, and, after worshipping the Bhagavat, he, at that very time, praised him in his presence with these Gâthâs[1]:

"O thou of immeasurable light, whose knowledge

[1] As the text of these Gâthâs is far from satisfactory, I have given a translation of the Chinese translation by Saṅghavarman at the end of my edition, Anecdota Oxoniensia, I, part ii, p. 79.

is endless and incomparable; not any other light can shine here (where thou art)! The rays of the moon of *S*iva and of the jewel of the sun, were not bright here in the whole world. (1)

"The form also is infinite in the best of beings[1]; thus also the voice of Buddha is of infinite sound; his virtue likewise, with meditation, knowledge[2], strength; like unto thee there is no one in this world. (2)

"The Law (dharma) is deep, wide, and subtle; the best of Buddhas is incomprehensible, like the ocean; therefore there is no further exaltation of the teacher; having left all faults, he is gone to the other shore[3]. (3)

"Then the best of Buddhas[4], of endless light, lights up all regions, he the king of kings; and I, having become Buddha, and a master of the Law, may I deliver mankind from old age and death! (4)

"And I, on the strength of generosity, equanimity, virtue, forbearance, power, meditation and absorption, undertake here the first and best duties, and shall become a Buddha, the saviour of all beings. (5)

"And I, seeking for the knowledge of the best of the Blessed Ones, shall always worship many hundred thousands of ko*t*is of Buddhas, endless like the sand of the Gaṅgâ, the incomparable lords. (6)

---

[1] It would be better to read sattvasâra as a vocative. See p. 22, l. 5.

[2] I have translated as if the reading were pra*g*ñâ, which would, however, have spoiled the metre.

[3] The text has -dhikâlam, and -bdhipâram is suggested as a conjecture only.

[4] I translate buddhavara.

"Whatever worlds there are, similar (in number) to the sand of the Gaṅgâ, and the endless countries which exist besides, there everywhere I shall send out light, because I have attained such power[1]. (7)

"My land is (to be) noble, the first and the best; the Bodhi-tree excellent in this world[2]. There is incomparable happiness arising from Nirvâ*n*a, and this also I shall explain as vain. (8)

"Beings[3] come hither from the ten quarters; having arrived there they quickly show my happiness. May Buddha there teach me the truth,—I form a desire full of true strength and vigour. (9)

"I, knowing the worlds of the ten quarters, possessed of absolute knowledge—they also always proclaim my thought! May I, gone to Avi*k*i hell, always abide there, but I shall never cease to practise the power of prayer! [i. e. May I remain in hell, if I cease to pray.]" (10)

§ 5. 'Then, O Ânanda, that Bhikshu Dharmâkara, having praised the Bhagavat, the Tathâgata Loke*s*vararâ*g*a, in his presence, with those Gâthâs, spoke thus: "O Bhagavat, I wish to know the highest perfect knowledge. Again and again I raise and incline my thoughts towards the highest perfect knowledge. May therefore the Bhagavat, as a teacher, thus teach me the Law, that I may quickly know the highest perfect knowledge. May I become in the world a Tathâgata, equal to the

[1] The text is obscure, Saṅghavarman translates: 'My light will shine over all these countries, thus my strength and power will be immeasurable.'

[2] According to the Chinese translation.

[3] Should it be sattvâ?

unequalled. And may the Bhagavat proclaim those signs by which I may comprehend the perfection of all good qualities of a Buddha country."

'After this, O Ânanda, the Bhagavat Lokesvararâga, the Tathâgata, thus spoke to that Bhikshu:

"Do you by yourself, O Bhikshu, know the perfection of all excellences and good qualities of a Buddha country?"

'He said: "O Bhagavat, I could not do this, but the Bhagavat alone. Explain the perfection of the excellences and all the good qualities of Buddha countries of the other Tathâgatas, after hearing which we may fulfil every one of their signs."

'Then, O Ânanda, the Tathâgata Lokesvararâga, holy and fully enlightened, knowing the good disposition of that Bhikshu, taught for a full koti of years the perfection of all the excellences and good qualities of Buddha countries belonging to eighty-one hundred thousand niyutas of kotis of Buddhas, together with the signs, indication, and description, desiring welfare, wishing for benefits, compassionate, full of compassion, so that there might never be an end of Buddha countries, having conceived great pity for all beings. The measure of life of that Tathâgata was full forty kalpas.

§ 6. 'Then, O Ânanda, that Bhikshu Dharmâkara, taking the perfections of all the excellences and good qualities of those Buddha countries, of those eighty-one hundred thousand niyutas of kotis of Buddhas, and concentrating them all on one Buddha country, worshipped with his head the feet of the Bhagavat Lokesvararâga, the Tathâgata, turned respectfully round him to the right, and walked away from the presence of this Bhagavat. And afterwards, for the space of five kalpas, he thus concentrated the perfection of all the excellences and good qualities of the Buddha countries, such as had never been known before in the ten quarters of the whole world, more excellent, and more perfect than any, and composed the most excellent prayer.

§ 7. 'Thus, O Ânanda, that Bhikshu concentrated in his mind a perfection of a Buddha country eighty-one times more immeasurable, noble, and excellent than the perfection of the eighty-one hundred thousand niyutas of ko*t*is of Buddha countries that had been told him by the Bhagavat Loke*s*vararâ*g*a, the Tathâgata. And then, proceeding to where the Tathâgata was, he worshipped the feet of the Bhagavat with his head, and said: "O Bhagavat, the perfection of all the excellences and good qualities of the Buddha countries has been concentrated by me."

'After this, O Ânanda, the Tathâgata Loke*s*vararâ*g*a thus spoke to the Bhikshu: "Preach then, O Bhikshu;—the Tathâgata allows it. Now is the proper time, O Bhikshu. Delight the assembly, produce joy, let the lion's voice be heard, so that now and hereafter, noble-minded Bodhisattvas, hearing it, may comprehend the different subjects (or occasions) of the prayers for the perfection of the good qualities of a Buddha country."

'Then, O Ânanda, that Bhikshu Dharmâkara thus spoke at that time to the Bhagavat: "May the Bhagavat thus listen to me, to what my own prayers are, and how, after I shall have obtained the highest perfect knowledge, my own Buddha country will then be endowed with all inconceivable excellences and good qualities.

§ 8. 1. "O Bhagavat, if in that Buddha country of mine there should be either hell, brute-creation [1], the realm of departed spirits, or the body of Asuras, then may I not obtain the highest perfect knowledge.

2. "O Bhagavat, if in that Buddha country of mine the beings who are born there should fall away (die), and fall into hell, the brute-creation, the realm of departed spirits, or into the body of Asuras, then may I not obtain the highest perfect knowledge.

3. "O Bhagavat, if in that Buddha country of mine the beings who are born there should not all be of one colour, viz. a golden colour, then may I not obtain the highest perfect knowledge.

4. "O Bhagavat, if in that Buddha country of mine there should be perceived any difference between gods and men, except when people count and tell, saying: 'These are gods and men, but only in ordinary and imperfect parlance,' then may I not obtain the highest perfect knowledge.

5. "O Bhagavat, if in that Buddha country of mine the beings who are born there should not be possessed of the highest Pâramitâs of miraculous power and self-control, so that they could at least in the shortest moment of one thought step over a hundred thousand niyutas of ko*t*is of Buddha countries, then may I not obtain the highest perfect knowledge.

6. "O Bhagavat, if in that Buddha country of mine the beings who are born there should not all be possessed of the recollection of their former births, so as at least to remember a hundred thousand

[1] Birth as an animal.

niyutas of ko*t*is of kalpas, then may I not obtain the highest perfect knowledge.

7. "O Bhagavat, if in that Buddha country of mine the beings who are born there should not all acquire the divine eye, so as at least to be able to see a hundred thousand niyutas of ko*t*is of worlds, then may I not obtain the highest perfect knowledge.

8. "O Bhagavat, if in that Buddha country of mine the beings who are born there should not all acquire the divine ear, so as at least to be able to hear at the same time the good Law from a hundred thousand niyutas of ko*t*is of Buddha countries, then may I not obtain the highest perfect knowledge.

9. "O Bhagavat, if in that Buddha country of mine the beings who are born there should not all be skilled in the knowledge of the thoughts of other people, so as at least to be able to know the deeds and thoughts of beings belonging to a hundred thousand niyutas of ko*t*is of Buddha countries, then may I not obtain the highest perfect knowledge.

10. "O Bhagavat, if in that Buddha country of mine the beings who are born there should form any idea of property, even with regard to their own body, then may I not obtain the highest perfect knowledge.

11. "O Bhagavat, if in that Buddha country of mine the beings who are born there should not all be firmly established, viz. in absolute truth, till they have reached Mahâparinirvâ*n*a, then may I not obtain the highest perfect knowledge.

12. "O Bhagavat, if any being should be able to count the pupils belonging to me after I have

obtained the highest perfect knowledge in that Buddha country of mine, even if all beings who are contained in those three millions of spheres of worlds[1], after having become Pratyekabuddhas[2], should be counting for a hundred thousand niyutas of ko*t*is of kalpas, then may I not obtain the highest perfect knowledge.

13. "O Bhagavat, if, after I have obtained the highest perfect knowledge, my light should be liable to be measured in this Buddha country of mine, even by the measure of a hundred thousand niyutas of ko*t*is of Buddha countries, then may I not obtain the highest perfect knowledge.

14. "O Bhagavat, if the measure of the life of the beings in that Buddha country of mine, after I have obtained the highest perfect knowledge, should be liable to be measured, excepting always by their own power of prayer, then may I not obtain the highest perfect knowledge.

15. "O Bhagavat, if the measure of my life after I have obtained Bodhi (Buddha knowledge) should be limited, even by numbering a hundred thousand niyutas of ko*t*is of kalpas, then may I not obtain the highest perfect knowledge.

16. "O Bhagavat, if, for the beings in this Buddha country of mine, after I have obtained Bodhi, even the name of sin should exist, then may I not obtain the highest perfect knowledge.

17. "O Bhagavat, if immeasurable and innumerable blessed Buddhas in immeasurable Buddha

---

[1] Trisâhasra mahâsâhasra.

[2] Men ready for Buddhaship, but who decline to preach or communicate their knowledge.

countries do not glorify my name, after I have obtained the Bodhi (knowledge); if they do not preach my fame and proclaim my praise, and utter it together, then may I not obtain the highest perfect knowledge.

18[1]. "O Bhagavat, if those beings who have directed their thought towards the highest perfect knowledge in other worlds, and who, after having heard my name, when I have obtained the Bodhi (knowledge), have meditated on me with serene thoughts; if at the moment of their death, after having approached them, surrounded by an assembly of Bhikshus, I should not stand before them, worshipped by them, that is, so that their thoughts should not be troubled, then may I not obtain the highest perfect knowledge.

19. "O Bhagavat, if those beings who in immeasurable and innumerable Buddha countries, after they have heard my name, when I shall have obtained Bodhi, should direct their thought to be born in that Buddha country of mine, and should for that purpose bring their stock of merit to maturity, if these should not be born in that Buddha country, even those who have only ten times repeated the thought (of that Buddha country), barring always those beings who have committed the (five) Ânantarya sins[2], and who have caused an obstruction and abuse of the good Law, then may I not obtain the highest perfect knowledge.

20. "O Bhagavat, if those beings who have been

[1] On Pra*n*idhânas 18 to 21, see note at the end.

[2] The five sins which bring immediate retribution. Cf. Childers, s. v.

born in that Buddha country of mine, after I have obtained Bodhi, should not all be bound to one birth only, before reaching the highest perfect knowledge, barring always the special prayers of those very noble-minded Bodhisattvas who have put on the whole armour (of the Law), who understand the welfare of all beings, who are devoted to all beings, who work for the attainment of Nirvâ*n*a of all beings, who wish to perform the duty of a Bodhisattva in all worlds, who wish to serve all Buddhas, and to bring beings, in number like grains of sand of the river Gaṅgâ, to the highest perfect knowledge, and who besides are turned towards the higher practice[1], and perfect in the practice of the Samantabhadra[2] discipline, then may I not obtain the highest perfect knowledge.

21. "O Bhagavat, if the Bodhisattvas who are born in that Buddha country of mine, after I have obtained Bodhi, should not all be able, after having gone to other Buddha countries, after their one morning-meal, to worship many hundreds of Buddhas, many thousands of Buddhas, many hundred thousands of Buddhas, many ko*t*is of Buddhas, &c., till up to many hundred thousand niyutas of ko*t*is of Buddhas, with objects which give every kind of pleasure, and this through the grace of the Buddha, then may I not obtain the highest perfect knowledge.

22. "O Bhagavat, if those Bodhisattvas in that Buddha country of mine, after I have obtained Bodhi, should wish their stock of merit to grow

---

[1] Possibly the same as the uttarimagga, Arhatship.

[2] See note at the end.

in the following shapes, viz. either in gold, in silver, in jewels, in pearls, in beryls, in shells, in stones, in corals, in crystal, in amber, in red pearls, in diamond, &c., or in any one of the other jewels; or in all kinds of perfumes, in flowers, in garlands, in ointment, in incense-powder, in cloaks, in umbrellas, in flags, in banners, or in lamps; or in all kinds of dancing, singing, and music;—and if such gifts should not appear for them, from being produced as soon as thought of, then may I not obtain the highest perfect knowledge.

23. "O Bhagavat, if those beings who are born in that Buddha country of mine, after I have obtained Bodhi, should not all recite the story of the Law which is accompanied by omniscience, then may I not obtain the highest perfect knowledge.

24. "O Bhagavat, if the Bodhisattvas in that Buddha country of mine, after I have obtained Bodhi, should think thus: May we, remaining in this world, honour, revere, esteem, and worship the blessed Buddhas in immeasurable and innumerable Buddha countries, viz. with cloaks, alms-bowls, beds, stools, refreshments, medicines, utensils, with flowers, incense, lamps, perfumes, garlands, ointment, powder, cloaks, umbrellas, flags, banners, with different kinds of dancing, singing, and music, and with showers of jewels,—and if the blessed Buddhas should not accept them, when they are produced as soon as thought of, viz. from compassion, then may I not obtain the highest perfect knowledge.

25. "O Bhagavat, if the Bodhisattvas who are born in that Buddha country of mine, after I have obtained Bodhi, should not all be in possession of strength of body as strong as the diamond (or thunderbolt?) of

Nârâya*n*a, then may I not obtain the highest perfect knowledge.

26. "O Bhagavat, if any being in that Buddha country of mine, after I have obtained Bodhi, should learn the limit of the beauty of (its) ornament, even if he be possessed of the divine eye, and should know (its) various beauty, saying: 'That Buddha country possesses so much beauty and so much magnificence,' then may I not obtain the highest perfect knowledge.

27. "O Bhagavat, if in that Buddha country of mine, after I have obtained Bodhi, a Bodhisattva possessed even of a very small stock of merit, should not perceive the Bodhi-tree of noble beauty, at least a hundred yo*g*anas in height, then may I not obtain the highest perfect knowledge.

28. "O Bhagavat, if in that Buddha country of mine, after I have obtained Bodhi, either teaching or learning should have to be made by any being, and they should not all be in possession of the perfect knowledge, then may I not obtain the highest perfect knowledge.

29. "O Bhagavat, if that Buddha country of mine, after I have obtained Bodhi, should not be so brilliant, that in it could be seen on all sides immeasurable, innumerable, inconceivable, incomparable, immense Buddha countries, as a round face is seen in a highly burnished round mirror, then may I not obtain the highest perfect knowledge.

30. "O Bhagavat, if in that Buddha country of mine, after I have obtained Bodhi, there should not be a hundred thousand of vases full of different sweet perfumes, made of all kinds of jewels, always smoking with incense, fit for the worship of Bodhi-

sattvas and Tathâgatas, rising into the sky beyond gods, men, and all things, then may I not obtain the highest perfect knowledge.

31. "O Bhagavat, if in that Buddha country of mine, after I have obtained Bodhi, there should not be showers of sweet jewel-flowers, always pouring down, and if there should not be sweet-sounding music-clouds, always playing, then may I not obtain the highest perfect knowledge.

32. "O Bhagavat, if the beings belonging to me, after I have obtained Bodhi, who are visible by their splendour, in immeasurable, innumerable, inconceivable, incomparable worlds, should not all be filled with pleasure, far beyond gods and men, then may I not obtain the highest perfect knowledge.

33. "O Bhagavat, if, after I have obtained Bodhi, the noble-minded Bodhisattvas in immeasurable, inconceivable, incomparable, immense Buddha countries on all sides, after having heard my name, should not be delivered from birth, through the merit arising from that hearing, and should not be strong in the knowledge of Dhâra*n*îs, until they have obtained the very throne of Bodhi, then may I not obtain the highest perfect knowledge.

34. "O Bhagavat, if, after I have obtained Bodhi, women in immeasurable, innumerable, inconceivable, incomparable, immense Buddha countries on all sides, after having heard my name, should allow carelessness to arise, should not turn their thoughts towards Bodhi, should, when they are free from birth, not despise their female nature; and if they, being born again, should assume a second female nature, then may I not obtain the highest perfect knowledge.

35. "O Bhagavat, if, after I have obtained Bodhi, the Bodhisattvas who in immeasurable, innumerable, inconceivable, incomparable, immense Buddha countries round about in the ten quarters having heard my name, and having fallen down, shall worship me with prostrate reverence, should not, when performing the duty of Bodhisattvas, be honoured by the world and by the gods, then may I not obtain the highest perfect knowledge.

36. "O Bhagavat, if, after I have obtained Bodhi, the work of dyeing, sewing, drying, washing of his cloaks should have to be performed by any Bodhisattva, and they should not perceive themselves, as quick as thought, covered by newly-produced excellent cloaks, granted to them by the Tathâgata, then may I not obtain the highest perfect knowledge.

37. "O Bhagavat, if the beings who are born at the same time in that Buddha country, after I have obtained Bodhi, should not obtain such happiness as that of the holy Bhikshu who is free from pain and has obtained the third meditation, then may I not obtain the highest perfect knowledge.

38. "O Bhagavat, if those Bodhisattvas who are born in that Buddha country of mine, after I have obtained Bodhi, should not produce from different jewel-trees such a mass of excellent ornaments in that Buddha country, as they should wish for, then may I not obtain the highest perfect knowledge.

39. "O Bhagavat, if the Bodhisattvas who are born in other Buddha countries, when they have heard my name, after I shall have obtained Bodhi, should suffer any diminution in the strength of their senses, then may I not obtain the highest perfect knowledge.

40. "O Bhagavat, if, after I have obtained Bodhi, the Bodhisattvas, from hearing my name in a place of a different Buddha country, should not obtain the Samâdhi (ecstacy) called Suvibhaktavatî, in which Samâdhi the Bodhisattvas will see immeasurable, innumerable, inconceivable, incomparable, immense, blessed Buddhas one moment after another; and if that Samâdhi of theirs should come to an end meanwhile, then may I not obtain the highest perfect knowledge.

41. "O Bhagavat, if, after I have obtained Bodhi, beings, having heard my name in Buddha countries different from this, should not, through the stock of merit which follows on that hearing, obtain birth in a noble family, till they arrive at Bodhi, then may I not obtain the highest perfect knowledge.

42. "O Bhagavat, if, after I have obtained Bodhi, the Bodhisattvas who live in other Buddha countries, after hearing my name, till they have reached Bodhi by the stock of merit which follows on that hearing, should not all obtain a combination of their stock of merit with the joy and gladness of their Bodhisattva life, then may I not obtain the highest perfect knowledge.

43. "O Bhagavat, if, after I have obtained Bodhi, the Bodhisattvas, as soon as they have heard my name, in other worlds, should not obtain the Samâdhi called Samantânugata, in which Bodhisattvas honour one moment after another immeasurable, innumerable, inconceivable, incomparable, immense, blessed Buddhas, and if that Samâdhi of theirs should come to an end before they have reached the throne of Bodhi, then may I not obtain the highest perfect knowledge.

44. "O Bhagavat, if the beings who are born in that Buddha country of mine, after I have obtained Bodhi, should not hear, as quick as thought, such a teaching of the Law as they wish to hear, then may I not obtain the highest perfect knowledge.

45. "O Bhagavat, if, after I have obtained Bodhi, the Bodhisattvas in this and other Buddha countries, as soon as they have heard my name, should ever turn back from the highest perfect knowledge, then may I not obtain the highest perfect knowledge.

46. "O Bhagavat, if, after I have obtained Bodhi, and have become a Buddha-teacher, the Bodhisattvas who hear my name in Buddha countries, and obtain the first, the second, and the third degrees of endurance, as soon as they have heard my name, should turn away again from Buddha, the Law, and the Church, then may I not obtain the highest perfect knowledge."

§ 9. 'And again, O Ânanda, when he had spoken such prayers, that Bhikshu Dharmâkara, at that time, through the grace of Buddha spoke these verses[1]:

1. "If, when I have obtained Bodhi, there should not be for me an excellent Pra*n*idhâna of such a character, then, O Prince, O Best of beings, may I not be endowed with the ten powers, incomparable, worthy of offerings[2].

2. "If there should not be for me such a country, endowed with many and various mighty and divine

---

[1] The translation of these verses, owing to the imperfect state of the text, is in many places tentative only.

[2] See verse 10.

endowments, I should gladly go to hell, suffering pain, and not be a King of treasures[1].

3. "If, when I have approached the Bodhi throne, my name should not quickly reach the ten quarters, the broad and many endless Buddha countries, may I not be a lord of the world, endowed with power.

4. "If indeed I should delight in the enjoyments of love, being deprived of zeal, understanding and prudence, even after having reached the incomparable and blessed Bodhi, may I not be a teacher in the world, endowed with power.

5. "The lord of vast light, incomparable and infinite, has illuminated all Buddha countries in all the quarters, he has quieted passions, all sins and errors, he has quieted the fire in the walk of hell.

6. "After making his broad eye lustrous, after driving away the darkness from all men, after removing all untimely misfortunes, he led hither those who dwell in Svarga (heaven) and who shine with endless light.

7. "The splendour of sun and moon does not shine in heaven, nor the fiery splendour of the maze of jewels of the gods; the Lord overcomes all splendour, he, the bright one, who has performed his former discipline.

8. "He is the best of men, the treasure of all who suffer; there is no one like him in all the quarters. Having completed a hundred thousand of good works, he, in his assembly, raised the lion-voice of Buddha.

9. "After having worshipped former self-existing *G*inas, after having performed immeasurable ko*t*is

---

[1] A Nâga king?

of vows and penances, he became in this, his best of spiritual existences, the best of beings, possessed of the full power of prayers.

10. "As the Bhagavat, the Lord, who is possessed of unlimited light of knowledge, knows the three kinds of knowledge in the world, may I also be worthy of equal offerings[1], the best of sages, the leader of men.

11. "If, O Lord, this my prayer succeeds, after I have obtained Bodhi, may this sphere of a thousand worlds tremble, and may a shower of flowers descend on the hosts of gods."

12. 'Then the earth trembled, flowers were showered down, hundreds of instruments resounded in the sky, powder of heavenly sweet sandal-wood was scattered, and there was a voice saying: "Thou wilt be a Buddha in the world."

§ 10. 'That Bhikshu Dharmâkara, the noble-minded Bodhisattva, O Ânanda, was possessed of this perfection of prayers. And a few Bodhisattvas only, O Ânanda, are possessed of such a perfection of prayers. There is on this earth an appearance of a few only of such prayers. Of a few, however, existence cannot be denied.

'Then again, O Ânanda, this Bhikshu Dharmâkara having recited these peculiar prayers before the Bhagavat Loke*s*vararâ*g*a, the Tathâgata, and before the world including gods, Mâra, and Brahman, and before people consisting of *S*rama*n*as and Brâhma*n*as with gods, men, and Asuras, was established in the attainment of the true promise. And proclaiming this purity of the Buddha country, this

[1] See verse 1.

greatness and excellency of the Buddha country, and performing the duty of a Bodhisattva, he never conceived the remotest thoughts of lust, malevolence, and cruelty, during a hundred thousand niyutas of ko*t*is of years, immeasurable, innumerable, inconceivable, incomparable, measureless, immense, inexpressible; and he never conceived the idea of lust, malevolence, and cruelty, nay, he never conceived the idea of form, sound, smell, taste, and touch. He was gentle, charming indeed, and compassionate; pleasant to live with, agreeable, amiable, content, of few wishes, satisfied, retired, not evil, not foolish, not suspicious, not crooked, not wicked, not deceitful, tender [1], kindly speaking, always zealous, docile in the searching after the pure Law. And for the good of all beings, he recited the great prayer, showing respect to friends, teachers, masters, the Church, the Law, and Buddha, always girded for the performance of the duties of the Bodhisattva, righteous, gentle, not deceitful, not flattering, virtuous, a leader for the sake of rousing others to perform all good laws, producing by his activity the ideas of emptiness, causelessness, and purposelessness, and he was well guarded in his speech. Then, performing the duties of a Bodhisattva, after having given up all speaking which, when spoken, serves to injure one's self or others or both, he employed only such speech as served the pleasure and benefit of himself, others, or both. And he was so wise that, when entering into capitals, kingdoms, countries, towns, cities, and villages, he was always perfectly restrained with regard to all objects of sense. Performing

[1] Sukhiloma, for sukhulâma or sukhumâla (i.e. sukumâra).

himself the duties of the Bodhisattva without interruption, he walked himself in the highest perfection (pâramitâ) of liberality, and he also roused others to walk in the same. And himself walking in the highest perfections of knowledge, meditation, strength, patience, and virtue, he roused others also to walk in the same. And he has collected so large a stock of merit that, wherever he is born, there arise for him many hundreds of thousands of niyutas of ko*t*îs of treasures from out the earth.

'By him, while he was thus performing the duties of a Bodhisattva, immeasurable and innumerable hundreds of thousands of niyutas of ko*t*îs of beings were established in perfect enlightenment, of whom it is not easy to know the limit by means of speech. So many immeasurable and innumerable holy Buddhas were honoured, revered, esteemed, and worshipped, and enabled to touch whatever causes pleasure, such as cloaks, alms-bowls, couches, seats, refreshments, medicines, and other furniture. It is not easy to know the limit by pointing it out in words, as to how many beings were established by him in the noble families of Brâhma*n*as, Kshatriyas, ministers, householders, and merchants. In the same manner they were established in the sovereignty of *G*ambûdvîpa (India), and they were established in the character of *K*akravartins, Lokapâlas, *S*akras, Suyâmas, Sutushitas, Sunirmitas, Va*s*avartins, Devarâ*g*as, and Mahâbrahmans. So many immeasurable and innumerable Buddhas were honoured, revered, esteemed, and worshipped, and requested to turn the wheel of the Law, of whom it is not easy to know the limit by means of words.

'And he collected such virtue, that out of his

mouth, while performing the duties of a Bodhisattva, during immeasurable, innumerable, inconceivable, incomparable, immense, measureless, inexpressible ko*t*is of kalpas, there breathed a sweet and more than heavenly smell of sandal-wood. From all the pores of his hair there arose the smell of lotus, and he was pleasing to everybody, gracious and beautiful, endowed with the fulness of the best bright colour[1]. As his body was adorned with all the good signs and marks, there arose from the pores (of his hair) and from the palms of his hands all sorts of precious ornaments in the shape of all kinds of cloaks and vestments, in the shape of all kinds of flowers, incense, scents, garlands, ointments, umbrellas, flags, and banners, and in the shape of all kinds of instrumental music. And there appeared also, streaming forth from the palms of his hands, all kinds of viands and drink, food, hard and soft, and sweetmeats, and all kinds of enjoyments and pleasures. Thus then that Bhikshu Dharmâkara, O Ânanda, had obtained the command of all necessaries, after performing the duties of a Bodhisattva.'

§ 11. After this, the blessed Ânanda thus spoke to the Bhagavat: 'O Bhagavat, has that Bhikshu Dharmâkara, the noble-minded Bodhisattva, after having obtained the highest perfect knowledge, passed away, having entered Nirvâ*n*a, or has he not yet been enlightened, or is he now living and enlightened, and does he dwell now, remain, support himself, and teach the Law?'

The Bhagavat said: 'Not indeed, O Ânanda, has

[1] See Lal. Vist. p. 337.

that Tathâgata passed away, nor has he not yet come, but the Tathâgata, the holy, after having obtained the highest perfect knowledge, dwells now, remains, supports himself, and teaches the Law, in the western quarter, in the Buddha country, distant from this world by a hundred thousand niyutas of ko*t*îs of Buddha countries, in the world which is called Sukhâvatî, being called Amitâbha, the Tathâgata, holy and fully enlightened. He is surrounded by innumerable Bodhisattvas, and worshipped by endless *S*râvakas, and in possession of the endless perfection of his Buddha country.

§ 12. 'And his light is immeasurable, so that it is not easy to know the limit of its measure, saying, he stands illuminating so many hundreds of Buddha countries, so many thousands of Buddha countries, so many hundred thousands of Buddha countries, so many ko*t*îs of Buddha countries, so many hundred ko*t*îs of Buddha countries, so many thousand ko*t*îs of Buddha countries, so many hundred thousands of ko*t*îs of Buddha countries, so many hundred thousands of niyutas of ko*t*îs of Buddha countries. But indeed, O Ânanda, to put it briefly, a hundred thousand niyutas of ko*t*îs of Buddha countries, equal to the sands of the river Gaṅgâ, are always lighted up in the eastern quarter, by the light of that Bhagavat Amitâbha. Thus on every side in the southern, western, northern quarter, in the zenith and nadir, in every one of these quarters, there are a hundred thousand niyutas of ko*t*îs of Buddha countries, like the sands of the river Gaṅgâ, always lighted up by the light of that Bhagavat Amitâbha, excepting the Buddhas, the Bhagavats, who, through the practice of their former prayers, have lighted up the world by their own light, which is a fathom in length, or by their light which is one, two, three, four, five, ten, twenty, thirty, forty, or fifty yo*g*anas in length, or a hundred or thousand or hundred thousand yo*g*anas in length, until their brightness reaches many hundred thousand niyutas of ko*t*is of yo*g*anas in length. There is not, O Ânanda, any case of likeness, by which the extent of the light of that Tathâgata Amitâbha could be understood. Hence, O Ânanda, for that reason that Tathâgata is called Amitâbha (possessed of infinite light), and he is called Amitaprabha (possessed of infinite splendour), Amitaprabhâsa (possessed of infinite brilliancy), Asamâptaprabha (whose light is never finished), Asaṅgataprabha (whose light is not conditioned), Prabhâ*s*ikhots*ri*sh*t*aprabha (whose light proceeds from flames of light), Sadivyama*n*iprabha (whose light is that of heavenly jewels), Apratihatara*s*mirâgaprabha (whose light has the colour of unimpeded rays), Râ*g*anîyaprabha (possessed of beautiful light), Prema*n*îyaprabha (possessed of lovely light), Pramodanîyaprabha (possessed of delightful light), Saṅgamanîyaprabha (possessed of attractive light), Uposha*n*îyaprabha (possessed of pleasant light), Anibandhanîyaprabha [1] (possessed of light that cannot be stopped), Ativîryaprabha (possessed of extremely powerful light), Atulyaprabha (possessed of incomparable light), Abhibhûyanarendrâbhûtrayendraprabha [2] (possessed of light greater than that of

[1] This seems better than nibandhanîyaprabha, as printed in the text.

[2] This reading is conjectural and the translation doubtful. Perhaps the text was anabhibhûyanarendrâbhûtrayendra-prabha*h*.

the lords of men, nay, the lords of the three worlds), *S*rântasa*ñk*ayendusûrya*g*ihmîkara*n*aprabha (possessed of light which bends the full moon and the sun), Abhibhûyalokapâla*s*akrabrahma*s*uddhâvâsamahe*s*varasarvadeva*g*ihmîkara*n*aprabha (possessed of light which bends all the conquered gods, Mahe*s*vara, the *S*uddhâvâsas, Brahman, *S*akra, and the Lokapâlas).

'This splendour of the Ârya (noble) is pure, great, producing bodily pleasure, happiness of mind, producing happiness, delight, and joy for men and not-men, Kinnaras, Mahoragas, Garu*d*as, Gandharvas, Yakshas, Nâgas, Asuras, and Devas; and producing the pleasure of beings of good disposition [1].

'And in this manner, O Ânanda, the Tathâgata [2] might speak for a whole kalpa on the work of the Tathâgata Amitâbha, beginning with his light, and yet he would not be able to reach the end of the virtues of that light of that Tathâgata, neither would there be any failure of the self-confidence in the Tathâgata himself. And why? Because, O Ânanda, both these things are immeasurable, innumerable, inconceivable, and endless, viz. first, the greatness of the excellence of the light of that Tathâgata Amitâbha, the Bhagavat, and secondly, the unsurpassed light of the knowledge possessed by the Tathâgata (by myself).

[1] Here the text adds (p. 30, l. 4), kalyaku*s*alamimi*n*evadviprâmodyakara*n*î. The whole sentence is unintelligible.

[2] This refers to the Bhagavat *S*âkyamuni himself, who speaks of himself as the Tathâgata. What he means to say is that the light of Amitâbha is infinite and that therefore even the Tathâgata could not finish the description of it. Yet this would not detract from the infinite power of the Tathâgata or diminish his vai*s*âradya because that power too is infinite.

§ 13. 'And, O Ânanda, the assembly of the hearers of that Tathâgata Amitâbha is immeasurable, so that it is not easy to learn its measure, so as to be able to say, there are so many ko*t*is of the hearers, so many hundreds, thousands, hundred-thousands, kaṅkaras, vimbaras, nayutas (niyutas?), ayutas, akshobhyas, vivâhas (masc.), srotas (?), o*g*as[1], so many periods, called immeasurable, innumerable, countless, incomparable, inconceivable. Now, for instance, O Ânanda, the Bhikshu Maudgalyâyana having obtained miraculous power, might, if he wished, count[2] in one day and night, how many kinds of stars there are in the universal world. Then, let there be a hundred thousand niyutas of ko*t*îs of such men, endowed with miraculous powers, and let them do nothing else but count the first company (only) of the hearers of the Tathâgata Amitâbha, during a hundred thousand niyutas of ko*t*îs of years, and yet by them thus counting even the hundredth part would not be counted, even the thousandth, even the hundred thousandth; nay, not even so far as the minutest part, or likeness, or approach[3] towards it would have been counted.

'Thus, for instance, O Ânanda, a man might throw out from the great ocean, which is not to be measured across by less than eighty-four thousand yo*g*anas, one single drop of water by the sharp end of hair, which is divided a hundred times. What do you think then, Ânanda,—which would be greater, one drop of water which has been thrown up by the

[1] All these are names of fanciful measures.

[2] Nâgare*n*a, 'with an instrument' or 'by some clever contrivance.'

[3] See Kern's translation of the Saddharmapu*nd*arîka, p. 317, note 2.

sharp pointed hair divided a hundred times, or the mass of water left in the great ocean?'

Ânanda said: 'Even a thousand yo*g*anas, O Bhagavat, would be a small portion of the great ocean, how much more then one drop of water thrown out by the sharp pointed hair divided a hundred times!'

Bhagavat said: 'As that one drop of water, exactly so large (so small in proportion) was the first company of the hearers. And let there be reckoning made by those Bhikshus, who are like Maudgalyâyana, counting for a hundred thousand niyutas of ko*t*îs of years, and yet, as to the mass of water left in the great ocean, it would even then have to be considered as not counted. How much more with regard to the second, third, and the rest of the companies of the hearers! Therefore the mass of hearers of the Bhagavat is endless and boundless, and receives the name of "immeasurable and innumerable."'

§ 14. 'And, O Ânanda, the length of the life of that Bhagavat Amitâbha, the Tathâgata, is immeasurable, so that it is not easy to know its length, so as to be able to say (that it comprises) so many hundreds of kalpas, so many thousands of kalpas, so many hundred thousands of kalpas, so many ko*t*îs of kalpas, so many hundreds of ko*t*îs of kalpas, so many thousands of ko*t*îs of kalpas, so many hundred thousands of ko*t*îs of kalpas, so many hundred thousands of niyutas of ko*t*îs of kalpas. Therefore, O Ânanda, the limit of the measure of the life of that Bhagavat is immeasurable indeed. Therefore that Tathâgata is called Amitâyus.

'And as, O Ânanda, the rule of making known the reckoning of kalpas exists here in this world, ten kalpas have passed now since Bhagavat Amitâyus, the Tathâgata, arose and awoke to the highest perfect knowledge.

§ 15. 'And, O Ânanda, the world called Sukhâvatî belonging to that Bhagavat Amitâbha is prosperous, rich, good to live in, fertile, lovely, and filled with many gods and men. Then, O Ânanda, in that world there are neither hells, nor the brute creation, nor the realm of departed spirits, nor bodies of Asuras, nor untimely births[1]. And there do not appear in this world such gems as are known in the world Sukhâvatî.

§ 16. 'Now, O Ânanda, that world Sukhâvatî is fragrant with several sweet-smelling scents, rich in manifold flowers and fruits, adorned with gem trees, and frequented by tribes of manifold sweet-voiced birds, which have been made by the Tathâgata (on purpose[2]). And, O Ânanda, those gem trees are of several colours, of many colours, and of many hundred thousand colours. There are gem trees there of golden-colour, and made of gold. There are those of silver-colour, and made of silver. There are those of beryl-colour, and made of beryl. There are those of crystal-colour, and made of crystal. There are those of coral-colour, and made of coral. There are those of red pearl-colour, and made of red pearls. There are those of diamond-colour, and made of diamonds.

'There are some trees of two gems, viz. gold and silver. There are some of three gems, viz. gold, silver, and beryl. There are some of four gems,

[1] These untimely births, i. e. being born out of time, when there are no Buddhas to listen to, are not mentioned in the first Pranidhâna; nor the jewels.

[2] Cf. the eighth paragraph in the Smaller Sukhâvatî-vyûha.

viz. gold, silver, beryl, and crystal. There are some of five gems, viz. gold, silver, beryl, crystal, and coral. There are some of six gems, viz. gold, silver, beryl, crystal, coral, and red pearls. There are some of seven gems, viz. gold, silver, beryl, crystal, coral, red pearls, and diamonds as the seventh.

'And there, O Ânanda, of the trees made of gold, the flowers, leaves, small branches, branches, trunks, and roots are made of gold, and the fruits are made of silver. Of trees made of silver, the flowers, leaves, small branches, branches, trunks, and roots are made of silver only, and the fruits are made of beryl. Of trees made of beryl, the flowers, leaves, small branches, branches, trunks, and roots are made of beryl, and the fruits are made of crystal. Of trees made of crystal, the flowers, leaves, small branches, branches, trunks, and roots are made of crystal only, and the fruits are made of coral. Of trees made of coral, the flowers, leaves, small branches, branches, trunks, and roots are made of coral only, and the fruits are made of red pearls. Of trees made of red pearls, the flowers, leaves, small branches, branches, trunks, and roots are made of red pearls only, and the fruits are made of diamonds. Of trees made of diamonds, the flowers, leaves, small branches, branches, trunks, and roots are made of diamonds only, and the fruits are made of gold.

'Of some trees, O Ânanda, the roots are made of gold, the trunks of silver, the branches of beryl, the small branches of crystal, the leaves of coral, the flowers of red pearls, and the fruits of diamonds. Of some trees, O Ânanda, the roots are made of silver, the trunks of beryl, the branches of crystal, the small branches of coral, the leaves of red pearls, the flowers of diamonds, and the fruits of gold. Of some trees, O Ânanda, the roots are made of beryl, the trunks of crystal, the branches of coral, the small branches of red pearls, the leaves of diamonds, the flowers of gold, and the fruits of silver. Of some trees, O Ânanda, the roots are made of crystal, the trunks of coral, the branches of red pearls, the small branches of diamonds, the leaves of gold, the flowers of silver, and the fruits of beryl. Of some trees, O Ânanda, the roots are made of coral, the trunks of red pearls, the branches of diamonds, the small branches of gold, the leaves of silver, the flowers of beryl, and the fruits of crystal. Of some trees, O Ânanda, the roots are made of red pearls, the trunks of diamonds, the branches of gold, the small branches of silver, the leaves of beryl, the flowers of crystal, and the fruits of coral. Of some trees, O Ânanda, the roots are made of diamonds, the trunks of gold, the branches of silver, the small branches of beryl, the leaves of crystal, the flowers of coral, and the fruits of red pearls. Of some trees, O Ânanda, the roots are made of the seven gems, the trunks of the seven gems, the branches of the seven gems, the small branches of the seven gems, the leaves of the seven gems, the flowers of the seven gems, and the fruits of the seven gems.

'And, O Ânanda, the roots, trunks, branches, small branches, leaves, flowers, and fruits of all those trees are pleasant to touch, and fragrant. And, when those (trees) are moved by the wind, a sweet and delightful sound proceeds from them, never tiring, and never disagreeable to hear. That Buddha country, O Ânanda, is always on every side surrounded by such trees made of the seven gems, by masses of Kadalî (banana) trees, and rows of palm-trees made of the seven gems, and entirely surrounded with golden nets, and wholly covered with lotus flowers, made of all kinds of gems.

'There are lotus flowers there, half a yo*g*ana in circumference. There are others, one yo*g*ana in circumference; and others, two, three, four, or five yo*g*anas in circumference; nay, there are some, as much as ten yo*g*anas in circumference. And from each gem-lotus there proceed thirty-six hundred thousand ko*t*is of rays of light. And from each ray of light there proceed thirty-six hundred thousand ko*t*is of Buddhas, with bodies of golden-colour, possessed of the thirty-two marks of great men, who go and teach the Law to beings in the immeasurable and innumerable worlds in the eastern quarter. Thus also in the southern, western, and northern quarters, above and below, in the cardinal and intermediate points, they go their way to the immeasurable and innumerable worlds and teach the Law to beings in the whole world.

§ 17. 'And again, O Ânanda, there are no black mountains anywhere in that Buddha country, nor anywhere jewel mountains, nor anywhere Sumerus, kings of mountains, nor anywhere *K*akravâ*d*as, great *K*akravâ*d*as, kings of mountains. And that Buddha country is level on every side, lovely, like the palm of the hand, with districts full of jewels and treasures of every kind.'

After this, the blessed Ânanda spoke thus to the Bhagavat: 'But in that case, O Bhagavat, where do the gods consisting of the companies of the four Mahârâ*g*as who dwell on the side of the Sumeru, and where do the Trâyastri*ms*a gods who dwell on the top of the Sumeru, find their place?'

Bhagavat said: 'What do you think, O Ânanda, where do these other beings find their place, who in this world dwell above the king of mountains, Sumeru, namely, the Yâmadevas, Tushitas, Nirmâ*n*aratis, Paranirmitava*s*avartins, Brahmakâyikas, Brahmapurohitas, Mahâbrahmans, as far as the Akanish*th*as?'

Ânanda replied: 'O Bhagavat, the result of works and the outcome of works are inconceivable' (i.e. I do not understand it).

Bhagavat said: 'Here, you see, the result of works and the outcome of works are inconceivable. But to the blessed Buddhas the position of Buddhas is not inconceivable, while to thee the holy and miraculous power of virtuous beings, whose stock of merit has become ripened, seems inconceivable.'

Ânanda said: 'I had no doubt on this, no difference of opinion, or hesitation; on the contrary, I ask only the Tathâgata about this matter in order to destroy the doubts, the differences of opinion, and the hesitations of future beings.'

Bhagavat said: 'All right, Ânanda, this is what you ought to do.

§ 18. 'In that world Sukhâvatî, O Ânanda, there flow different kinds of rivers; there are great rivers there, one yo*g*ana in breadth; there are rivers up to twenty, thirty, forty, fifty yo*g*anas in breadth, and up to twelve yo*g*anas in depth. All these rivers are delightful, carrying water of different sweet odour, carrying bunches of flowers adorned with various gems, resounding with sweet voices. [1] And, O Ânanda, there proceeds from an instrument which consists of hundred thousand ko*t*is of parts, which embodies heavenly music and is played by clever people, the same delightful sound which proceeds from those great rivers, the sound which is deep, unknown, incomprehensible, clear, pleasant to the ear, touching the heart, beloved, sweet, delightful, never tiring, never disagreeable, pleasant to hear, as if it always said, "Non-eternal, peaceful, unreal." Such a sound comes to be heard by these beings.

'And again, O Ânanda, the borders of those great rivers on both sides are filled with jewel trees of various scents, from which bunches of flowers, leaves, and branches of all kinds hang down. And if the beings, who are on the borders of those rivers, wish to enjoy sport full of heavenly delights, the water rises to the ankle only after they have stepped into the rivers, if they wish it to be so; or if they wish it, the water rises to their knees, to their hips, to their sides, and to their ears. And heavenly pleasures arise. Again, if the beings then wish the water to be cold, it is cold; if they wish it to be hot, it is hot; if they wish it to be hot and cold, it is hot and cold, according to their pleasure.

'And those great rivers flow along, full of water scented with the best perfumes of the Uragasâra sandal-wood, of Tagaras, Kâlânusârin (dark, fragrant sandal-wood) trees, Agarus, and heavenly Tamâla-pattras; covered with flowers of the white water-lilies, and heavenly Utpalas, Padmas, Kumudas, and Pu*nd*arîkas; full of delightful sounds of peacocks,

[1] Instead of tâsâm, it is better to read tathâ.

sparrows, ku*n*âlas, cuckoos, *s*ârikas, parrots, ducks, geese, herons, cranes, swans[1] and others; with small islands inhabited by flocks of birds, created by the Tathâgata; adorned with fields, full of metals; with fords on which it is easy to drink, free from mud, and covered with gold dust. And when these beings there desire, thinking what kind of wishes should be fulfilled for them, then exactly such wishes are fulfilled for them according to the Law[2].

'And, O Ânanda, the sound which rises from that water is delightful, and the whole Buddha country is aroused by it. And if beings, who stand on the borders of the river, wish that the sound should not come within their ear-shot, then it does not come within their ear-shot, even if they are possessed of the heavenly ear. And whatever sound a man wishes to hear, exactly that delightful sound he hears, as for instance, the sound "Buddha, Dharma (the Law), Saṅgha (the Church), the Pâramitâs (highest perfections), the Bhûmis (stages), the Balas (powers), Vai*s*âradya (perfections), Âve*n*ikabuddhadharma (freedom from attachment), Pratisa*m*vit (consciousness); *S*ûnyatâ (emptiness), Animitta (unconditioned), Apra*n*ihita (free from desire), Anabhisa*m*skâra (not made), A*g*âta (not born), Anutpâda (without origin), Abhâva (not being), and Nirodha (cessation); *S*ânta, pra*s*ânta, and upa*s*ânta (peace); Mahâmaitrî (great love), Mahâkaru*n*â (great pity), Mahâmuditâ (great rejoicing), and Mahopekshâ (great forgiveness); Anutpattikadharmakshânti

[1] The Tibetan translation puts these birds as follows: geese, swans, cranes, ducks, kâra*nd*avas, parrots, *grouse* (kokilas), ku*n*âlas, kalaviṅkas, and peacocks.

[2] Instead of Dharmâ*h*, the Tibetan translator seems to have read Dharmavat.

(resignation to consequences which have not yet arisen), and Abhishekabhûmipratilambha (attainment of the royal stage)."

'And having heard these sounds, everybody feels the highest delight and pleasure accompanied by retirement, passionlessness, quiet, cessation, law, and a stock of merit leading to the perfect knowledge.

'And, O Ânanda, there is nowhere in that Sukhâvatî world any sound of sin, obstacle, misfortune, distress, and destruction; there is nowhere any sound of pain, even the sound of perceiving what is neither pain nor pleasure is not there, O Ânanda, how much less the sound of pain. For that reason, O Ânanda, that world is called Sukhâvatî, shortly, but not in full. For, O Ânanda, the whole kalpa would come to an end, while the different causes of the pleasure of the world Sukhâvatî are being praised, and even then the end of those causes of happiness could not be reached.

§ 19. 'And again, O Ânanda, the beings, who have been and will be born in that world Sukhâvatî, will be endowed with such colour, strength, vigour, height and breadth, dominion, accumulation of virtue[1]; with such enjoyments of dress, ornaments, gardens, palaces, and pavilions; and such enjoyments of touch, taste, smell, and sound; in fact with all enjoyments and pleasures, exactly like the Paranirmitavasavartin gods.

'And again, O Ânanda, in that world Sukhâvatî, beings do not take food consisting of gross materials of gravy or molasses; but whatever food they desire, such food they perceive, as if it were taken,

[1] Here the text seems corrupt.

and become delighted in body and mind. Yet they need not put it into their mouth.

'And if, after they are satisfied, they wish different kinds of perfumes, then with these very heavenly kinds of perfumes the whole Buddha country is scented. And whosoever wishes to perceive there such perfume, every perfume of every scent of the Gandharvarâ*g*a does always reach his nose[1].

'And in the same manner, if they desire musical instruments, banners, flags, umbrellas, cloaks, powders, ointments, garlands, and scents, then the whole Buddha country shines with such things. If they desire cloaks of different colours and many hundred thousand colours, then with these very best cloaks the whole Buddha country shines. And the people feel themselves covered with them.

'And if they desire such ornaments, as for instance, head-ornaments, ear-ornaments, neck-ornaments, hand and foot ornaments, namely, diadems, earrings, bracelets, armlets, necklaces, chains, ear-jewels, seals, gold strings, girdles, gold nets[2], pearl nets, jewel nets, nets of bells made of gold and jewels, then they see that Buddha country shining with such ornaments adorned with many hundred thousand jewels, that are fastened to ornament-trees. And they perceive themselves to be adorned with these ornaments.

'And if they desire a palace, with colours and emblems of such and such height and width, adorned with hundred thousand gates made with different

[1] The Tibetan translator seems to have read: tatra yas ta*m* gandham âghrâtukâmo na bhavati, tasya sarva*s*o gandhasa*ñg*ñâ vâsanâ *k*a na samudâ*k*arati.

[2] The Tibetan translation suggests the reading svar*n*a*g*âlâ.

jewels, covered with different heavenly flowers[1], full of couches strewn with beautiful cushions, then exactly such a palace appears before them. And in these delightful palaces they dwell, play, sport, walk about, being honoured, and surrounded by seven times seven thousands of Apsarases.

§ 20. 'And in that world, there is no difference between gods and men, except when they are spoken of in ordinary and imperfect parlance as gods and men. And, O Ânanda, as a low man and impotent man, before the face of the mighty king, is neither bright, nor warm, nor brilliant, nor is he self-confident and radiant,—thus *S*akra, king of the Devas, if before the face of the Paranirmitava*s*avartin gods, is neither bright, nor warm, nor brilliant, namely, with regard to his gardens, palaces, dresses, ornaments, his dominion, his perfection, his miraculous power, or his supremacy, his comprehension of the Law, and his full enjoyment of the Law. And, O Ânanda, as the Paranirmitava*s*avartin gods are there, thus men must be considered in the world Sukhâvatî.

§ 21. 'And again, O Ânanda, in that world Sukhâvatî, when the time of forenoon has come, the winds are greatly agitated and blowing everywhere in the four quarters. And they shake and drive many beautiful, graceful, and many-coloured stalks of the gem trees, which are perfumed with sweet heavenly scents, so that many hundred beautiful flowers of delightful scent fall down on the great earth, which is all full of jewels. And with these flowers that

[1] Instead of pushpa the Tibetan translator seems to have read dûshya, 'garment.'

Buddha country is adorned on every side seven fathoms deep. As a clever man might spread out a flower-bed on the earth and make it even with both his hands, beautiful and charming, even thus with those flowers of various scents and colours that Buddha country is shining on every side seven fathoms deep. And these many flowers are soft, pleasant to touch, if one may use a comparison, like Kâ*k*ilindika (some kind of soft substance). If one puts one's foot on them, they sink down four inches; if one raises one's foot, they rise again four inches. When the time of the forenoon has gone again, those flowers vanish without leaving anything behind. Then that Buddha country is again clean, pleasant, beautiful, and without fading flowers. The winds blow again everywhere in the four quarters, and scatter down fresh flowers as before. And as it is in the forenoon, so it is at noon, at twilight, in the first, middle, and last watch of the night. And the beings, if touched by those winds which blow perfume with various scents, are as full of happiness as a Bhikshu (mendicant) who has obtained Nirvâ*n*a.

§ 22. 'And in that Buddha country, O Ânanda, no mention is ever made of the names of fire, sun, moon, planets, Nakshatras (constellations), and stars, or of blinding darkness. There is no mention even of day and night, except in the conversation of the Tathâgata. Nor is there any idea of predial property belonging to monasteries.

§ 23. 'And again, O Ânanda, in that world Sukhâvatî at the proper time clouds full of heavenly perfumed water pour down heavenly flowers of all colours; heavenly seven jewels, heavenly sandalwood-powder, and heavenly umbrellas, flags, and banners are poured down. And in the sky, the heavenly flowers of all colours, and heavenly canopies are held, likewise heavenly excellent umbrellas and all kinds of ornaments, heavenly musical instruments are played, and heavenly Apsarases dance.

§ 24. 'And again, O Ânanda, in that Buddha country whatever beings have been born, and are being born, and will be born, are always constant in absolute truth, till they have reached Nirvâ*n*a. And why is that? Because there is no room or mention there of the other two divisions (râ*s*is), such as beings not constant or constant in falsehood.

'On this wise, O Ânanda, that world is briefly called Sukhâvatî, not at full length. Even a kalpa, O Ânanda, would come to an end, while the causes of happiness which exist in that world Sukhâvatî are being praised, and yet it would be impossible to reach the end of them.'

§ 25. Then the Bhagavat at that time spoke the following verses[1]:

'Thus, O Ânanda, the world Sukhâvatî is endowed with immeasurable good qualities and excellences.

§ 26. 'And again, O Ânanda, in the ten quarters, and in each of them, in all the Buddha countries equal in number to the sand of the Gaṅgâ, the

[1] The text of these verses is so corrupt that I thought it best to follow the example of the five Chinese translators, all of whom leave them out. They only repeat what was said before, that people might go on for ever praising the excellences of Sukhâvatî, yet they would never reach the end of them, and that the merit of hearing even the name of Sukhâvatî is greater than all other blessings on earth. The best thing, however, is to have faith in *G*ina, and to drive away all doubt. The Tibetan translator gives a translation of seven verses, but his translation also seems as obscure as the original.

blessed Buddhas equal in number to the sand of the Gaṅgâ, glorify the name of the blessed Amitâbha, the Tathâgata, they preach his fame, they proclaim his glory, they extol his virtue. And why? Because all beings who hear the name of the blessed Amitâbha, and having heard it, raise their thought with joyful longing, even for once only, will not turn away again from the highest perfect knowledge.

§ 27. 'And before the eyes of those beings, O Ânanda, who again and again think of the Tathâgata reverently, and who make the great and unmeasured stock of good works grow, turning their thought towards Bodhi (knowledge), and who pray to be born in that world, Amitâbha, the Tathâgata, holy and fully enlightened, when the time of their death has approached, will appear, surrounded by many companies of Bhikshus and honoured by them. And then these beings, having seen the Bhagavat, their thoughts filled with joy, will, when they have died, be-born in that world of Sukhâvatî. And if, O Ânanda, any son or daughter of a good family should wish —What?—How then may I see that Tathâgata Amitâbha visibly, then he must raise his thought on to the highest perfect knowledge, he must direct his thought with perseverance and excessive desire towards that Buddha country, and direct the stock of his good works towards being born there.

§ 28. 'But before the eyes of those who do not care much about the Tathâgata Amitâbha, and who do not vigorously increase the great and unmeasured stock of their good works, the Tathâgata Amitâbha, holy and fully enlightened, will appear, at the time of death, with the company of Bhikshus, in breadth and height and form and beauty, very like (the former), and very like (the real Tathâgata), but only created by thought. And they, through their meditation that dwells on perceiving the sight of the Tathâgata, and with unfailing memory, will, when they have died, be born in the same Buddha country.

§ 29. 'And again, O Ânanda, those beings who meditate on the Tathâgata by giving him the ten thoughts, and who will direct their desire towards that Buddha country, and who will feel satisfaction when the profound doctrines are being preached, and who will not fall off, nor despair, nor fail, but will meditate on that Tathâgata, if it were by one thought only, and will direct their desire toward that Buddha country, they also will see the Tathâgata Amitâbha, while they are in a dream, they will be born in the world Sukhâvatî, and will never turn away from the highest perfect knowledge.

§ 30. 'And, O Ânanda, after thus seeing the cause and effect, the Tathâgatas of the ten quarters, in immeasurable and innumerable worlds, glorify the name of the Tathâgata Amitâbha, preach his fame, and proclaim his praise. And again, O Ânanda, in that Buddha country, Bodhisattvas equal in number to the sand of the Gaṅgâ approach, from the ten quarters, and in each quarter towards that Tathâgata Amitâbha, in order to see him, to bow before him, to worship him, to consult him, and likewise in order to see that company of Bodhisattvas, and the different kinds of perfection in the multitude of ornaments and excellences belonging to that Buddha country.'

§ 31. Then at that time, the Bhagavat, in order

to illustrate this matter in fuller measure, recited these verses[1]:

1. 'As there are Buddha countries equal to the sand of the river Gaṅgâ in the eastern quarter, whence all the Bodhisattvas come to worship the Buddha, the lord Amitâyu;

2. 'And they having taken many bunches of flowers of different colours, sweetly-scented and delightful, shower them down on the best leader of men, on Amitâyu, worshipped by gods and men;—

3. 'In the same manner there are as many Buddha countries in the southern, western, and northern quarters, whence they come with the Bodhisattvas to worship the Buddha, the lord Amitâyu.

4. 'And they having taken many handfulls of scents of different colours, sweetly-scented and delightful, shower them down on the best leader of men, on Amitâyu, worshipped by gods and men.

5. 'These many Bodhisattvas having worshipped and revered the feet of Amitaprabha, and having walked round him respectfully, speak thus: "Oh, the country of Buddha shines wonderfully!"

6. 'And they cover him again with handfulls of flowers, with thoughts jubilant, with incomparable joy, and proclaim their wish before that lord: "May our country also be such as this."

7. 'And what was thrown there as handfulls of flowers arose in the form of an umbrella extending over a hundred yoganas, and the beautiful country shines and is well adorned, and flowers cover the whole body of Buddha.

---

[1] In these verses there are again many doubtful passages which could be rendered tentatively only.

8. 'These Bodhisattvas having thus honoured him, how do they act?—Delighted they pronounce this speech: "Gains by those people are well gained, by whom the name of the best man has been heard.

9. '" By us also all the gain has been well gained, because we have come to this Buddha country. See this dream-like country[1] how beautiful it is, which was made by the teacher during a hundred thousand kalpas.

10. '"Look, the Buddha possessed of a mass of the best virtues shines, surrounded by Bodhisattvas. Endless is his splendour[2], and endless the light, and endless the life, and endless the assembly."

11. 'And the lord Amitâyu makes a smile of thirty-six niyutas of ko*t*is of rays, which rays having issued from the circle of his mouth light up the thousand ko*t*is of Buddha countries.

12. 'And all these rays having returned there again settle on the head of the lord; gods and men produce (perceive) the delight, because they have seen there this light of him.

13. 'There rises the Buddha-son, glorious, he indeed the mighty Avalokite*s*vara, and says: "What is the reason there, O Bhagavat, what is the cause, that thou smilest, O lord of the world?

14. '"Explain this, for thou knowest the sense, and art full of kind compassion, the deliverer of many living beings. All beings will be filled with joyful thoughts, when they have thus heard this excellent and delightful speech.

15. '"And the Bodhisattvas who have come from

---

[1] Maitra, 'love,' possibly 'kindness,' or was it kshetra?
[2] Amitâ asyâbhâ?

many worlds to Sukhâvatî in order to see the Buddha, having heard it and having perceived the great joy, will quickly inspect this country.

16. '"And beings, come to this noble country, (quickly) obtain miraculous power, divine eye and divine ear, they remember their former births, and know the highest wisdom."

17. 'Then Buddha Amitâyu preaches: "This prayer was mine formerly, so that beings having in any way whatever heard my name should for ever go to my country.

18. '"And this my excellent prayer has been fulfilled, and beings having quickly come here from many worlds into my presence, never return from here, not even for one birth."

19. 'If a Bodhisattva wishes here that his country should be such as this, and that he also should deliver many beings, through his name, through his preaching, and through his sight,

20. 'Let him quickly and with speed go to the world Sukhâvatî, and having gone near Amitaprabha, let him worship a thousand ko*t*îs of Buddhas.

21. 'Having worshipped many ko*t*îs of Buddhas, and having gone to many countries by means of their miraculous power, and having performed adoration in the presence of the Sugatas, they will go to Sukhâvatî with devotion[1].

§ 32. 'And again, O Ânanda, there is a Bodhi-tree belonging to Amitâyus, the Tathâgata, holy and fully enlightened. That Bodhi-tree is ten hun-

[1] The Tibetan translation has 'in the morning,' as if the text had been pûrvabhakta.

dred yo*g*anas in height, having petals, leaves, and branches spread over eight hundred yo*g*anas, having a circumference near the base of the root of five hundred yo*g*anas, always in leaf, always in flower, always in fruit, of different colours, of many hundred thousand colours, of different leaves, of different flowers, of different fruits, adorned with many beautiful ornaments, shining with precious jewels, bright like the moon, beautified with precious jewels (such as are) fastened on *S*akra's head, strewn with *K*intâma*n*i[1] jewels, well adorned with the best jewels of the sea, more than heavenly, hung with golden strings, adorned with hundreds of gold chains, jewel-garlands, necklaces, bracelets, strings of red pearls and blue pearls, lion twists (Si*m*halatâ), girdles, bunches, strings of jewels, and all kinds of jewels, covered with nets of bells, nets of all kinds of jewels, nets of pearls, and nets of gold, adorned with the emblems of the dolphin, the Svastika, the Nandyâvarta, and the moon, adorned with nets of jewels and of bells, and with ornaments of gold and of all kinds of jewels, in fact adorned according to the desires of beings whatever their wishes may be.

'And again, O Ânanda, the sound and noise of that Bodhi-tree, when it is moved by the wind, reaches immeasurable worlds. And, O Ânanda, for those beings whose hearing that Bodhi-tree reaches, no disease of the ear is to be feared until they reach Bodhi (highest knowledge). And for those immeasurable, innumerable, inconceivable, incomparable, measureless, immense, and inexpressible beings, whose sight that Bodhi-tree reaches, no disease of the eye

[1] Jewels yielding every wish.

is to be feared until they reach Bodhi. And again, O Ânanda, for those beings who smell the scent of that Bodhi-tree, no disease of the nose is to be feared until they reach Bodhi. For those beings who taste the fruits of that Bodhi-tree, no disease of the tongue is to be feared until they reach Bodhi. For those beings who are lighted up by the light of that Bodhi-tree, no disease of the body is to be feared until they reach Bodhi. And again, O Ânanda, for those beings who meditate on that Bodhi-tree according to the Law, henceforward until they reach the Bodhi, no perplexity of their thought is to be feared. And all those beings, through the seeing of that Bodhi-tree, never turn away, namely, from the highest perfect knowledge. And they obtain three kinds of kshânti or resignation, namely, Ghoshânugâ, Anulomikî (resignation to natural consequences), and Anutpattika-dharma-kshânti (resignation to consequences which have not yet arisen), through the power of the former prayers of that same Tathâgata Amitâyus, through the service rendered by them to the former *G*inas, and through the performance of the former prayers, to be well accomplished, and to be well conceived, without failure or without flaw.

§ 33. 'And again, O Ânanda, those Bodhisattvas who have been born, are being born, or will be born there, are all bound to one birth only[1], and will thence indeed obtain the highest perfect knowledge; barring always the power of prayers, as in the case of those Bodhisattvas who are preaching with the voice of lions, who are girded with the noble armour

[1] Their present birth.

(of the Law), and who are devoted to the work of helping all people to attain Parinirvâ*n*a.—

§ 34. 'And again, O Ânanda, in that Buddha country, those who are *S*râvakas are possessed of the light of a fathom, and those who are Bodhisattvas are possessed of the light of a hundred thousand ko*t*is of yo*g*anas; barring always the two Bodhisattvas, by whose light that world is everywhere shining with eternal splendour.'

Then the blessed Ânanda said this to the Bhagavat: 'What are the names, O Bhagavat, of those two noble-minded Bodhisattvas?'

The Bhagavat said: 'One of them, O Ânanda, is the noble-minded Bodhisattva Avalokite*s*vara, and the second is Mahâsthâmaprâpta by name. And, O Ânanda, these two were born there, having left this Buddha country here[1].

§ 35. 'And, O Ânanda, those Bodhisattvas who have been born in that Buddha country are all endowed with the thirty-two marks of a great man, possessed of perfect members, skilled in meditation and wisdom, clever in all kinds of wisdom, having sharp organs, having well-restrained organs, having organs of sense capable of thorough knowledge, not mean, possessed of the five kinds of strength, of patience under censure, and of endless and boundless good qualities.

---

[1] Saṅghavarman translates this passage: 'These two Bodhisattvas practised the discipline of Bodhisattva in this country, and after death they were miraculously born in that Buddha country.' Bodhiru*k*i translates: 'O Ânanda, these two Bodhisattvas went to be born in that country from the world Sahâ, when they had exhausted the measure of their life (here).' The world Sahâ belongs to the Buddha *S*âkyamuni.

§ 36. 'And again, O Ânanda, all those Bodhisattvas who have been born in that Buddha country are not deprived of the sight of Buddha, nor liable to fall down (to the evil states), until they reach the Bodhi. Henceforward they all will never be forgetful of their former births[1]; barring always those who are devoted to their former place, during the disturbances of the kalpas, and while the five kinds of corruption prevail, when there is the appearance of blessed Buddhas in the world, as for instance, that of me at present.

§ 37. 'And again, O Ânanda, all the Bodhisattvas who have been born in that Buddha country, having gone during one morning meal to the other world, worship many hundred thousand niyutas of ko*t*îs of Buddhas, as many as they like, through the favour of Buddha. They consider in many ways that they should worship (Buddhas) with such and such flowers, incense, lamps, scents, garlands, ointments, powder, cloaks, umbrellas, flags, banners, ensigns, music, concerts, and musical instruments; and, as soon as they have considered this, there arise also on their hands exactly such materials for every kind of worship. And while performing worship for those blessed Buddhas with those materials, beginning with flowers and ending with musical instruments, they lay up for themselves much immeasurable and innumerable merit. Again, if they wish that such handfulls of flowers should be produced on their hands, then such handfulls of heavenly flowers, of different colours, of many colours, of different scents, are produced on their hands as soon as thought of. They shower

[1] 'Na' must be left out, or we must read na*g*âtva*g*âtismarâ.

again and again such handfulls of flowers upon those blessed Buddhas. And the very smallest handfull of flowers, being thrown on high, appears above in the sky as an umbrella of flowers ten yo*g*anas in circumference. And when the second has been thrown after it, the first does not fall down on the earth. There are handfulls of flowers there, which having been thrown up, appear in the sky as umbrellas of flowers twenty yo*g*anas in circumference. There appear in the sky some flower-umbrellas, thirty, forty, or fifty yo*g*anas in circumference, as far as a hundred thousand yo*g*anas in circumference. Those (Bodhisattvas) there who perceive the noble pleasure and joy, and obtain the noble strength of thought, having caused a great and immeasurable and innumerable stock of good works to ripen, and having worshipped many hundred thousand niyutas of ko*t*îs of Buddhas, turn again to the world Sukhâvatî in one morning, through the favour of practising the former prayers of the same Tathâgata Amitâyus, owing to the hearing of the Law formerly given, owing to the stock of good works produced under former *G*inas, owing to the perfect completion in the success of former prayers, owing to the well-ordered state of mind[1].

§ 38. 'And again, O Ânanda, all those beings who have been born in that Buddha country recite the story of the Law, which is accompanied by omniscience[2]. And for the beings in that Buddha

[1] The text of this passage is very imperfect in all the MSS. Comparing the sentence with the last sentence of Chapter XXXII, it might seem possible to read paripûr*n*ânûnatayâ, or paripûryatayânûnatayâ, for paripûryâtmabhûtayâ. On suvibhakta, see Childers, s. v. vibha*g*ati.

[2] See the twenty-third Pra*n*idhâna.

country there exists no idea of property whatever[1]. And all those going and walking through that Buddha country feel neither pleasure nor pain; stepping forward they have no desire, and with desire they do not step forward. They give no thought to any beings. And again, O Ânanda, for those beings who have been born in that world Sukhâvatî, there is no idea of others, no idea of self, no idea of inequality, no strife, no dispute, no opposition. Full of equanimity, of benevolent thought, of tender thought, of affectionate thought, of useful thought, of serene thought, of firm thought, of unbiassed thought, of undisturbed thought, of unagitated thought, of thought (fixed on) the practice of discipline and transcendent wisdom, having entered on knowledge which is a firm support to all thoughts, equal to the ocean in wisdom, equal to the mountain Meru in knowledge, rich in many good qualities, delighting in the music of the Bodhyaṅgas[2], devoted to the music of Buddha, they discard the eye of flesh, and assume the heavenly eye. And having approached the eye of wisdom, having reached the eye of the Law, producing the eye of Buddha, showing it, lighting it, and fully exhibiting it, they attain perfect wisdom. And being bent on the equilibrium of the three elements[3], having subdued and calmed their thoughts, endowed with a perception of the causes of all

[1] See the tenth Pra*n*idhâna.

[2] 'Requisites for attaining the supreme knowledge of a Buddha.'—Childers, Pâli Dictionary, p. 93 b.

[3] Probably the three dhâtus, Kâmadhâtu, Rûpadhâtu, and Arûpadhâtu; see Childers, s. v. dhâtu.

things, clever in explanation of causes, endowed with the power of explaining the Law (or things such as they really are), clever in taking and refusing, clever in leading and not leading, clever in resting[1], they, being regardless of worldly stories, derive true pleasures from stories transcending the world. They are clever in examining all things, familiar with the knowledge of the cessation of the working of all things, perceiving even what cannot be seen, caring for nothing, attached to nothing, without cares, without pain, free without clinging to anything, free from impurity[2], of blameless behaviour, not clinging to anything, intent on the deep or profound laws, they do not sink, elevated to the entrance into the knowledge of Buddha difficult to comprehend, having obtained the path of one vehicle[3], free from doubt, beyond the reach of questionings, knowing the thoughts of others, free from self-confidence. Being elevated in knowledge, they are like the Sumeru; being imperturbable in thought, they are like the ocean; they surpass the light of the sun and moon, by the light of wisdom, and by the whiteness, brilliancy, purity, and beauty of their knowledge; by their light and splendour, they are like the colour of molten gold; by their patiently bearing the good and evil deeds of all beings, they are like the earth; by their cleaning and carrying off the taint[4] of all sins, they are

---

[1] The text may originally have been sthânâsthânakus*a*lâ*h*.

[2] The next words aparyasthâyina*h* and abhig*ñ*âsvamûlasthâyina*h* seem to have a technical meaning, but neither the Tibetan nor the Chinese translators give an intelligible rendering.

[3] Saṅghavarman translates 'one vehicle.'

[4] The Tibetan translation presupposes mala instead of mûla.

like water; by their burning the evil of pride[1] in anything, they are like the king of fire; by not clinging to anything, they are like the wind; by pervading all things and yet not caring for anything, they are like the ether; by not being tainted by the whole world, they are like lotuses; by their shouting forth the Law, they are like the great cloud at the rainy season; by showering down the whole ocean of the Law, they are like the great rain; by overpowering great troops, they are like bulls; by the highest restraint of their thoughts, they are like great elephants; by being well trained, they are like noble horses; by their fearlessness, confidence, and heroism, they are like the lion, the king of beasts; by affording protection to all beings, they are like the Nyagrodha (fig-tree), the king of trees; by not being shaken by any calumniators, they are like the (Sumeru), the king of mountains; by their feeling of unlimited love, they are like the sky; by their precedence, owing to their command of the Law, and their stock of all merit, they are like the great Brahman; by their not dwelling in what they have accumulated, they are like birds; by their scattering all calumniators, they are like Garu*d*a, king of birds; by their not being averse to our obtaining difficult things, they are like the Udumbara flowers; calm like elephants[2], because their senses are neither crooked nor shaken; clever in decision, full of the sweet flavour of patience; without envy, because they do not hanker after the happiness of others; wise, because in their search after the Law, never

[1] Mâna, 'pride,' is one of the Kle*s*as.

[2] The Tibetan translator seems to have read sagaravat, instead of nâgavat.

tired of discussions on the Law; like the precious beryl, through their value; (like) jewel-mines [1], by their sacred knowledge; sweet-sounding by the noise of the great drum of the Law, striking the great kettledrum of the Law, blowing the great trumpet-shell of the Law, raising the great banner of the Law, lighting the torch of the Law, looking for wisdom, not foolish, faultless, passionless, pure, refined, not greedy, fond of distributing, generous, open-handed, fond of distributing gifts, not stingy in giving instruction and food, not attached, without fear, without desires, wise, patient, energetic, bashful, orderly, fearless [2], full of knowledge, happy, pleasant to live with, obliging, enlightening the world [3], free from sorrow, free from taint, having left off the winking of the eye, possessing lightly acquired knowledge, strong in reasoning, strong in prayer, not crooked, not perverse; then, having accumulated a hundred thousand niyutas of ko*t*is of lakshas [4] of virtue, delivered from the thorns of pride, free from illusion, hatred, and passion; pure, devoted to what is pure, famous by the *G*ina-power, learned in the world, elevated by their purified knowledge, sons of the *G*ina, endowed with the vigour of thought, heroes, firm, unselfish [5], free from faults, unequalled, free from anger, collected, noble, heroes, bashful, energetic, possessed of memory, understanding, and prudence;

---

[1] The Tibetan translation seems to have read ratnâkarasad*r*i*s*â*h*.

[2] If the same as nirgahana.

[3] The next words are unintelligible in their present form.

[4] The Tibetan translation has Buddha for laksha.

[5] Asamâ*h* in the Tibetan translation.

sending forth the weapons of knowledge, possessed of purity, shining, free from faults and taints, endowed with memory, resting on serene knowledge. And such, O Ânanda, are the beings in that Buddha country, stated briefly. But if the Tathâgatas should describe them fully, even in a length of life that should last for a hundred thousand niyutas of ko*t*is of kalpas, yet the end of the virtues of those good people would not be reached, and yet there would be no failure of the self-confidence of the Tathâgata. And why? Because, O Ânanda, both are indeed inconceivable and incomparable, viz. first, the virtues of those Bodhisattvas, and secondly, the unsurpassed light of knowledge of the Tathâgata[1].

§ 39. 'And now, O Ânanda, stand up, facing westward, and having taken a handful of flowers, fall down. This is the quarter where that Bhagavat Amitâbha, the Tathâgata, holy and fully enlightened, dwells, remains, supports himself, and teaches the Law, whose spotless and pure name, famed in every quarter of the whole world with its ten quarters, the blessed Buddhas, equal to (the grains of) the sand of the river Gaṅgâ, speaking and answering again and again without stopping, extol, praise, and eulogize.'

After this, the blessed Ânanda said this to the Bhagavat: 'I wish, O Bhagavat, to see that Amitâbha, Amitaprabha, Amitâyus, the Tathâgata, holy and fully enlightened, and those noble-minded Bodhisattvas, who are possessed of a stock of merit amassed under many hundred thousand niyutas of ko*t*is of Buddhas.'

---

[1] For these passages, see the end of Chapter XII.

At that moment this speech was spoken by the blessed Ânanda, and immediately that Amitâbha, the Tathâgata, holy and fully enlightened, let such a ray of light go out of the palm of his own hand, that even the most distant Buddha country was shining with the great splendour. And again at that time, whatever black mountains, or jewel-mountains, or Merus, great Merus, Mu*k*ilindas, great Mu*k*ilindas, *K*akravâ*d*as, great *K*akravâ*d*as, or erections, or pillars, trees, woods, gardens, palaces, belonging to the gods and men, exist everywhere in hundred thousand ko*t*is of Buddha countries; all these were pervaded and overcome by the light of that Tathâgata. And as a man, followed by another at a distance of a fathom only, would see the other man, when the sun has risen, exactly in the same manner the Bhikshus, Bhikshu*n*is, Upâsakas (laymen), Upâsikâs (lay-women), gods, Nâgas, Yakshas, Râkshasas, Gandharvas, Asuras, Garu*d*as, Kinnaras, Mahoragas, men and not-men, in this Buddha country, saw at that time that Amitâbha, the Tathâgata, holy and fully enlightened, like the Sumeru, the king of mountains, elevated above all countries, surpassing all quarters, shining, warming, glittering, blazing; and they saw that great mass of Bodhisattvas, and that company of Bhikshus, viz. by the grace of Buddha, from the pureness of that light. And as this great earth might be, when all covered with water, so that no trees, no mountains, no islands, no grasses, bushes, herbs, large trees, no rivers, chasms, water-falls, would be seen, but only the one great earth which had all become an ocean, in exactly the same manner there is neither mark nor sign whatever to be seen in that Buddha country, except *S*râvakas, spreading their light over a fathom, and those Bodhisattvas, spreading their light over a hundred thousand ko*t*îs of yo*g*anas. And that Bhagavat Amitâbha, the Tathâgata, holy and fully enlightened, overshadowing that mass of *S*râvakas and that mass of Bodhisattvas, is seen, illuminating all quarters. Again at that time all those Bodhisattvas, *S*râvakas, gods and men in that world Sukhâvatî, saw this world Sahâ and *S*âkyamuni, the Tathâgata, holy and fully enlightened, surrounded by a holy company of Bhikshus, teaching the Law.

§ 40. Then, the Bhagavat addressed the noble-minded Bodhisattva A*g*ita, and said: 'Do you see, O A*g*ita, the perfection of the array of ornaments and good qualities in that Buddha country; and above in the sky (places) with charming parks[1], charming gardens, charming rivers and lotus lakes, scattered with many precious Padmas, Utpalas, Kumudas, and Pu*nd*arîkas; and below, from the earth to the abode of the Akanish*th*as, the surface of the sky, covered with flowers, ornamented with wreaths of flowers, shining on the rows of many precious columns, frequented by flocks of all kinds of birds created by the Tathâgata?'

The Bodhisattva A*g*ita said: 'I see, O Bhagavat.'

The Bhagavat said: 'Do you see again, O A*g*ita, those flocks of immortal birds, making the whole Buddha country resound with the voice of Buddha, so that those Bodhisattvas are never without meditating on Buddha?'

A*g*ita said: 'I see, O Bhagavat.'

---

[1] A substantive seems to be wanting to which all these adjectives would refer.

The Bhagavat said: 'Do you see again, O A*g*ita, those beings, who have ascended to the palaces which extend over a hundred thousand yo*g*anas in the sky, walking about respectfully?'

A*g*ita said: 'I see, O Bhagavat.'

The Bhagavat said: 'What do you think, O A*g*ita, is there any difference between the gods called Paranirmitava*s*avartins, and men in the world Sukhâvatî?'

A*g*ita said: 'I do not, O Bhagavat, perceive even one difference, so far as the men in that world of Sukhâvatî are endowed with great supernatural powers.'

The Bhagavat said: 'Do you see again, O A*g*ita, those men dwelling within the calyx of excellent lotus-flowers in that world Sukhâvatî?'

He said: 'As gods called Trâyastri*ms*as or Yâmas, having entered into palaces of fifty or hundred or five hundred yo*g*anas in extent, are playing, sporting, walking about, exactly in the same manner I see, O Bhagavat, these men dwelling within the calyx of excellent lotus-flowers in the world Sukhâvatî.

§ 41. 'Again there are, O Bhagavat, beings who, being born miraculously, appear sitting cross-legged in the lotus-flowers. What is there, O Bhagavat, the cause, what the reason, that some dwell within the calyx, while others, being born miraculously, appear sitting cross-legged in the lotus-flowers?'

The Bhagavat said: 'Those Bodhisattvas, O A*g*ita, who, living in other Buddha countries, entertain doubt about being born in the world Sukhâvatî, and with that thought amass a stock of merit, for them there is the dwelling within the calyx. Those, on the contrary, who are filled with faith, and being free from doubt, amass a stock of merit in order to be born in the world Sukhâvatî, and conceive, believe, and trust in the perfect knowledge of the blessed Buddhas, they, being born miraculously, appear sitting cross-legged in the flowers of the lotus. And those noble-minded Bodhisattvas, O A*g*ita, who, living in other Buddha countries, raise their thought in order to see Amitâbha, the Tathâgata, holy and fully enlightened, who never entertain a doubt, believe in the perfect knowledge of Buddha and in their own stock of merit, for them, being born miraculously, and appearing cross-legged, there is, in one minute, such a body as that of other beings who have been born there long before. See, O A*g*ita, the excellent, immeasurable, unfailing, unlimited wisdom, that namely for their own benefit they are deprived during five hundred years of seeing Buddhas, seeing Bodhisattvas, hearing the Law, speaking about the Law (with others), and thus collecting a stock of merit; they are indeed deprived of the successful attainment of every stock of merit, and that through their forming ideas tainted with doubt.

'And, O A*g*ita, there might be a dungeon belonging to an anointed Kshatriya king, inlaid entirely with gold and beryl, in which cushions, garlands, wreaths and strings are fixed, having canopies of different colours and kind, covered with silk cushions, scattered over with various flowers and blossoms, scented with excellent scents, adorned with arches, courts, windows, pinnacles, fire-places, and terraces, covered with nets of bells of the seven kinds of gems, having four angles, four pillars, four doors, four stairs; and the son of that king having been thrown into the dungeon for some misdeed is there, bound with a chain made of the *G*âmbûnada gold. And suppose there is a couch prepared for him, covered with many woollen cloths, spread over with cotton and feather cushions, having Kâlinga coverings, and carpets, together with coverlids[1], red on both sides, beautiful and charming. There he might be then either sitting or resting. And there might be brought to him much food and drink, of various kinds, pure and well prepared. What do you think, O A*g*ita, would the enjoyment be great for that prince?'

A*g*ita said: 'Yes[2], it would be great, O Bhagavat.'

The Bhagavat said: 'What do you think, O A*g*ita, would he even taste it there, and notice it, or would he feel any satisfaction from it?'

He said: 'Not indeed, O Bhagavat; but on the contrary, when he had been led away by the king and thrown into the dungeon, he would only wish for deliverance from there. He would seek for the nobles, princes, ministers, women[3], elders (rich merchants), householders, and lords of castles, who might deliver him from that dungeon. Moreover, O Bhagavat, there is no pleasure for that prince in that dungeon, nor is he liberated, until the king shows him favour.'

The Bhagavat said: 'Thus, O A*g*ita, it is with those Bodhisattvas who, having fallen into doubt, amass a stock of merit, but doubt the knowledge of Buddha. They are born in that world Sukhâ-

[1] The text is corrupt. One might begin a new word with sottarapada*kk*hada*h*.

[2] One expects, No.

[3] Stryâgâra, like the German Frauenzimmer.

vatî, through the hearing of Buddha's name, and through the serenity of thought only; they do not, however, appear sitting cross-legged in the flowers of the lotus, being born miraculously, but dwell only in the calyx of the lotus-flowers. Moreover for them there exist ideas of palaces and gardens [1]. There is no discharge, there is no phlegm or mucus, there is nothing disagreeable to the mind. But they are deprived of seeing Buddhas, hearing the Law, seeing Bodhisattvas, speaking about and ascertaining the Law, (gathering) any (new) stock of merit, and practising the Law, during five hundred years. Moreover they do not rejoice there or perceive satisfaction. But they wish to remove one another, and then they step out behind. And it is not known whether their exit takes place above, below, or across. See, O A*g*ita, there might be worshippings of many hundred thousand niyutas of ko*t*îs of Buddhas during those five hundred years, and also many, immense, innumerable, immeasurable stocks of merit to be amassed. But all this they destroy by the fault of doubt. See, O A*g*ita, to how great an injury the doubt of the Bodhisattvas leads. Therefore now, O A*g*ita, after the Bodhisattvas without doubting have quickly raised their thoughts towards the Bodhi, in order to obtain power of conferring happiness for the benefit of all creatures, their stock of merit should be turned towards their being born in the world Sukhâvatî, where the blessed Amitâbha, the Tathâgata, holy and fully enlightened, dwells.'

§ 42. After these words, the Bodhisattva A*g*ita

[1] They imagine they are living in palaces and gardens.

thus spoke to the Bhagavat: 'O Bhagavat, will the Bodhisattvas, who have gone away from this Buddha country, or from the side of other blessed Buddhas, be born in the world Sukhâvatî?'

The Bhagavat said: 'Indeed, O Agita, seventy-two niyutas of kotîs of Bodhisattvas are gone away from this Buddha country, who will be born in the world Sukhâvatî; Bodhisattvas, who will never return, thanks to the stock of merit, which they have accumulated under many hundred thousand niyutas of kotîs of Buddhas. What then shall be said of those with smaller stocks of merit[1]? 1. Eighteen hundred niyutas of kotîs of Bodhisattvas will be born in the world Sukhâvatî from the place of the Tathâgata Dushprasaha. 2. There lives in the Eastern quarter the Tathâgata named Ratnâkara. From his place ninety kotîs of Bodhisattvas will be born in the world Sukhâvatî. 3. Twenty-two kotîs of Bodhisattvas will be born in the world Sukhâvatî from the place of the Tathâgata Gyotishprabha. 4. Twenty-five kotîs of Bodhisattvas will be born in the world Sukhâvatî from the place of the Tathâgata Amitaprabha. 5. Sixty kotîs of Bodhisattvas will be born in the world Sukhâvatî from the place of the Tathâgata Lokapradîpa. 6. Sixty-four kotîs of Bodhisattvas will be born in the world Sukhâvatî from the place of the Tathâgata Nâgâbhibhû. 7. Twenty-five kotîs of Bodhisattvas will be born in the world Sukhâvatî from the place of the Tathâgata Viragahprabha. 8. Sixteen kotîs of Bodhisattvas will be born in the world Sukhâvatî from the place of the Tathâgata Simha. 9. Eighteen thousand

[1] What is meant is that their number is much larger.

Bodhisattvas will be born in the world Sukhâvatî from the place of the Tathâgata Simha (sic). 10. Eighty-one niyutas of kotîs of Bodhisattvas will be born in the world Sukhâvatî from the place of the Tathâgata Srîkûta. 11. Ten niyutas of kotîs of Bodhisattvas will be born in the world Sukhâvatî from the place of the Tathâgata Narendrarâga. 12. Twelve thousand Bodhisattvas will be born in the world Sukhâvatî from the place of the Tathâgata Balâbhigña. 13. Twenty-five kotîs of Bodhisattvas[1], who have obtained strength, having gone to one place in one week of eight days, and having turned to the West during ninety hundred thousand niyutas of kotîs of kalpas[2], will be born in the world Sukhâvatî from the place of the Tathâgata Pushpadhvaga. 14. Twelve kotîs of Bodhisattvas will be born in the world Sukhâvatî from the place of the Tathâgata Gvalanâdhipati. 15. From the place of the Tathâgata Vaisâradyaprâpta, sixty-nine kotîs of Bodhisattvas will be born in the world Sukhâvatî, in order to see the Tathâgata Amitâbha, to bow before him, to worship him, to ask questions of him, and to consult him. For this reason, O Agita, I might proclaim during a full niyuta of kotîs of kalpas the names of those Tathâgatas, from whom the Bodhisattvas proceed in order to see that Tathâgata Amitâbha in the world Sukhâvatî, to

[1] It should be pañkavimsatir.

[2] Saṅghavarman's translation of this passage is: 'Within seven days they can take hold of the firm conditions (dharmas) practised by a noble-minded one during hundred thousands of kotîs of kalpas.' Bodhiruki's is: 'Within seven days they can cause beings to separate from their state of transmigration during hundred thousands of niyutas of kotîs.'

bow before him, and to worship him, and yet the end could not be reached.

§ 43. 'See, O A*g*ita, what easy gains are gained by those beings who will hear the name of the Tathâgata Amitâbha, holy and fully enlightened. Nor will those beings be of little faith [1], who will obtain at least one joyful thought of that Tathâgata and of this treatise of the Law. Therefore now, O A*g*ita, I invite you, and command you to proclaim this treatise of the Law, before the world together with the gods. Having plunged into the vast universe full of fire, no one ought to turn back, if he has but once conceived the thought of going across. And why? Because ko*t*is of Bodhisattvas indeed, O A*g*ita, return from the highest perfect knowledge, on account of not hearing such treatises of the Law as this. Therefore, from a wish for this treatise of the Law, a great effort should be made to hear, learn, and remember it, and to study it for the sake of fully grasping it and widely making it known. A good copy of it should be kept, after it has been copied in a book, if only during one night and day, or even during the time necessary for milking a cow. The name of Master should be given to a teacher who desires to conduct quickly innumerable beings to the state of never returning from the highest perfect knowledge, namely, in order that they may see the Buddha country of that blessed Amitâbha, the Tathâgata, and to acquire the excellent perfection of the array of good qualities peculiar to his own Buddha country.

---

[1] Hînâdhimuktika, see Va*g*ra*kkh*edikâ XV; or 'following the lower Law.'

'And, O A*g*ita, such beings will have easily gained their gains who, having amassed a stock of merit, having performed service under former *G*inas, and having been guided by Buddhas, shall hear in future, until the destruction of the good Law, such-like excellent treatises of the Law, treatises which are praised, eulogized, and approved of by all Buddhas, and convey quickly the great knowledge of omniscience. And those also who, when they have heard it, shall obtain excellent delight and pleasure, and will learn, retain, recite and grasp, and wisely preach it to others, and be delighted by its study, or, having copied it at least, will worship it, will certainly produce much good work, so that it is difficult to count it.

'Thus indeed, O A*g*ita, I have done what a Tathâgata ought to do. It is now for you to devote yourself to it without any doubt. Do not doubt the perfect and unfailing knowledge of Buddha. Do not enter into the dungeon made of gems built up in every way. For indeed, the birth of a Buddha, O A*g*ita, is difficult to be met with, so is the instruction in the Law, and also a timely birth [1]. O A*g*ita, the way to gain the perfection (pâramitâ) of all stocks of merit has been proclaimed by me. Do now exert yourselves and move forward. O A*g*ita, I grant indeed a great favour to this treatise of the Law. Be valiant so that the laws of Buddhas may not perish or disappear. Do not break the command of the Tathâgata.'

§ 44. Then at that time, the Bhagavat spoke these verses:

[1] Of the hearer; so that the student should be born at a time when there is a Buddha on earth.

1. 'Such hearings of me will not be for people who have not done good; but those who are heroes and perfect, they will hear this speech.

2. 'And those by whom the Lord of the world, the enlightened and the light-giver, has been seen, and the law been heard reverentially, will obtain the highest joy.

3. 'Low people of slothful minds cannot find any delight in the laws of Buddha; those who have worshipped in the Buddha countries learn the service of the Lords of the three worlds.

4. 'As a blind man in darkness does not know the way, and much less can show it, so also he who is (only) a *S*râvaka[1] in the knowledge of Buddha; how then should beings who are ignorant!

5. 'The Buddha only knows the virtues of a Buddha; but not gods, Nâgas, Asuras, Yakshas, and *S*râvakas (disciples); even for Anekabuddhas[2] there is no such way, as when the knowledge of a Buddha is being manifested.

6. 'If all beings had attained bliss, knowing the highest meaning in pure wisdom, they would not in ko*t*is of kalpas or even in a longer time tell all the virtues of one Buddha.

7. 'Thereupon they would attain Nirvâ*n*a, preaching for many ko*t*is of kalpas, and yet the measure of the knowledge of a Buddha would not be reached, for such is the wonderfulness of the knowledge of the *G*inas.

8. 'Therefore a learned man of an intelligent race[3] who believes my words, after having perceived

[1] Those who are as yet hearers only of the Law.

[2] Should it be Pratyekabuddhas?

[3] The text is evidently corrupt, and the translation conjectural.

all paths of the knowledge of the *G*inas, should utter speech, saying, "Buddha is wise."

9. 'Now and then a man is found, now and then a Buddha appears, knowledge of the object of faith is acquired after a long time,—therefore one should strive to acquire (the knowledge of) the object (of faith) [1].'

§ 45. And while this treatise of the Law was being delivered, twelve ko*t*îs of niyutas of beings obtained the pure and spotless eye of the Law with regard to Laws. Twenty-four hundred thousand niyutas of ko*t*îs of beings obtained the Anâgâmin [2] reward. Eight hundred Bhikshus had their thoughts delivered from faults so as to cling no more to anything. Twenty-five ko*t*îs of Bodhisattvas obtained resignation to things to come. And by forty hundred thousand niyutas of ko*t*îs of the human and divine race, thoughts such as had never risen before were turned toward the highest perfect knowledge, and their stocks of merit were made to grow toward their being born in the world Sukhâvatî, from a desire to see the Tathâgata, the blessed Amitâbha. And all of them having been born there, will in proper order be born in other worlds, as Tathâgatas, called Ma*ñg*usvara (sweet-voiced). And eighty ko*t*îs of niyutas having acquired resignation under the Tathâgata Dîpańkara, never turning back again from the highest perfect knowledge, rendered perfect by the

[1] The tenth verse is again unintelligible, but may have meant something like that 'those who having heard the best Laws, are joyful in remembering Sugata, are our friends in time past, and they also who wish for enlightenment.'

[2] One who is not born again, except in the Brahma world, and then may obtain Nirvâ*n*a.

Tathâgata Amitâyus, practising the duties of former Bodhisattvas, will carry out, after they are born in the world Sukhâvatî, the duties enjoined in the former Pra*n*idhânas (prayers).

§ 46. At that time this universe (the three millions of worlds) trembled in six ways. And various miracles were seen. On earth everything was perfect, and human and divine instruments were played, and the shout of joy was heard as far as the world of the Akanish*th*as.

§ 47. Thus spoke the Bhagavat enraptured, and the noble-minded Bodhisattva A*g*ita, and the blessed Ânanda, the whole Assembly, and the world, with gods, men, spirits, mighty birds, and fairies, applauded the speech of the Bhagavat.

The praise of the beauty of the excellences of Sukhâvatî, the country of the blessed Amitâbha, the Tathâgata, the entry of the Bodhisattva on the stage of 'never returning,' the story of Amitâbha, the Mahâyânasûtra of the Description of Sukhâvatî is finished.

NOTE

BY THE REV. BŬNYIU NANJIO, M.A.,

ON THE TWO PRA*N*IDHÂNAS, THE 18TH AND 21ST, MISSING IN THE TEXT.

In the Chinese translations of the Larger Sukhâvatîvyûha, made by Saṅghavarman, A.D. 252, and Bodhiru*k*i, A.D. 693–713, there are altogether 48 Pra*n*idhânas, not 46, as in the Sanskrit text. The 18th and the 21st in the translations are evidently wanting in the Sanskrit text, and the latter part of the 19th Pra*n*idhâna in that text is the latter part of the lost 18th, according to the translations. This 18th Pra*n*idhâna, however, is so important that it is called by Gen-ku, the teacher of Shin-ran, the founder of the Shin-shiu sect, 'the king of the Pra*n*idhânas.'

Saṅghavarman's translation of the 18th, 20th, and 21st is as follows:—

18. 'When I have obtained Buddhahood, if those beings who are in the ten quarters should believe in me with serene thoughts, and should wish to be born in my country, and should have say ten times thought of me (or repeated my name),—if they should not be born there, may I not obtain the perfect knowledge;—barring only those beings who have committed the five deadly sins, and who have spoken evil of the good Law.'

The 18th Pra*n*idhâna in the Sanskrit text agrees with the 19th in both Chinese translations; but the 20th in these translations is somewhat shorter than the 19th in the Sanskrit text. The shorter translation is as follows:—

20. 'When I have obtained Buddhahood, if those beings who are in the ten quarters, after they have heard my name, should direct their thoughts towards my country and should plant the roots of merit (or prepare their stock of merit), and should bring them to maturity with their serene thoughts, and wish to be born in my country,—if they should not accomplish (their desire), may I not obtain the perfect knowledge.

21. 'When I have obtained Buddhahood, if gods and men in my country should not all be endowed perfectly with the thirty-two marks of the great man, may I not obtain the perfect knowledge.'

I have tried to restore the Sanskrit text for the above three Pra*n*idhânas, in accordance with the Chinese translations.

The 18th may be formed chiefly out of the 19th in the text, something as follows:—

॥ १८ ॥ सचेन्मे भगवन्बोधिप्राप्तस्य ये सत्त्वा अन्येषु लोकधातुषु मम नामधेयं श्रुत्वा तत्र बुद्धक्षेत्रे चित्तं प्रेरयेयुरुपपत्तये प्रसन्नचित्ता मामनुस्मरेयुस्ते तत्र बुद्धक्षेत्रे नोपपद्येरन्नंतशो दशभिश्चित्तोत्पादपरिवर्तैः स्थापयित्वानंतर्यकारिणः सद्धर्मप्रतिक्षेपावरणावृतांश्च सत्त्वान्मा तावदहमनुत्तरां सम्यक्संबोधिमभिसंबुध्येयं ॥

Note.—The fulfilment of this Pra*n*idhâna is given in the text (p. 47, ll. 1–4), as the reason of the fulfilment of the 17th:—

०। तत्कस्य हेतोः। ये केचित्सत्त्वास्तस्य भगवतोऽमिताभस्य नामधेयं शृण्वंति श्रुत्वा चांतश एकचित्तोत्पादमप्यध्याशयेन प्रसादसहगतेन चित्तमुत्पादयंति ते सर्वेऽवैवर्तिकतायां संत्यनुत्तरायाः सम्यक्संबोधेः ॥ २६ ॥

In the Chinese translations, the exception of two kinds of beings is repeated at the end of this fulfilment.

The 20th (i.e. 19th in the text) may then be shortened like this :—

॥२०॥ सचेन्मे भगवन्बोधिप्राप्तस्याप्रमेयासंख्येयेषु बुद्धक्षेत्रेषु ये
सत्त्वा मम नामधेयं श्रुत्वा तत्र बुद्धक्षेत्रे चित्तं प्रेरयेयुरुपपत्तये कुशल-
मूलानि च परिणामयेयुस्ते तत्र बुद्धक्षेत्रे नोपपद्येरन्मा तावदहमनुत्तरां
सम्यक्संबोधिमभिसंबुध्येयं ॥

The fulfilment of this Pra*n*idhâna may be the 27th chapter in the text, with the exception of some portion on the appearance of Amitâbha before a dying man, which belongs to the 19th (i.e. 18th in the text) Pra*n*idhâna.

ये चानंद केचित्सत्त्वास्तं तथागतं पुनः सत्कारमनसिकरिष्यंति
बह्वपरिमितं कुशलमूलमवरोपयिष्यंति बोधये चित्तं परिणाम्य तत्र
च लोकधातावुपपत्तये प्रणिधास्यंति ०। (ततस्)ते (तं भगवंतं दृष्ट्वा)
प्रसन्नचित्ताश्च्युताः संतस्तत्रैव सुखावत्यां लोकधातावुपपत्स्यंते। (p. 47.)

The 21st may be like this :—

॥२१॥ सचेन्मे भगवन्बोधिप्राप्तस्य तत्र बुद्धक्षेत्रे ये सत्त्वाः प्रत्याजाता
भवेयुस्ते सर्वे न द्वात्रिंशन्महापुरुषलक्षणसमन्वागता भवेयुर्मा तावदह-
मनुत्तरां सम्यक्संबोधिमभिसंबुध्येयं ॥

This Pra*n*idhâna is found in the Tibetan translation.

The fulfilment of this Pra*n*idhâna is to be found in chap. 35 (p. 56) as follows :—

तत्र चानंद बुद्धक्षेत्रे ये बोधिसत्त्वाः प्रत्याजाताः सर्वे ते द्वात्रिंशन्म-
हापुरुषलक्षणसमन्वागताः ०।

B. N.

INDEX OF WORDS.

Roman numerals refer to the chapters, Arabic figures with p. to the pages of the edition of the Sanskrit text in the Anecdota Oxoniensia, without p. to the verses in certain chapters. Arabic figures in parentheses give the number in the lists of names.

INDEX OF SUBJECTS.

THE SMALLER

SUKHÂVATÎ-VYÛHA.

THE SMALLER SUKHÂVATÎ-VYÛHA.

ADORATION TO THE OMNISCIENT!

§ 1. Thus it was heard by me: At one time the Blessed (Bhagavat, i.e. Buddha) dwelt at *S*râvastî [1], in the *G*eta-grove, in the garden of Anâthapi*nd*aka, together with a large company of Bhikshus (mendicant friars), viz. with twelve hundred and fifty Bhikshus, all of them acquainted with the five kinds of knowledge [2], elders, great disciples [3], and Arhats [4],

---

[1] *S*râvastî, capital of the Northern Ko*s*alas, residence of king Prasena*g*it. It was in ruins when visited by Fa-hian (init. V. Saec.); not far from the modern Fizabad. Cf. Burnouf, Introduction, p. 22.

[2] Abhi*gñ*ânâbhi*gñ*âtai*h*. The Japanese text reads abhi*gñ*âtâbhâ*gñ*âtai*h*, i.e. abhi*gñ*âtâbhi*gñ*âtai*h*. If this were known to be the correct reading, we should translate it by 'known by known people,' notus a viris notis, i.e. well known, famous. Abhi*gñ*âta in the sense of known, famous, occurs in Lalitavistara, p. 25, and the Chinese translators adopted the same meaning here. Again, if we preferred the reading abhi*gñ*ânâbhi*gñ*âtai*h*, this, too, would admit of an intelligible rendering, viz. known or distinguished by the marks or characteristics, i.e. the good qualities which belong to a Bhikshu. But the technical meaning is 'possessed of a knowledge of the five abhi*gñ*âs.' It would be better in that case to write abhi*gñ*âtâbhi*gñ*ânai*h*, but no MSS. seem to support that reading. The five abhi*gñ*âs or abhi*gñ*ânas which an Arhat ought to possess are the divine sight, the divine hearing, the knowledge of the thoughts of others, the remembrance of former existences, and magic power. See Burnouf, Lotus, Appendice, No. xiv. The larger text of the Sukhâvatî-vyûha has

[3, 4] See next page.

such as *S*âriputra, the elder, Mahâmaudgalyâyana, Mahâkâ*s*yapa, Mahâkapphi*n*a, Mahâkâtyâyana, Mâhâkaush*th*ila, Revata, *S*uddhipanthâka, Nanda, Ânanda, Râhula, Gavâmpati, Bharadvâ*g*a, Kâlodayin, Vakkula, and Aniruddha. He dwelt together with these and many other great disciples, and together with many noble-minded Bodhisattvas, such as Ma*ñg*u*s*rî, the prince, the Bodhisattva A*g*ita, the Bodhisattva Gandhahastin, the Bodhisattva Nityodyukta, the Bodhisattva Anikshiptadhura. He dwelt together with them and many other noble-minded Bodhisattvas, and with *S*akra, the Indra or King[5]

abhi*gñ*ânâbhi*gñ*ai*h*, and afterwards abhi*gñ*âtâbhi*gñ*ai*h*. The position of the participle as the uttara-pada in such compounds as abhi*gñ*ânâbhi*gñ*âtai*h* is common in Buddhist Sanskrit. Mr. Bendall has called my attention to the Pâli abhi*ññ*âta-abhi*ññ*âta (Vinaya-pi*t*aka, ed. Oldenberg, vol. i, p. 43), which favours the Chinese acceptation of the term.

[3] Mahâ*s*râvaka, the great disciples; sometimes the eighty principal disciples.

[4] Arhadbhi*h*. I have left the correct Sanskrit form, because the Japanese text gives the termination adbhi*h*. Hôgö's text has the more usual form arhantai*h*. The change of the old classical arhat into the Pâli arahan, and then back into Sanskrit arhanta, arahanta, and at last arihanta, with the meaning of 'destroyer of the enemies,' i e. the passions, shows very clearly the different stages through which Sanskrit words passed in the different phases of Buddhist literature. In Tibet, in Mongolia, and in China, Arhat is translated by 'destroyer of the enemy,' i.e. ari-hanta. See Burnouf, Lotus, p. 287, Introduction, p. 295. Arhat is really the title of the Bhikshu on reaching the fourth degree of perfection. Cf. Sûtra of the 42 Sections, cap. 2. Clemens of Alexandria (d. 220) speaks of the Σεμνοί who worshipped a pyramid erected over the relics of a god. This may be a translation of Arhat, as Lassen ('De nom. Ind. philosoph.' in Rhein. Museum, vol. i, p. 187) and Burnouf (Introduction, p. 295) supposed, or a transliteration of Samana. Clemens also speaks of Σεμναί (Stromat. p. 539, Potter).

[5] Indra, the old Vedic god, has come to mean simply lord, and

of the Devas, and with Brahman Sahâmpati. With these and many other hundred thousand nayutas[1] of sons of the gods, Bhagavat dwelt at *S*râvastî.

§ 2. Then Bhagavat addressed the honoured *S*âriputra and said, 'O *S*âriputra, after you have passed from here over a hundred thousand ko*t*îs of Buddha countries there is in the Western part a Buddha country, a world called Sukhâvatî (the happy country). And there a Tathâgata, called Amitâyus, an Arhat, fully enlightened, dwells now, and remains, and supports himself, and teaches the Law[2].

'Now what do you think, *S*âriputra, for what reason is that world called Sukhâvatî (the happy)? In that world Sukhâvatî, O *S*âriputra, there is neither bodily nor mental pain for living beings. The sources of happiness are innumerable there. For that reason is that world called Sukhâvatî (the happy).

§ 3. 'And again, O *S*âriputra, that world Sukhâvatî is adorned with seven terraces, with seven rows of

---

in the *K*anda Paritta (Journal Asiatique, 1871, p. 220) we actually find Asurinda, the Indra or Lord of the Asuras.

[1] The numbers in Buddhist literature, if they once exceed a ko*t*i or ko*t*î, i.e. ten millions, become very vague, nor is their value always the same. Ayuta, i.e. a hundred ko*t*îs; niyuta, i.e. a hundred ayutas; and nayuta, i.e. 1 with 22 zeros, are often confounded; nor does it matter much so far as any definite idea is concerned which such numerals convey to our mind. See Prof. H. Schubert, 'On large numbers,' in Open Court, Dec. 14, 1893.

[2] Tish*th*ati dhriyate yâpayati dharma*m* *k*a de*s*ayati. This is an idiomatic phrase, which occurs again and again in the Nepalese text of the Sukhâvatî-vyûha (MS. 26 b, ll. 1, 2; 55 a, l. 2, &c.). It seems to mean, he stands there, holds himself, supports himself, and teaches the law. Burnouf translates the same phrase by, 'ils se trouvent, vivent, existent' (Lotus, p. 354). On yâpeti in Pâli, see Fausböll, Dasaratha-*g*âtaka, pp. 26, 28; and yâpana in Sanskrit.

palm-trees, and with strings of bells[1]. It is enclosed on every side[2], beautiful, brilliant with the four gems, viz. gold, silver, beryl, and crystal[3]. With

---

[1] Kiṅki*n*î*g*âla. The texts read kaṅka*n*a*g*alai*s* *k*a and kaṅka*n*î*g*alais *k*a, and again later kaṅka*n*î*g*alunâm (also lû) and kaṅka*n*î*g*alânâm. Mr. Beal translates from Chinese 'seven rows of exquisite curtains,' and again 'gemmous curtains.' First of all, it seems clear that we must read *g*âla, net, web, instead of *g*ala. Secondly, kaṅka*n*a, bracelet, gives no sense, for what could be the meaning of nets or strings of bracelets? I prefer to read kiṅki*n*î*g*âla, nets or strings or rows of bells. Such rows of bells served for ornamenting a garden, and it may be said of them that, if moved by the wind, they give forth certain sounds. In the commentary on Dhammapada 30, p. 191, we meet with kiṅkinika*g*âla, from which likewise the music proceeds; see Childers, s.v. *g*âla. In the MSS. of the Nepalese Sukhâvatî-vyûha (R.A.S.), p. 39 a, l. 4, I likewise find svar*n*aratnakiṅki*n*î*g*âlâni, which settles the matter, and shows how little confidence we can place in the Japanese texts.

[2] Anuparikshipta, enclosed; see parikkhepo in Childers' Dictionary, and compare pairidaêza, paradise.

[3] The four and seven precious things in Pâli are (according to Childers):—

1. suva*nn*a*m*, gold.
2. ra*g*ata*m*, silver.
3. muttâ, pearls.
4. ma*n*i, gems (as sapphire, ruby).
5. ve*l*uriya*m*, cat's eye.
6. va*g*ira*m*, diamond.
7. pavâ*l*am, coral.

Here Childers translates cat's eye; but s.v. ve*l*uriyam, he says, a precious stone, perhaps lapis lazuli.

In Sanskrit (Burnouf, Lotus, p. 320):—

1. suvar*n*a, gold.
2. rûpya, silver.
3. vai*d*ûrya, lapis lazuli.
4. spha*t*ika, crystal.
5. lohitamukti, red pearls.
6. a*s*magarbha, diamond.
7 musâragalva, coral.

such arrays of excellences peculiar to a Buddha country is that Buddha country adorned.

§ 4. 'And again, O *S*âriputra, in that world Sukhâvatî there are lotus lakes, adorned with the seven gems, viz. gold, silver, beryl, crystal, red pearls, diamonds, and corals as the seventh. They are full of water which possesses the eight good qualities[1], their waters rise as high as the fords and bathing-places, so that even crows[2] may drink there; they are

---

Julien (Pèlerins Buddhistes, vol. ii, p. 482) gives the following list:—

1. spha*t*ika, rock crystal.
2. vaidûrya, lapis lazuli.
3. a*s*magarbha, cornaline.
4. musâragalva, amber.
5. padmarâga, ruby.

Vai*d*ûrya (or Vaidûrya) is mentioned in the Tathâgatagu*n*a-*gñ*âna*k*intyavishayâvatâranirde*s*a (Wassilief, p. 161) as a precious stone which, if placed on green cloth, looks green, if placed on red cloth, red. The fact that vai*d*ûrya is often compared with the colour of the eyes of a cat would seem to point to the cat's eye (see Borooah's Engl.-Sanskrit Dictionary, vol. ii, preface, p. ix), certainly not to lapis lazuli. Cat's eye is a kind of chalcedony. I see, however, that vai*d*ûrya has been recognised as the original of the Greek βήρυλλος, a very ingenious conjecture, either of Weber's or of Pott's, considering that lingual *d* has a sound akin to r, and ry may be changed to ly and ll (Weber, Omina, p. 326). The Persian billaur or ballûr, which Skeat gives as the etymon of βήρυλλος, is of Arabic origin, means crystal, and could hardly have found its way into Greek at so early a time. See 'India, what can it teach us?' p. 267.

[1] The eight good qualities of water are limpidity and purity, refreshing coolness, sweetness, softness, fertilising qualities, calmness, power of preventing famine, productiveness. See Beal, Catena, p. 379.

[2] Kâkâpeya. One text reads kâkapeya, the other kâkâpeya.. It is difficult to choose. The more usual word is kâkapeya, which is explained by Pâ*n*ini, II, 1, 33. It is uncertain, however, whether kâkapeya is meant as a laudatory or as

strewn with golden sand. And in these lotus-lakes there are all around on the four sides four stairs, beautiful and brilliant with the four gems, viz. gold, silver, beryl, crystal. And on every side of these lotus-lakes gem-trees are growing, beautiful and brilliant with the seven gems, viz. gold, silver, beryl, crystal, red pearls, diamonds, and corals as the seventh. And in those lotus-lakes lotus-flowers are growing, blue, blue-coloured, of blue splendour, blue to behold; yellow, yellow-coloured, of yellow splendour, yellow to behold; red, red-coloured, of red splendour, red to behold; white, white-coloured, of white splendour, white to behold; beautiful, beautifully-coloured, of beautiful splendour, beautiful to behold, and in circumference as large as the wheel of a chariot.

---

a depreciatory term. Böhtlingk takes it in the latter sense, and translates nadî kâkapeyâ, by a shallow river that could be drunk up by a crow. Târânâtha takes it in the former sense, and translates nadî kâkapeyâ, as a river so full of water that a crow can drink it without bending its neck (kâkair anatakandharai*h* pîyate; pûr*n*odakatvena prasasye kâkai*h* peye nadyâdau). In our passage kâkapeya must be a term of praise, and we therefore could only render it by 'ponds so full of water that crows could drink from them.' But why should so well known a word as kâkapeya have been spelt kâkâpeya, unless it was done intentionally? And if intentionally, what was it intended for? We must remember that Pâ*n*ini, II, 1, 42 schol., teaches us how to form the word tîrthakâka, a crow at a tîrtha, which means a person in a wrong place. It would seem therefore that crows were considered out of place at a tîrtha or bathing-place, either because they were birds of ill omen, or because they defiled the water. From that point of view, kâkâpeya would mean a pond not visited by crows, free from crows. Professor Pischel has called my attention to Mahâparinibbâna Sutta (J. R. A. S. 1875, p. 67, p. 21), where kâkapeyâ clearly refers to a full river. Samati*tth*ika, if this is the right reading, occurs in the same place as an epithet of

§ 5. 'And again, O *S*âriputra, in that Buddha country there are heavenly musical instruments always played on, and the earth is lovely and of golden colour. And in that Buddha country a flower-rain of heavenly Mândârava blossoms pours down three times every day, and three times every night. And the beings who are born there worship before their morning meal[1] a hundred thousand ko*t*îs of Buddhas by going to other worlds; and having showered a hundred thousand ko*t*îs of flowers upon each Tathâgata, they return to their own world in time for the afternoon rest[2]. With such arrays of excellences peculiar to a Buddha country is that Buddha country adorned.

§ 6. 'And again, O *S*âriputra, there are in that Buddha country swans, curlews[3], and peacocks. Three times every night, and three times every day, they

---

a river, by the side of kâkapeya, and I think it most likely that it means rising to a level with the tîrthas, the fords or bathing-places. Mr. Rhys Davids informs me that the commentary explains the two words by samatittikâ ti samaharitâ, kâkapeyyâ ti yatthatatthak*i* tîre *th*itena kâkena sakkâ patum ti.

[1] Purobhaktena. The text is difficult to read, but it can hardly be doubtful that purobhaktena corresponds to Pâli purebhatta*m* (i.e. before the morning meal), opposed to pa*k*-*kh*âbhatta*m*, after the noonday meal (i.e. in the afternoon). See Childers, s.v. Pûrvabhaktikâ would be the first repast, as Prof. Cowell informs me.

[2] Divâvihârâya, for the noonday rest, the siesta. See Childers, s.v. vihâra.

[3] Krau*ñk*â*h*. Snipe, curlew. Is it meant for Kuravîka, or Karavîka, a fine-voiced bird (according to Kern, the Sk. karâyikâ), or for Kalaviṅka, Pâli Kalavîka? See Childers, s.v. opapâtiko; Burnouf, Lotus, p. 566. I see, however, the same birds mentioned together elsewhere, as ha*m*sakrau*ñk*amayûra*s*uka*s*âlikakokila, &c. On mayûra see Mahâv., Introd. p. xxxix; Rv. I, 191, 14.

come together and perform a concert, each uttering his own note. And from them thus uttering proceeds a sound proclaiming the five virtues, the five powers, and the seven steps leading towards the highest knowledge[1]. When the men there hear that sound, remembrance of Buddha, remembrance of the Law, remembrance of the Church, rises in their mind.

'Now, do you think, O *S*âriputra, that there are beings who have entered into the nature of animals (birds, &c.)? This is not to be thought of. The

[1] Indriyabalabodhyaṅga*s*abda. These are technical terms, but their meaning is not quite clear. Spence Hardy, in his Manual, p. 498, enumerates the five indrayas, viz. (1) sardhâwa, purity (probably *s*raddhâ, faith); (2) wiraya, persevering exertion (vîrya); (3) sati or smirti, the ascertainment of truth (sm*ri*ti); (4) samâdhi, tranquillity; (5) pragnâwa, wisdom (pra*gñ*â).

The five balayas (bala), he adds, are the same as the five indrayas.

The seven bowdyânga (bodhyaṅga) are according to him: (1) sihi or smirti, the ascertainment of the truth by mental application; (2) dharmmawicha, the investigation of causes; (3) wîraya, persevering exertion; (4) prîti, joy; (5) passadhi, or prasrabdhi, tranquillity; (6) samâdhi, tranquillity in a higher degree, including freedom from all that disturbs either body or mind; (7) upekshâ, equanimity.

It will be seen from this that some of these qualities or excellences occur both as indriyas and bodhyaṅgas, while balas are throughout identical with indriyas.

Burnouf, however, in his Lotus, gives a list of five balas (from the Vocabulaire Pentaglotte) which correspond with the five indriyas of Spence Hardy; viz. *s*raddhâ-bala, power of faith; vîrya-bala, power of vigour; sm*ri*ti-bala, power of memory; samâdhi-bala, power of meditation; pra*gñ*â-bala, power of knowledge. They precede the seven bodhyaṅgas both in the Lotus, the Vocabulaire Pentaglotte, and the Lalita-vistara.

To these seven bodhyaṅgas Burnouf has assigned a special treatise (Appendice xii, p. 796). They occur both in Sanskrit and Pâli. See also Dharmasaṅgraha s.v. in the Anecdota Oxoniensia.

very name of hells is unknown in that Buddha country, and likewise that of (descent into) animal bodies and of the realm of Yama (the four apâyas)[1]. No, these tribes of birds have been made on purpose by the Tathâgata Amitâyus, and they utter the sound of the Law. With such arrays of excellences, &c.

§ 7. 'And again, O *S*âriputra, when those rows of palm-trees and strings of bells in that Buddha country are moved by the wind, a sweet and enrapturing sound proceeds from them. Yes, O *S*âriputra, as from a heavenly musical instrument consisting of a hundred thousand ko*t*is of sounds, when played by Âryas, a sweet and enrapturing sound proceeds, a sweet and enrapturing sound proceeds from those rows of palm-trees and strings of bells moved by the wind. And when the men hear that sound, reflection on Buddha arises in them, reflection on the Law, reflection on the Church. With such arrays of excellences, &c.

§ 8. 'Now what do you think, O *S*âriputra, for what reason is that Tathâgata called Amitâyus? The length of life (âyus), O *S*âriputra, of that Tathâgata and of those men there is immeasurable (amita). Therefore is that Tathâgata called Amitâyus. And ten kalpas have passed, O *S*âriputra, since that Tathâgata awoke to perfect knowledge.

§ 9. 'And what do you think, O *S*âriputra, for what reason is that Tathâgata called Amitâbha? The

[1] Niraya, the hells, also called Naraka. Yamaloka, the realm of Yama, the judge of the dead, is explained as the four apâyas, i.e. Naraka, hell; Tiryagyoni, birth as animals; Pretaloka, realm of the departed; Asuraloka, realm of evil spirits. The three terms which are here used together occur likewise in a passage translated by Burnouf, Introduction, p. 544.

splendour (âbhâ), O *S*âriputra, of that Tathâgata is unimpeded over all Buddha countries. Therefore is that Tathâgata called Amitâbha.

'And there is, O *S*âriputra, an innumerable assembly of disciples with that Tathâgata, purified and venerable persons, whose number it is not easy to count. With such arrays of excellences, &c.

§ 10. 'And again, O *S*âriputra, of those beings also who are born in the Buddha country of the Tathâgata Amitâyus as purified Bodhisattvas, never to return again and bound by one birth only, of those Bodhisattvas also, O *S*âriputra, the number is not easy to count, except they are reckoned as infinite in number [1].

'Then again all beings, O *S*âriputra, ought to make fervent prayer for that Buddha country. And why? Because they come together there with such excellent men. Beings are not born in that Buddha country of the Tathâgata Amitâyus as a reward and result of good works performed in this present life [2].

---

[1] Iti saṅkhyâ*m* ga*kkh*anti, they are called; cf. Childers, s.v. saṅkhyâ. Asaṅkhyeya, even more than aprameya, is the recognised term for infinity. Burnouf, Lotus, p. 852.

[2] Avaramâtraka. This is the Pâli oramattako, 'belonging merely to the present life,' and the intention of the writer seems to be to inculcate the doctrine, that salvation can be obtained by mere repetitions of the name of Amitâbha, in direct opposition to the original doctrine of Buddha, that as a man soweth, so he reapeth. Buddha would have taught that the ku*s*alamûla, the root or the stock of good works performed in this world (avaramâtraka), will bear fruit in the next, while here 'vain repetitions' seem all that is enjoyed. The Chinese translators take a different view of this passage. But from the end of this section, where we read kulaputre*n*a vâ kuladuhitrâ vâ tatra buddhakshetre *k*ittaprâ*n*idhâna*m* kartavyam, it seems clear that the locative (buddhakshetre) forms the object of the pra*n*idhâna, the fervent prayer or longing. The Satpurushas already in the Buddhakshetra would be the innumerable men (manushyâs) and Bodhisattvas mentioned before.

No, whatever son or daughter of a family shall hear the name of the blessed Amitâyus, the Tathâgata, and having heard it, shall keep it in mind, and with thoughts undisturbed shall keep it in mind for one, two, three, four, five, six or seven nights,—when that son or daughter of a family comes to die, then that Amitâyus, the Tathâgata, surrounded by an assembly of disciples and followed by a host of Bodhisattvas, will stand before them at their hour of death, and they will depart this life with tranquil minds. After their death they will be born in the world Sukhâvatî, in the Buddha country of the same Amitâyus, the Tathâgata. Therefore, then, O *S*âriputra, having perceived this cause and effect[1], I with reverence say thus, Every son and every daughter of a family ought with their whole mind to make fervent prayer for that Buddha country.

§ 11. 'And now, O *S*âriputra, as I here at present glorify that world, thus in the East, O *S*âriputra, other blessed Buddhas, led by the Tathâgata Akshobhya, the Tathâgata Merudhva*g*a, the Tathâgata Mahâmeru, the Tathâgata Meruprabhâsa, and the Tathâgata Ma*ñg*udhva*g*a, equal in number to the sand of the river Gaṅgâ, comprehend their own Buddha countries in their speech, and then reveal them[2].

[1] Arthava*s*a, lit. the power of the thing; cf. Dhammapada, p. 388, v. 289.

[2] I am not quite certain as to the meaning of this passage, but if we enter into the bold metaphor of the text, viz. that the Buddhas cover the Buddha countries with the organ of their tongue and then unrol it, what is intended can hardly be anything but that they first try to find words for the excellences of those countries, and then reveal or proclaim them. Burnouf, however (Lotus, p. 417), takes the expression in a literal sense, though he is shocked by its grotesqueness. On these Buddhas and their countries, see Burnouf, Lotus, p. 113.

Accept this repetition of the Law, called the "Favour of all Buddhas," which magnifies their inconceivable excellences.

§ 12. 'Thus also in the South do other blessed Buddhas, led by the Tathâgata *K*andrasûryapradîpa, the Tathâgata Ya*s*a*h*prabha, the Tathâgata Mahâr*k*iskandha, the Tathâgata Merupradîpa, the Tathâgata Anantavîrya, equal in number to the sand of the river Gaṅgâ, comprehend their own Buddha countries in their speech, and then reveal them. Accept, &c.

§ 13. 'Thus also in the West do other blessed Buddhas, led by the Tathâgata Amitâyus, the Tathâgata Amitaskandha, the Tathâgata Amitadhva*g*a, the Tathâgata Mahâprabha, the Tathâgata Mahâratnaketu, the Tathâgata *S*uddhara*s*miprabha, equal in number to the sand of the river Gaṅgâ, comprehend, &c.

§ 14. 'Thus also in the North do other blessed Buddhas, led by the Tathâgata Mahâr*k*iskandha, the Tathâgata Vai*s*vânaranirghosha, the Tathâgata Dundubhisvaranirghosha, the Tathâgata Dushpradharsha, the Tathâgata Âdityasambhava, the Tathâgata *G*aleniprabha (*G*valanaprabha ?), the Tathâgata Prabhâkara, equal in number to the sand, &c.

§ 15. 'Thus also in the Nadir do other blessed Buddhas, led by the Tathâgata Si*m*ha, the Tathâgata Ya*s*as, the Tathâgata Ya*s*a*h*prabhâva, the Tathâgata Dharma, the Tathâgata Dharmadhara, the Tathâgata Dharmadhva*g*a, equal in number to the sand, &c.

§ 16. 'Thus also in the Zenith do other blessed Buddhas, led by the Tathâgata Brahmaghosha, the Tathâgata Nakshatrarâ*g*a, the Tathâgata Indraketudhva*g*arâ*g*a, the Tathâgata Gandhottama, the Tathâgata Gandhaprabhâsa, the Tathâgata Mahâr*k*iskandha, the Tathâgata Ratnakusumasampushpitagâtra, the Tathâgata Sâlendrarâ*g*a, the Tathâgata Ratnotpala*s*rî, the Tathâgata Sarvârthadar*s*a, the Tathâgata Sumerukalpa, equal in number to the sand, &c.[1]

§ 17. 'Now what do you think, O *S*âriputra, for what reason is that repetition (treatise) of the Law called the Favour of all Buddhas? Every son or daughter of a family who shall hear the name of that repetition of the Law and retain in their memory the names of those blessed Buddhas, will be favoured by the Buddhas, and will never return again, being once in possession of the transcendent true knowledge. Therefore, then, O *S*âriputra, believe[2], accept, and do not doubt of me and those blessed Buddhas!

'Whatever sons or daughters of a family shall make mental prayer for the Buddha country of that blessed Amitâyus, the Tathâgata, or are making it now or have made it formerly, all these will never return again, being once in possession of the transcendent true knowledge. They will be born in that Buddha country, have been born, or are being born

---

[1] It should be remarked that the Tathâgatas here assigned to the ten quarters differ entirely from those assigned to them in the Lalita-vistara, Book XX. Not even Amitâbha is mentioned there.

[2] Pratîyatha. The texts give again and again pattîyatha, evidently the Pâli form, instead of pratîyata. I have left tha, the Pâli termination of the 2 p. pl. in the imperative, instead of ta, because that form was clearly intended, while pa for pra may be an accident. Yet I have little doubt that patîyatha was in the original text. That it is meant for the imperative, we see from *s*raddadhâdhvam, &c., further on. Other traces of the influence of Pâli or Prâkrit on the Sanskrit of our Sûtra appear in arhantai*h*, the various reading for arhadbhi*h*, which I preferred; sambahula for bahula; dhriyate yâpayati; purobhaktena; anyatra; saṅkhyâ*m* ga*kkh*anti; avaramâtraka; ve*th*ana instead of vesh*t*ana, in nirve*th*ana; dharmaparyâya (Corp. Inscript. plate xv), &c.

now. Therefore, then, O *S*âriputra, mental prayer is to be made for that Buddha country by faithful sons and daughters of a family.

§ 18. 'And as I at present magnify here the inconceivable excellences of those blessed Buddhas, thus, O *S*âriputra, do those blessed Buddhas magnify my own inconceivable excellences.

'A very difficult work has been done by *S*âkyamuni, the sovereign of the *S*âkyas. Having obtained the transcendent true knowledge in this world Sahâ, he taught the Law which all the world is reluctant to accept, during this corruption of the present kalpa, during this corruption of mankind, during this corruption of belief, during this corruption of life, during this corruption of passions.

§ 19. 'This is even for me, O *S*âriputra, an extremely difficult work that, having obtained the transcendent true knowledge in this world Sahâ, I taught the Law which all the world is reluctant to accept, during this corruption of mankind, of belief, of passion, of life, and of this present kalpa.'

§ 20. Thus spoke Bhagavat joyful in his mind. And the honourable *S*âriputra, and the Bhikshus and Bodhisattvas, and the whole world with the gods, men, evil spirits and genii, applauded the speech of Bhagavat.

This is the Mahâyânasûtra [1]
called Sukhâvatî-vyûha.

---

[1] The Sukhâvatî-vyûha, even in its shortest text, is called a Mahâyâna-sûtra, nor is there any reason why a Mahâyâna-sûtra should not be short. The meaning of Mahâyâna-sûtra is simply a Sûtra belonging to the Mahâyâna school, the school of the Great Boat. It was Burnouf who, in his Introduction to the History of Buddhism, tried very hard to establish a distinction between the

Vaipulya or developed Sûtras, and what he calls the simple Sûtras. Now, the Vaipulya Sûtras may all belong to the Mahâyâna school, but that would not prove that all the Sûtras of the Mahâyâna school are Vaipulya or developed Sûtras. The name of simple Sûtra, in opposition to the Vaipulya or developed Sûtras, is not recognised by the Buddhists themselves; at least, I know no name for simple Sûtras. No doubt there is a great difference between a Vaipulya Sûtra, such as the Lotus of the Good Law, translated by Burnouf, and the Sûtras which Burnouf translated, for instance, from the Divyâvadâna. But what Burnouf considers as the distinguishing mark of a Vaipulya Sûtra, viz. the occurrence of Bodhisattvas, as followers of the Buddha *S*âkyamuni, would no longer seem to be tenable *, unless we classed our short Sukhâvatî-vyûha as a Vaipulya or developed Sûtra. For this there is no authority. Our Sûtra is a Mahâyâna Sûtra, but never called a Vaipulya Sûtra, and yet in this Sûtra the Bodhisattvas constitute a very considerable portion among the followers of Buddha. But more than that, Amitâbha, the Buddha of Sukhâvatî, another personage whom Burnouf looks upon as peculiar to the Vaipulya Sûtras, who is, in fact, one of the Dhyâni-buddhas, though not called by that name in our Sûtra, forms the chief object of its teaching, and is represented as known to Buddha *S*âkyamuni, nay, as having become a Buddha long before the Buddha *S*âkyamuni †. The larger text of the Sukhâvatî-vyûha would certainly, according to Burnouf's definition, seem to fall into the category of the Vaipulya Sûtras. But it is not so called in the MSS. which I have seen, and Burnouf himself gives an analysis of that Sûtra (Introduction, p. 99) as a specimen of a Mahâyâna, but not of a Vaipulya Sûtra.

* 'La présence des Bodhisattvas ou leur absence intéresse donc le fonds même des livres où on la remarque, et il est bien évident que ce seul point trace une ligne de démarcation profonde entre les Sûtras ordinaires et les Sûtras développés.'—Burnouf, Introduction, p. 112.

† 'L'idée d'un ou de plusieurs Buddhas surhumains, celle de Bodhisattvas créés par eux, sont des conceptions aussi étrangères à ces livres (les Sûtras simples) que celle d'un Âdibuddha ou d'un Dieu.'—Burnouf, Introduction, p. 120.

INDEX OF NAMES AND SUBJECTS

IN THE SMALLER SUKHÂVATÎ-VYÛHA.

INDEX OF SANSKRIT WORDS,

CHIEFLY THOSE EXPLAINED IN THE NOTES.

THE

VA*G*RA*KKH*EDIKÂ.

THE

VAGRAKKHEDIKÂ

OR

DIAMOND-CUTTER.

ADORATION to the blessed Ârya-pragñâ-pâramitâ (perfection of wisdom).

I.

Thus it was heard by me: At one time Bhagavat (the blessed Buddha) dwelt in Srâvastî, in the grove of *G*eta [1], in the garden of Anâthapi*nd*ada [2], together with a large company of Bhikshus (mendicants), viz. with 1250 Bhikshus [3], with many noble-minded Bodhisattvas [4].

---

[1] *G*eta, son of king Prasena*g*it, to whom the park belonged before it was sold to Anâthapi*nd*ada.

[2] Another name of Sudatta, meaning, literally, he who gives food to the poor.

[3] The number of 1250 is explained by a Chinese priest Luṅ-hiṅ, in his commentary on the Amitâyur-dhyâna-sûtra. According to the Dharmagupta-vinaya, which he quotes, the number consisted of 500 disciples of Uruvilva-kâsyapa, 300 of Gayâ-kâsyapa, 200 of Nadî-kâsyapa, 150 of Sâriputra, and 100 of Maudgalyâyana. The Chinese translators often mistook the Sanskrit expression 'half-thirteen hundred,' i.e. 1250. See Bunyiu Nanjio, Catalogue of Tripi*t*aka, p. 6.

[4] Higher beings on the road to Bodhi or perfect knowledge. They are destined hereafter to become Buddhas themselves.

Then Bhagavat having in the forenoon put on his undergarment[1], and having taken his bowl and cloak, entered the great city of *S*râvastî to collect alms. Then Bhagavat, after he had gone to the great city of *S*râvastî to collect alms, performed the act of eating[2], and having returned from his round in the afternoon[3], he put away his bowl and cloak, washed his feet, and sat down on the seat intended[4] for him, crossing his legs[5], holding his body upright, and turning his reflection upon himself. Then many Bhikshus approached to where Bhagavat was, saluted his feet with their heads, turned three times round him to the right, and sat down on one side. (1)

II.

At that time again the venerable Subhûti came to that assembly and sat down. Then rising from his seat and putting his robe over one shoulder, kneeling on the earth with his right knee, he stretched out his folded hands towards Bhagavat and said to him: 'It is wonderful, O Bhagavat, it is exceedingly wonderful, O Sugata, how much the noble-minded Bodhisattvas have been favoured with the highest favour by the Tathâgata, the holy and

[1] In Pâli pubba*m*hasamaya*m* nivâsetva, the technical expression for putting on the robes early in the morning; see Childers, s. v. nivâseti.

[2] In Pâli katabhattaki*kk*o, see Childers, s. v.

[3] In Pâli pa*kkh*âbhatta*m* pi*nd*apâtapa*t*ikkânta, see Childers, s. v. pi*nd*apâta. Vig. observes that pa*kkh*abhatta*m* pi*nd*apâtapa*t*ikkânto is a ὕστερον πρότερον, as it means, having returned from his rounds, and then made his meal on the food obtained on his rounds.

[4] Pâli pa*ññ*ata.

[5] Burnouf, Lotus, p. 334.

fully enlightened! It is wonderful how much the noble-minded Bodhisattvas have been instructed[1] with the highest instruction by the Tathâgata, the holy and fully enlightened! How then, O Bhagavat, should the son or the daughter of a good family, after having entered on the path of the Bodhisattvas, behave, how should he advance, and how should he restrain his thoughts?'

After the venerable Subhûti had thus spoken, Bhagavat said to him: 'Well said, well said, Subhûti! So it is, Subhûti, so it is, as you say. The noble-minded Bodhisattvas have been favoured with the highest favour by the Tathâgata, the noble-minded Bodhisattvas have been instructed with the highest instruction by the Tathâgata. Therefore, O Subhûti, listen and take it to heart, well and rightly. I shall tell you, how any one who has entered on the path of Bodhisattvas should behave, how he should advance, and how he should restrain his thoughts.' Then the venerable Subhûti answered the Bhagavat and said: 'So be it, O Bhagavat.' (2)

III.

Then the Bhagavat thus spoke to him: 'Any one, O Subhûti, who has entered here on the path of the Bodhisattvas must thus frame his thought: As many beings as there are in this world of beings, comprehended under the term of beings (either born of eggs, or from the womb, or from moisture, or miraculously), with form or without form, with name or without name, or neither with nor without name, as far as

[1] I have followed the Chinese translator, who translates parîndita by instructed, entrusted, not by protected.

any known world of beings is known, all these must be delivered by me in the perfect world of Nirvâna. And yet, after I have thus delivered immeasurable beings, not one single being has been delivered. And why? If, O Subhûti, a Bodhisattva had any idea of (belief in) a being, he could not be called a Bodhisattva (one who is fit to become a Buddha). And why? Because, O Subhûti, no one is to be called a Bodhisattva, for whom there should exist the idea of a being, the idea of a living being, or the idea of a person.' (3)

IV.

'And again, O Subhûti, a gift should not be given by a Bodhisattva, while he believes[1] in objects; a gift should not be given by him, while he believes in anything; a gift should not be given by him, while he believes in form; a gift should not be given by him, while he believes in the special qualities of sound, smell, taste, and touch. For thus, O Subhûti, should a gift be given by a noble-minded Bodhisattva, that he should not believe even in the idea of cause. And why? Because that Bodhisattva, O Subhûti, who gives a gift, without believing in anything, the measure of his stock of merit is not easy to learn.'—'What do you think, O Subhûti, is it easy to learn the measure of space in the eastern quarter?' Subhûti said: 'Not indeed, O Bhagavat.' —Bhagavat said: 'In like manner, is it easy to learn the measure of space in the southern, western, northern quarters, below and above (nadir and zenith), in quarters and subquarters, in the ten quarters all round?' Subhûti said: 'Not indeed,

[1] To believe here means to depend on or to accept as real.

O Bhagavat.' Bhagavat said: 'In the same manner, O Subhûti, the measure of the stock of merit of a Bodhisattva, who gives a gift without believing in anything, is not easy to learn. And thus indeed, O Subhûti, should one who has entered on the path of Bodhisattvas give a gift, that he should not believe even in the idea of cause.' (4)

V.

'Now, what do you think, O Subhûti, should a Tathâgata be seen (known) by the possession of signs[1]?' Subhûti said: 'Not indeed, O Bhagavat, a Tathâgata is not to be seen (known) by the possession of signs. And why? Because what has been preached by the Tathâgata as the possession of signs, that is indeed the possession of no-signs.'

After this, Bhagavat spoke thus to the venerable Subhûti: 'Wherever there is, O Subhûti, the possession of signs, there is falsehood; wherever there is no possession of signs, there is no falsehood. Hence the Tathâgata is to be seen (known) from no-signs as signs[2].' (5)

VI.

After this, the venerable Subhûti spoke thus to the Bhagavat: 'Forsooth, O Bhagavat, will there be any beings in the future, in the last time, in the last moment, in the last 500 years[3], during the time

---

[1] Qualities by which he could be known.

[2] It would be easier to read lakshanâlakshanatvatah, from the signs having the character of no-signs. M. de Harlez translates rightly, 'c'est par le non-marque de marquer que la Tathâgata doit être vu et reconnu.'

[3] I have changed Pañkâsatî into Pañkasatî, because what is

of the decay of the good Law, who, when these very words of the Sûtras are being preached, will frame a true idea[1]?' The Bhagavat said: 'Do not speak thus, Subhûti. Yes, there will be some beings in the future, in the last time, in the last moment, in the last 500 years, during the decay of the good Law, who will frame a true idea when these very words are being preached.

'And again, O Subhûti, there will be noble-minded Bodhisattvas, in the future, in the last time, in the last moment, in the last 500 years, during the decay of the good Law, there will be strong and good and wise beings, who, when these very words of the Sûtras are being preached, will frame a true idea. But those noble-minded Bodhisattvas, O Subhûti, will not have served one Buddha only, and the stock

intended here is evidently the last of the periods of 500 years each, which, according to the Mahâyâna-Buddhists, elapsed after the death of Buddha. The following extract from the Mahâsannipâta-sûtra (Ta-tsi-king, No. 61 in Tripi*t*aka), given to me by Mr. B. Nanjio, fully explains the subject. 'It is stated in the fifty-first section of the Mahâsannipâta-sûtra, that Buddha said: "After my Nirvâ*n*a, in the first 500 years, all the Bhikshus and others will be strong in deliberation in my correct Law. (Those who first obtain the 'holy fruit,' i.e. the Srota-âpannas, are called those who have obtained deliberation.) In the next or second 500 years, they will be strong in meditation. In the next or third 500 years, they will be strong in 'much learning,' i.e. bahu*s*ruta, religious knowledge. In the next or fourth 500 years, they will be strong in founding monasteries, &c. In the last or fifth 500 years, they will be strong in fighting and reproving. The pure (lit. white) Law will then become invisible."'

The question therefore amounts to this, whether in that corrupt age the law of Buddha will still be understood? and the answer is, that there will be always some excellent Boddhisattvas who, even in the age of corruption, can understand the preaching of the Law.

[1] Will understand them properly.

of their merit will not have been accumulated under one Buddha only; on the contrary, O Subhûti, those noble-minded Bodhisattvas will have served many hundred thousands of Buddhas, and the stock of their merit will have been accumulated under many hundred thousands of Buddhas; and they, when these very words of the Sûtras are being preached, will obtain one and the same faith [1]. They are known, O Subhûti, by the Tathâgata through his Buddha-knowledge; they are seen, O Subhûti, by the Tathâgata through his Buddha-eye; they are understood, O Subhûti, by the Tathâgata. All these, O Subhûti, will produce and will hold fast an immeasurable and innumerable stock of merit. And why? Because, O Subhûti, there does not exist in those noble-minded Bodhisattvas the idea of self, there does not exist the idea of a being, the idea of a living being, the idea of a person. Nor does there exist, O Subhûti, for these noble-minded Bodhisattvas the idea of quality (dharma), nor of no-quality. Neither does there exist, O Subhûti, any idea (sa*m*g*ñ*â) or no-idea. And why? Because, O Subhûti, if there existed for these noble-minded Bodhisattvas the idea of quality, then they would believe in a self, they would believe in a being, they would believe in a living being, they would believe in a person. And if there existed for them the idea of no-quality, even then they would believe in a self,

[1] I am doubtful about the exact meaning of eka*k*ittaprasâda. Childers gives eka*k*itta, as an adjective, with the meaning of 'having the same thought,' and *k*ittaprasâda, as faith in Buddha. But eka*k*ittaprasâda may also be 'faith produced by one thought,' 'immediate faith,' and this too is a recognised form of faith in Buddhism. See Sukhâvatî, pp. 71, 108.

they would believe in a being, they would believe in a living being, they would believe in a person. And why? Because, O Subhûti, neither quality nor no-quality is to be accepted by a noble-minded Bodhisattva. Therefore this hidden saying has been preached by the Tathâgata: "By those who know the teaching of the Law, as like unto a raft, all qualities indeed must be abandoned; much more no-qualities[1]."' (6)

VII.

And again Bhagavat spoke thus to the venerable Subhûti: 'What do you think, O Subhûti, is there anything (dharma) that was known by the Tathâgata under the name of the highest perfect knowledge, or anything that was taught by the Tathâgata?'

After these words, the venerable Subhûti spoke thus to Bhagavat: 'As I, O Bhagavat, understand the meaning of the preaching of the Bhagavat, there is nothing that was known by the Tathâgata under the name of the highest perfect knowledge, nor is there anything that is taught by the Tathâgata. And why? Because that thing which was known or taught by the Tathâgata is incomprehensible and inexpressible. It is neither a thing nor no-thing. And why? Because the holy persons[2] are of imperfect power[3].' (7)

---

[1] The same line is quoted in the Abhidharmakosha-vyâkhyâ.

[2] Âryapudgala need not be Bodhisattvas, but all who have entered on the path leading to Nirvâ*n*a.

[3] Harlez: 'Parceque les entités supérieures sont produites telles sans être réelles et parfaites pour cela.' If sa*m*skr*i*ta can be used in Buddhist literature in the sense of perfect, and prabhâvitâ as power, my translation might pass, but even then the 'because' remains difficult.

VIII.

Bhagavat said: 'What do you think, O Subhûti, if a son or daughter of a good family filled this sphere of a million millions of worlds[1] with the seven gems or treasures, and gave it as a gift to the holy and enlightened Tathâgatas, would that son or daughter of a good family on the strength of this produce a large stock of merit?' Subhûti said: 'Yes, O Bhagavat, yes, O Sugata, that son or daughter of a good family would on the strength of this produce a large stock of merit. And why? Because, O Bhagavat, what was preached by the Tathâgata as the stock of merit, that was preached by the Tathâgata as no-stock of merit. Therefore the Tathâgata preaches: "A stock of merit, a stock of merit[2] indeed!"' Bhagavat said: 'And if, O Subhûti, the son or daughter of a good family should fill this sphere of a million millions of worlds with the seven treasures and should give it as a gift to the holy and enlightened Tathâgatas, and if another after taking from this treatise of the Law one Gâthâ of four lines only should fully teach others and explain it, he indeed would on the strength of this produce a larger stock of merit immeasurable and innumerable. And why? Because, O Subhûti, the highest perfect knowledge of the holy and enlightened Tathâgatas is produced from it; the blessed Buddhas are produced from it. And why? Because, O Subhûti, when the Tathâgata preached:

[1] See Childers, s. v. Lokadhâtu.

[2] Or should it be, bhâshate *x* pu*n*yaskandha*h* pu*n*yaskandha iti, i.e. he preaches no-stock of merit is the stock of merit? It would not be applicable to later passages, but the style of the Sûtras varies.

"The qualities of Buddha, the qualities of Buddha indeed!" they were preached by him as no-qualities of Buddha. Therefore they are called the qualities of Buddha.' (8)

IX.

Bhagavat said[1]: 'Now, what do you think, O Subhûti, does a Srota-âpanna[2] think in this wise: The fruit of Srota-âpatti has been obtained by me?' Subhûti said: 'Not indeed, O Bhagavat, a Srota-âpanna does not think in this wise: The fruit of Srota-âpatti has been obtained by me. And why? Because, O Bhagavat, he has not obtained any particular state (dharma). Therefore he is called a Srota-âpanna. He has not obtained any form, nor sounds, nor smells, nor tastes, nor things that can be touched. Therefore he is called a Srota-âpanna. If, O Bhagavat, a Srota-âpanna were to think in this wise: The fruit of Srota-âpatti has been obtained by me, he would believe in a self, he would believe in a being, he would believe in a living being, he would believe in a person.'

Bhagavat said: 'What do you think, O Subhûti, does a Sak*ri*dâgâmin think in this wise: The fruit of a Sak*ri*dâgâmin has been obtained by me?' Subhûti said: 'Not indeed, O Bhagavat, a Sak*ri*-

[1] This phrase is wanting in the Sanskrit MSS., but it is found in the Chinese translation of Dharmagupta, of the Sui dynasty (A.D. 589–618).

[2] Srota-âpanna, a man who has obtained the first grade of sanctification, literally, who has entered the stream. The second grade is that of the Sak*ri*dâgâmin, who returns once. The third grade is that of the Anâgâmin, who does not return at all, but is born in the Brahman world from whence he becomes an Arhat and may obtain Nirvâ*n*a.

dâgâmin does not think in this wise: The fruit of a Sak*ri*dâgâmin has been obtained by me. And why? Because he is not an individual being (dharma), who has obtained the state of a Sak*ri*dâgâmin. Therefore he is called a Sak*ri*-dâgâmin.'

Bhagavat said: 'What do you think, O Subhûti, does an Anâgâmin think in this wise: The fruit of an Anâgâmin has been obtained by me?' Subhûti said: 'Not indeed, O Bhagavat, an Anâgâmin does not think in this wise: The fruit of an Anâgâmin has been obtained by me. And why? Because he is not an individual being, who has obtained the state of an Anâgâmin. Therefore he is called an Anâgâmin.'

Bhagavat said: 'What do you think, O Subhûti, does an Arhat think in this wise: The fruit of an Arhat has been obtained by me?' Subhûti said: 'Not indeed, O Bhagavat, an Arhat does not think in this wise: The fruit of an Arhat has been obtained by me. And why? Because he is not an individual being, who is called an Arhat. Therefore he is called an Arhat. And if, O Bhagavat, an Arhat were to think in this wise: The state of an Arhat has been obtained by me, he would believe in a self, he would believe in a being, he would believe in a living being, he would believe in a person.

'And why? I have been pointed out, O Bhagavat, by the holy and fully enlightened Tathâgata, as the foremost of those who dwell in virtue[1].

[1] Ara*n*âvihârin. Ra*n*a is strife, then sin, therefore ara*n*a might be peace and virtue, only the a would be short. Probably ara*n*a-vihârin was formed with reference to âra*n*ya-vihârin, living in

I, O Bhagavat, am an Arhat, freed from passion. And yet, O Bhagavat, I do not think in this wise: I am an Arhat, I am freed from passion. If, O Bhagavat, I should think in this wise, that the state of an Arhat has been obtained by me, then the Tathâgata would not have truly prophesied of me, saying: "Subhûti, the son of a good family, the foremost of those dwelling in virtue, does not dwell anywhere, and therefore he is called a dweller in virtue, a dweller in virtue indeed!"' (9)

X.

Bhagavat said: 'What do you think, O Subhûti, is there anything (dharma) which the Tathâgata has adopted from the Tathâgata Dîpankara[1], the holy and fully enlightened?' Subhûti said: 'Not indeed, O Bhagavat; there is not anything which the Tathâgata has adopted from the Tathâgata Dîpankara, the holy and fully enlightened.'

Bhagavat said: 'If, O Subhûti, a Bodhisattva should say: "I shall create numbers of worlds," he would say what is untrue. And why? Because, O Subhûti, when the Tathâgata preached: "Numbers of worlds, numbers of worlds indeed!" they were preached by him as no-numbers. Therefore they are called numbers of worlds.

'Therefore, O Subhûti, a noble-minded Bodhisattva should in this wise frame an independent

the forest, retired from the world, and in peace, just as arhan, worthy, was changed into arahan, the destroyer of sin. Beal translates, 'one who delights in the mortification of an Aranyaka (forest devotee).' De Harlez: 'chef de ceux qui ne sont plus attachés à la jouissance.'

[1] A former Buddha.

mind, which is to be framed as a mind not believing in anything, not believing in form, not believing in sound, smell, taste, and anything that can be touched. Now, for instance, O Subhûti, a man might have a body and a large body, so that his size should be as large as the king of mountains, Sumeru. Do you think then, O Subhûti, that his selfhood (he himself) would be large?' Subhûti said: 'Yes, O Bhagavat, yes, O Sugata, his selfhood would be large. And why? Because, O Bhagavat, when the Tathâgata preached: "Selfhood, selfhood indeed!" it was preached by him as no-selfhood. Therefore it is called selfhood.' (10)

XI.

Bhagavat said: 'What do you think, O Subhûti, if there were as many Gaṅgâ rivers as there are grains of sand in the large river Gaṅgâ, would the grains of sand be many?' Subhûti said: 'Those Gaṅgâ rivers would indeed be many, much more the grains of sand in those Gaṅgâ rivers.' Bhagavat said: 'I tell you, O Subhûti, I announce to you, If a woman or man were to fill with the seven treasures as many worlds as there would be grains of sand in those Gaṅgâ rivers and present them as a gift to the holy and fully enlightened Tathâgatas —What do you think, O Subhûti, would that woman or man on the strength of this produce a large stock of merit?' Subhûti said: 'Yes, O Bhagavat, yes, O Sugata, that woman or man would on the strength of this produce a large stock of merit, immeasurable and innumerable.' Bhagavat said: 'And if, O Subhûti, a woman or man having filled so many worlds with the seven treasures should give them as a gift to the holy and enlightened Tathâgatas, and if another son or daughter of a good family, after taking from this treatise of the Law one Gâthâ of four lines only, should fully teach others and explain it, he, indeed, would on the strength of this produce a larger stock of merit, immeasurable and innumerable.' (11)

XII.

'Then again, O Subhûti, that part of the world in which, after taking from this treatise of the Law one Gâthâ of four lines only, it should be preached or explained, would be like a *K*aitya (holy shrine) for the whole world of gods, men, and spirits; what should we say then of those who learn the whole of this treatise of the Law to the end, who repeat it, understand it, and fully explain it to others? They, O Subhûti, will be endowed with the highest wonder[1]. And in that place, O Subhûti, there dwells the teacher[2], or one after another holding the place of the wise preceptor[3].' (12)

XIII.

After these words, the venerable Subhûti spoke thus to Bhagavat: 'O Bhagavat, how is this treatise of the Law called, and how can I learn it?' After this, Bhagavat spoke thus to the venerable Subhûti: 'This treatise of the Law, O Subhûti, is called the Pra*g*ñâ-pâramitâ (Transcendent wisdom), and you should learn it by that name. And why? Because, O Subhûti, what was preached by the Tathâgata as the Pra*g*ñâ-pâramitâ, that was preached by the

[1] With what excites the highest wonder.

[2] *S*astâ, often the name of Buddha, Pâli sattha.

[3] This may refer to a succession of teachers handing down the tradition one to the other.

Tathâgata as no-Pâramitâ. Therefore it is called the Pragñâ-pâramitâ.

'Then, what do you think, O Subhûti, is there anything (dharma) that was preached by the Tathâgata?' Subhûti said: 'Not indeed, O Bhagavat, there is not anything that was preached by the Tathâgata.'

Bhagavat said: 'What do you think then, O Subhûti,—the dust of the earth which is found in this sphere of a million millions of worlds, is that much?' Subhûti said: 'Yes, O Bhagavat, yes, O Sugata, that dust of the earth would be much. And why? Because, O Bhagavat, what was preached by the Tathâgata as the dust of the earth, that was preached by the Tathâgata as no-dust. Therefore it is called the dust of the earth. And what was preached by the Tathâgata as the sphere of worlds, that was preached by the Tathâgata as no-sphere. Therefore it is called the sphere of worlds.'

Bhagavat said: 'What do you think, O Subhûti, is a holy and fully enlightened Tathâgata to be seen (known) by the thirty-two signs of a hero?' Subhûti said: 'No indeed, O Bhagavat; a holy and fully enlightened Tathâgata is not to be seen (known) by the thirty-two signs of a hero. And why? Because what was preached by the Tathâgata as the thirty-two signs of a hero, that was preached by the Tathâgata as no-signs. Therefore they are called the thirty-two signs of a hero.'

Bhagavat said: 'If, O Subhûti, a woman or man should day by day sacrifice his life (selfhood[1]) as

[1] Âtmabhâva seems to refer here to the living body, not to the spiritual Âtman, which, according to Buddha, can be got rid of by

many times as there are grains of sand in the river Gaṅgâ, and if he should thus sacrifice his life for as many kalpas as there are grains of sand in the river Gaṅgâ, and if another man, after taking from this treatise of the Law one Gâthâ of four lines only, should fully teach others and explain it, he indeed would on the strength of this produce a larger stock of merit, immeasurable and innumerable.' (13)

XIV.

At that time, the venerable Subhûti was moved by the power of the Law, shed tears, and having wiped his tears, he thus spoke to Bhagavat: 'It is wonderful, O Bhagavat, it is exceedingly wonderful, O Sugata, how fully this teaching of the Law has been preached by the Tathâgata for the benefit of those beings who entered on the foremost path (the path that leads to Nirvâ*n*a), and who entered on the best path, from whence, O Bhagavat, knowledge has been produced in me. Never indeed, O Bhagavat, has such a teaching of the Law been heard by me before. Those Bodhisattvas, O Bhagavat, will be endowed with the highest wonder[1], who when this Sûtra is being preached hear it and will frame to themselves a true idea. And why? Because what is a true idea is not a true idea. Therefore the Tathâgata preaches: "A true idea, a true idea indeed!"

'It is no wonder to me, O Bhagavat, that I accept and believe this treatise of the Law, which has been preached. And those beings also, O Bhagavat,

knowledge only. Buddha himself sacrificed his life again and again, and a willingness to die would probably be accepted for the deed.

[1] Will possess miraculous powers, and will be admired.

who will exist in the future, in the last time, in the last moment, in the last 500 years, during the time of the decay of the good Law, who will learn this treatise of the Law, O Bhagavat, remember it, recite it, understand it, and fully explain it to others, they will indeed be endowed with the highest wonder.

'But, O Bhagavat, there will not arise in them any idea of a self, any idea of a being, of a living being, or a person, nor does there exist for them any idea or no-idea. And why? Because, O Bhagavat, the idea of a self is no-idea, and the idea of a being, or a living being, or a person is no-idea. And why? Because the blessed Buddhas are freed from all ideas.'

After these words, Bhagavat thus spoke to the venerable Subhûti: 'So it is, O Subhûti, so it is. Those beings, O Subhûti, who when this Sûtra was being recited here will not be disturbed or frightened or become alarmed, will be endowed with the highest wonder. And why? Because, O Subhûti, this was preached by the Tathâgata, as the Paramapâramitâ, which is no-Pâramitâ. And, O Subhûti, what the Tathâgata preaches as the Paramapâramitâ, that was preached also by immeasurable blessed Buddhas. Therefore it is called the Paramapâramitâ.

'And, O Subhûti, the Pâramitâ or the highest perfection of endurance (kshânti) belonging to a Tathâgata, that also is no-Pâramitâ. And why? Because, O Subhûti, at the time when the king of Kaliṅga[1] cut my flesh from every limb, I had no idea of a self, of a being, of a living being, or of

[1] The Chinese text points to Kalirâgâ. On this Kalirâgâ or Kalinripa see Lalita-vistara, p. 191.

a person; I had neither an idea nor no-idea. And why? Because, O Subhûti, if I at that time had had an idea of a self, I should also have had an idea of malevolence. If I had had an idea of a being, or of a living being, or of a person, I should also have had an idea of malevolence. And why? Because, O Subhûti, I remember the past 500 births, when I was the *Ri*shi Kshântivâdin (preacher of endurance). At that time also, I had no idea of a self, of a being, of a living being, of a person. Therefore then, O Subhûti, a noble-minded Bodhisattva, after putting aside all ideas, should raise his mind to the highest perfect knowledge. He should frame his mind so as not to believe (depend) in form, sound, smell, taste, or anything that can be touched, in something (dharma), in nothing or anything. And why? Because what is believed is not believed (not to be depended on). Therefore the Tathâgata preaches: "A gift should not be given by a Bodhisattva[1] who believes in anything, it should not be given by one who believes in form, sound, smell, taste, or anything that can be touched."

'And again, O Subhûti, a Bodhisattva should in such wise give his gift for the benefit of all beings. And why? Because, O Subhûti, the idea of a being is no-idea. And those who are thus spoken of by the Tathâgata as all beings are indeed no-beings. And why? Because, O Subhûti, a Tathâgata says what is real, says what is true, says the things as they are; a Tathâgata does not speak untruth.

'But again, O Subhûti, whatever doctrine has been

[1] See before, chap. iv.

perceived, taught, and meditated on by a Tathâgata, in it there is neither truth nor falsehood. And as a man who has entered the darkness would not see anything, thus a Bodhisattva is to be considered who is immersed in objects, and who being immersed in objects gives a gift. But as a man who has eyes would, when the night becomes light, and the sun has risen, see many things, thus a Bodhisattva is to be considered who is not immersed in objects, and who not being immersed in objects gives a gift.

'And again, O Subhûti, if any sons or daughters of good families will learn this treatise of the Law, will remember, recite, and understand it, and fully explain it to others, they, O Subhûti, are known by the Tathâgata through his Buddha-knowledge, they are seen, O Subhûti, by the Tathâgata through his Buddha-eye. All these beings, O Subhûti, will produce and hold fast an immeasurable and innumerable stock of merit.' (14)

XV.

'And if, O Subhûti, a woman or man sacrificed in the morning as many lives as there are grains of sand in the river Gaṅgâ and did the same at noon and the same in the evening, and if in this way they sacrificed their lives for a hundred thousands of niyutas of ko*t*is of ages, and if another, after hearing this treatise of the Law, should not oppose it, then the latter would on the strength of this produce a larger stock of merit, immeasurable and innumerable. What should we say then of him who after having written it, learns it, remembers it, understands it, and fully explains it to others?

'And again, O Subhûti, this treatise of the Law is

incomprehensible and incomparable. And this treatise of the Law has been preached by the Tathâgata for the benefit of those beings who entered on the foremost path (the path that leads to Nirvâ*n*a), and who entered on the best path. And those who will learn this treatise of the Law, who will remember it, recite it, understand it, and fully explain it to others, they are known, O Subhûti, by the Tathâgata through his Buddha-knowledge, they are seen, O Subhûti, by the Tathâgata through his Buddha-eye. All these beings, O Subhûti, will be endowed with an immeasurable stock of merit, they will be endowed with an incomprehensible, incomparable, immeasurable and unmeasured stock of merit. All these beings, O Subhûti, will equally remember the Bodhi (the highest Buddha-knowledge), will recite it, and understand it. And why? Because it is not possible, O Subhûti, that this treatise of the Law should be heard by beings of little faith, by those who believe in self, in beings, in living beings, and in persons. It is impossible that this treatise of the Law should be heard by beings who have not acquired the knowledge of Bodhisattvas, or that it should be learned, remembered, recited, and understood by them. The thing is impossible.

'And again, O Subhûti, that part of the world in which this Sûtra will be propounded, will have to be honoured by the whole world of gods, men, and evil spirits, will have to be worshipped, and will become like a *K*aitya (a holy sepulchre).' (15)

XVI.

'And, O Subhûti, sons or daughters of a good family who will learn these very Sûtras, who will remember them, recite them, understand them, thoroughly take them to heart, and fully explain them to others, they will be overcome[1], they will be greatly overcome. And why? Because, O Subhûti, whatever evil deeds these beings have done in a former birth, deeds that must lead to suffering, those deeds these beings, owing to their being overcome, after they have seen the Law, will destroy, and they will obtain the knowledge of Buddha.

'I remember, O Subhûti, in the past, before innumerable and more than innumerable kalpas, there were eighty-four hundred thousands of niyutas of ko*t*is of Buddhas following after the venerable and fully enlightened Tathâgata Dîpaṅkara, who were pleased by me, and after being pleased were not displeased. And if, O Subhûti, these blessed Buddhas were pleased by me, and after being pleased were not displeased, and if on the other hand people at the last time, at the last moment, in the last 500 years, during the time of the decay of the good Law, will learn these very Sûtras, remember them, recite them, understand them, and fully explain them to others, then, O Subhûti, in comparison with their stock of merit that former stock of merit will not come to one hundredth part, nay, not to one thousandth part, not to a hundred thousandth part, not to a ten millionth part, not to a hundred millionth part, not to a hundred thousand ten millionth part, not to a hundred thousands of niyutas ten millionth part. It will not bear number, nor fraction, nor counting, nor comparison, nor approach, nor analogy.

'And if, O Subhûti, I were to tell you the stock of

[1] Paribhûta is explained by despised, but the sense, or even the non-sense, is difficult to understand.

merit of those sons or daughters of good families, and how large a stock of merit those sons or daughters of good families will produce, and hold fast at that time, people would become distracted and their thoughts would become bewildered. And again, O Subhûti, as this treatise of the Law preached by the Tathâgata is incomprehensible and incomparable, its rewards also must be expected (to be) incomprehensible.' (16)

XVII.

At that time the venerable Subhûti thus spoke to the Bhagavat: 'How should a person, after having entered on the path of the Bodhisattvas, behave, how should he advance, and how should he restrain his thoughts?' Bhagavat said: 'He who has entered on the path of the Bodhisattvas should thus frame his thought: All beings must be delivered by me in the perfect world of Nirvâ*n*a; and yet after I have thus delivered these beings, no being has been delivered. And why? Because, O Subhûti, if a Bodhisattva had any idea of beings, he could not be called a Bodhisattva, and so on[1] from the idea of a living being to the idea of a person; if he had any such idea, he could not be called a Bodhisattva. And why? Because, O Subhûti, there is no such thing (dharma) as one who has entered on the path of the Bodhisattvas.

'What do you think, O Subhûti, is there anything which the Tathâgata has adopted from the Tathâgata Dîpankara with regard to the highest perfect knowledge?' After this, the venerable Subhûti

[1] See chap. iii, p. 114.

spoke thus to the Bhagavat: 'As far as I, O Bhagavat, understand the meaning of the preaching of the Bhagavat, there is nothing which has been adopted by the Tathâgata from the holy and fully enlightened Tathâgata Dîpaṅkara with regard to the highest perfect knowledge.' After this, Bhagavat thus spoke to the venerable Subhûti: 'So it is, Subhûti, so it is. There is not, O Subhûti, anything which has been adopted by the Tathâgata from the holy and fully enlightened Tathâgata Dîpaṅkara with regard to the highest perfect knowledge. And if, O Subhûti, anything had been adopted by the Tathâgata, the Tathâgata Dîpaṅkara would not have prophesied of me, saying[1]: "Thou, O boy, wilt be in the future the holy and fully enlightened Tathâgata called *S*âkyamuni." Because then, O Subhûti, there is nothing that has been adopted by the holy and fully enlightened Tathâgata with regard to the highest perfect knowledge, therefore I was prophesied by the Tathâgata Dîpaṅkara, saying: "Thou, boy, wilt be in the future the holy and fully enlightened Tathâgata called *S*âkyamuni."

'And why, O Subhûti, the name of Tathâgata? It expresses true suchness. And why Tathâgata, O Subhûti? It expresses that he had no origin. And why Tathâgata, O Subhûti? It expresses the destruction of all qualities. And why Tathâgata, O Subhûti? It expresses one who had no origin whatever. And why this? Because, O Subhûti, no-origin is the highest goal.

'And whosoever, O Subhûti, should say that, by the holy and fully enlightened Tathâgata, the highest

[1] This prophecy is supposed to have been addressed by Dîpaṅkara to *S*âkyamuni, before he had become a Buddha.

perfect knowledge has been known, he would speak an untruth, and would slander me, O Subhûti, with some untruth that he has learned. And why? Because there is no such thing, O Subhûti, as has been known by the Tathâgata with regard to the highest perfect knowledge. And in that, O Subhûti, which has been known and taught by the Tathâgata, there is neither truth nor falsehood. Therefore the Tathâgata preaches: "All things are Buddha-things." And why? Because what was preached by the Tathâgata, O Subhûti, as all things, that was preached as no-things; and therefore all things are called Buddha-things.

'Now, O Subhûti, a man might have a body and a large body.' The venerable Subhûti said: 'That man who was spoken of by the Tathâgata as a man with a body, with a large body, he, O Bhagavat, was spoken of by the Tathâgata as without a body, and therefore he is called a man with a body and with a large body.'

Bhagavat said: 'So it is, O Subhûti; and if a Bodhisattva were to say: "I shall deliver all beings," he ought not to be called a Bodhisattva. And why? Is there anything, O Subhûti, that is called a Bodhisattva?' Subhûti said: 'Not indeed, Bhagavat, there is nothing which is called a Bodhisattva.' Bhagavat said: 'Those who were spoken of as beings, beings indeed, O Subhûti, they were spoken of as no-beings by the Tathâgata, and therefore they are called beings. Therefore the Tathâgata says: "All beings are without self, all beings are without life, without manhood[1], without a personality."

[1] Sans croissance, Harlez; see Childers, s. v. poriso.

'If, O Subhûti, a Bodhisattva were to say: "I shall create numbers of worlds," he would say what is untrue. And why? Because, what were spoken of as numbers of worlds, numbers of worlds indeed, O Subhûti, these were spoken of as no-numbers by the Tathâgata, and therefore they are called numbers of worlds.

'A Bodhisattva, O Subhûti, who believes that all things are without self, that all things are without self, he has faith, he is called a noble-minded Bodhisattva by the holy and fully enlightened Tathâgata.' (17)

XVIII.

Bhagavat said: 'What do you think, O Subhûti, has the Tathâgata the bodily eye?' Subhûti said: 'So it is, O Bhagavat, the Tathâgata has the bodily eye.'

Bhagavat said: 'What do you think, O Subhûti, has the Tathâgata the heavenly eye?' Subhûti said: 'So it is, O Bhagavat, the Tathâgata has the heavenly eye.'

Bhagavat said: 'What do you think, O Subhûti, has the Tathâgata the eye of knowledge?' Subhûti said: 'So it is, O Bhagavat, the Tathâgata has the eye of knowledge.'

Bhagavat said: 'What do you think, O Subhûti, has the Tathâgata the eye of the Law?' Subhûti said: 'So it is, O Bhagavat, the Tathâgata has the eye of the Law.'

Bhagavat said: 'What do you think, O Subhûti, has the Tathâgata the eye of Buddha?' Subhûti said: 'So it is, O Bhagavat, the Tathâgata has the eye of Buddha.'

Bhagavat said: 'What do you think, O Subhûti, as many grains of sand as there are in the great river Gaṅgâ—were they preached by the Tathâgata as grains of sand?' Subhûti said: 'So it is, O Bhagavat, so it is, O Sugata, they were preached as grains of sand by the Tathâgata.' Bhagavat said: 'What do you think, O Subhûti, if there were as many Gaṅgâ rivers as there are grains of sand in the great river Gaṅgâ; and, if there were as many worlds as there are grains of sand in these, would these worlds be many?' Subhûti said: 'So it is, O Bhagavat, so it is, O Sugata, these worlds would be many.' Bhagavat said: 'As many beings as there are in all those worlds, I know the manifold trains of thought of them all. And why? Because what was preached as the train of thoughts, the train of thoughts indeed, O Subhûti, that was preached by the Tathâgata as no-train of thoughts, and therefore it is called the train of thoughts. And why? Because, O Subhûti, a past thought is not perceived, a future thought is not perceived, and the present thought is not perceived.' (18)

XIX.

'What do you think, O Subhûti, if a son or a daughter of a good family should fill this sphere of a million millions of worlds with the seven treasures, and give it as a gift to holy and fully enlightened Buddhas, would that son or daughter of a good family produce on the strength of this a large stock of merit?' Subhûti said: 'Yes, a large one.' Bhagavat said: 'So it is, Subhûti, so it is; that son or daughter of a good family would produce on the strength of this a large stock of merit, immeasurable and innumerable. And why? Because what was preached as a stock of merit, a stock of merit indeed, O Subhûti, that was preached as no-stock of merit by the Tathâgata, and therefore it is called a stock of merit. If, O Subhûti, there existed a stock of merit, the Tathâgata would not have preached: "A stock of merit, a stock of merit indeed!"' (19)

XX.

'What do you think then, O Subhûti, is a Tathâgata to be seen (known) by the shape of his visible body?' Subhûti said: 'Not indeed, O Bhagavat, a Tathâgata is not to be seen (known) by the shape of his visible body. And why? Because, what was preached, O Bhagavat, as the shape of the visible body, the shape of the visible body indeed, that was preached by the Tathâgata as no-shape of the visible body, and therefore it is called the shape of the visible body.'

Bhagavat said: 'What do you think, O Subhûti, should a Tathâgata be seen (known) by the possession of signs?' Subhûti said: 'Not indeed, O Bhagavat, a Tathâgata is not to be seen (known) by the possession of signs. And why? Because, what was preached by the Tathâgata as the possession of signs, that was preached as no-possession of signs by the Tathâgata, and therefore it is called the possession of signs.' (20)

XXI.

Bhagavat said: 'What do you think, O Subhûti, does the Tathâgata think in this wise: The Law has been taught by me?' Subhûti said: 'Not indeed, O Bhagavat, does the Tathâgata think in this wise: The Law has been taught by me.' Bhagavat said: 'If a man should say that the Law has been taught by the Tathâgata, he would say what is not true; he would slander me with untruth which he has learned. And why? Because, O Subhûti, it is said the teaching of the Law, the teaching of the Law indeed. O Subhûti, there is nothing that can be perceived by the name of the teaching of the Law.'

After this, the venerable Subhûti spoke thus to the Bhagavat: 'Forsooth, O Bhagavat, will there be any beings in the future, in the last time, in the last moment, in the last 500 years, during the time of the decay of the good Law, who, when they have heard these very Laws, will believe?' Bhagavat said: 'These, O Subhûti, are neither beings nor no-beings. And why? Because, O Subhûti, those who were preached as beings, beings indeed, they were preached as no-beings by the Tathâgata, and therefore they are called beings.' (21)

XXII.

'What do you think then, O Subhûti, is there anything which has been known by the Tathâgata in the form of the highest perfect knowledge?' The venerable Subhûti said: 'Not indeed, O Bhagavat, there is nothing, O Bhagavat, that has been known by the Tathâgata in the form of the highest perfect knowledge.' Bhagavat said: 'So it is, Subhûti, so it is. Even the smallest thing is not known or perceived there, therefore it is called the highest perfect knowledge.' (22)

XXIII.

'Also, Subhûti, all is the same there, there is no difference there, and therefore it is called the highest perfect knowledge. Free from self, free from being, free from life, free from personality, that highest perfect knowledge is always the same, and thus known with all good things. And why? Because, what were preached as good things, good things indeed, O Subhûti, they were preached as no-things by the Tathâgata, and therefore they are called good things.' (23)

XXIV.

'And if, O Subhûti, a woman or man, putting together as many heaps of the seven treasures as there are Sumerus, kings of mountains, in the sphere of a million millions of worlds, should give them as a gift to holy and fully enlightened Tathâgatas; and, if a son or a daughter of a good family, after taking from this treatise of the Law, this Pra*gñ*âpâramitâ, one Gâthâ of four lines only, should teach it to others, then, O Subhûti, compared with his stock of merit, the former stock of merit would not come to the one hundredth part,' &c.[1], till 'it will not bear an approach.' (24)

XXV.

'What do you think then, O Subhûti, does a Tathâgata think in this wise: Beings have been delivered by me? You should not think so, O Subhûti. And why? Because there is no being, O Subhûti, that has been delivered by the Tathâgata. And, if there were a being, O Subhûti, that has been delivered by the Tathâgata, then the Tathâgata would believe in self, believe in a being, believe in a living being, and believe in a person. And what is called a belief in self, O Subhûti, that is preached

[1] As before, in chap. xvi.

as no-belief by the Tathâgata. And this is learned by children and ignorant persons; and they who were preached as children and ignorant persons, O Subhûti, were preached as no-persons by the Tathâgata, and therefore they are called children and ignorant persons.' (25)

XXVI.

'What do you think then, O Subhûti, is the Tathâgata to be seen (known) by the possession of signs?' Subhûti said: 'Not indeed, O Bhagavat. So far as I know the meaning of the preaching of the Bhagavat, the Tathâgata is not to be seen (known) by the possession of signs.' Bhagavat said: 'Good, good, Subhûti, so it is, Subhûti; so it is, as you say; a Tathâgata is not to be seen (known) by the possession of signs. And why? Because, O Subhûti, if the Tathâgata were to be seen (known) by the possession of signs, a wheel-turning king also would be a Tathâgata[1]; therefore a Tathâgata is not to be seen (known) by the possession of signs.' The venerable Subhûti spoke thus to the Bhagavat: 'As I understand the meaning of the preaching of the Bhagavat, a Tathâgata is not to be seen (known) by the possession of signs.' Then the Bhagavat at that moment preached these two Gâthâs:

They who saw me by form, and they who heard me by sound,
They engaged in false endeavours, will not see me.

---

[1] This probably refers to the auspicious signs discovered in *S*âkyamuni at his birth, which left it open whether he should become a king or a Buddha.

A Buddha is to be seen (known) from the Law; for
the Lords (Buddhas) have the Law-body;
And the nature of the Law cannot be understood,
nor can it be made to be understood. (26)

XXVII.

'What do you think then, O Subhûti, has the highest perfect knowledge been known by the Tathâgata through the possession of signs? You should not think so, O Subhûti. And why? Because, O Subhûti, the highest perfect knowledge would not be known by the Tathâgata through the possession of signs. Nor should anybody, O Subhûti, say to you that the destruction or annihilation of any thing is proclaimed by those who have entered on the path of the Bodhisattvas.' (27)

XXVIII.

'And if, O Subhûti, a son or a daughter of a good family were to fill worlds equal to the number of grains of sand of the river Gaṅgâ with the seven treasures, and give them as a gift to holy and fully enlightened Tathâgatas; and if a Bodhisattva acquired endurance in selfless and uncreated things, then the latter will on the strength of this produce a larger stock of merit, immeasurable and innumerable.

'But, O Subhûti, a stock of merit should not be appropriated by a noble-minded Bodhisattva.' The venerable Subhûti said: 'Should a stock of merit, O Bhagavat, not be appropriated by a Bodhisattva?' Bhagavat said: 'It should be appropriated, O Subhûti; it should not be appropriated; and therefore it is said: It should be appropriated.' (28)

XXIX.

'And again, O Subhûti, if anybody were to say that the Tathâgata goes, or comes, or stands, or sits, or lies down, he, O Subhûti, does not understand the meaning of my preaching. And why? Because the word Tathâgata means one who does not go to anywhere, and does not come from anywhere; and therefore he is called the Tathâgata (truly come), holy and fully enlightened.' (29)

XXX.

'And again, O Subhûti, if a son or a daughter of a good family were to take as many worlds as there are grains of earth-dust in this sphere of a million millions of worlds, and reduce them to such fine dust as can be made with immeasurable strength, like what is called a mass of the smallest atoms, do you think, O Subhûti, would that be a mass of many atoms?' Subhûti said: 'Yes, Bhagavat, yes, Sugata, that would be a mass of many atoms. And why? Because, O Bhagavat, if it were a mass of many atoms, Bhagavat would not call it a mass of many atoms. And why? Because, what was preached as a mass of many atoms by the Tathâgata, that was preached as no-mass of atoms by the Tathâgata; and therefore it is called a mass of many atoms. And what was preached by the Tathâgata as the sphere of a million millions of worlds, that was preached by the Tathâgata as no-sphere of worlds; and therefore it is called the sphere of a million millions of worlds. And why? Because, O Bhagavat, if there were a sphere of worlds, there would exist a belief in matter; and what was preached as a belief in matter by the Tathâgata, that was preached as no-belief by the Tathâgata; and therefore it is called a belief in matter.' Bhagavat said: 'And a belief in matter itself, O Subhûti, is unmentionable and inexpressible; it is neither a thing nor no-thing, and this is known by children and ignorant persons.' (30)

XXXI.

'And why? Because, O Subhûti, if a man were to say that belief in self, belief in a being, belief in life, belief in personality had been preached by the Tathâgata, would he be speaking truly?' Subhûti said: 'Not indeed, Bhagavat, not indeed, Sugata; he would not be speaking truly. And why? Because, O Bhagavat, what was preached by the Tathâgata as a belief in self, that was preached by the Tathâgata as no-belief; therefore it is called belief in self.'

Bhagavat said: 'Thus then, O Subhûti, are all things to be perceived, to be looked upon, and to be believed by one who has entered on the path of the Bodhisattvas. And in this wise are they to be perceived, to be looked upon, and to be believed, that a man should believe neither in the idea of a thing nor in the idea of a no-thing. And why? Because, by saying: The idea of a thing, the idea of a thing indeed, it has been preached by the Tathâgata as no-idea of a thing.' (31)

XXXII.

'And, O Subhûti, if a noble-minded Bodhisattva were to fill immeasurable and innumerable spheres of worlds with the seven treasures, and give them as a gift to holy and fully enlightened Tathâgatas;

and if a son or a daughter of a good family, after taking from this treatise of the Law, this Pragñâpâramitâ, one Gâthâ of four lines only, should learn it, repeat it, understand it, and fully explain it to others, then the latter would on the strength of this produce a larger stock of merit, immeasurable and innumerable. And how should he explain it? As in the sky:

Stars, darkness, a lamp, a phantom, dew, a bubble.
A dream, a flash of lightning, and a cloud—thus we should look upon the world (all that was made).

Thus he should explain; therefore it is said: He should explain.'

Thus spoke the Bhagavat enraptured. The elder Subhûti, and the friars, nuns, the faithful laymen and women, and the Bodhisattvas also, and the whole world of gods, men, evil spirits and fairies, praised the preaching of the Bhagavat. (32)

Thus is finished the Diamond-cutter, the blessed Pragñâpâramitâ.

THE LARGER

PRAGÑÂ-PÂRAMITÂ-HRIDAYA-SÛTRA.

THE LARGER

PRAG*Ñ*Â-PÂRAMITÂ-H*RI*DAYA-SÛTRA.

ADORATION TO THE OMNISCIENT !

This I heard: At one time the Bhagavat dwelt at Râ*g*agr*i*ha, on the hill G*ri*dhrakû*t*a, together with a large number of Bhikshus and a large number of Bodhisattvas.

At that time the Bhagavat was absorbed in a meditation, called Gambhîrâvasambodha. And at the same time the great Bodhisattva Âryâvalokite*s*vara, performing his study in the deep Pra*gñâ*pâramitâ, thought thus: 'There are the five Skandhas, and those he (the Buddha?) considered as something by nature empty.'

Then the venerable *S*âriputra, through Buddha's power, thus spoke to the Bodhisattva Âryâvalokite*s*vara: 'If the son or daughter of a family wishes to perform the study in the deep Pra*gñ*âpâramitâ, how is he to be taught?'

On this the great Bodhisattva Âryâvalokite*s*vara thus spoke to the venerable *S*âriputra: 'If the son or daughter of a family wishes to perform the study in the deep Pra*gñ*âpâramitâ, he must think thus:

'There are five Skandhas, and these he considered as by their nature empty. Form is emptiness, and emptiness indeed is form. Emptiness is not different from form, form is not different from emptiness. What is form that is emptiness, what is emptiness that is form. Thus perception, name, conception, and knowledge also are emptiness. Thus, O *S*âriputra, all things have the character of emptiness, they have no beginning, no end, they are faultless and not faultless, they are not imperfect and not perfect. Therefore, O *S*âriputra, here in this emptiness there is no form, no perception, no name, no concept, no knowledge. No eye, ear, nose, tongue, body, and mind. No form, sound, smell, taste, touch, and objects. There is no eye,' &c., till we come to 'there is no mind, no objects, no mind-knowledge. There is no knowledge, no ignorance, no destruction (of ignorance),' till we come to 'there is no decay and death, no destruction of decay and death; there are not (the Four Truths, viz.) that there is pain, origin of pain, stoppage of pain, and the path to it. There is no knowledge, no obtaining, no not-obtaining of Nirvâ*n*a. Therefore, O *S*âriputra, as there is no obtaining (of Nirvâ*n*a), a man who has approached the Pra*gñ*âpâramitâ of the Bodhisattvas, dwells (for a time) enveloped in consciousness. But when the envelopment of consciousness has been annihilated, then he becomes free of all fear, beyond the reach of change, enjoying final Nirvâ*n*a.

'All Buddhas of the past, present, and future, after approaching the Pra*gñ*âpâramitâ, have awoke to the highest perfect knowledge.

'Therefore we ought to know the great verse of the Pra*gñ*âpâramitâ, the verse of the great wisdom, the unsurpassed verse, the verse which appeases all pain—it is truth, because it is not false[1]—the verse proclaimed in the Pragñâpâramitâ[2]: "O wisdom, gone, gone, gone to the other shore, landed at the other shore, Svâhâ!"

'Thus, O Sâriputra, should a Bodhisattva teach in the study of the deep Pragñâpâramitâ.'

Then when the Bhagavat had risen from that meditation, he gave his approval to the venerable Bodhisattva Avalokitesvara, saying: 'Well done, well done, noble son! So it is, noble son. So indeed must this study of the deep Pragñâpâramitâ be performed. As it has been described by thee, it is applauded by Arhat Tathâgatas.' Thus spoke Bhagavat with joyful mind. And the venerable Sâriputra, and the honourable Bodhisattva Avalokitesvara, and the whole assembly, and the world of gods, men, demons, and fairies praised the speech of the Bhagavat.

Here ends the Pragñâpâramitâhridayasûtra.

---

[1] It is truth, not falsehood, W text.

[2] Fit for obtaining Pragñâpâramitâ, W text.

THE SMALLER

PRAG*Ñ*Â-PÂRAMITÂ-HR*I*DAYA-SÛTRA.

THE SMALLER

PRAG*Ñ*Â-PÂRAMITÂ-H*R*IDAYA-SÛTRA.

ADORATION TO THE OMNISCIENT!

The venerable Bodhisattva Avalokite*s*vara, performing his study in the deep Prag*ñ*âpâramitâ (perfection of wisdom), thought thus: 'There are the five Skandhas, and these he considered as by their nature empty (phenomenal).'

'O *S*âriputra,' he said, 'form here is emptiness, and emptiness indeed is form. Emptiness is not different from form, form is not different from emptiness. What is form that is emptiness, what is emptiness that is form.'

'The same applies to perception, name, conception, and knowledge.'

'Here, O *S*âriputra, all things have the character of emptiness, they have no beginning, no end, they are faultless and not faultless, they are not imperfect and not perfect. Therefore, O *S*âriputra, in this emptiness there is no form, no perception, no name, no concepts, no knowledge. No eye, ear, nose, tongue, body, mind. No form, sound, smell, taste, touch, objects.'

'There is no eye,' &c., till we come to 'there is no mind.'

(What is left out here are the eighteen Dhâtus or aggregates, viz. eye, form, vision; ear, sound, hearing; nose, odour, smelling; tongue, flavour, tasting; body, touch, feeling; mind, objects, thought.)

'There is no knowledge, no ignorance, no destruction of knowledge, no destruction of ignorance,' &c., till we come to 'there is no decay and death, no destruction of decay and death; there are not (the four truths, viz. that there) is pain, origin of pain, stoppage of pain, and the path to it. There is no knowledge, no obtaining (of Nirvâna).'

'A man who has approached the Pragñâpâramitâ of the Bodhisattva dwells enveloped in consciousness [1]. But when the envelopment of consciousness has been annihilated, then he becomes free of all fear, beyond the reach of change, enjoying final Nirvâna.'

'All Buddhas of the past, present, and future, after approaching the Pragñâpâramitâ, have awoke to the highest perfect knowledge.'

'Therefore one ought to know the great verse of the Pragñâpâramitâ, the verse of the great wisdom, the unsurpassed verse, the peerless verse, which appeases all pain—it is truth, because it is not false—the verse proclaimed in the Pragñâpâramitâ: "O wisdom, gone, gone, gone to the other shore, landed at the other shore, Svâhâ!"'

Thus ends the heart of the Pragñâpâramitâ.

---

[1] See Childers, s.v. *k*ittam.

INDEX OF NAMES AND SUBJECTS

IN THE VAGRAKKHEDIKÂ AND THE PRAGÑÂ-PÂRAMITÂ-HRIDAYA-SÛTRA.

INDEX OF SANSKRIT WORDS,

CHIEFLY THOSE EXPLAINED IN THE NOTES.

AMITÂYUR-DHYÂNA-SÛTRA,

THE SÛTRA OF THE MEDITATION ON AMITÂYUS.

MEDITATION

ON

BUDDHA AMITÂYUS[1].

PART I.

§ 1. Thus it was heard by me: At one time the Buddha dwelt in Râgagriha, on the mountain Gridhrakûta, with a large assembly of Bhikshus and with thirty-two thousands of Bodhisattvas; with Mañgusrî, Prince of the Law[2], at the head of the assembly.

§ 2. At that time, in the great city of Râgagriha there was a prince, the heir-apparent, named Agâtasatru. He listened to the wicked counsel of Devadatta and other friends and forcibly arrested Bimbisâra his father, the king, and shut him up by himself in a room with seven walls, proclaiming to all the courtiers that no one should approach (the king). The chief consort of the king, Vaidehî by

---

[1] Nanjio's Catalogue of Tripitaka, No. 198; translated into Chinese A. D. 424, by Kâlayasas, a Sramana from India.

[2] Sanskrit Kumârabhûta, 'prince' or 'princely,' but Chinese has 'prince of the law;' according to the commentator, K'-kö, he was called so because he was (skilled in) converting men by (teaching) the Law. K'-kö seems to have understood that Mañgusrî was not a royal prince, but the name Kumârabhûta was given him as an honorific title. Max Müller, 'the prince' (p. 350, vol. ii, Selected Essays); Kern, 'the prince royal,' but he gives an alternative 'still a youth' (p. 4, Saddharmapundarika).

name, was true and faithful to her lord, the king. She supported him in this wise: having purified herself by bathing and washing, she anointed her body with honey and ghee mixed with corn-flour, and she concealed the juice of grapes in the various garlands she wore (in order to give him food without being noticed by the warder). As she stole in and made an offering to him, he was able to eat the flour and to drink the juice (of grapes). Then he called for water and rinsed his mouth. That done, the king stretched forth his folded hands towards the Mount G*ri*dhrakû*t*a and worshipped duly and respectfully the World-Honoured One, who at that time abode there. And he uttered the following prayer: 'Mahâmaudgalyâyana is my friend and relative; let him, I pray, feel compassion towards me, and come and communicate to me the eight prohibitive precepts[1] (of Buddha).' On this, Mahâmaudgalyâyana at once appeared before the king, coming with a speed equal to the flight of a falcon or an eagle, and communicated to him the eight precepts.

Day after day did he come. The World-Honoured One sent also his worthy disciple Pûr*n*a to preach the Law to the king. Thus a period of three weeks passed by. The king showed by his countenance that he was happy and contented when he had an opportunity of hearing the Law as well as of enjoying the honey and flour.

§ 3. At that time, A*g*âta*s*atru asked the warder

[1] According to the commentator, Shân-tâo, 'killing, stealing, adultery, lying, drinking, applying ointment, &c., music, and using ornamented chairs, &c.'

of the gate whether his father was yet alive. On this, the warder answered him: 'O Exalted king, the chief consort (of thy father) brought (food) and presented it to him by anointing her body with honey and flour and filling her garlands with the juice (of grapes), and the *S*rama*n*as, Mahâmaudgalyâyana and Pûr*n*a, approached the king through the sky in order to preach the Law to him. It is, O king, impossible to prevent them coming.' When the prince heard this answer his indignation arose against his mother: 'My mother,' he cried, 'is, indeed, a rebel, for she was found in company with that rebel. Wicked people are those *S*rama*n*as, and it is their art of spells causing illusion and delusion that delayed the death of that wicked king for so many days.' Instantly he brandished his sharp sword, intending to slay his mother. At that moment, there intervened a minister named *K*andraprabha, who was possessed of great wisdom and intelligence, and *G*îva (a famous physician). They saluted the prince and remonstrated with him, saying: 'We, ministers, O Great king, heard that since the beginning of the kalpas there had been several wicked kings, even to the number of eighteen thousand, who killed their own fathers, coveting the throne of (their respective) kingdoms, as mentioned in the Sûtra of the discourse of the Veda[1]. Yet never have we heard of a man killing his mother, though he be void of virtue. Now, if thou, O king, shouldst dare to commit such a deadly sin, thou wouldst bring a stain upon the blood of the Kshatriyas (the kingly race). We cannot even

[1] This is non-Buddhistic, according to Shân-tâo.

bear to hear of it. Thou art indeed a *Kandâla* (the lowest race); we shall not stay here with thee.' After this speech, the two great ministers retired stepping backward, each with his hand placed on his sword. A*g*âta*s*atru was then frightened, and greatly afraid of them, and asked *G*îva, saying: 'Wilt thou not be friendly to me?' In reply *G*îva said to him: 'Do not then, O Great king, by any means think of injuring thy mother.' On hearing this, the prince repented and sought for mercy, and at once laid down his sword and did his mother no hurt. He finally ordered the officers of the inner chambers to put the queen in a hidden palace and not to allow her to come out again.

§ 4. When Vaidehî was thus shut up in retirement she became afflicted by sorrow and distress. She began to do homage to Buddha from afar, looking towards the Mount G*ri*dhrakû*t*a. She uttered the following words: 'O Tathâgata! World-Honoured One! In former times thou hast constantly sent Ânanda to me for enquiry and consolation. I am now in sorrow and grief. Thou, O World-Honoured One, art majestic and exalted; in no way shall I be able to see thee. Wilt thou, I pray thee, command Mahâmaudgalyâyana and thy honoured disciple, Ânanda, to come and have an interview with me?' After this speech, she grieved and wept, shedding tears like a shower of rain. Before she raised her head from doing homage to the distant Buddha, the World-Honoured One knew what Vaidehî was wishing in her mind, though he was on the Mount G*ri*dhrakû*t*a. Therefore, he instantly ordered Mahâmaudgalyâyana and Ânanda to go to her through the sky. Buddha himself disappeared from that mountain and appeared in the royal palace.

When the queen raised her head as she finished homage to Buddha, she saw before her the World-Honoured Buddha *S*âkyamuni, whose body was purple gold in colour, sitting on a lotus-flower which consists of a hundred jewels, with Mahâmaudgalyâyana attending on his left, and with Ânanda on his right. *S*akra (Indra), Brahman, and other gods that protect the world were seen in the midst of the sky, everywhere showering heavenly flowers with which they made offerings to Buddha in their worship. Vaidehî, at the sight of Buddha the World-Honoured One, took off her garlands and prostrated herself on the ground, crying, sobbing, and speaking to Buddha: 'O World-Honoured One! what former sin of mine has produced such a wicked son? And again, O Exalted One, from what cause and circumstances hast thou such an affinity (by blood and religion) with Devadatta (Buddha's wicked cousin and once his disciple)?'

§ 5. 'My only prayer,' she continued, 'is this: O World-Honoured One, mayst thou preach to me in detail of all the places where there is no sorrow or trouble, and where I ought to go to be born anew. I am not satisfied with this world of depravities[1], with *G*ambudvîpa (India)[2], which is full of hells, full of hungry spirits (pretas), and of the brute creation. In this world of depravities, there is many an assemblage of the wicked. May I not

[1] For five depravities vide Smaller Sukhâvatî, § 18; Saddharmapu*nd*arîka by Kern, p. 58, § 140 note.

[2] But Japanese Buddhists take this in a wider sense.

hear, I pray, the voice of the wicked in the future; and may I not see any wicked person.

'Now I throw my five limbs down to the ground before thee, and seek for thy mercy by confessing my sins. I pray for this only that the Sun-like Buddha may instruct me how to meditate on a world wherein all actions are pure.' At that moment, the World-Honoured One flashed forth a golden ray from between his eyebrows. It extended to all the innumerable worlds of the ten quarters. On its return the ray rested on the top of Buddha's head and transformed itself into a golden pillar just like the Mount Sumeru, wherein the pure and admirable countries of the Buddhas in the ten quarters appeared all at once illuminated.

One was a country consisting of seven jewels, another was a country all full of lotus-flowers; one was like the palace of Mahesvara Deva (god Siva), another was like a mirror of crystal, with the countries in the ten quarters reflected therein. There were innumerable countries like these, resplendent, gorgeous, and delightful to look upon. All were meant for Vaidehî to see (and choose from).

Thereupon Vaidehî again spoke to Buddha: 'O World-Honoured One, although all other Buddha countries are pure and radiant with light, I should, nevertheless, wish myself to be born in the realm of Buddha Amitâyus (or Amitâbha), in the world of Highest Happiness (Sukhâvatî). Now I simply pray thee, O World-Honoured One, to teach me how to concentrate my thought so as to obtain a right vision (of that country).'

§ 6. Thereupon the World-Honoured One gently smiled upon her, and rays of five colours issued forth out of his mouth, each ray shining as far as the head of king Bimbisâra.

At that moment, the mental vision of that exalted king was perfectly clear though he was shut up in lonely retirement, and he could see the World-Honoured One from afar. As he paid homage with his head and face, he naturally increased and advanced (in wisdom), whereby he attained to the fruition of an Anâgâmin (the third of the four grades to Nirvâ*n*a).

§ 7. Then the World-Honoured One said: 'Now dost thou not know, O Vaidehî, that Buddha Amitâyus is not very far from here? Thou shouldst apply thy mind entirely to close meditation upon those who have already perfected the pure actions necessary for that Buddha country.

'I now proceed to fully expound them for thee in many parables, and thereby afford all ordinary persons of the future who wish to cultivate these pure actions an opportunity of being born in the Land of Highest Happiness (Sukhâvatî) in the western quarter. Those who wish to be born in that country of Buddha have to cultivate a threefold goodness. Firstly, they should act filially towards their parents and support them; serve and respect their teachers and elders; be of compassionate mind, abstain from doing any injury, and cultivate the ten virtuous actions[1]. Secondly, they should take and observe the vow of seeking refuge with the Three Jewels, fulfil all moral precepts, and not lower their dignity or neglect any ceremonial observance. Thirdly, they should give their whole mind

[1] I. e. observe the ten prohibitive precepts of Buddha.

to the attainment of the Bodhi (perfect wisdom), deeply believe in (the principle of) cause and effect, study and recite (the Sûtras of) the Mahâyâna doctrine, and persuade and encourage others who pursue the same course as themselves.

'These three groups as enumerated are called the pure actions (leading to the Buddha country).' 'O Vaidehî!' Buddha continued, 'dost thou not understand now? These three classes of actions are the efficient cause of the pure actions taught by all the Buddhas of the past, present, and future.'

§ 8. Buddha then addressed Ânanda as well as Vaidehî: 'Listen carefully, listen carefully! Ponder carefully on what you hear! I, Tathâgata, now declare the pure actions needful (for that Buddha country) for the sake of all beings hereafter, that are subject to the misery (inflicted) by the enemy, i. e. passion. Well done, O Vaidehî! Appropriate questions are those which thou hast asked[1]! O Ânanda, do thou remember these words of me, of Buddha, and repeat them openly to many assemblies. I, Tathâgata, now teach Vaidehî and also all beings hereafter in order that they may meditate on the World of Highest Happiness (Sukhâvatî) in the western quarter.

'It is by the power of Buddha only that one can see that pure land (of Buddha) as clear as one sees the image of one's face reflected in the transparent mirror held up before one.

'When one sees the state of happiness of that country in its highest excellence, one greatly re-

[1] Vide supra, § 4; but those two questions, though appropriate, have not after all been answered by Buddha in this Sûtra.

joices in one's heart and immediately attains a spirit of resignation prepared to endure whatever consequences may yet arise[1].' Buddha, turning again to Vaidehî, said: 'Thou art but an ordinary person; the quality of thy mind is feeble and inferior.

'Thou hast not as yet obtained the divine eye and canst not perceive what is at a distance. All the Buddhas, Tathâgatas have various means at their disposal and can therefore afford thee an opportunity of seeing (that Buddha country).' Then Vaidehî rejoined: 'O World-Honoured One, people such as I, can now see that land by the power of Buddha, but how shall all those beings who are to come after Buddha's Nirvâ*n*a, and who, as being depraved and devoid of good qualities, will be harassed by the five worldly sufferings[2]—how shall they see the World of Highest Happiness of the Buddha Amitâyus?'

PART II.

§ 9. Buddha then replied: 'Thou and all other beings besides ought to make it their only aim, with concentrated thought, to get a perception of the western quarter. You will ask how that perception is to be formed. I will explain it now. All beings, if not blind from birth, are uniformly possessed of sight, and they all see the setting sun. Thou shouldst sit down properly, looking in the western direction, and prepare thy thought for a close medi-

[1] Anutpatikadharmakshânti, cf. Larger Sukhâvatî, § 19, p. 39, and § 32, p. 5. Kern, 'the acquiescence in the eternal law,' Saddharmapu*nd*arîka XI, p. 254.

[2] 1. Birth, 2. Old age, 3. Sickness, 4. Death, 5. Parting.

tation on the sun; cause thy mind to be firmly fixed (on it) so as to have an unwavering perception by the exclusive application (of thy thought), and gaze upon it (more particularly) when it is about to set and looks like a suspended drum.

'After thou hast thus seen the sun, let (that image) remain clear and fixed, whether thine eyes be shut or open;—such is the perception of the sun, which is the First Meditation.

§ 10. 'Next thou shouldst form the perception of water; gaze on the water clear and pure, and let (this image) also remain clear and fixed (afterwards); never allow thy thought to be scattered and lost.

'When thou hast thus seen the water thou shouldst form the perception of ice. As thou seest the ice shining and transparent, thou shouldst imagine the appearance of lapis lazuli.

'After that has been done, thou wilt see the ground consisting of lapis lazuli, transparent and shining both within and without. Beneath this ground of lapis lazuli there will be seen a golden banner with the seven jewels, diamonds and the rest, supporting the ground[1]. It extends to the eight points of the compass, and thus the eight corners (of the ground) are perfectly filled up. Every side of the eight quarters consists of a hundred jewels, every jewel has a thousand rays, and every ray has eighty-four thousand colours which, when reflected in the ground of lapis lazuli, look like a thousand millions of suns, and it is difficult to see them all one by one. Over the surface of that ground of lapis lazuli there are

---

[1] 'A banner supporting or lifting up the ground' is rather strange, but there is no other way of translating it.

stretched golden ropes intertwined crosswise; divisions are made by means of (strings of) seven jewels with every part clear and distinct.

'Each jewel has rays of five hundred colours which look like flowers or like the moon and stars. Lodged high up in the open sky these rays form a tower of rays, whose storeys and galleries are ten millions in number and built of a hundred jewels. Both sides of the tower have each a hundred millions of flowery banners furnished and decked with numberless musical instruments. Eight kinds of cool breezes proceed from the brilliant rays. When those musical instruments are played, they emit the sounds "suffering," "non-existence," "impermanence," and "non-self;"—such is the perception of the water, which is the Second Meditation.

§ 11. 'When this perception has been formed, thou shouldst meditate on its (constituents) one by one and make (the images) as clear as possible, so that they may never be scattered and lost, whether thine eyes be shut or open. Except only during the time of thy sleep, thou shouldst always keep this in thy mind. One who has reached this (stage of) perception is said to have dimly seen the Land of Highest Happiness (Sukhâvatî).

'One who has obtained the Samâdhi (the state of supernatural calm) is able to see the land (of that Buddha country) clearly and distinctly: (this state) is too much to be explained fully;—such is the perception of the land, and it is the Third Meditation.

'Thou shouldst remember, O Ânanda, the Buddha words of mine, and repeat this law for attaining to the perception of the land (of the Buddha country) for the sake of the great mass of the people hereafter who may wish to be delivered from their sufferings. If any one meditates on the land (of that Buddha country), his sins (which bind him to) births and deaths during eighty millions of kalpas shall be expiated; after the abandonment of his (present) body, he will assuredly be born in the pure land in the following life. The practice of this kind of meditation is called the "right meditation." If it be of another kind it is called "heretical meditation."'

§ 12. Buddha then spoke to Ânanda and Vaidehî: 'When the perception of the land (of that Buddha country) has been gained, you should next meditate on the jewel-trees (of that country). In meditating on the jewel-trees, you should take each by itself and form a perception of the seven rows of trees; every tree is eight hundred yoganas high, and all the jewel-trees have flowers and leaves consisting of seven jewels all perfect. All flowers and leaves have colours like the colours of various jewels:—from the colour of lapis lazuli there issues a golden ray; from the colour of crystal, a saffron ray; from the colour of agate, a diamond ray; from the colour of diamond, a ray of blue pearls. Corals, amber, and all other gems are used as ornaments for illumination; nets of excellent pearls are spread over the trees, each tree is covered by seven sets of nets, and between one set and another there are five hundred millions of palaces built of excellent flowers, resembling the palace of the Lord Brahman; all heavenly children live there quite naturally; every child has a garland consisting of five hundred millions of precious gems like those that are fastened on *S*akra's (Indra's) head[1], the rays of which shine over a hundred yo*g*anas, just as if a hundred millions of suns and moons were united together; it is difficult to explain them in detail. That (garland) is the most excellent among all, as it is the commixture of all sorts of jewels. Rows of these jewel-trees touch one another; the leaves of the trees also join one another.

'Among the dense foliage there blossom various beautiful flowers, upon which are miraculously found fruits of seven jewels. The leaves of the trees are all exactly equal in length and in breadth, measuring twenty-five yo*g*anas each way; every leaf has a thousand colours and a hundred different pictures on it, just like a heavenly garland. There are many excellent flowers which have the colour of *G*âmbûnada gold and an appearance of fire-wheels in motion, turning between the leaves in a graceful fashion. All the fruits are produced just (as easily) as if they flowed out from the pitcher of the God *S*akra. There is a magnificent ray which transforms itself into numberless jewelled canopies with banners and flags. Within these jewelled canopies the works of all the Buddhas of the Great Chiliocosm appear illuminated; the Buddha countries of the ten quarters also are manifested therein. When you have seen these trees you should also meditate on them one by one in order. In meditating on the trees, trunks, branches, leaves, flowers, and fruits, let them all be distinct and clear;—such is the perception of the trees (of that Buddha country), and it is the Fourth Meditation.

[1] The text has *S*akrâbhilagnama*n*iratna, vide infra, §§ 16, 19.

§ 13. 'Next, you should perceive the water (of that country). The perception of the water is as follows:—

'In the Land of Highest Happiness there are waters in eight lakes; the water in every lake consists of seven jewels which are soft and yielding. Deriving its source from the king of jewels that fulfils every wish [1], the water is divided into fourteen streams; every stream has the colour of seven jewels; its channel is built of gold, the bed of which consists of the sand of variegated diamonds.

'In the midst of each lake there are sixty millions of lotus-flowers, made of seven jewels; all the flowers are perfectly round and exactly equal (in circumference), being twelve *yoganas*. The water of jewels flows amidst the flowers and rises and falls by the stalks (of the lotus); the sound of the streaming water is melodious and pleasing, and propounds all the perfect virtues (Parâmitâs), "suffering," "non-existence," "impermanence," and "non-self;" it proclaims also the praise of the signs of perfection [2], and minor marks of excellence [2] of all Buddhas. From the king of jewels that fulfils every wish, stream forth the golden-coloured rays excessively beautiful, the radiance of which transforms itself into birds possessing the colours of a hundred jewels, which sing out harmonious notes, sweet and delicious, ever praising the remembrance of Buddha, the remembrance of the Law, and the remembrance of the Church;—such is the perception

[1] Sanskrit *K*intâma*n*i, i.e. 'wishing-pearl.'

[2] For thirty-two signs and eighty minor marks vide Dharmasangraha by Kasawara, p. 53 seq. (vol. i, part v, Anecdota Oxoniensia, Aryan Series, 1885).

of the water of eight good qualities, and it is the Fifth Meditation.

§ 14. 'Each division of that (Buddha) country, which consists of several jewels, has also jewelled storeys and galleries to the number of five hundred millions; within each storey and gallery there are innumerable Devas engaged in playing heavenly music. There are some musical instruments that are hung up in the open sky, like the jewelled banners of heaven; they emit musical sounds without being struck, which, while resounding variously, all propound the remembrance of Buddha, of the Law and of the Church, Bhikshus, &c. When this perception is duly accomplished, one is said to have dimly seen the jewel-trees, jewel-ground, and jewel-lakes of that World of Highest Happiness (Sukhâvatî);—such is the perception formed by meditating on the general (features of that Land), and it is the Sixth Meditation.

'If one has experienced this, one has expiated the greatest sinful deeds which would (otherwise lead one) to transmigration for numberless millions of kalpas; after his death he will assuredly be born in that land.

§ 15[1]. 'Listen carefully! listen carefully! Think over what you have heard! I, Buddha, am about to explain in detail the law of delivering one's self from trouble and torment. Commit this to your memory in order to explain it in detail before a great assembly.' While Buddha was uttering these words, Buddha Amitâyus stood in the midst of the sky

[1] § 15. Hereafter, for brevity's sake, I take the liberty of omitting several passages which seem to be unnecessary repetitions.

with Bodhisattvas Mahâsthâma and Avalokitesvara, attending on his right and left respectively. There was such a bright and dazzling radiance that no one could see clearly; the brilliance was a hundred thousand times greater than that of gold (*G*âmbû-nada). Thereupon Vaidehî saw Buddha Amitâyus and approached the World-Honoured One, and worshipped him, touching his feet; and spoke to him as follows: 'O Exalted One! I am now able, by the power of Buddha, to see Buddha Amitâyus together with the two Bodhisattvas. But how shall all the beings of the future meditate on Buddha Amitâyus and the two Bodhisattvas?'

§ 16. Buddha answered: 'Those who wish to meditate on that Buddha ought first to direct their thought as follows: form the perception of a lotus-flower on a ground of seven jewels, each leaf of that lotus exhibits the colours of a hundred jewels, and has eighty-four thousand veins, just like heavenly pictures; each vein possesses eighty-four thousand rays, of which each can be clearly seen. Every small leaf and flower is two hundred and fifty yo*g*anas in length and the same measurement in breadth. Each lotus-flower possesses eighty-four thousand leaves, each leaf has the kingly pearls to the number of a hundred millions, as ornaments for illumination; each pearl shoots out a thousand rays like bright canopies. The surface of the ground is entirely covered by a mixture of seven jewels. There is a tower built of the gems which are like those that are fastened on *S*akra's head. It is inlaid and decked with eighty thousand diamonds, Ki*ms*uka jewels, Brahma-ma*n*i and excellent pearl nets.

'On that tower there are miraculously found four posts with jewelled banners; each banner looks like a hundred thousand millions of Sumeru mountains.

'The jewelled veil over these banners is like that of the celestial palace of Yama, illuminated with five hundred millions of excellent jewels, each jewel has eighty-four thousand rays, each ray has various golden colours to the number of eighty-four thousand, each golden colour covers the whole jewelled soil, it changes and is transformed at various places, every now and then exhibiting various appearances; now it becomes a diamond tower, now a pearl net, again clouds of mixed flowers, freely changing its manifestation in the ten directions it exhibits the state of Buddha;—such is the perception of the flowery throne, and it is the Seventh Meditation.'

Buddha, turning to Ânanda, said: 'These excellent flowers were created originally by the power of the prayer of Bhikshu, Dharmâkara[1]. All who wish to exercise the remembrance of that Buddha ought first to form the perception of that flowery throne. When engaged in it one ought not to perceive vaguely, but fix the mind upon each detail separately. Leaf, jewel, ray, tower, and banner should be clear and distinct, just as one sees the image of one's own face in a mirror. When one has achieved this perception, the sins which would produce births and deaths during fifty thousand kalpas are expiated, and he is one who will most assuredly be born in the World of Highest Happiness.

§ 17. 'When you have perceived this, you should

[1] Vide Larger Sukhâvatî, p. 7, § 3.

next perceive Buddha himself. Do you ask how? Every Buddha Tathâgata is one whose (spiritual) body is the principle of nature (Darmadhâtu-kâya), so that he may enter into the mind of any beings. Consequently, when you have perceived Buddha, it is indeed that mind of yours that possesses those thirty-two signs of perfection and eighty minor marks of excellence (which you see in Buddha). In fine, it is your mind that becomes Buddha, nay, it is your mind that is indeed Buddha. The ocean of true and universal knowledge of all the Buddhas derives its source from one's own mind and thought. Therefore you should apply your thought with an undivided attention to a careful meditation on that Buddha Tathâgata, Arhat, the Holy and Fully Enlightened One. In forming the perception of that Buddha, you should first perceive the image of that Buddha; whether your eyes be open or shut, look at an image like *G*âmbûnada gold in colour, sitting on that flower (throne mentioned before).

'When you have seen the seated figure your mental vision will become clear, and you will be able to see clearly and distinctly the adornment of that Buddha country, the jewelled ground, &c. In seeing these things, let them be clear and fixed just as you see the palms of your hands. When you have passed through this experience, you should further form (a perception of) another great lotus-flower which is on the left side of Buddha, and is exactly equal in every way to the above-mentioned lotus-flower of Buddha. Still further, you should form (a perception of) another lotus-flower which is on the right side of Buddha. Perceive that an image of Bodhisattva Avalokite*s*vara is sitting on the left-hand flowery throne, shooting forth golden rays exactly like those of Buddha. Perceive then that an image of Bodhisattva Mahâsthâma is sitting on the right-hand flowery throne.

'When these perceptions are gained the images of Buddha and the Bodhisattvas will all send forth brilliant rays, clearly lighting up all the jewel-trees with golden colour. Under every tree there are also three lotus-flowers. On every lotus-flower there is an image, either of Buddha or of a Bodhisattva; thus (the images of the Bodhisattvas and of Buddha) are found everywhere in that country. When this perception has been gained, the devotee should hear the excellent Law preached by means of a stream of water, a brilliant ray of light, several jewel-trees, ducks, geese, and swans. Whether he be wrapped in meditation or whether he has ceased from it, he should ever hear the excellent Law. What the devotee hears must be kept in memory and not be lost, when he ceases from that meditation; and it should agree with the Sûtras, for if it does not agree with the Sûtras, it is called an illusory perception, whereas if it does agree, it is called the rough perception of the World of Highest Happiness;—such is the perception of the images, and it is the Eighth Meditation.

'He who has practised this meditation is freed from the sins (which otherwise involve him in) births and deaths for innumerable millions of kalpas, and during this present life he obtains the Samâdhi due to the remembrance of Buddha.

§ 18. 'Further, when this perception is gained, you should next proceed to meditate on the bodily marks and the light of Buddha Amitâyus.

'Thou shouldst know, O Ânanda, that the body of Buddha Amitâyus is a hundred thousand million times as bright as the colour of the *G*âmbûnada gold of the heavenly abode of Yama; the height of that Buddha is six hundred thousand niyutas of ko*t*is of yo*g*anas innumerable as are the sands of the river Gaṅgâ.

'The white twist of hair between the eyebrows all turning to the right, is just like the five Sumeru mountains.

'The eyes of Buddha are like the water of the four great oceans; the blue and the white are quite distinct.

'All the roots of hair of his body issue forth brilliant rays which are also like the Sumeru mountains.

'The halo of that Buddha is like a hundred millions of the Great Chiliocosms; in that halo there are Buddhas miraculously created, to the number of a million of niyutas of ko*t*is innumerable as the sands of the Gaṅgâ; each of these Buddhas has for attendants a great assembly of numberless Bodhisattvas who are also miraculously created.

'Buddha Amitâyus has eighty-four thousand signs of perfection, each sign is possessed of eighty-four minor marks of excellence, each mark has eighty-four thousand rays, each ray extends so far as to shine over the worlds of the ten quarters, whereby Buddha embraces and protects all the beings who think upon him and does not exclude (any one of them). His rays, signs, &c., are difficult to be explained in detail. But in simple meditation let the mind's eye dwell upon them.

'If you pass through this experience, you will at the same time see all the Buddhas of the ten quarters. Since you see all the Buddhas it is called the Samâdhi of the remembrance of the Buddhas.

'Those who have practised this meditation are said to have contemplated the bodies of all the Buddhas. Since they have meditated on Buddha's body, they will also see Buddha's mind. It is great compassion that is called Buddha's mind. It is by his absolute compassion that he receives all beings.

'Those who have practised this meditation will, when they die, be born in the presence of the Buddhas in another life, and obtain a spirit of resignation wherewith to face all the consequences which shall hereafter arise.

'Therefore those who have wisdom should direct their thought to the careful meditation upon that Buddha Amitâyus. Let those who meditate on Buddha Amitâyus begin with one single sign or mark—let them first meditate on the white twist of hair between the eyebrows as clearly as possible; when they have done this, the eighty-four thousand signs and marks will naturally appear before their eyes. Those who see Amitâyus will also see all the innumerable Buddhas of the ten quarters. Since they have seen all the innumerable Buddhas, they will receive the prophecy of their future destiny (to become Buddha), in the presence of all the Buddhas;—such is the perception gained by a complete meditation on all forms and bodies (of Buddha), and it is the Ninth Meditation.

§ 19. 'When you have seen Buddha Amitâyus distinctly, you should then further meditate upon Bodhisattva Avalokitesvara, whose height is eight hundred thousands of niyutas of yo*g*anas; the colour of his body is purple gold, his head has a turban (ush*n*îsha*s*iraskatâ), at the back of which there is a halo; (the circumference of) his face is a hundred thousand yo*g*anas. In that halo, there are five hundred Buddhas miraculously transformed just like those of *S*âkyamuni Buddha, each transformed Buddha is attended by five hundred transformed Bodhisattvas who are also attended by numberless gods.

'Within the circle of light emanating from his whole body, appear illuminated the various forms and marks of all beings that live in the five paths [1] of existence.

'On the top of his head is a heavenly crown of gems like those that are fastened (on Indra's head), in which crown there is a transformed Buddha standing, twenty-five yo*g*anas high.

'The face of Bodhisattva Avalokite*s*vara is like *G*âmbûnada gold in colour.

'The soft hair between the eyebrows has all the colours of the seven jewels, from which eighty-four kinds of rays flow out, each ray has innumerable transformed Buddhas, each of whom is attended by numberless transformed Bodhisattvas; freely changing their manifestations they fill up the worlds of the ten quarters; (the appearance) can be compared with the colour of the red lotus-flower.

'(He wears) a garland consisting of eight thousand rays, in which is seen fully reflected a state of perfect beauty. The palm of his hand has a mixed colour of five hundred lotus-flowers. His hands have ten

[1] Men, gods, hell, the departed spirits, the brute creation.

(tips of) fingers, each tip has eighty-four thousand pictures, which are like signet-marks, each picture has eighty-four thousand colours, each colour has eighty-four thousand rays which are soft and mild and shine over all things that exist. With these jewel hands he draws and embraces all beings. When he lifts up his feet, the soles of his feet are seen to be marked with a wheel of a thousand spokes (one of the thirty-two signs) which miraculously transform themselves into five hundred million pillars of rays. When he puts his feet down to the ground, the flowers of diamonds and jewels are scattered about, and all things are simply covered by them. All the other signs of his body and the minor marks of excellence are perfect, and not at all different from those of Buddha, except the signs of having the turban on his head and the top of his head invisible, which two signs of him are inferior to those of the World-Honoured One;—such is the perception of the real form and body of Bodhisattva Avalokite*s*vara, and it is the Tenth Meditation.'

Buddha, especially addressing Ânanda, said: 'Whosoever wishes to meditate on Bodhisattva Avalokite*s*vara must do so in the way I have explained. Those who practise this meditation will not suffer any calamity; they will utterly remove the obstacle that is raised by Karma, and will expiate the sins which would involve them in births and deaths for numberless kalpas. Even the hearing of the name of this Bodhisattva will enable one to obtain immeasurable happiness. How much more, then, will the diligent contemplation of him!

'Whosoever will meditate on Bodhisattva Avalokite*s*vara should first meditate on the turban of his head, and then on his heavenly crown.

'All the other signs should also be meditated on according to their order, and they should be clear and distinct just as one sees the palms of one's hands.

'Next you should meditate on Bodhisattva Mahâsthâma, whose bodily signs, height, and size are equal to those of Avalokite*s*vara; the circumference (lit. surface) of his halo is one hundred and twenty-five yo*g*anas, and it shines as far as two hundred and fifty yo*g*anas. The rays of his whole body shine over the countries of the ten quarters, they are purple gold in colour, and can be seen by all beings that are in favourable circumstances.

'If one but sees the ray that issues from a single root of the hair of this Bodhisattva, he will at the same time see the pure and excellent rays of all the innumerable Buddhas of the ten quarters.

'For this reason this Bodhisattva is named the Unlimited Light; it is with this light of wisdom that he shines over all beings and causes them to be removed from the three paths of existence (Hells, Pretas, and the brute creation), and to obtain the highest power. For the same reason this Bodhisattva is called the Bodhisattva of Great Strength (Mahâsthâma). His heavenly crown has five hundred jewel-flowers; each jewel-flower has five hundred jewel-towers; in each tower are seen manifested all the pure and excellent features of the far-stretching Buddha countries in the ten quarters. The turban on his head is like a padma- (lotus) flower; on the top of the turban there is a jewel-pitcher, which is filled with various brilliant rays fully manifesting the state of Buddha. All his other bodily signs are quite equal to those of Avalokitesvara. When this Bodhisattva walks about, all the regions of the ten quarters tremble and quake. Wherever the earth quakes there appear five hundred millions of jewel-flowers; each jewel-flower with its splendid dazzling beauty looks like the World of Highest Happiness (Sukhâvatî).

'When this Bodhisattva sits down, all the countries of seven jewels at once tremble and quake: all the incarnate (lit. divided) Âmitâyus's, innumerable as the dust of the earth, and all the incarnate Bodhisattvas (Aval. and Mahâs.) who dwell in the middlemost Buddha countries (situated) between the Buddha country of the lower region (presided over) by a Buddha called the "Golden Light," and the country of the upper region (presided over) by a Buddha called the "King of Light,"—all these assemble in the World of Highest Happiness (Sukhâvatî), like gathering clouds, sit on their thrones of lotus-flowers, which fill the whole sky, and preach the excellent Law in order to deliver all the beings that are plunged in suffering;—such is the perception of the form and body of Bodhisattva Mahâsthâma, and it is the Eleventh Meditation.

'Those who practise this meditation are freed from the sins (which would otherwise involve them) in births and deaths for innumerable asankhya kalpas.

'Those who have practised this meditation do not live in an embryo state but obtain free access to the excellent and admirable countries of Buddhas. Those who have experienced this are said to have perfectly meditated upon the two Bodhisattvas Avalokitesvara and Mahâsthâma.

§ 20. 'After thou hast had this perception, thou shouldst imagine thyself to be born in the World of Highest Happiness in the western quarter, and to be seated, cross-legged, on a lotus-flower there. Then imagine that the flower has shut thee in and has afterwards unfolded; when the flower has thus unfolded, five hundred coloured rays will shine over thy body, thine eyes will be opened so as to see the Buddhas and Bodhisattvas who fill the whole sky; thou wilt hear the sounds of waters and trees, the notes of birds, and the voices of many Buddhas preaching the excellent Law, in accordance with the twelve divisions[1] of the scriptures. When thou hast ceased from that meditation, thou must remember the experience ever after.

'If thou hast passed through this experience thou art said to have seen the World of Highest Happiness in the realm of the Buddha Amitâyus;—this is the perception obtained by a complete meditation on that Buddha country, and is called the Twelfth Meditation.

'The innumerable incarnate bodies of Amitâyus, together with those of Aval. and Mahâs., constantly come and appear before such devotees (as above mentioned).'

§ 21. Buddha then spoke to Ânanda and Vaidehî: 'Those who wish, by means of their serene thoughts, to be born in the western land, should first meditate on an image of the Buddha, who is sixteen cubits

[1] Vide Max Müller, Dhammapada, Introduction, p. xxxiii, and Kasawara, Dharmasaṅgraha, LXII, p. 48.

high[1], seated on (a lotus-flower in) the water of the lake. As it was stated before, the (real) body and its measurement are unlimited, incomprehensible to the ordinary mind.

'But by the efficacy of the ancient prayer of that Tathâgata, those who think of and remember him shall certainly be able to accomplish their aim.

'Even the mere perceiving of the image of that Buddha brings to one immeasurable blessings. How much more, then, will the meditating upon all the complete bodily signs of that Buddha! Buddha Amitâyus has supernatural power; since everything is at his disposal, he freely transforms himself in the regions of the ten quarters. At one time he shows himself as possessing a magnificent body, which fills the whole sky, at another he makes his body appear small, the height being only sixteen or eighteen cubits. The body he manifests is always pure gold in colour; his halo—(bright with) transformed Buddhas—and his jewel lotus-flowers are as mentioned above. The bodies of the two Bodhisattvas are the same always.

'All beings can recognise either of the two Bodhisattvas by simply glancing at the marks of their heads. These two Bodhisattvas assist Amitâyus in his work of universal salvation;—such is the meditation that forms a joint perception of the Buddha and Bodhisattvas, and it is the Thirteenth Meditation.'

---

[1] This is said to have been the height of *S*âkyamuni; the cubit is Chinese, but as it varied from time to time, it is difficult to determine his real height. Spence Hardy, in his Manual of Buddhism, p. 364, says, 'Buddha is sometimes said to be twelve cubits in height, and sometimes eighteen cubits.'

PART III.

§ 22. Buddha then spoke to Ânanda and Vaidehî: 'The beings who will be born in the highest form of the highest grade (i. e. to Buddhahood) are those, whoever they may be, who wish to be born in that country and cherish the threefold thought whereby they are at once destined to be born there. What is the threefold thought, you may ask. First, the True Thought; second, the Deep Believing Thought; third, the Desire to be born in that Pure Land by bringing one's own stock of merit to maturity. Those who have this threefold thought in perfection shall most assuredly be born into that country.

'There are also three classes of beings who are able to be born in that country. What, you may ask, are the three classes of beings? First, those who are possessed of a compassionate mind, who do no injury to any beings, and accomplish all virtuous actions according to Buddha's precepts; second, those who study and recite the Sûtras of the Mahâyâna doctrine, for instance, the Vaipulya Sûtras[1]; third, those who practise the sixfold remembrance[2]. These three classes of beings who wish to be born in that country by bringing (their respective stocks of merit) to maturity, will become destined to be born there if they have accomplished any of those meritorious deeds for one day or even for seven days.

[1] Nanjio's Catalogue of Tripiṭaka, Nos. 23, 24–28, and many others.

[2] Sixfold remembrance, i. e. of the Three Jewels, the precepts, the charity of Buddha, and Bodhisattvas and the world of Devas.

'When one who has practised (these merits) is about to be born in that country, Buddha Amitâyus, together with the two Bodhisattvas Aval. and Mahâs., also numberless created Buddhas, and a hundred thousand Bhikshus and *S*râvakas, with their whole retinue, and innumerable gods, together with the palaces of seven jewels, will appear before him out of regard for his diligence and courage; Aval., together with Mahâs., will offer a diamond seat to him; thereupon Amitâyus himself will send forth magnificent rays of light to shine over the dying person's body. He and many Bodhisattvas will offer their hands and welcome him, when Aval., Mahâs., and all the other Bodhisattvas will praise the glory of the man who practised the meritorious deeds, and convey an exhortation to his mind. When the new-comer, having seen these, rejoicing and leaping for joy, looks at himself, he will find his own body seated on that diamond throne; and as he follows behind Buddha he will be born into that country, in a moment. When he has been born there, he will see Buddha's form and body with every sign of perfection complete, and also the perfect forms and signs of all the Bodhisattvas; he will also see brilliant rays and jewel-forests and hear them propounding the excellent Law, and instantly be conscious of a spirit of resignation to whatever consequences may hereafter arise. Before long he will serve every one of the Buddhas who live in the regions of the ten quarters. In the presence of each of those Buddhas he will obtain successively a prophecy of his future destiny. On his return to his own land (Sukhâvatî, in which he has just been born) he will obtain countless hundreds of thousands of Dhâra*n*î formulas (mystic form of prayer);—such are those who are to be born in the highest form of the highest grade (to Buddhahood).

§ 23. 'Next, the beings who will be born in the middle form of the highest grade are those who do not necessarily learn, remember, study, or recite those Vaipulya Sûtras, but fully understand the meaning of the truth (contained in them), and having a firm grasp of the highest truth do not speak evil of the Mahâyâna doctrine, but deeply believe in (the principle of) cause and effect; who by bringing these good qualities to maturity seek to be born in that Country of Highest Happiness. When one who has acquired these qualities is about to die, Amitâyus, surrounded by the two Bodhisattvas Aval. and Mahâs., and an innumerable retinue of dependents, will bring a seat of purple gold and approach him with words of praise, saying: "O my son in the Law! thou hast practised the Mahâyâna doctrine; thou hast understood and believed the highest truth; therefore I now come to meet and welcome thee." He and the thousand created Buddhas offer hands all at once.

'When that man looks at his own body, he will find himself seated on that purple gold seat; he will, then, stretching forth his folded hands, praise and eulogise all the Buddhas. As quick as thought he will be born in the lake of seven jewels, of that country. That purple gold seat on which he sits is like a magnificent jewel-flower, and will open after a night; the new-comer's body becomes purple gold in colour, and he will also find under his feet a lotus-flower consisting of seven jewels. Buddha and the

Bodhisattvas at the same time will send forth brilliant rays to shine over the body of that person whose eyes will instantaneously be opened and become clear. According to his former usage (in the human world) he will hear all the voices that are there, preaching primary truths of the deepest significance.

'Then he will descend from that golden seat and worship Buddha with folded hands, praising and eulogising the World-Honoured One. After seven days, he will immediately attain to the state of the highest perfect knowledge (anuttarasa*m*yaksa*m*bodhi) from which he will never fall away (avaivartya); next he will fly to all the ten regions and successively serve all the Buddhas therein; he will practise many a Samâdhi in the presence of those Buddhas. After the lapse of a lesser kalpa he will attain a spirit of resignation to whatever consequences may hereafter arise, and he will also obtain a prophecy of his future destiny in the presence of Buddhas.

§ 24. 'Next are those who are to be born in the lowest form of the highest grade: this class of beings also believes in (the principle of) cause and effect, and without slandering the Mahâyâna doctrine, simply cherishes the thought of obtaining the highest Bodhi and by bringing this good quality to maturity seeks to be born in that Country of Highest Happiness. When a devotee of this class dies, Amitâyus, with Aval., Mahâs., and all the dependents, will offer him a golden lotus-flower; he will also miraculously create five hundred Buddhas in order to send and meet him. These five hundred created Buddhas will, all at once, offer hands and praise him, saying: "O my son in the Law! thou art pure now; as thou hast cherished the thought of obtaining the highest Bodhi, we come to meet thee." When he has seen them, he will find himself seated on that golden lotus-flower. Soon the flower will close upon him; following behind the World-Honoured One he will go to be born in the lake of seven jewels. After one day and one night the lotus-flower will unfold itself. Within seven days he may see Buddha's body, though his mind is not as yet clear enough to perceive all the signs and marks of the Buddha, which he will be able to see clearly after three weeks; then he will hear many sounds and voices preaching the excellent Law, and he himself, travelling through all the ten quarters, will worship all the Buddhas, from whom he will learn the deepest significance of the Law. After three lesser kalpas he will gain entrance to the knowledge of a hundred (divisions of) nature (*s*atadharma-vidyâdvâra) and become settled in the (first) joyful stage[1] (of Bodhisattva). The perception of these three classes of beings is called the meditation upon the superior class of beings, and is the Fourteenth Meditation.

§ 25. 'The beings who will be born in the highest form of the middle grade are those who observe the five prohibitive precepts, the eight prohibitive precepts and the fasting, and practise all the moral precepts; who do not commit the five deadly sins[2], and who bring no blame or trouble upon any being; and who by bringing these good qualities to maturity seek to be born in the World of Highest Happiness in the western quarter. On the eve of such a person's departure from this life, Amitâyus, surrounded by

[1] There are ten stages which a Bodhisattva goes through.

[2] Childers' Pâli Dictionary, s. v. abhi*th*ânam.

Bhikshus and dependents, will appear before him, flashing forth rays of golden colour, and will preach the Law of suffering, non-existence, impermanence, and non-self. He will also praise the virtue of homelessness that can liberate one from all sufferings. At the sight of Buddha, that believer will excessively rejoice in his heart; he will soon find himself seated on a lotus-flower. Kneeling down on the ground and stretching forth his folded hands he will pay homage to Buddha. Before he raises his head he will reach that Country of Highest Happiness and be born there. Soon the lotus-flower will unfold, when he will hear sounds and voices praising and glorifying the Four Noble Truths (of suffering). He will immediately attain to the fruition of Arhatship, gain the threefold knowledge and the six supernatural faculties, and complete the eightfold emancipation.

§ 26. 'The beings who will be born in the middle form of the middle grade are those who either observe the eight prohibitive precepts, and the fasting for one day and one night, or observe the prohibitive precept for *S*rama*n*era (a novice) for the same period, or observe the perfect moral precepts, not lowering their dignity nor neglecting any ceremonial observance for one day and one night, and by bringing their respective merits to maturity seek to be born in the Country of Highest Happiness. On the eve of departure from this life, such a believer who is possessed of this moral virtue, which he has made fragrant by cultivation during his life, will see Amitâyus, followed by all his retinue; flashing forth rays of golden colour, this Buddha will come before him and offer a lotus-flower of seven jewels.

'He will hear a voice in the sky, praising him and saying: "O son of a noble family, thou art indeed an excellent man. Out of regard for thy obedience to the teachings of all the Buddhas of the three worlds I, now, come and meet thee." Then the new-comer will see himself seated on that lotus-flower. Soon the lotus-flower will fold around him, and being in this he will be born in the jewel-lake of the World of Highest Happiness in the western quarter.

'After seven days that flower will unfold again, when the believer will open his eyes, and praise the World-Honoured One, stretching forth his folded hands. Having heard the Law, he will rejoice and obtain the fruition of a Srota-âpanna[1] (the first grade to Nirvâ*n*a).

'In the lapse of half a kalpa he will become an Arhat.

§ 27. 'Next are the beings who will be born in the lowest form of the middle grade (to Buddhahood). If there be sons or daughters of a noble family who are filial to their parents and support them, besides exercising benevolence and compassion in the world, at their departure from this life, such persons will meet a good and learned teacher who will fully describe to them the state of happiness in that Buddha country of Amitâyus, and will also explain the forty-eight prayers of the Bhikshu Dharmâkara[2]. As soon as any such person has heard these details, his life will come to an end. In a brief moment[3] he

[1] Vide Va*g*ra*kkh*edikâ, § 9.

[2] Vide Larger Sukhâvatî, §§ 7, 8.

[3] Lit. 'In the time in which a strong man can bend his arm or stretch his bended arm.'

will be born in the World of Highest Happiness in the western quarter.

'After seven days he will meet Aval. and Mahâs., from whom he will learn the Law and rejoice. After the lapse of a lesser kalpa he will attain to the fruition of an Arhat. The perception of these three sorts of beings is called the meditation of the middle class of beings, and is the Fifteenth Meditation.

§ 28. 'Next are the beings who will be born in the highest form of the lowest grade. If there be any one who commits many evil deeds, provided that he does not speak evil of the Mahâvaipulya Sûtras, he, though himself a very stupid man, and neither ashamed nor sorry for all the evil actions that he has done, yet, while dying, may meet a good and learned teacher who will recite and laud the headings and titles of the twelve divisions of the Mahâyâna scriptures. Having thus heard the names of all the Sûtras, he will be freed from the greatest sins which would involve him in births and deaths during a thousand kalpas.

'A wise man also will teach him to stretch forth his folded hands and to say, "Adoration to Buddha Amitâyus" (Namo-mitâbhâya Buddhâya, or, Namo-mitâyushe Buddhâya). Having uttered the name of the Buddha, he will be freed from the sins which would otherwise involve him in births and deaths for fifty millions of kalpas. Thereupon the Buddha will send a created Buddha, and the created Bodhisattvas Aval. and Mahâs., to approach that person with words of praise, saying: "O son of a noble family, as thou hast uttered the name of that Buddha, all thy sins have been destroyed and expiated, and therefore we now come to meet thee." After this speech the devotee will observe the rays of that created Buddha flooding his chamber with light, and while rejoicing at the sight he will depart this life. Seated on a lotus-flower he will follow that created Buddha and go to be born in the jewel-lake.

'After the lapse of seven weeks, the lotus-flower will unfold, when the great compassionate Bodhisattvas Aval. and Mahâs. will stand before him, flashing forth magnificent rays, and will preach to him the deepest meaning of the twelve divisions of the scriptures. Having heard this, he will understand and believe it, and cherish the thought of attaining the highest Bodhi. In a period of ten lesser kalpas he will gain entrance to the knowledge of the hundred (divisions of) nature, and be able to enter upon the first (joyful) stage (of Bodhisattva). Those who have had an opportunity of hearing the name of Buddha, the name of the Law, and the name of the Church—the names of the Three Jewels—can also be born (in that country).'

§ 29. Buddha continued: 'Next are the beings who will be born in the middle form of the lowest grade. If there be any one who transgresses the five and the eight prohibitive precepts, and also all the perfect moral precepts; he, being himself so stupid as to steal things that belong to the whole community[1], or things that belong to a particular Bhikshu, and not be ashamed nor sorry for his impure preaching of the Law (in case of preacher), but magnify and glorify himself with many wicked deeds:—such a

[1] The text has 'saṅghika things,' which is probably saṅghika lâbha, i.e. 'gains of the whole community' opposed to gains of a single monk, Childers' Pâli Dictionary, s. v. saṅghiko, p. 449.

sinful person deserves to fall into hell in consequence of those sins. At the time of his death, when the fires of hell approach him from all sides, he will meet a good and learned teacher who will, out of great compassion, preach the power and virtue of the ten faculties of Amitâyus and fully explain the supernatural powers and brilliant rays of that Buddha; and will further praise moral virtue, meditation, wisdom, emancipation, and the thorough knowledge that follows emancipation. After having heard this, he will be freed from his sins, which would involve him in births and deaths during eighty millions of kalpas; thereupon those violent fires of hell will transform themselves into a pure and cool wind blowing about heavenly flowers. On each of these flowers will stand a created Buddha or Bodhisattva to meet and receive that person. In a moment he will be born in a lotus-flower growing in the lake of seven jewels. After six kalpas the lotus-flower will open, when Avalokitesvara and Mahâsthâma will soothe and encourage him with their Brahma-voices, and preach to him the Mahâyâna Sûtras of the deepest significance.

'Having heard this Law, he will instantaneously direct his thought toward the attainment of the highest Bodhi.

§ 30. 'Lastly, the beings who will be born in the lowest form of the lowest grade. If there be any one who commits evil deeds, and even completes the ten wicked actions, the five deadly sins[1] and the like; that

---

[1] The five deadly sins, according to Mahâvyutpatti, § 118, are Mât*ri*ghâta, Pit*ri*ghâta, Arhatghâta, Saṅghabheda, Tathâgatasyântike dush*t*a*k*ittarudhirotpâdana, which are unpardonable in the Larger Sukhâvatî; vide Nanjio's note and Pra*n*idhâna 19 (§ 8), the

man, being himself stupid and guilty of many crimes, deserves to fall into a miserable path of existence and suffer endless pains during many kalpas. On the eve of death he will meet a good and learned teacher who will, soothing and encouraging him in various ways, preach to him the excellent Law and teach him the remembrance of Buddha, but, being harassed by pains, he will have no time to think of Buddha. Some good friend will then say to him: "Even if thou canst not exercise the remembrance of Buddha, thou mayst, at least, utter the name, 'Buddha Amitâyus[1].'" Let him do so serenely with his voice uninterrupted; let him be (continually) thinking of Buddha until he has completed ten times the thought, repeating (the formula), "Adoration to Buddha Amitâyus" (Namo*mitâyushe Buddhâya). On the strength of (his merit of) uttering Buddha's name he will, during every repetition, expiate the sins which involve him in births and deaths during eighty millions of kalpas. He will, while dying, see a golden lotus-flower like the disk of the sun appearing before his eyes; in a moment he will be born in the World of Highest Happiness. After twelve greater kalpas the lotus-flower will unfold; thereupon the Bodhisattvas Aval. and Mahâs., raising their voices in great compassion, will preach to him in detail the real state of all the elements of nature and the law of the expiation of sins.

Ânantarya sins. Cf. the six crimes enumerated in Childers' Pâli Dictionary, p. 7 b, Abhi*th*ânam; vide supra, p. 192, § 25.

[1] The Corean text and the two other editions of the T'ang and Sung dynasties have 'Namo*mitâyushe Buddhâya' instead of 'Buddha Amitâyus,' which is the reading of the Japanese text and the edition of the Ming dynasty.

'On hearing them he will rejoice and will immediately direct his thought toward the attainment of the Bodhi;—such are the beings who are to be born in the lowest form of the lowest grade (to Buddhahood). The perception of the above three is called the meditation of the inferior class of beings, and is the Sixteenth Meditation.'

PART IV.

§ 31. When Buddha had finished this speech, Vaidehî, together with her five hundred female attendants, could see, as guided by the Buddha's words, the scene of the far-stretching World of the Highest Happiness, and could also see the body of Buddha and the bodies of the two Bodhisattvas. With her mind filled with joy she praised them, saying: 'Never have I seen such a wonder!' Instantaneously she became wholly and fully enlightened, and attained a spirit of resignation, prepared to endure whatever consequences might yet arise[1]. Her five hundred female attendants too cherished the thought of obtaining the highest perfect knowledge, and sought to be born in that Buddha country.

§ 32. The World-Honoured One predicted that they would all be born in that Buddha country, and be able to obtain the Samâdhi (the supernatural calm) of the presence of many Buddhas. All the innumerable Devas (gods) also directed their thought toward the attainment of the highest Bodhi.

Thereupon Ânanda rose from his seat, approached

[1] Vide supra, §§ 8, 22, 23.

Buddha, and spoke thus: 'O World-Honoured One, what should we call this Sûtra? And how should we receive and remember it (in the future)?'

Buddha said in his reply to Ânanda: 'O Ânanda, this Sûtra should be called the meditation on the Land of Sukhâvatî, on Buddha Amitâyus, Bodhisattva Avalokitesvara, Bodhisattva Mahâsthâma, or otherwise be called "(the Sûtra on) the entire removal of the obstacle of Karma[1], (the means of) being born in the realm of the Buddhas." Thou shouldst take and hold it, not forgetting nor losing it. Those who practise the Samâdhi (the supernatural calm) in accordance with this Sûtra will be able to see, in the present life, Buddha Amitâyus and the two great Bodhisattvas.

'In case of a son or a daughter of a noble family, the mere hearing of the names of the Buddha and the two Bodhisattvas will expiate the sins which would involve them in births and deaths during innumerable kalpas. How much more will the remembrance (of Buddha and the Bodhisattvas)!

'Know that he who remembers that Buddha is the white lotus (pu*n*d*a*rîka) among men, it is he whom the Bodhisattvas Avalokite*s*vara and Mahâsthâma consider an excellent friend. He will, sitting in the Bodhi-ma*nd*ala[2], be born in the abode of Buddhas.'

---

[1] Sanskrit karmâvara*n*a-vi*s*uddhi.

[2] Bodhi-ma*nd*ala = Bodhi-ma*nd*a, i. e. the Circle of Bodhi; 'the round terrace of enlightenment,' see Kern, Saddharmapu*nd*arîka, p. 155 note. This circle is the ground on which stood the A*s*vattha tree near which *S*âkyamuni defeated the assaults of Mâra, and finally obtained Bodhi or enlightenment. The tree is called Bodhidruma, the ground round its stem the bodhima*nd*ala. In the Saddharmapu*nd*arîka VII, 7, it is called Bodhima*nd*avara, which

Buddha further spoke to Ânanda: 'Thou shouldst carefully remember these words. To remember these words is to remember the name of Buddha Amitâyus.'

When Buddha concluded these words, the worthy disciples Mahâmaudgalyâyana, and Ânanda, Vaidehî, and the others were all enraptured with excessive joy.

§ 33. Thereupon the World-Honoured One came back, walking through the open sky, to the Mount Gridhrakûta. Ânanda soon after spoke before a great assembly of all the occurrences as stated above. On hearing this, all the innumerable Devas (gods), Nâgas (snakes), and Yakshas (demi-gods) were inspired with great joy; and having worshipped the Buddha they went their way.

Here ends the Sûtra of the Meditation on Buddha Amitâyus, spoken by Buddha (*S*âkyamuni).

Dr. Kern translates by the terrace of enlightenment, vára meaning circuit. A different idea is expressed by bodhimandapa in the Buddha-karita XIV, 90, which would mean a hall or pavilion, unless we ought to read here also bodhimandala.

INDEX OF NAMES AND SUBJECTS

IN THE AMITÂYUR-DHYÂNA-SÛTRA.

TRANSLITERATION OF ORIENTAL ALPHABETS ADOPTED FOR THE TRANSLATIONS OF THE SACRED BOOKS OF THE EAST.

CONSONANTS.	MISSIONARY ALPHABET. I Class.	II Class.	III Class.	Sanskrit.	Zend.	Pehlevi.	Persian.	Arabic.	Hebrew.	Chinese.
Gutturales.										
1 Tenuis	k	...	...	क	𐬐	𐬐	ک	ك	כּ	k
2 ,, aspirata	kh	...	...	ख	𐬑	[illegible]	...	...	כ	kh
3 Media	g	...	...	ग	𐬔	[illegible]	گ	...	גּ	...
4 ,, aspirata	gh	...	...	घ	𐬖	[illegible]	...	...	ג	...
5 Gutturo-labialis	q	...	...	...	...	...	ق	ق	ק	...
6 Nasalis	ṅ (ng)	...	...	ङ	{𐬧 (ng) / 𐬣 (N)}	...	...	...	...	...
7 Spiritus asper	h	...	...	ह	𐬵 (𐬓 hv)	[illegible]	ه	ه	ה	h, hs
8 ,, lenis	'	...	...	...	...	...	ا	ا	א	...
9 ,, asper faucalis	ʽh	...	...	...	...	...	ح	ح	ח	...
10 ,, lenis faucalis	ʼh	...	...	...	...	...	ع	ع	ע	...
11 ,, asper fricatus	...	ʽ*h*	...	...	...	...	خ	خ	ח	...
12 ,, lenis fricatus	...	ʼ*h*	...	...	...	...	غ	غ	...	...
Gutturales modificatae (palatales, &c.)										
13 Tenuis	...	*k*	...	च	𐬗	[illegible]	چ	...	...	*k*
14 ,, aspirata	...	*kh*	...	छ	...	...	...	...	...	*kh*
15 Media	...	*g*	...	ज	𐬘	[illegible]	ج	ج	...	...
16 ,, aspirata	...	*gh*	...	झ	...	...	ژ	...	...	...
17 ,, Nasalis	...	*ñ*	...	ञ	...	...	...	...	...	...

CONSONANTS (continued).	MISSIONARY ALPHABET. I Class.	II Class.	III Class.	Sanskrit.	Zend.	Pehlevi.	Persian.	Arabic.	Hebrew.	Chinese.
18 Semivocalis	y	...	...	य	[illegible] / [illegible] init.	[illegible]	ي	ي	י	y
19 Spiritus asper	...	(ẏ)	...	...	...	...	...	...	...	...
20 „ lenis	...	(ẏ)	...	...	...	...	...	...	...	...
21 „ asper assibilatus	...	*s*	...	श	[illegible]	[illegible]	ش	ش	...	...
22 „ lenis assibilatus	...	*s*	...	...	[illegible]	[illegible]	ژ	...	...	*s*
Dentales.										
23 Tenuis	t	...	...	त	[illegible]	[illegible]	ت	ت	תּ	t
24 „ aspirata	th	...	...	थ	[illegible]	...	...	...	ת	th
25 „ assibilata	...	...	TH	...	...	...	ث	ث	...	...
26 Media	d	...	...	द	[illegible]	[illegible]	د	د	דּ	...
27 „ aspirata	dh	...	...	ध	[illegible]	...	...	...	ד	...
28 „ assibilata	...	...	DH	...	...	...	ذ	ذ	...	...
29 Nasalis	n	...	...	न	[illegible]	[illegible]	ن	ن	נ	n
30 Semivocalis	l	...	...	ल	...	[illegible]	ل	ل	ל	l
31 „ mollis 1	...	*l*	...	ळ	...	...	...	...	...	...
32 „ mollis 2	...	...	L	...	...	...	...	...	...	...
33 Spiritus asper 1	s	...	...	स	[illegible]	[illegible]	س (ث)	س	שׂ	s
34 „ asper 2	...	...	s (ʃ)	...	...	...	...	...	ס	...
35 „ lenis	z	...	...	...	[illegible]	[illegible]	ز (ذ)	ز	ז	z
36 „ asperrimus 1	...	...	z (ʒ)	...	...	...	ص	ص	צ	ʒ, ʒh
37 „ asperrimus 2	...	...	ƶ (ʒ)	...	...	...	ض	...	...	...

Dentales modificatae (linguales, &c.)										
38 Tenuis	...	*t*	....	ट	....	...	ط	ط	ט	...
39 „ aspirata	...	*th*	....	ठ	....	...	ط	ط	...	...
40 Media	...	*d*	....	ड	[illegible]	[illegible]	...	...	...	...
41 „ aspirata	...	*dh*	....	ढ	....	...	...	ض	...	...
42 Nasalis	...	*n*	....	ण	[illegible]	...	...	...	...	...
43 Semivocalis	r	...	....	र	[illegible]	[illegible]	ر	ر	ר	...
44 „ fricata	...	*r*	....	...	....	...	...	...	...	*r*
45 „ diacritica	...	...	R	...	....	...	...	...	...	...
46 Spiritus asper	sh	...	....	ष	[illegible]	[illegible]	...	...	...	sh
47 „ lenis	zh	...	....	...	....	...	...	...	...	...
Labiales.										
48 Tenuis	p	...	....	प	[illegible]	[illegible]	پ	...	פּ	p
49 „ aspirata	ph	...	....	फ	....	...	...	...	פ	ph
50 Media	b	...	....	ब	[illegible]	[illegible]	ب	ب	בּ	...
51 „ aspirata	bh	...	....	भ	....	...	...	...	ב	...
52 Tenuissima	...	*p*	....	...	....	...	...	...	...	...
53 Nasalis	m	...	....	म	[illegible]	[illegible]	م	م	מ	m
54 Semivocalis	w	...	....	...	[illegible]	...	...	...	...	w
55 „ aspirata	hw	...	....	...	....	...	...	...	...	...
56 Spiritus asper	f	...	....	...	[illegible]	[illegible]	ف	ف	...	f
57 „ lenis	v	...	....	व	[illegible]	[illegible]	و	و	ו	...
58 Anusvâra	...	*m*	....	अं	[illegible]	...	...	...	...	...
59 Visarga	...	*h*	....	अः	....	...	...	...	...	...

VOWELS.	MISSIONARY ALPHABET. I Class.	II Class.	III Class.	Sanskrit.	Zend.	Pehlevi.	Persian.	Arabic.	Hebrew.	Chinese.
1 Neutralis	0	...	...	...	...	...	...	...	ְ	ă
2 Laryngo-palatalis	ĕ	...	...	...	...	...	...	...	...	...
3 „ labialis	ŏ	...	...	...	...	𐭥 fin.	...	...	...	...
4 Gutturalis brevis	a	...	...	अ	𐬀	𐭠 init.	ـَ	ـَ	ַ	a
5 „ longa	â	(a)	...	आ	𐬁	𐭠	ـَا	ـَا	ָ	â
6 Palatalis brevis	i	...	...	इ	𐬌	...	ـِ	ـِ	ִ	i
7 „ longa	î	(i)	...	ई	𐬍	𐭩	ـِي	ـِي	ִי	î
8 Dentalis brevis	li	...	...	ऌ	...	...	...	...	...	...
9 „ longa	lî	...	...	ॡ	...	...	...	...	...	...
10 Lingualis brevis	ri	...	...	ऋ	...	...	...	...	...	...
11 „ longa	rî	...	...	ॠ	...	...	...	...	...	...
12 Labialis brevis	u	...	...	उ	𐬎	...	ـُ	ـُ	ֻ	u
13 „ longa	û	(u)	...	ऊ	𐬏	𐭥	ـُو	ـُو	וּ	û
14 Gutturo-palatalis brevis	e	...	...	...	𐬈 (e) 𐬉 (e)	...	...	...	ֶ	e
15 „ longa	ê (ai)	(e)	...	ए	𐬀𐬉, 𐬀𐬊	𐭩	...	...	ֵ	ê
16 Diphthongus gutturo-palatalis	âi	(ai)	...	ऐ	...	...	ـَيْ	ـَيْ	...	âi
17 „ „	ei (ĕi)	...	...	...	...	...	...	...	...	ei, êi
18 „ „	oi (ŏu)	...	...	...	...	...	...	...	...	...
19 Gutturo-labialis brevis	o	...	...	...	𐬊	...	...	...	ָ	o
20 „ longa	ô (au)	(o)	...	ओ	𐬋	𐭥	...	...	וֹ	...
21 Diphthongus gutturo-labialis	âu	(au)	...	औ	𐬃𐬎 (au)	...	ـَوْ	ـَوْ	...	âu
22 „ „	eu (ĕu)	...	...	...	...	...	...	...	...	...
23 „ „	ou (ŏu)	...	...	...	...	...	...	...	...	...
24 Gutturalis fracta	ä	...	...	...	...	...	...	...	...	...
25 Palatalis fracta	ï	...	...	...	...	...	...	...	...	...
26 Labialis fracta	ü	...	...	...	...	...	...	...	...	ü
27 Gutturo-labialis fracta	ö	...	...	...	...	...	...	...	...	...

SACRED BOOKS OF THE EAST

TRANSLATED BY

VARIOUS ORIENTAL SCHOLARS

AND EDITED BY

F. MAX MÜLLER

*** *This Series is published with the sanction and co-operation of the Secretary of State for India in Council.*

REPORT presented to the ACADÉMIE DES INSCRIPTIONS, May 11, 1883, by M. ERNEST RENAN.

'M. Renan présente trois nouveaux volumes de la grande collection des "Livres sacrés de l'Orient" (Sacred Books of the East), que dirige à Oxford, avec une si vaste érudition et une critique si sûre, le savant associé de l'Académie des Inscriptions, M. Max Müller. . . . La première série de ce beau recueil, composée de 24 volumes, est presque achevée. M. Max Müller se propose d'en publier une seconde, dont l'intérêt historique et religieux ne sera pas moindre. M. Max Müller a su se procurer la collaboration des savans les plus éminens d'Europe et d'Asie. L'Université d'Oxford, que cette grande publication honore au plus haut degré, doit tenir à continuer dans les plus larges proportions une œuvre aussi philosophiquement conçue que savamment exécutée.'

EXTRACT from the QUARTERLY REVIEW.

'We rejoice to notice that a second series of these translations has been announced and has actually begun to appear. The stones, at least, out of which a stately edifice may hereafter arise, are here being brought together. Prof. Max Müller has deserved well of scientific history. Not a few minds owe to his enticing words their first attraction to this branch of study. But no work of his, not even the great edition of the Rig-Veda, can compare in importance or in usefulness with this English translation of the Sacred Books of the East, which has been devised by his foresight, successfully brought so far by his persuasive and organising power, and will, we trust, by the assistance of the distinguished scholars he has gathered round him, be carried in due time to a happy completion.'

Professor E. HARDY, Inaugural Lecture in the University of Freiburg, 1887.

'Die allgemeine vergleichende Religionswissenschaft datirt von jenem grossartigen, in seiner Art einzig dastehenden Unternehmen, zu welchem auf Anregung Max Müllers im Jahre 1874 auf dem internationalen Orientalistencongress in London der Grundstein gelegt worden war, die Übersetzung der heiligen Bücher des Ostens' (*the Sacred Books of the East*).

The Hon. ALBERT S. G. CANNING, 'Words on Existing Religions.'

'The recent publication of the "Sacred Works of the East" in English is surely a great event in the annals of theological literature.'

Oxford

AT THE CLARENDON PRESS

LONDON: HENRY FROWDE

OXFORD UNIVERSITY PRESS WAREHOUSE, AMEN CORNER, E.C.

FIRST SERIES.

VOL. I. The Upanishads.

Translated by F. MAX MÜLLER. Part I. The *Kh*ândogya-upanishad, The Talavakâra-upanishad, The Aitareya-âra*n*yaka, The Kaushîtaki-brâhma*n*a-upanishad, and The Vâ*g*asaneyi-sa*m*hitâ-upanishad. 8vo, cloth, 10*s*. 6*d*.

The Upanishads contain the philosophy of the Veda. They have become the foundation of the later Vedânta doctrines, and indirectly of Buddhism. Schopenhauer, speaking of the Upanishads, says: 'In the whole world there is no study so beneficial and so elevating as that of the Upanishads. It has been the solace of my life, it will be the solace of my death.'

[See also Vol. XV.]

VOL. II. The Sacred Laws of the Âryas,

As taught in the Schools of Âpastamba, Gautama, Vâsish*th*a, and Baudhâyana. Translated by GEORG BÜHLER. Part I. Âpastamba and Gautama. 8vo, cloth, 10*s*. 6*d*.

The Sacred Laws of the Âryas contain the original treatises on which the Laws of Manu and other lawgivers were founded.

[See also Vol. XIV.]

VOL. III. The Sacred Books of China.

The Texts of Confucianism. Translated by JAMES LEGGE. Part I. The Shû King, The Religious Portions of the Shih King, and The Hsiâo King. 8vo, cloth, 12*s*. 6*d*.

Confucius was a collector of ancient traditions, not the founder of a new religion. As he lived in the sixth and fifth centuries B.C. *his works are of unique interest for the study of Ethology.*

[See also Vols. XVI, XXVII, XXVIII, XXXIX, and XL.]

VOL. IV. The Zend-Avesta.

Translated by JAMES DARMESTETER. Part I. The Vendîdâd. 8vo, cloth, 10*s*. 6*d*.

The Zend-Avesta contains the relics of what was the religion of Cyrus, Darius, and Xerxes, and, but for the battle of Marathon, might have become the religion of Europe. It forms to the present day the sacred book of the Parsis, the so-called fire-worshippers. Two more volumes will complete the translation of all that is left us of Zoroaster's religion.

[See also Vols. XXIII and XXXI.]

VOL. V. Pahlavi Texts.

Translated by E. W. WEST. Part I. The Bundahis, Bahman Yast, and Shâyast lâ-shâyast. 8vo, cloth, 12*s*. 6*d*.

The Pahlavi Texts comprise the theological literature of the revival of Zoroaster's religion, beginning with the Sassanian dynasty. They are important for a study of Gnosticism.

VOLS. VI AND IX. The Qur'ân.

Parts I and II. Translated by E. H. PALMER. 8vo, cloth, 21*s*.

This translation, carried out according to his own peculiar views of the origin of the Qur'ân, was the last great work of E. H. Palmer, before he was murdered in Egypt.

VOL. VII. The Institutes of Vishnu.

Translated by JULIUS JOLLY. 8vo, cloth, 10*s*. 6*d*.

A collection of legal aphorisms, closely connected with one of the oldest Vedic schools, the Kathas, *but considerably added to in later time. Of importance for a critical study of the Laws of Manu.*

VOL. VIII. The Bhagavadgîtâ, with The Sanatsugâtîya, and The Anugîtâ.

Translated by KÂSHINÂTH TRIMBAK TELANG. 8vo, cloth, 10*s*. 6*d*.

The earliest philosophical and religious poem of India. It has been paraphrased in Arnold's 'Song Celestial.'

VOL. X. The Dhammapada,

Translated from Pâli by F. MAX MÜLLER; and

The Sutta-Nipâta,

Translated from Pâli by V. FAUSBÖLL; being Canonical Books of the Buddhists. 8vo, cloth, 10*s*. 6*d*.

The Dhammapada contains the quintessence of Buddhist morality. The Sutta-Nipâta gives the authentic teaching of Buddha on some of the fundamental principles of religion.

VOL. XI. Buddhist Suttas.

Translated from Pâli by T. W. RHYS DAVIDS. 1. The Mahâparinibbâna Suttanta; 2. The Dhamma-*k*akka-ppavattana Sutta. 3. The Tevi*gg*a Suttanta; 4. The Âkaṅkheyya Sutta; 5. The *K*etokhila Sutta; 6. The Mahâ-sudassana Suttanta; 7. The Sabbâsava Sutta. 8vo, cloth, 10*s*. 6*d*.

A collection of the most important religious, moral, and philosophical discourses taken from the sacred canon of the Buddhists.

VOL. XII. The *S*atapatha-Brâhma*n*a, according to the Text of the Mâdhyandina School.

Translated by JULIUS EGGELING. Part I. Books I and II. 8vo, cloth, 12*s*. 6*d*.

A minute account of the sacrificial ceremonies of the Vedic age. It contains the earliest account of the Deluge in India.

[See also Vols. XXVI, XLI.]

VOL. XIII. Vinaya Texts.

Translated from the Pâli by T. W. RHYS DAVIDS and HERMANN OLDENBERG. Part I. The Pâtimokkha. The Mahâvagga, I–IV. 8vo, cloth, 10*s*. 6*d*.

The Vinaya Texts give for the first time a translation of the moral code of the Buddhist religion as settled in the third century B.C.

[See also Vols. XVII and XX.]

VOL. XIV. The Sacred Laws of the Âryas,

As taught in the Schools of Âpastamba, Gautama, Vâsish*th*a, and Baudhâyana. Translated by GEORG BÜHLER. Part II. Vâsish*th*a and Baudhâyana. 8vo, cloth, 10*s*. 6*d*.

VOL. XV. The Upanishads.

Translated by F. MAX MÜLLER. Part II. The Ka*th*a-upanishad, The Mu*nd*aka-upanishad, The Taittirîyaka-upanishad, The B*ri*hadâra*n*yaka-upanishad, The *S*vetâ*s*vatara-upanishad, The Pra*s*ña-upanishad, and The Maitrâya*n*a-brâhma*n*a-upanishad. 8vo, cloth, 10*s*. 6*d*.

VOL. XVI. The Sacred Books of China.

The Texts of Confucianism. Translated by JAMES LEGGE. Part II. The Yî King. 8vo, cloth, 10*s*. 6*d*.

[See also Vols. XXVII, XXVIII.]

VOL. XVII. Vinaya Texts.

Translated from the Pâli by T. W. RHYS DAVIDS and HERMANN OLDENBERG. Part II. The Mahâvagga, V–X. The *K*ullavagga, I–III. 8vo, cloth, 10*s*. 6*d*.

VOL. XVIII. Pahlavi Texts.

Translated by E. W. WEST. Part II. The Dâdistân-î Dînîk and The Epistles of Mânûskîhar. 8vo, cloth, 12*s.* 6*d.*

VOL. XIX. The Fo-sho-hing-tsan-king.

A Life of Buddha by Asvaghosha Bodhisattva, translated from Sanskrit into Chinese by Dharmaraksha, A.D. 420, and from Chinese into English by SAMUEL BEAL. 8vo, cloth, 10*s.* 6*d.*

This life of Buddha was translated from Sanskrit into Chinese, A.D. 420. It contains many legends, some of which show a certain similarity to the Evangelium infantiae, &c.

VOL. XX. Vinaya Texts.

Translated from the Pâli by T. W. RHYS DAVIDS and HERMANN OLDENBERG. Part III. The Kullavagga, IV–XII. 8vo, cloth, 10*s.* 6*d.*

VOL. XXI. The Saddharma-pundarîka; or, The Lotus of the True Law.

Translated by H. KERN. 8vo, cloth, 12*s.* 6*d.*

'The Lotus of the true Law,' a canonical book of the Northern Buddhists, translated from Sanskrit. There is a Chinese translation of this book which was finished as early as the year 286 A.D.

VOL. XXII. Gaina-Sûtras.

Translated from Prâkrit by HERMANN JACOBI. Part I. The Âkârâṅga-Sûtra and The Kalpa-Sûtra. 8vo, cloth, 10*s.* 6*d.*

The religion of the Gainas was founded by a contemporary of Buddha. It still counts numerous adherents in India, while there are no Buddhists left in India proper.

Part II, *in preparation.*

VOL. XXIII. The Zend-Avesta.

Translated by JAMES DARMESTETER. Part II. The Sîrôzahs, Yasts, and Nyâyis. 8vo, cloth, 10*s.* 6*d.*

VOL. XXIV. Pahlavi Texts.

Translated by E. W. WEST. Part III. Dînâ-î Maînôg-Khirad, Sikand-gûmânîk Vigâr, and Sad Dar. 8vo, cloth, 10*s.* 6*d.*

SECOND SERIES.

VOL. XXV. Manu.

Translated by GEORG BÜHLER. 8vo, cloth, 21*s*.

This translation is founded on that of Sir William Jones, which has been carefully revised and corrected with the help of seven native Commentaries. An Appendix contains all the quotations from Manu which are found in the Hindu Law-books, translated for the use of the Law Courts in India. Another Appendix gives a synopsis of parallel passages from the six Dharma-sûtras, the other Sm*ri*tis, the Upanishads, the Mahâbhârata, &c.

VOL. XXVI. The *S*atapatha-Brâhma*n*a.

Translated by JULIUS EGGELING. Part II. Books III and IV. 8vo, cloth, 12*s*. 6*d*.

VOLS. XXVII AND XXVIII. The Sacred Books of China.

The Texts of Confucianism. Translated by JAMES LEGGE. Parts III and IV. The Lî *K*î, or Collection of Treatises on the Rules of Propriety, or Ceremonial Usages. 8vo, cloth, 12*s*. 6*d*. each.

VOL. XXIX. The G*ri*hya-Sûtras, Rules of Vedic Domestic Ceremonies.

Part I. *S*âṅkhâyana, Â*s*valâyana, Pâraskara, Khâdira. Translated by HERMANN OLDENBERG. 8vo, cloth, 12*s*. 6*d*.

These rules of Domestic Ceremonies describe the home life of the ancient Âryas with a completeness and accuracy unmatched in any other literature. Some of these rules have been incorporated in the ancient Law-books.

VOL. XXX. The G*ri*hya-Sûtras, Rules of Vedic Domestic Ceremonies.

Part II. Gobhila, Hira*n*yake*s*in, Âpastamba. Translated by HERMANN OLDENBERG. Âpastamba, Ya*gñ*a-paribhâshâ-sûtras. Translated by F. MAX MÜLLER. 8vo, cloth, 12*s*. 6*d*.

VOL. XXXI. The Zend-Avesta.

Part III. The Yasna, Visparad, Âfrînagân, Gâhs, and Miscellaneous Fragments. Translated by L. H. MILLS. 8vo, cloth, 12*s*. 6*d*.

VOL. XXXII. Vedic Hymns.

Translated by F. MAX MÜLLER. Part I. 8vo, cloth, 18*s*. 6*d*.

VOL. XXXIII. The Minor Law-books.
Translated by JULIUS JOLLY. Part I. Nârada, B*ri*haspati. 8vo, cloth, 10*s*. 6*d*.

VOL. XXXIV. The Vedânta-Sûtras, with the Commentary by *S*aṅkarâ*k*ârya. Part I.
Translated by G. THIBAUT. 8vo, cloth, 12*s*. 6*d*.

VOL. XXXV. The Questions of King Milinda. Part I.
Translated from the Pâli by T. W. RHYS DAVIDS. 8vo, cloth, 10*s*. 6*d*.

VOL. XXXVI. The Questions of King Milinda. Part II.
[*In the Press.*]

VOL. XXXVII. The Contents of the Nasks, as stated in the Eighth and Ninth Books of the Dînka*r*d.
Part I. Translated by E. W. WEST. 8vo, cloth, 15*s*.

VOL. XXXVIII. The Vedânta-Sûtras. Part II. [*In the Press.*]

VOLS. XXXIX AND XL. The Sacred Books of China.
The Texts of Tâoism. Translated by JAMES LEGGE. 8vo, cloth, 21*s*.

VOL. XLI. The *S*atapatha-Brâhma*n*a. Part III.
Translated by JULIUS EGGELING. 8vo, cloth, 12*s*. 6*d*.

VOL. XLII. Hymns of the Atharva-veda.
Translated by M. BLOOMFIELD. [*In preparation.*]

VOLS. XLIII AND XLIV. The *S*atapatha-Brâhma*n*a.
Parts IV and V. [*In preparation.*]

VOL. XLV. The *G*aina-Sûtras. Part II. [*In the Press.*]

VOL. XLVI. The Vedânta-Sûtras. Part III. [*In preparation.*]

VOL. XLVII. The Contents of the Nasks. Part II.
[*In preparation.*]

VOL. XLVIII. Vedic Hymns. Part II. [*In preparation.*]

VOL. XLIX. Buddhist Mahâyâna Texts. Buddha-*k*arita, translated by E. B. COWELL. Sukhâvatî-vyûha, Va*g*ra*kk*hedikâ, &c., translated by F. MAX MÜLLER. Amitâyur-Dhyâna-Sûtra, translated by J. TAKAKUSU. [*Now ready.*]

Anecdota Oxoniensia.

ARYAN SERIES.

Buddhist Texts from Japan. I. Vagra*kkh*edikâ; *The Diamond-Cutter.*

Edited by F. MAX MÜLLER, M.A. Small 4to, 3*s.* 6*d.*

One of the most famous metaphysical treatises of the Mahâyâna Buddhists.

Buddhist Texts from Japan. II. Sukhâvatî-Vyûha: *Description of Sukhâvatî, the Land of Bliss.*

Edited by F. MAX MÜLLER, M.A., and BUNYIU NANJIO. With two Appendices: (1) Text and Translation of Saṅghavarman's Chinese Version of the Poetical Portions of the Sukhâvatî-Vyûha; (2) Sanskrit Text of the Smaller Sukhâvatî-Vyûha. Small 4to, 7*s.* 6*d.*

The *editio princeps* of the Sacred Book of one of the largest and most influential sects of Buddhism, numbering more than ten millions of followers in Japan alone.

Buddhist Texts from Japan. III. *The Ancient Palm-Leaves containing the* Pragñâ-Pâramitâ-H*ri*daya-Sûtra *and the* Ush*n*îsha-Vigaya-Dhâra*n*î.

Edited by F. MAX MÜLLER, M.A., and BUNYIU NANJIO, M.A. With an Appendix by G. BÜHLER, C.I.E. With many Plates. Small 4to, 10*s.*

Contains facsimiles of the oldest Sanskrit MS. at present known.

Dharma-Sa*m*graha, *an Ancient Collection of Buddhist Technical Terms.*

Prepared for publication by KENJIU KASAWARA, a Buddhist Priest from Japan, and, after his death, edited by F. MAX MÜLLER and H. WENZEL. Small 4to, 7*s.* 6*d.*

Kâtyâyana's Sarvânukrama*n*î of the *Ri*gveda.

With Extracts from Sha*d*guru*s*ishya's Commentary entitled Vedârthadîpikâ. Edited by A. A. MACDONELL, M.A., Ph.D. 16*s.*

Oxford

AT THE CLARENDON PRESS

LONDON: HENRY FROWDE

OXFORD UNIVERSITY PRESS WAREHOUSE, AMEN CORNER, E.C.